More Praise for
ROSE KENNEDY

"A more complete portrait of the matriarch of one of America's eminent political family dynasties." —*Los Angeles Times*

"A fuller picture than ever before. . . . Perry writes with compassion and brings keen insight into what Rose Kennedy's own words tell us about this complex woman." —Amy Scribner, *BookPage*

"Perry's engrossing biography allows us at last to understand Rose, thorns and all." —*Mail on Sunday*

"Barbara Perry has done it again! *Rose Kennedy* is the much needed, balanced biography of the grand matriarch of American politics. Whether it was helping the disabled, raising children, or playing ward boss, Mrs. Kennedy was a force of nature."
—Douglas Brinkley,
professor of history at Rice University and author of *Cronkite*

"At the core of most families, frequently out of the public spotlight, is the matriarch. She personifies and by example extends the values and mores that make that family unique. Mrs. Rose Kennedy was such a woman. Raised in a high-profile political family, she nurtured one of America's most influential families. Her influence continues to be a force in American culture. *Rose Kennedy* captures the essence of this exceptional leader. It places her in the spotlight she avoided but richly deserves." —Bob Graham, U.S. senator

"Rose Fitzgerald Kennedy was one of the most inspiring women of the twentieth century. . . . Barbara Perry brilliantly and sensitively shows us Rose's world. . . . You will be deeply moved by Perry's magnificently researched account of this remarkable centenarian, whose steely optimism and unshakeable religious faith overcame life's darkest detours." —Larry J. Sabato,
director, University of Virginia Center for Politics

"Perry, a senior fellow in the Presidential Oral History Program at the University of Virginia's Miller Center, has carried out extensive research—including her subject's papers made available in 2006 at the John F. Kennedy Library—to produce a fond but not fawning biography."   —*Richmond Times-Dispatch*

"In this magnificent biography, Perry brilliantly recounts the fascinating and at times heartbreaking life of a complex and determined woman and illuminates that life through Rose's extraordinary vantage point in history."   —Examiner.com

"Empathetic."   —Jonathan Yardley, *Washington Post*

"Well written."   —Kitty Kelley,
Washington Independent Review of Books

"Perry's biography is a finely crafted, comprehensive account of one of the most driven women in the shadows of American political history. . . . While there are untold numbers of books on the Kennedys, Perry adds archival details and nuance to our understanding of Rose. Kennedy completists and novices alike are sure to find the book fascinating as it further reveals the perspective of the strong woman behind the dynasty."   —Lisa Guardarini, *Library Journal*

ALSO BY BARBARA A. PERRY

Jacqueline Kennedy: First Lady of the New Frontier

ROSE KENNEDY

THE LIFE AND TIMES OF A
POLITICAL MATRIARCH

Barbara A. Perry

W. W. NORTON & COMPANY
New York   London

For information about permission to reproduce selections from this book,
write to Permissions, W. W. Norton & Company, Inc.,
500 Fifth Avenue, New York, NY 10110

For information about special discounts for bulk purchases, please contact
W. W. Norton Special Sales at specialsales@wwnorton.com or 800-233-4830

Manufacturing by Courier Westford
Book design by JAM Design
Production manager: Devon Zahn

Library of Congress Cataloging-in-Publication Data

Perry, Barbara A. (Barbara Ann), 1956–
Rose Kennedy : the life and times of a political matriarch / Barbara A. Perry. — First edition.
       pages cm.
Includes bibliographical references and index.
ISBN 978-0-393-06895-5 (hardcover)
1. Kennedy, Rose Fitzgerald, 1890–1995. 2. Mothers of presidents—United States—Biography.
3. Kennedy family. I. Title.
E748.K378P47 2013
973.9092—dc23
[B]
                                                          2013006529

ISBN 978-0-393-34946-7 pbk.

W. W. Norton & Company, Inc.
500 Fifth Avenue, New York, N.Y. 10110
www.wwnorton.com

W. W. Norton & Company Ltd.
Castle House, 75/76 Wells Street, London W1T 3QT

1 2 3 4 5 6 7 8 9 0

For Rose and Rob Capon

Contents

ROSE
KENNEDY

Prologue

"I WILL NEVER ALLOW MYSELF TO BE VANQUISHED OR ANNIHI-lated. I have always enjoyed living and working, and I believe I have had a great life," Rose Fitzgerald Kennedy declared as she neared eighty. Citing British theologian John Cardinal Newman, she believed that God had created her to perform "some definite service. . . . I may never know it in this life, but I shall be told it in the next."[1] If such an afterlife exists, Rose Kennedy arrived there on January 22, 1995, at age 104. At the pearly gates she would have reviewed her life's stunning intersection with the twentieth century's most historic events and told Saint Peter *her* version of life as a Boston belle, devoted wife, award-winning mother, devout Irish Catholic, indefatigable campaigner, charitable fund-raiser, and stoic heroine. She would have asked for the most stylish heavenly gown for the reunion with her husband and four children, who had preceded her in death. If they had not yet achieved beatific perfection, Rose would surely have offered advice about how to do so. On Earth she had been absent for more than a decade from the public stage she occupied most of her life. Usually a supporting actor, Rose relished portraying the leading lady. Yet she also embraced less glamorous theatrical duties: stage manager, playwright, dresser, makeup artist, and casting director for her family's successful political productions. Often upstaged by her father, husband, and sons, she outlived all but one and fashioned a family mythology that endures.

Debilitated by strokes in her final years, Rose couldn't plan her funeral, but she surely would have approved the tasteful familial service, filled with ritualistic Catholic liturgy. Three Kennedy generations had gathered for a traditional Irish wake at their storied Cape Cod compound. Then they accompanied Rose's remains to Boston's historic North End, site of her 1890 birth. A few blocks from her birthplace stands St. Stephen's, its edifice purchased from Congregationalists by Boston's Catholic diocese in 1862 to serve the waves of Irish Catholic immigrants flooding into surrounding tenements. Restored in 1964, under Kennedy prelate Richard Cardinal Cushing's direction, the church's red-brick facade, decorated with white pilasters and crowned by a clock tower and belfry, epitomizes classic Federal-era architecture.

On a chilly, gray January morning, the black hearse carrying Rose Kennedy's elegant mahogany casket approached the church's front entrance. Baby Rose had crossed the same threshold for her 1890 christening, as had her legendary father, John F. (Honey Fitz) Fitzgerald, in 1863. Across the narrow street, with its old-world ambience, stood respectful spectators, bundled against the biting New England cold, hoping to glimpse the celebrated Kennedys.

Rose's final act didn't disappoint them or C–SPAN viewers watching the two-hour Mass of Resurrection. As funeral directors slipped a white shroud over her coffin, the matriarch's children and their progeny gathered around. The oldest grandchildren served as pallbearers, accompanying Grandma Kennedy's casket up the church's center aisle. Their names recalled her "agony and ecstasy," as Rose had labeled life's dramas. Kathleen, assassinated Senator Robert F. Kennedy's eldest, bears the name of Rose's beloved daughter, nicknamed Kick, whose love life broke her mother's heart. Kick perished in a 1948 plane crash on her way to the south of France with her married boyfriend. (Kick's first husband, a Protestant British nobleman, died from a Nazi sniper's bullet in 1944. Only a few weeks before, Rose's cherished oldest child, Joseph P. [Joe] Kennedy Jr., a Navy pilot, died when his plane exploded over the English countryside.) Caroline, daughter of murdered President John F. Kennedy, was still overcoming the 1994 cancer death of her mother, First Lady Jacqueline Kennedy Onassis. Christopher, the tall, handsome son of Patricia Kennedy Lawford and her former husband, the late Hollywood actor Peter Lawford, struggled with another of the family's curses—substance abuse, which had also hastened his father's death.

Robert S. (Bobby) Shriver III hailed from the most stable family in the Kennedy clan, led by his mother, Eunice, named for Rose's sister (a tuberculosis victim at age twenty-three) and founder of the Special Olympics, and her husband, R. Sargent (Sarge) Shriver Jr., first director of JFK's Peace Corps and former ambassador to France. Yet they had been embarrassed over Bobby's 1970 drug bust for pot possession. Police had arrested him, along with his cousin, Robert Kennedy Jr. Kara, Senator Edward M. (Teddy) Kennedy's eldest, represented him and his former wife, Joan, who both suffered from public bouts of alcoholism, as would their youngest son, Congressman Patrick Kennedy (D-RI). Kara's brother, Teddy Jr., limped into Rose's funeral on a prosthetic leg, resulting from his battle with cancer as a twelve-year-old.

Steve Smith Jr.'s mother, Jean Kennedy Smith, bore the title of US ambassador to Ireland, following in the footsteps of her late father, Joseph P. (Joe) Kennedy Sr., ambassador to the Court of St. James's at the start of World War II. In 1969 Joe had succumbed to the aftereffects of a devastating stroke suffered eight years before. Steve's father, Steve Smith Sr., had served as the business manager of the Kennedys' campaigns and Kennedy Foundation. Steve Sr. had died of cancer in 1990 before his younger son, William Kennedy Smith, faced 1991 rape charges after Good Friday barhopping in Palm Beach with uncle Teddy and cousin Patrick. Having admitted in court that he had displayed poor judgment in carousing with his son and nephew on one of the Catholic Church's most solemn nights, Teddy was relieved when the jury acquitted young Willie, then a medical student. Forever tied to Chappaquiddick, where his car careened off a rustic bridge in 1969 and drowned Mary Jo Kopechne, Teddy had begun to reform his dissolute private life. After a public confession of past mistakes, he married Victoria Reggie in 1992. By all accounts, their happy union set him on a straighter path and made him an even more effective legislator as well as family patriarch.

Before the 1990s gave way to the twenty-first century, two more of Rose's grandchildren would join in death their cousin David Kennedy, Robert's son, who fell victim to a 1984 drug overdose at a seedy Palm Beach motel. David's brother, Michael, ran head-on into a tree on an Aspen ski slope while playing "ice football" with his siblings on New Year's Eve 1997. Two years later, John F. Kennedy Jr. crashed his private plane off Martha's Vineyard on a hazy July 1999 evening, killing himself, his wife, and her sister.

At St. Stephen's the bright interior and happy remembrances of Rose's full life lifted the gloom of the leaden skies and grieving family. Boston's Bernard Cardinal Law delivered Pope John Paul II's condolences. Rose would have savored that honor. In 1964 she had told a journalist that among the most meaningful events in her life were a 1939 audience with Pope Pius XII and a 1936 meeting with the future pontiff and President Franklin Roosevelt at Hyde Park.[2] Robert Kennedy's widow, Ethel, mother of their eleven children, gave the first reading. As early as 1983, when her mother-in-law's health began to deteriorate, the family had chosen a passage from the book of Proverbs to summarize Rose's life:

> Strength and dignity are her clothing, and she laughs at the time to come. She opens her mouth with wisdom, and the teaching of kindness is on her tongue. She looks well to the ways of her household, and does not eat the bread of idleness. Her children rise up and call her happy; her husband too, and he praises her; "Many women have done excellently but you surpass them all." Charm is deceitful, and beauty is vain, but a woman who fears the Lord is to be praised. Give her a share

in the fruit of her hands, and let her works praise her in the city gates.[3]

Rose's son-in-law Sargent Shriver followed Ethel at the pulpit to read a passage from the First Letter of Peter. The scripture perfectly encapsulated Rose's faith that had buffered the unfathomable tragedies befalling her family. "You may for [a] time have to suffer the distress of many trials," declared Apostle Peter, "but this is so that your faith, which is more precious than the passing splendor of fire-tried gold, may by its genuineness lead to . . . your salvation."[4] Within a few years, ebullient Sarge would begin to exhibit Alzheimer's symptoms and ultimately fall prey to the disease.

Six of Rose's twenty-nine grandchildren delivered the Prayers of the Faithful, petitions citing "Grandma's own words and wishes" for preventing mental retardation, strengthening faith, increasing public service, and embracing life's simple pleasures of love, laughter, flowers, music, and dancing. Television correspondent Maria Shriver prayed for "joy in heaven," where Rose was now reunited with her deceased children—Joe, Kathleen, Jack, and Bobby.

After Communion for hundreds of mourners, Rose's children eulogized her. Although she was survived by five of her nine, only four—Eunice, Patricia, Jean, and Teddy—could attend. Her oldest daughter, Rosemary, resided in a Wisconsin institution for the developmentally disabled, the victim of a failed lobotomy in 1941. Eunice Shriver recalled her mother as a loving teacher. "The mother's heart is the child's schoolroom," Eunice quoted Henry Ward Beecher. Rose would ask, "Now, Eunice, where is Pakistan; where is Wales?" as they studied a wall map. "She taught us to listen to Dad's dinner-table conversations about politics," even though they "seemed boring to a young child." Yet those political dialogues around the family table "became the basis for our life's work." Rose had "sparked her daughter's imagination with bedtime stories— excerpts from *Little Women* . . . and, of course, the Gospel." "But as smart as she was," Mrs. Shriver recalled, "she would never let us forget our special sister, Rosemary. . . . Mother's acts of intelligence, inclusion, respect, and love of motherhood created unbreakable bonds of love and support between my brothers and sisters. Her acts of goodness were this child's schoolroom. They were my mother's heart," Eunice concluded, "and I loved her."[5] Rose's empathy for Rosemary inspired Eunice to embrace the least gifted Kennedy and, ultimately, a life's passion for serving the mentally retarded.

Fulfilling the role practiced all too often in his star-crossed family, Teddy delivered the perfect eulogy. As he had done after brother Bobby's 1968 assassination, Joe and Rose Kennedy's sole surviving son captured his mother's essence in poetic phrases, with a tender, occasionally quavering voice. Beginning with a self-deprecating anecdote about Rose's ubiquitous grammar lessons, Teddy revealed, "On my office wall, there is a note from Mother, reacting to a comment I once made in an interview. 'Dear Teddy,' she wrote in the note, 'I just saw a story in which you said: 'If I was President. . . .' You should have said, 'if I were President. . . .' which is correct because it is a condition contrary to fact.'"[6] Throughout his life, Teddy understood and appreciated his mother. In letters and visits, he appeared to know just how far his teasing of her could go. She adored his attentiveness and patience with her maternal guidance.

Again poking fun at Rose's punctilious nature, Teddy eulogized, "Mother always thought her children should strive for the highest place. But inside the family, with love and laughter, she knew how to put each of us in our place. She was ambitious not only for our success, but for our souls. From our youth, we remember how, with effortless ease, she could bandage a cut, dry a tear, recite from memory 'The Midnight Ride of Paul Revere,' and spot a hole in a sock from a hundred yards away." Turning more serious, his voice breaking, the Massachusetts senator recalled, "She sustained us in our saddest times by her faith in God, which was the greatest gift she gave us—and by the strength of her character, which was the combination of the sweetest gentleness and the most tempered steel. . . . What any of us has done—whatever contribution we have made—begins and ends with Rose and Joe Kennedy. For all of us, Dad was the spark. Mother was the light of our lives. He was our greatest fan. She was our greatest teacher." Teddy looked to the future when Rose would "welcome the rest of us home [to heaven]." Until then, Teddy concluded, "Mother's prayers will continue to be more than enough to see us through." Returning to his pew, the sixty-two-year-old senator reached toward Rose's coffin and whispered, "I love you, Mother."

To Handel's "Hallelujah" chorus, the family followed Rose's casket out of St. Stephen's. Clouds had broken and sun shone, bathing the hearse in soft winter light. Still hobbled by the effects of his broken back, suffered in a 1964 plane crash that killed his pilot and Senate aide, Teddy gingerly folded his ample body into the lead limousine's front seat. Before he departed for Brookline's Holyhood Cemetery, where Rose would be interred next to her husband, the senator spied several veteran Senate colleagues exiting from the church. He left the car's warmth to shake hands, clasp them on the shoulder, and thank them for coming. Close friends, like Democratic senator Christopher Dodd of Connecticut and Republican senator Orrin Hatch of Utah, merited special attention, and he led them to the limousine's open door to speak with his sisters. There Teddy stood on the sidewalk, with the funeral procession idling, until he had shaken the hand of every mourner departing the church. Just like Rose's father, Honey Fitz, born in a nearby Irish tenement and destined to become a North End ward boss, state senator, US congressman, and mayor, Senator Kennedy never missed an opportunity to press the flesh, especially now that he was locked in a tough reelection campaign with Mitt Romney. It was a simple and fitting coda for the celebrated Irish American matriarch who had given birth to the most influential political dynasty of the twentieth century.

CHAPTER I

Honey Fitz's Daughter

APPROACHING THE JOHN F. KENNEDY LIBRARY, HOME TO ROSE'S three hundred archival boxes, takes the visitor along Boston's Dorchester Bay. On a sunny day the water's sparkle accents the small Harbor Islands. Dead ahead rises the nine-story library, I. M. Pei's modern edifice of white poured concrete and glass, dramatically poised at the bay's edge like a gleaming ship ready to launch. On the bay side of the building sits JFK's twenty-six-foot sailboat, *Victura*, displayed on a manicured point of land. Onshore breezes produce an invigorating burst of fresh salt air that recalls Kennedy sailing excursions off Hyannis Port.

The contrast of arriving at the library from the northwest couldn't be more pronounced. Condos line the beach, blocking bay views. Suddenly the street that seems to be heading directly to the library turns sharply, detouring around a monstrous Boston Public Works building behind a chain-link fence. Constructed of dreary gray granite, the Gothic castle might once have camouflaged a pumping station. It has fallen into utter disrepair, punctuated by broken windows, decaying walls, and boarded-up entries. The grounds are equally squalid. Mounds of mulch and road salt spill out of storage sheds. Occasionally a city dump truck roars off the property, spewing a cloud of dust. On hot days a nauseating stench wafts from grates outside the fence. The scene evokes F. Scott Fitzgerald's valley of ashes—the wasteland Jay Gatsby traversed to reach New York City from his Long Island mansion.

Whereas evil forces in *The Great Gatsby* ultimately destroyed the eponymous character, Rose Kennedy declared after her sons' assassinations, "I'm going to carry on."[1] Indeed, she did, struggling to rise above the darkness that threatened to envelop her. She reached for the light and clarity now symbolized in the Kennedy Library's facade. Her mission included mitigating or dispelling any blot on her family's public image, which she meticulously strove to create and convey. "Mother is a perfectionist," Teddy Kennedy explained.[2] She demanded perfection from herself and attempted to perfect everyone and everything around her. What she couldn't perfect, she ignored or masked.

Born Rose Elizabeth, on July 22, 1890, to John Francis and Mary Josephine (Josie) Hannon Fitzgerald, she was only two generations removed from the muck and mire of Ireland's peat bogs and peasant farms. Fleeing the blighted isle in the midst of the 1840s potato famine, Rose's paternal grandparents, Thomas Fitzgerald, a farmer, and Rose Mary Murray, both left County Wexford for a better life in the New World. They sailed to Boston on filthy death traps dubbed "coffin ships," where a quarter of émigrés typically perished en route. The couple met, wed, and produced eleven children in Boston. One of them, Rose's father, was born during the American Civil War in an eight-family North End tenement. Rose began her revisionist family history by labeling John Fitzgerald's birthplace "a modest flat."[3] She accurately pinpointed the source of her interest in American history by noting her father's fascination with North End landmarks, starting with the Old North Church, where Paul Revere's comrade signaled that the British army was indeed coming to quell the American revolutionaries.

A bundle of frenetic energy, Rose's father married beautiful but reserved Josie Hannon from Acton, Massachusetts, in 1889. Her parents hailed from County Limerick. A graduate of Boston Latin

School, established in 1635, making it America's first public school, John Fitzgerald studied medicine at Harvard for less than a year before leaving to care for his six younger brothers after their parents died in close succession. He acquired a civil service clerkship in Boston's Customs House, earning $1,200 to $1,800 annually.

At the North End's 4 Garden Court Street, John and Josie welcomed baby Rose, their firstborn. The little girl exhibited physical and personality traits acquired from both parents. Her flashing blue eyes matched her father's, but she developed lush dark hair like her mother's thick tresses. To the ghostwriter of her 1974 memoir, journalist Robert Coughlan, Rose observed admiringly that her mother's hair "never was gray. Her hair always stayed its natural color—even when she was quite old her hair was quite dark. . . . Everybody thinks that the reason my hair isn't gray is that I have it done so expertly that it doesn't look gray, doesn't look dyed."[4]

John Fitzgerald sported a compact, athletic frame, and Josie, a petite woman, stood perfectly erect well into her tenth decade. Rose maintained ramrod posture for most of her life, along with her girlish figure. A "nervous tummy," which she inherited from her father, prompted her to eat birdlike portions of bland foods. For years she existed on baked potatoes, toast, custard, and sponge cake. Most photos of Rose as an adult picture her holding one hand behind her back and turning at an angle toward the camera. She advised her children and grandchildren to do the same in order to appear thinner. In modern parlance, Rose exhibited "body image" issues.

Rose also inherited her father's broad jaw line and aquiline nose, making her face appear more mature at an early age. Her sister, Agnes, two years younger, acquired their mother's softer, more refined, facial features. Rose admitted, "My sister was very attractive. In fact, she was the beauty of the family."[5] Self-deprecatingly, she often told the story that when her father took Agnes and her to meet William McKinley in 1897, the president exclaimed to Agnes, "You are the prettiest girl who has entered the White House!" A teenaged John F. Kennedy would tease, "Why didn't he say that to you, Mother?"[6]

If the genetic lottery denied her Josie's natural beauty, Rose enhanced her attractive features and exhibited the best of her mother's common sense. "There was no use in getting excited over little things, getting nervous, getting upset," Rose reported about her mother's equanimity.[7] Yet her whirling-dervish father bestowed an energy and joie de vivre on her firstborn. "He talked to me incessantly when I was a child . . . about everything in sight," especially Boston's historic landmarks. She so completely adopted his rapid-fire speaking manner that teachers called on young Rose for class recitations if the bell was about to ring. Although exhibiting none of her mother's introversion, Rose's self-contained personality allowed her to sit quietly alone and read as a child or travel by herself and spend long solitary hours as an adult. Yet she was completely at ease before crowds. She frequently observed with pride, "I'd been in the limelight since I was practically five years old,"[8] when her father won election to the US House of Representatives. He had already served on the Boston Common Council (1891 to 1892) and in the state senate (1892 to 1894). Possessing a leprechaun's twinkle, charm, and mischievousness, John Fitzgerald exemplified the paradigmatic Irish politician. Crooning "Sweet Adeline," and displaying Irish loquaciousness, he earned the label "Fitzblarney" for his presentations and the nickname "Honey Fitz."

Rose attended first grade at St. John School in her North Square neighborhood. Founded in 1873, the school is located on Boston's Freedom Trail, which includes Paul Revere's North End home. The school's current mission recalls its goal in Rose's era: teach the children of new immigrants. Although Rose wouldn't attend Catholic schools again until after high school, she maintained a devotion to Jesus's mother throughout her life and remembered St. John as "where I learned my prayers."[9]

At age seven Rose and her family, now joined by sister Agnes and brother Tom, left Boston, moving northwest twenty miles to 391 Main Street in West Concord, near historic and picturesque Concord. The Fitzgerald family was now closer to Josie's parents in adjacent Acton, where she had grown up on a farm. Making the half-hour trip by horse and buggy to visit the Hannons nearly every summer day provided some of Rose's happiest childhood memories. She loved rural life, with its predictable seasonal rhythms, the freedom to explore nature, and family traditions like making home-churned ice cream using farm-fresh ingredients.

Yet Rose sometimes begrudged being the oldest child in a growing brood that eventually numbered six after the addition of her sister Eunice and brothers John Jr. and Frederick. She remembered her mother teaching the older children catechism while feeding the infants. "There was always a baby in the house," she recalled, "which I rather resented . . . because most of my friends had only a brother or sister. They didn't have six members in their family. I couldn't get much attention because I was the oldest and left to go on my own." She admitted, however, that being the eldest gave her "self-confidence" and made her "independent."[10] Catholic Rose, both as daughter and mother, always found herself at odds with American birthrates. From her own birth in 1890, until her last child's arrival in 1932, the average number of children born to women who lived to age fifty continued a decline from a high of seven in 1800 to a low of two by 1940.[11]

Rose's youthful disquietude may also have stemmed from her father's frequent absences. In 1894, three years before the family moved from Boston, Honey Fitz had won election to the US House of Representatives, where he served until 1901. As a young girl, she accompanied her father to scores of dedications, parades, banquets, and political rallies. There she absorbed his lessons of maintaining the common touch. Rose discovered the balance between making her privileged life intriguing to voters while portraying herself as approachable and empathetic. Foreshadowing her own married life, Rose had to adjust to her father being in Washington during the week and returning on weekends during his congressional career. Sometimes both her mother and father left her and the Fitzgerald siblings behind to vacation at health spas. A nursemaid and housekeeper cared for the children.

A stern disciplinarian, Rose's mother ran a strict household, trying to control the chaos of having five children in the span of less than a decade, followed by the sixth four years later. Believing that rod-sparing spoiled children, Josie inflicted corporal punishment if they violated punctuality, neatness, or etiquette rules. She expected them to study secular and religious lessons assiduously. In 1968 Rose wrote to a journalist that her father had "exercised the greatest influence" on her, in part, because as "a devout Catholic, my father brought me up in a religious atmosphere. He often discussed the great heritage of art and learning as well as of faith and morals which the Church had bequeathed to its members."[12] Yet she credited her mother with imparting religious faith to her. Although Honey Fitz followed the Catholic Church's requirement of weekly and holy-day Mass attendance, Rose claimed that he did so as much to engage with friends and constituents as to commune with the Almighty.

In contrast, Josie incorporated Catholicism into the household's routine. Each May, the month that the Church devotes to Mother Mary, Rose and her siblings erected a shrine to the Blessed Virgin and decorated it with fresh flowers. For a devout Catholic girl who loved gathering blossoms in West Concord's idyllic meadows, this ritual made a lifelong impression. More painfully, Rose remembered how her mother insisted that the children pray the rosary with her each of Lent's forty nights, while they knelt on the hard floor of their darkened living room.[13] Nevertheless, Rose rhapsodized about the comfort that fingering rosary beads gave her during the most tragic times in her adult life. She suggested to her grown children that they turn to the rosary rather than alcohol, pills, or cigarettes to relieve their anxiety. "Instead, if they said a 'Hail Mary,' it would be much better for their figures than an extra drink."[14] Given the Kennedy family's well-documented addiction problems, Rose's descendants would have saved more than their physiques by heeding her advice.

One of Rose's favorite childhood pastimes was driving her horse-drawn carriage to the town library and borrowing books by Louisa May Alcott, who lived in Concord from 1845 to 1888. As a preteen, Rose devoured Alcott's works, including *An Old-Fashioned Girl*, *Little Men*, *Eight Cousins*, and the classic *Little Women*. The March daughters' adoration for their heroic, absent father must have resonated with Rose. "I think her books inspired me to lead a studious, poised life . . ." Rose remembered.[15] Alcott also offered a model for creating fictional images that masked painful realities.[16]

Alcott's Concord was imbued with Transcendental values, including striving for perfection, Rose's lifelong pursuit. Bronson Alcott, Louisa's father, joined his neighboring philosophers, Ralph Waldo Emerson and Henry David Thoreau, in attempting to perfect human beings, to be at one with nature, God, and reason. Unfortunately for Bronson's theory, Louisa's nature proved rebellious. Perhaps *Little Women*'s rosy interpretation of childhood is Louisa's homage to her father. Yet Jo, nearly every girl's favorite character in the book, is so beloved because of her obstreperous streak. Rose would soon enough challenge her own father's efforts to corral her teenage passions.

Another influence on Rose's childhood and, ultimately, her own maternal instincts were prevailing Victorian social mores. As women's historian Kathryn Sklar writes, "Seeing it possible to exert in early childhood an influence of lifelong personal and social significance, Victorians were far more sensitive than their ancestors had been to the importance of the right kind of mothering."[17] Republican Motherhood, a New England movement that encouraged women to produce patriotic sons who would serve in government, specified the goal of successful mothering. It also emphasized women's education so that they could teach republican virtues to their children.[18]

Exploring Concord's environs, most happily with her gregarious father, Rose embraced history lessons permeating the cradle of American independence. Born in the shadow of the Old North Church, educated initially in Paul Revere's neighborhood, she had then moved near the destination of Revere's legendary ride, where 1775's "shot heard 'round the world" at Lexington signaled the colonists' revolt from England. No wonder Longfellow's "The Midnight Ride of Paul Revere" remained one of her favorite poems, cited by son Teddy in his eulogy to her. For her eighty-fifth birthday, Rose requested that each of her grandchildren memorize a stanza. "Some of the naughtier ones misquoted a verse or two to

test Mother's memory," Teddy reported, "but she caught them."[19]
When several of her grandchildren, including Caroline Kennedy,
attended Concord Academy, Rose penned a letter to its headmaster,
inquiring whether the school took students to America's founding
landmarks.[20] She also instructed Caroline to visit the Alcott house,
telling her how much she had loved reading Louisa's novels as a girl.

Rose had continued her own education at Edward Everett
Grammar School and studied a year at Concord High School,
always achieving top marks. "My father was in Congress and that
put me in a unique position as far as my school friends were concerned in public school," she remarked in 1972, clearly relishing
those days when she first began to stand out among her peers.[21]

In 1901, having served three terms in the US House of Representatives, Honey Fitz left Congress when hometown Democratic
bosses, including Patrick Joseph (P. J.) Kennedy, blocked his renom-
ination. Undeterred, Honey Fitz set his sights on Boston's mayoral
office. In the meantime Fitzgerald purchased and became the publisher of a weekly newspaper, *The Republic*. Under his guidance, it
thrived, and in 1903 he moved the family closer to downtown Boston, into another rambling home. Located in suburban Dorchester's
Ashmont Hill, the sprawling Italianate house with mansard eaves
sat above Welles Avenue. While Rose compiled superb grades at
Dorchester High School and played intramural sports, her father
maintained his position as the North End's ward boss and formed a
temporary alliance with his counterpart in East Boston, P. J. Kennedy. Like Fitzgerald's mother and father, Kennedy's parents had
emigrated from Ireland and settled in Boston, where his father died
in middle age. A successful tavern owner, liquor importer, and
banker, Kennedy had risen into the Irish American middle class and
served eight terms in the state legislature.[22]

When Mayor Patrick Collins died suddenly in 1905, John Fitzgerald pounced on the opportunity to run for the Democratic
nomination. Kennedy and other ward bosses opposed him, but they
were no match for the "Little General," another moniker the
diminutive Fitzgerald earned. "The energetic forty-two-year-old
Fitzgerald . . . traveled from one ward to another in the back seat of

a large open-air touring car, delivering more than ten speeches a day to enthusiastic crowds. On primary eve [he] organized the city's first motorcade, complete with honking horns and blazing red flares, during which he spoke in every one of the city's twenty-five wards." Completing the campaigning in his beloved "dear old North End," where his supporters dubbed themselves "Dearos," Fitzgerald captured the nomination by nearly 4,000 votes. In the general election he won the mayor's office with 44,171 votes, more than 8,000 ahead of his nearest rival.[23]

Taking the oath in Boston's old City Hall on New Year's Day 1906, John F. Fitzgerald became the city's first native-born Irish Catholic mayor. The pastor of St. Stephen's Church, site of John's and Rose's baptisms, offered the invocation. Once in office, Mayor Fitzgerald launched into a blur of activity, implementing his slogan, "A Bigger, Better, Busier, Boston." "Because my father was in Congress and then he was mayor for six years, I was always more or less prominent. . . ," Rose explained about her youthful fame in Boston. "When I graduated [from Dorchester High School in 1905], he was the one who gave me my diploma, so . . . eyes were focused on me when I was graduating from school. And I went abroad with him and we had special suites on the boat. . . ."[24] She embraced public life with the same gusto as her extroverted father, and he chose her to accompany him to numerous official functions. Dressed like the iconic Gibson girl, Rose proudly stood next to Mayor Fitzgerald as he acknowledged passing soldiers in a festive 1910 parade.[25]

When asked by her memoirist why Josie Fitzgerald abdicated her role as the mayor's wife, Rose initially took issue with that characterization, defending her mother's choices. "[S]he was so . . . devoted and . . . really gave me my character, gave me my religious instructions. . . . And she was very attractive and always kept a girlish figure, which was great. Which my father viewed with great pride because a good many of his contemporar[ies] had wives who were rather fat and rugged looking, and she always maintained that very chic slim figure, which all the pictures show."[26]

Justifying her mother's choices, Rose responded, "You see the woman had six children," and women did not participate in politics "in those days. In the White House or in the social world, you didn't hear anything about the women's movement."[27] Perhaps Rose didn't hear about it in her circles, but the women's suffrage movement shifted into high gear during her father's tenure as mayor, especially during his second term between 1910 and 1914. Alice Paul of the National American Woman Suffrage Association, founded in Rose's birth year, 1890, had organized more than five thousand women to parade down Pennsylvania Avenue on the eve of Woodrow Wilson's 1913 inauguration.[28]

Rose's indifference to women's political issues marked most of her life. Although the Kennedy men used her to attract female votes, she did so usually by talking about her family and encouraging women to vote for her sons, rarely by discussing women's issues related to health, jobs, wages, childcare, or education. In 1962 she encouraged women to support Teddy's first run for the US Senate because no Kennedy had lost an election since females garnered the right to vote in 1920. She also visited his campaign headquarters to bolster women volunteers.[29]

Rose translated her secondary role into a primary one: asked if she would rather be a senator or president herself or the mother of one, she chose the latter. She was a Victorian who had trained her sons to be important contributors to society in a post-Victorian age when women wanted to serve society directly rather than through their children. Holding her first baby (Joe Jr.) in her arms was the most meaningful event in her life.[30]

Rose asserted that her mother's absence from public events resulted from her devotion to "children, church, and kitchen." "That was [women's] main function, and they were quite happy to do that. And [Mother] was happy that way."[31] Rose claimed that initially her mother "upheld the duties [of] hostess for the mayor very well. There wasn't very much to do, but there were tea parties, and she belonged to . . . a club for Catholic women."[32] Displaying youthful enthusiasm for public duties, Rose embraced more of them.[33]

As Mayor Fitzgerald's companion, Rose attracted her own headlines. At sixteen she accompanied him to Philadelphia to christen the *Bunker Hill*, a large steamship named for her hometown's Revolutionary War battle. Newspapers announced her upcoming trip to the launching ceremonies. By train, she traveled to Philadelphia with her father, along with a Boston contingent and group of New York City officials.[34] She was especially pleased that the steamship company presented her with a "handsome locket of pearls and diamonds."[35]

Soon after, the *Boston Sunday Globe* published a feature story on Rose's autograph collection. Writing to statesmen, kings, and rulers throughout the world, she asked for their signatures. A photograph of her most prized acquisition, President Theodore Roosevelt's autograph on a White House calling card, appeared in the paper.[36] Rose adored being near important personages. Her lifelong autograph pursuit gave her a sense of proximity to influence, especially when she collected a VIP's signature in person.

Although Honey Fitz had transitioned his political career from Washington to Boston, his continued absence from the Fitzgerald household earned Rose's criticism years later. "I was certainly not happy about that. . . . I'm sure none of us were, especially my mother." Yet Rose justified his absence as the price a "political family" has to pay. "I watched my own sons and their wives and children go through the same strains and disappointments."[37]

Honey Fitz's initial disapproval of her future husband also strained relations between Rose and her father. For years the Fitzgerald family had vacationed each summer at Old Orchard Beach, Maine, where other Irish Catholic Bostonians gathered, including P. J. Kennedy and his family. His oldest child, Joseph P. Kennedy, two years Rose's senior, first laid eyes on her when he was ten. A Boston newspaper photo shows the two children standing a few feet apart, but neither remembered this encounter in later years. Meeting again as teenagers on the Maine beach, Rose fell deeply in love with the fair-haired boy and his warm smile. Attired in their Victorian bathing costumes—for women, long woolen dresses and stockings—Rose relaxed on the beach with P. J. Kennedy and his son Joe. Sitting several feet from her future husband, Rose smiled broadly, betraying her happiness.[38] The object of Rose's teenage affection possessed her father's energy and drive, attended his alma mater (Boston Latin School), and starred on its baseball team.

Believing she deserved a more suitable beau, however, Honey Fitz disapproved of Rose's crush on his political rival's son.

Rose had earned her high school diploma through a three-year course prevalent in the early twentieth century. The *Boston Post* ran a photo of Rose receiving her diploma from her father, the mayor. Only fifteen when she graduated, Rose took a year of college preparatory courses, hoping to attend Wellesley, the premier women's college, located in a Boston suburb. In fact, Rose wrote to a friend that she would "soon [be] at Wellesley."[39] To her lifelong disappointment, Honey Fitz vetoed her enrollment. She maintained that he thought her too young, only seventeen if she had matriculated in 1907. Doris Kearns Goodwin offers another explanation: Boston's archbishop convinced Mayor Fitzgerald that such a prominent Irish Catholic should not enroll his daughter in a secular college.[40] Instead, he sent her to the Sacred Heart Convent in downtown Boston. Rose also took classes at the New England Conservatory of Music, honing her skills as an amateur pianist. Well into her seventies, she would play her father's theme song, "Sweet Adeline," hitting all the right notes in a slightly arrhythmic tempo. All her life she regretted Honey Fitz's decision barring her from Wellesley, but, typically, she claimed it disguised a blessing.

AFTER LOSING HIS 1908 reelection, amid charges of cronyism and administrative incompetence, Honey Fitz took Josie and their two oldest daughters to Europe for what Rose presumed was a brief vacation. Yet Honey Fitz used the trip to place an ocean between her and young Joe Kennedy. Just four days shy of her eighteenth birthday, Rose began her first overseas adventure. She and her family waved farewell with billowing red handkerchiefs to two launches accompanying the ship out of Boston harbor that sultry July afternoon. One carried her father's friends, another her aunts and uncles. The departing Fitzgeralds signaled to the launches until the small boats disappeared over the horizon.

The ex-mayor's family found their staterooms filled with flowers and candy to wish them well. Always worried about her "tummy," its sensitivity now compounded by possible seasickness, Rose "did not dare eat any" of the candy the first night out of port "except a little butterscotch." They sailed through fog and drizzle, making their way through the choppy North Atlantic, bound for London. On the second day, Rose received an invitation "to participate in Sunday service of the Church of England but declined . . . to play the piano for the singing of hymns."[41] The Roman Catholic Church instructed its adherents not to participate in other religions' services or even enter a non-Catholic church.

After a brief London stay, the Fitzgeralds crossed the Irish Sea to Dublin and their ancestors' Emerald Isle. Rose's diary didn't rhapsodize over Eire. Her family, like many with immigrant roots, was becoming a full-fledged participant in the American dream.[42] After touring Dublin, Killarney, and Cork, the family returned to England via Stratford-on-Avon, where Honey Fitz showed them Shakespeare's grave and regaled them with stories of the bard's plays. Taking the train back to London, Rose caught her first glimpse of Windsor Castle. "One part reserved now, where present king lives, but which we only saw from a distance," Rose recorded.[43] She couldn't know that it would become a prominent landmark in her life story.

Then the Boston quartet sailed across the English Channel and journeyed by train to Paris, which captured Rose's heart. She seemed most intrigued by all things Napoleonic, even more so than by Catholic landmarks. Stunning Sacré Coeur, atop Montmartre, earned only "Church of Sacred Heart on high hill" in her diary. On to Switzerland and Germany the family traveled, where Rose noted all the "honey-mooners" in Lucerne and the "beautiful cathedral" in Cologne.[44] Honey Fitz predicted that "there was sure to be a war later because Germans, an ambitious and industrious race, were crowded into a congested area and were bound to seek more territory."[45] Honey Fitz and Josie bid a sad farewell to Rose and Agnes in Holland. There they enrolled in Blumenthal, a Sacred Heart convent, near the convergence of the Dutch, Belgian, and Prussian borders. It would shape Rose's life, but not in the way her father had hoped.

CHAPTER 2

❧

"Your Obedient Child"

DESPITE HONEY FITZ'S MOTIVE FOR SENDING ROSE TO THE convent—in order to cool her ardor for Joe Kennedy—she later described the decision more benignly. Asked whether her father had sent her abroad as an "escape" from young Joe, she responded, "Well, I don't think that was it. [Father] said, 'You have been talking about studying abroad.' That was one of my great ambitions to study abroad. . . . I was crazy about traveling. I used to spend Saturday afternoons" going to travel lectures on Paris, London, and Rome and to presentations delivered in French or German to maintain foreign language skills.[1]

Rose would have preferred to study in France, but in 1905 the French government had mandated strict separation of church and state, prohibiting state recognition, funding, or endorsement of religious groups. Without government resources, convents could no longer operate their schools.[2] Across the border, Germany's Protestant chancellor Otto von Bismarck had battled the Catholic Church, seized its schools in 1871, and expelled Jesuits from the empire.[3] Although church-state conflict eased over the next decade, many nuns fled Prussian tyranny. Blumenthal provided refuge to

French and Prussian nuns, and they taught in their native languages. The convent was located in Vaals, Holland, a small town near the Prussian border city of Aachen, which the French called Aix-la-Chapelle, historic capital of Charlemagne's empire. Although Rose's classmates were primarily from Germany, several other Americans enrolled with the Fitzgerald sisters. Students from France and other European countries added to the school's national diversity, though most students came from wealthy Catholic families. Rose polished her French and German language skills, serving as a trilingual interpreter for fellow students.[4] Her linguistic fluency would serve her well in future travels and in her duties as a mayor's daughter, ambassador's wife, and president's mother.

Rose's convent life couldn't have been more strictly organized.[5] The nuns' routine combined British boarding-school regimentation with Marine boot-camp discipline. At least Rose could rely on her sister for company, but they both suffered painful homesickness. Whatever her upset over spartan conditions and separation from Joe, Rose practiced her lifelong discipline of hiding negative feelings. Letters home always put a sunny gloss on even the most dreary aspects of convent life. "Well, here we both are safely packed away at last in Blumenthal," she wrote. "We have a dear little room . . . and after we put our rugs in, and the pictures on the walls, I am sure it will look real homelike. The nuns are simply lovely to us, and do all in their power to make everything as agreeable as possible."[6] After the first week of classes she reported with relief, "I am glad because I think the first week is always the longest." Anyone who ever pined for family while far away from home, in an era without phone or Internet, feels the poignancy of Rose telling her parents, "Your pictures are standing on our writing tables, whenever we raise our eyes from our books there you are." She didn't tell her parents that she also displayed Joe's photo.[7]

All girls who have worn an unflattering Catholic school uniform, especially one as Victorian as the convent's, could appreciate Rose's sardonic description: "Our black uniforms [with high collars and black aprons] are all made and really are not *very* repulsive looking after all."[8] At least the girls could wear festive white dresses on religious holidays. The convent rules didn't require head coverings for the students, but Rose's and Agnes's beautiful tresses had to be pulled straight back in braids tied with ribbons. Every three weeks they submitted to a thorough "rubbing and scrubbing" of their hair.

As a youngster, Rose tended to run late for appointments, but the convent's strict schedule made her punctual. When she scolded son Jack for his tardiness, she never admitted that it might have been congenital.

The convent's frenetic pace, however, didn't mask Rose's wistfulness. "We have not wasted a second," she wrote home. "I am rather glad, for when I have a great deal more to do the time goes more quickly, and I feel as though a year ought not to be very long in passing, and then I can go home, and never have to go away again." Years later, she reported that her youngest son, Teddy, survived boarding-school loneliness by remembering that his older brothers had soldiered through homesickness. Rose always used this example to illustrate how training older children to be strong and responsible redounded to younger siblings. She overlooked or ignored just how lonely her children were, though they wrote to her constantly about missing their family while away at school or when their parents left them home with household staff and family friends.

As late as the 1960s, American Catholic schools proscribed talking everywhere except classrooms (but only when called on by the teacher) and playgrounds (unless the "silence bell" had rung). At Blumenthal Rose and Agnes could only converse with each other just before bedtime. The nuns allowed the students to chat for a few minutes at breakfast. During lunch, they listened to German readings; dinnertime featured French recitations. Rose asked her parents to send newspapers and magazines, along with sheet music from popular favorites like "Take Me Out to the Ball Game." Realizing that Boston politics remained contentious, she wrote, "So glad Pa is not bothering with [it]." The convent's isolation precluded updates on the 1908 presidential election, so Rose asked her parents to report the victor. It was Republican William Howard Taft.

Making the best of this sober lifestyle, Rose joined the student sodality and began to rise through its ranks. She started as an "angel," the lowest level of membership. Each morning she arose at 6 a.m., a quarter-hour earlier than required, for prayerful meditation. "So you see my piety is increasing," she wrote home. "If I am extremely angelic, I may become an aspirant for the Children of Mary; later I may become a Child of Mary. This is the highest honor a child of the Sacred Heart can receive. So I shall have to be a model of *perfection* for the next few months."[9] Now Rose added religious perfection to the secular variety from her Victorian childhood.

Devotion to the Blessed Virgin is a revealing aspect of Rose's commitment to flawlessness. The Catholic Church's doctrine regarding the mother of Jesus Christ centers on her purity: God chose Mary to bear His Son because she was virginal, untainted by man. She conceived the Savior through the Holy Spirit's power. Chosen for this sacred role, Mary's conception had been "immaculate," without the stain of original sin on her soul. Because her body bore the Christ Child, God didn't expose it to death's decay. With her life on earth complete, Mary was "assumed" into heaven—body and soul. These aspects of the Blessed Virgin's story repeat themselves in the rosary's Glorious and Joyful Mysteries— two themes pondered while reciting five decades, or sets of ten beads, each representing the prayer Hail, Mary. When life's trage- dies enveloped her, Rose would identify with the rosary's Sorrow- ful Mysteries, including Mary's vigil at her Son's Crucifixion.

Rose continued her musical training at the convent and enjoyed attending symphony concerts in Aachen conducted by famed Ger- man composer Richard Strauss. The Germans' "industry, ambi- tion, and ready acceptance of hard tasks; [as well as] respect for learning," especially study of foreign language, impressed young Rose. "I admired the respect [German] children had for the authority of their parents and the deep sense of spiritual responsi- bility parents felt for their children, demonstrated in such a lovely, open way. I often saw the sign of the cross made on a child's fore- head when he and his parents met after a separation," Rose observed.[10] All that she appreciated about German values she would try to practice in her own life.

Writing to Honey Fitz in November 1908, Rose asked for permission to travel with Agnes during their two-week Christmas break. Rose pulled out all the rhetorical stops in making her case. "I have something very important and exciting to tell you so I hope my words will be persuasive and you will say 'Yes,'" Rose began. Dropping a smidgen of guilt on her parents, she continued, "We love Blumenthal very dearly, but we do not at all relish the idea of spending our vacation here, when all the others are home, having a happy time with their families. We can take a two-week round trip from Aachen to Hanover, to Berlin, to Dresden, to Leipzig, to Cologne and back to Aachen, with room and board and incidentals, for about $140 [$3,300 in 2012]. This amount seems very large, but I hate to get away and not have enough," she wrote. "The cities we want to visit will prove interesting. They contain famous picture galleries and churches. An opportunity would also be afforded us to go to the theater, and see some of Goethe's and Schiller's plays." Rose assured her father that she and Agnes would have a proper chaperone, the nuns approved of their plan, and the sisters would write ahead to convents for lodging. After outlining her rationale, Rose tugged at Honey Fitz's heartstrings: "We do not want to spend the holidays here. It would make us too lonesome. I do hope Mother will approve. If I could only talk to her I am sure she would. We will think of you when you cut the [Thanksgiving] *Turkey* tomorrow."[11] In case her father approved, Rose told him where to send money for the trip.

With letters crisscrossing the Atlantic, Rose received a troubling message from her parents suggesting that the girls might consider staying another year at the convent. "It is very nice for girls who are used to boarding school life, but I prefer to be home in America," Rose frankly informed her parents. She turned to the issue of Christmas travel and pleaded, "So you see all we are waiting for is a word from you and then we can trot off. Send us a cablegram and just say 'Yes.' We would understand what you mean." Rose's prayers and supplications produced the answer she and Agnes desired. Expressing their gratitude, Rose wrote home: "We both were so happy and vowed that you and Pa were the best and the dearest

father and mother in the world. We shall both think of you at the
[Christmas] midnight Mass, and pray for you. We have a great deal
of opportunity to pray here. Happy New Year. Your loving and
devoted daughter."

The Fitzgerald sisters embraced their travel opportunity. Spending New Year's in Berlin, they saw the German royal family in the
loge directly below them at Wagner's *Tannhäuser*. As she would for
the rest of her adult life, Rose described in detail her attire. "We
had to wear 'décolleté' gowns and you should have seen us," she
wrote, clearly excited about wearing a strapless, low-cut dress, particularly after enduring high-necked convent uniforms and Victorian styles at home. The sisters moved on to Dresden and enjoyed
its "beautiful galleries," then traveled to Leipzig. After a quick visit
to Weimar and Eisenach, they returned to their austere convent
existence.[12] Although the "Reverend Mothers" and "Mother General" stayed up late to welcome the girls back to the convent and
allowed them to relate the adventures of their trip, they soon began
a three-day retreat of contemplative silence. "Of course the retreat
is a great blessing," Rose solemnly informed her parents.

Rose kept track of all her expenses to report to Honey Fitz
because she had "borrow[ed] more money than I expected." She
alerted him that their "school books are only loaned us like they are
in the public schools," but they would have to purchase school supplies. In addition, they bought curtains, facecloths, hair ribbons,
emery boards, pins, needles, and laundry bags. They also had to pay
for a carriage to take them across the border to Aachen, as well as a
chaperone to accompany them. They even had to hire someone to
supervise their walks. Agnes's white skirt was their most expensive
purchase ($22), along with a pair of black gloves ($7.50). Souvenir
cards, stationery, stamps, and cakes rounded out Rose's schoolgirl
necessities.[13] From then on she kept meticulous lists of all her travel
needs and expenditures.

As spring approached, the girls received more letters from home
about staying abroad another year. Rose skillfully cited her parents
as part of the reason that Agnes and she should return home. "It
would be too much of a sacrifice for you and for us to remain away

another year. If I did not *love* you all so *madly*, I might consider another year or two. But I often think, how could I ever forgive myself if anything should ever happen to you and Papa while we are over here."[14] From the convent Rose wrote that she hoped her father would avoid the next mayoral race so as not "to use all his strength and tire himself out, bothered with politics. It is so much better to have him in good health and free from worry."

With the 1908–9 school year ending, Rose proudly reported that she had "received my medal for the Child of Mary . . . the highest honor and blessing a Sacred Heart girl can get and one which we all strive for. We are supposed to be a model and help in the school, and someone to be depended upon." The nuns had selected her as one of the most responsible girls because she had mastered the order's commitment to faith, sacrifice, discipline, and piety. From then on, she closed letters to all Catholic clergy and nuns, "Your obedient child." Such subservience never bothered her, nor did the Catholic Church's patriarchy. In her future maternal role, she would try to instill obedience, discipline, and responsibility in all her children—with varying degrees of success.

In June 1909 Honey Fitz informed his daughters that he would run again for mayor. Giving them permission to return home, at least for the summer break, he sailed for Europe to escort them. His welcome news seemed "like some lovely dream" to Rose, but she worried about his leaving in the midst of the campaign to spend weeks abroad collecting her and Agnes. Rose assured Honey Fitz that they could make the return trip home unescorted. All they needed would be a "stunning" outfit to wear for their arrival in the port of Boston. She so wanted to be reunited with her family, and Joe no doubt, that she wrote, "I dare not think about home much because my imagination runs away with me. . . ."

WHEN SCHOOL ENDED in mid-July, the Fitzgerald girls departed for Amsterdam and a visit to the tiny Zuiderzee island of Marken. After a quick stop in The Hague, they went to Brussels, where they received a cable from their father that he had arrived in Paris. There they reunited and crossed the Channel to London, discovering that a national holiday had closed down the city. Honey Fitz took his daughters to Cowes, the seaside resort near the Isle of Wight. "A great regatta of boats of every description" had amassed offshore. England's King Edward VII had invited his nephew, Germany's Kaiser Wilhelm II, aboard the British royal yacht *Victoria and Albert III*. "What an eye dazzling display with all the yachts, big and little, decorated with gay flags and gala colors," remembered Rose, "and little motor boats darting back and forth filled with pretty girls visiting the yachts."[15]

Her father recognized Irish tea magnate Sir Thomas Lipton's boat *Erin III* bobbing in the waves. Honey Fitz so wanted to go aboard and introduce his beautiful daughters to his old friend. "As we were sitting rather disconsolately on the wharf, tweedling [*sic*] our thumbs, Father noticed a launch dock with the royal coat of arms on the front manned by a couple of sleek officers. With his accustomed initiative for trying everything once," Rose described, "he stepped up to one of them telling them that we had arrived unexpectedly from the United States and wanted to reach the *Erin*, at which news the young Britishers with the courtesy so characteristic of the race saluted and asked us all three to step aboard." Sailors wearing the royal ensign set off for Lipton's boat. "Imagine the excitement and flurry there was aboard the *Erin* when the officer on watch beheld the King's launch approaching," a bemused Rose recorded. "The rumor was broadcast to the guests who rushed to the deck in a mad scene of unparalleled excitement. The American guests aboard had to be coached as to how to curtsy, how to address the King and Queen as Sir and Ma'am, etc. The picture was of extreme disappointment when no one more important than a couple of Boston school girls mounted the yacht's ladder."[16]

Rose and Agnes were thrilled when Sir Thomas invited them to stay the night. Sipping Lipton tea served in china demitasse cups, stamped with a shamrock-and-flag emblem, the girls noted photos in silver shamrock picture frames, commemorating European royalty who had visited the yacht.[17] A photographer captured the Fitzgeralds' visit on *Erin III*, with Agnes sitting on deck at Lipton's feet and Rose posing at his side. The elderly tea mogul, wearing his captain's hat, smiled beneath his white walrus mustache.[18] His ruddy face glowed from the brisk winds or perhaps the charm of Honey Fitz and his pretty daughters. The adventure was Rose's first experience of pomp and attention abroad. Basking in the royal treatment, she would crave it for the rest of her life.

On to Scotland the trio traveled and made three more stops in Ireland (Belfast, Cork, and Dublin) before they sailed for the States. Decades later Rose wrote about seeing "all the pretty Irish colleens embarking there to seek their fortunes in America and their old feeble mothers weeping and saying good-bye to their loved daughters many of whom they would never see again." "I cried myself in sympathy thinking how lucky I was—comparing my lot with theirs."[19] She rarely displayed tearful emotion in public or admitted to such introspection. By the time Rose composed her 1951 remembrances of past sea voyages, however, she had lost literally and metaphorically her "loved daughters" Kathleen and Rosemary. The thought of Irish mothers bidding farewell to their girls forever undoubtedly resurrected sad memories, though she never cited her reason for rethinking her forty-year-old diary. Notably, that year, her son Jack began to prepare for his 1952 Senate race, and Rose campaigned for him around Massachusetts. Irish American voters would be impressed by her stories of sailing with Sir Thomas Lipton; they might even shed a tear over colleens departing the "Old Sod" for America.

More than one year after Rose and Agnes had embarked on their first European trip, they returned to Boston wearing two giant white Parisian feathers in their hats to avoid paying duty on them. "We must have looked a little overdressed," Rose conceded.[20] She had just celebrated her nineteenth birthday and was facing an uncertain future. Harboring no long-term career ambitions, Rose thought she "might teach music because I had played piano, [and] taken lessons at the Conservatory of Music" for many years.[21] Honey Fitz hadn't acquiesced to her romance with Joe Kennedy, nor had her ardor for him dimmed, despite the distraction and isolation of an exciting thirteen months abroad. Joe still had three years left at Harvard, so Rose turned to traditional activities for women of her age and social status.

"We arrived from Europe, and I then spent a year in a New York convent [Academy of the Sacred Heart, a girls' boarding school] and graduated from Manhattanville College."[22] But Rose couldn't receive an earned degree from the college, which had evolved from the academy, because it possessed no state charter to award degrees until 1917. The college bestowed an honorary doctorate on Rose in 1953, and it now ranks her as its most famous alumna. Rose's gender clearly fettered her education. She possessed an inquiring intellect, a facility for languages, and a prodigious academic work ethic, but her father confined her to stultifying convents and Catholic finishing schools.

"In those days girls from well-to-do families never thought much of getting a job, but rather spent their lives in games of bridge, sewing for charities and bazaars, besides a modest round of social engagements and travel," Rose explained.[23] These activities divided along the vast religious and social schism between Protestants and Catholics. She dismissed the divide's impact on her young life: "I was perfectly happy to be in my own group because I knew all the boys and girls or the men and the women."[24] "We just grew up thinking that the [Protestant] Yankees, as we called them, were in one group and the Irish Catholics were in another group. And it was understood, and I knew that when I grew up that I would not be admitted to their clubs. I knew I was as educated as them [a rare grammatical slip for Rose, who should have used the subjective pronoun]. At my debut I had all Catholics. And you knew you would marry a Catholic. In some ways it was much easier."[25]

Rose's dismissal of Boston's religious and socioeconomic cleavages during her youth reflects her characteristic optimism. Ironically, the dual social systems allowed her to thrive as the daughter of the city's most prominent Irish Catholic. Barred from Yankee clubs, including the prestigious Junior League, Rose took the opportunity to establish her own. In 1910 she founded the Lenox

Club, named for the hotel where it held monthly meetings. She changed its name to Ace of Clubs when a guest speaker, an English Jesuit priest, suggested it would designate the group as the premier club for Catholic women who had traveled abroad. Rose became its first president, insisting that the club not simply organize card parties. Instead, she made its mission educational, with current-events discussions and speakers on political and social issues. It provided an early proving ground for Rose to organize peers and focus on public affairs,[26] presaging future dinner-table conversations about public policy with her children and grandchildren that launched many of their public-service careers. She also learned effective public speaking in the safe and supportive environment of female friends. Additionally, the Ace of Clubs sponsored an annual ball that attracted Boston's prominent Catholics. Rose would later excel at festive social gatherings for voters in her sons' campaigns.

Despite her many social, economic, and educational advantages, Rose took no leadership roles in her era's major reform causes. Many women who led the late-nineteenth-century self-improvement-club movement, and supported women's suffrage and settlement houses, had received their higher education in new secular women's institutions (Mount Holyoke, Vassar, Wellesley, Smith, and Bryn Mawr) or in coed universities. Rose's conservative women's Catholic education, with its emphasis on homemaking, child rearing, and religious doctrine, hardly prepared her to become a suffragette or activist for the poor. She did volunteer, however, to teach catechism and sewing to Italian immigrant children in her old North End neighborhood.

The Catholic Church promoted such good deeds as "corporal and spiritual works of mercy," delineating them in the *Catholic Encyclopedia*, written and published during Rose's formative years. Matthew's Gospel, chapter 25, describes merciful acts in Jesus's parable of the shepherd separating his sheep from unwanted goats. Similarly, at the second coming Jesus will welcome to heaven those believers who have tended the hungry, thirsty, naked, homeless, sick, imprisoned, and dead. According to Catholic doctrine, spiritual as opposed to corporal acts include teaching, counseling, comforting, praying, and forgiving, as well as admonishing sinners and patiently accepting trespasses.[27]

THE YEAR 1910 thrust Rose back into the political limelight when her father retook the mayor's office, defeating the Republican candidate by a mere 1,402 votes. Storming the wards of the city in a showy motorcade, again promising "A Bigger, Better, Busier Boston," and closing with a chorus of "Sweet Adeline" had earned Honey Fitz the new four-year tenure for Boston mayors.[28]

Young women of Rose's social milieu looked forward to debuts as their twenty-first birthdays approached. High society's "coming out" parties signaled that a female had passed from girl to woman and could begin searching for a husband. Few Boston debutantes, however, could compete with the festivities surrounding Rose's debut. Part social reception, part political event, it reflected Rose's public life as Honey Fitz's favored daughter. Although Rose claimed that her "debut was not lavish, at least by standards of those times,"[29] it had a fairy-tale quality that made headlines. "Miss Fitzgerald's Debut Is Attended by Notables," proclaimed the *Boston Globe*, with the subheading, "Mayor's Home Rose-Garlanded for Occasion."

Mayor Fitzgerald's Dorchester residence overflowed with roses, palms, ferns, and garlands. "Miss Rose E. Fitzgerald, Gowned in White, Receives More Than 500 Friends at Mayor's Home," trumpeted the *Boston Post*. Each paper ran a photo of Rose and her mother, looking a bit dour in light of the happy occasion. Rose wore a white satin floor-length gown with a short train, but no jewelry, and topped her hair with a simple white ribbon. White kid gloves demurely covered her hands and arms. For more than three hours, she received hundreds of guests, shaking hands and welcoming them to the Fitzgerald home. The experience would prepare her for the long days of campaigning that lay ahead.

Held the day after New Year's 1911, the reception and tea featured Massachusetts's governor-elect, two congressmen, and Boston's City Council, which took a holiday at the mayor's suggestion.[30] Rose particularly cherished a telegram from family friend and admirer Sir Thomas Lipton: "I extend my congratulations to you on the occasion of your coming-out. I suppose that in a short time I will be sending congratulations for another occasion of great joy. Before that occurs I hope that you pick out a man who is the equal of your father."[31]

Rose had already done so, and Joe Kennedy attended her debut. Still hoping that he could change her mind, however, Honey Fitz invited another suitor. If Mayor Fitzgerald had his way, Rose would become Mrs. Hugh Nawn. The Nawns were well-to-do neighbors, and Hugh's father headed Boston's most successful Catholic contracting business. A member of Harvard's Class of 1910, Hugh seemed the perfect match for Rose. "[H]e was one of my beaux," she recalled, "and he was nice and I would have married him. He did have a car, and he did have a business to go into."[32] But he lacked Joe's charisma. In modern parlance, Rose and Hugh had no "chemistry." Honey Fitz's loving dedication to Rose would become a two-edged sword as she entered adulthood, for he refused to concede on her choice of a marriage partner.

Enrolling at Harvard as an undergraduate, just after Rose went abroad in 1908, Joe Kennedy began the education dream that John Fitzgerald had truncated when he dropped out of Harvard to care for his orphaned brothers. Only two generations removed from his grandfather Patrick Kennedy's immigration to the Irish slums of Boston, Joe began his competition to surpass Protestant elites by enrolling at their premier college. Never a first-rate student (he needed an extra year to complete his studies at Boston Latin School), Joe plodded through his Harvard classes, earning only average grades at best. His failure to make the first-string varsity baseball team proved a more serious blow to his considerable ego, which absorbed another beating when the Brahmins blackballed him at their most elite undergraduate clubs. Joe famously vowed that he would find a way to get even and spent the rest of his life plotting to do so. His radiant smile, piercing blue eyes, athletic build, ballroom dance prowess, and charming personality impressed other girls than Rose. Even while courting her, and certainly during her trips away from Boston, he sought the company of less prominent females. He always had an eye for chorus girls and would become an incorrigible womanizer.[33] Yet Rose's ardent attention, made more alluring by her father's disapproval, and her ties to the city's power structure attracted him to the prize Irish Catholic Boston belle.

"My father didn't think I should marry the first man who asked me, and still I was very much in love, and still I didn't want to offend my parents so we used to have these rendezvous," Rose remembered. Reminiscing decades later about her clandestine courtship, she expressed a youthful giggle: "We used to have these dance orders in those days, little cards, where your dancing partners put their names for different dances. You'd have perhaps, I don't know, fifteen or twenty dances. So [Joe] had fictitious initials that he put on so people wouldn't think that he was monopolizing my whole card. . . . And then we used to go to lectures, and just meet him by chance coming home. We'd walk a good deal in those days."[34]

For the first time in her life, Rose defied her father's wishes. Joe's accomplishments captivated her; he seemed like the perfect man. "He was captain of the baseball team, manager of the football team, president of his class, and colonel of his regiment [at Boston Latin School]," she explained. "I used to recite these things to tell my parents what great possibilities he had," Rose recalled with a smile. "[I]n school he had acquired all these honors and all these posts of responsibilities and . . . he was on [his way] to do great things. . . ."[35]

Responsibility: Rose sprinkled the word liberally throughout her conversations and writing. To be perfect, she had to be responsible. Assuming her mother's public responsibilities, Rose became the hostess for her father's events and his travel companion. Her beau epitomized responsibility, she argued to her parents, and therefore became a proper marriage candidate. Practicing responsible Victorian mores and "republican motherhood," she would train her sons to influence the world for all eternity. Acting responsibly, by making others responsible, became a major component of Rose's striving for perfection.

But, first, she had to convince her father that Joe should become her husband. His invitation to Harvard's 1911 Harvard junior prom thrilled her. Although she had "come out" the previous winter and was nearly twenty-one, Rose couldn't persuade Honey Fitz to approve. Joe even arranged a double date for the prom, but Mayor Fitzgerald wouldn't budge. In 1911 the median age for women's first marriage was twenty-one,[36] yet Rose couldn't even attend a college dance in a quartet of friends without her father's acquiescence. Her parents warned that marrying young might tie her down with children and limit travel opportunities. Again they arranged a trip to remove her from Joe's orbit. Rose made her first journey to a new winter resort, Palm Beach.[37] Oil-and-railroad magnate Henry Flagler had constructed rail lines down Florida's east coast, bringing "snow birds" from the frozen northeast to sunny climes.

All the way to Florida Rose prayed that business would call her father back to Boston "so I could go with my beau, but alas for youthful romance, I went on my way uneventfully and left my disappointed swain to himself." Rose remembered only two hotels in Palm Beach from that first vacation there with her father in 1911. "Rich, very rich people like the Astors, medium rich, and people of ordinary circumstances like me all were accommodated at the same place. I was very thrilled in those days to see the Vincent Astors, the Vanderbilts, and especially the Wideners all promenading up and down the foyer of the hotel after dinner." (The Wideners later would donate two million dollars to Harvard in honor of their son who perished on the *Titanic*.)

Prior to the Roaring Twenties' relaxed dress codes for women, Rose wore elaborate clothing, even in a resort setting: dresses with hemlines down to her stocking-covered ankles, high-heeled shoes, straw hats, and three-quarter jackets.[38] Swimming brought little respite from social mores prescribing that ladies cover their bodies. Rose worried about her long hair in Florida's steamy climate, and she spent endless hours rolling her tresses on curlers. She dared not try a "permanent," for the new chemical treatment left its early users with frizzy, brittle locks.

The nearby casino, where patrons wore formal attire, titillated her. Although she hadn't reached the age of majority, the bouncers always admitted her and other young women because "evidently no young girl ever gambled profligately." With few automobiles, tourists either walked to the beach or hired a rickshaw propelled by "a darkie on a bicycle." Rose used that term for blacks as late as 1951, but she followed it with a less offensive noun in her description of "the cakewalk, a dance performed by a dozen colored maids and waiters." After several weeks, Rose and her parents began the trip north. She lay in her sleeper-car, fretting about the possibility of a catastrophic crash: trains going in opposite directions had to share a single track. On the journey home, Rose observed the wealthiest travelers who hooked their own private railcars to the trains. "That seemed the height of luxury," she thought. Yet, avoiding the sin of covetousness, Rose reported that "we often viewed the [private] cars . . . not with envy but with amazement." By 1951 Rose tallied her trips to Palm Beach at fifty, but she never had another opportunity to attend Harvard's junior prom. "How wrong parents can be," she concluded.

Rose continued to accompany her father abroad while her mother managed hearth and home in Dorchester. Honey Fitz knew that his invitations to Rose appealed to her sense of fulfillment in serving as her father's travel companion and softened the blow of weeks away from Joe Kennedy. "Father was making trips and took me along because he enjoyed me, and I was just through school, and it was a good opportunity. My mother didn't care about going and leaving five children at home in the winter, which is always a worry for any mother and which was for me [when I became a mother]. . . . Because they are subject to colds and child[hood] diseases," Rose recalled. Before antibiotics and vaccines for measles, mumps, chicken pox, whooping cough, and polio, mothers had good reason to worry.

Rose later criticized her father for showering all of his paternal attention on her. "He did take me on most all these trips. He should have done as my husband did, see that the younger [siblings] participated, too. As I had been to Europe a couple of times, and the next time that he went he should have taken one of my brothers, for instance. But he didn't do that; he took me. . . . I did speak French and German, and he was very proud of me." Rose admitted to her memoirist that her brothers, Thomas, John, and Frederick, didn't inherit their father's energy or curiosity, but she placed some of the blame on Honey Fitz. "I don't think that he gave them as much encouragement as he did me. Because, I suppose, I had the disposition to absorb it and enjoy it and that, in turn, gave him more encouragement or more reason to talk to me." Although Honey Fitz also included his daughter Agnes in these trips abroad, Rose described her as "more like my mother, more shy and more inhibited." When they would throw parties, Agnes "would arrange the flowers and arrange the menu or do things that . . . took less output."[39] Rose, on the other hand, happily played the belle of the ball. In fact, Alice Roosevelt Longworth's acerbic quip about her extroverted father, Theodore, applied to both Rose and Honey Fitz. They wanted to be the "corpse at every funeral, the bride at every wedding, and the baby at every christening!"[40] Rose and her father became the center of attention simply by entering a room, and they passed this innate charisma to their progeny. Ultimately besting her father, Rose skillfully trained her children to turn heads through their appearance, personality, knowledge, wit, and eloquence.

Following the 1911 Palm Beach trip, Rose and Agnes departed for Europe with their father for yet another grand tour of the Continent. Honey Fitz ostensibly made the trip to visit the port cities of Hamburg and Brussels for the Boston Chamber of Commerce.[41] After a quick stop in Ireland and another meeting with Sir Thomas Lipton, they sailed for Belgium by way of Dover. The girls visited Blumenthal and sadly discovered that two of the nuns had died in the intervening years.[42] The presence of Hugh Nawn, as a newly minted Boston businessman, on the continental portion of the trip bolstered the mayor's scheme to distract Rose from Joe Kennedy's advances. She viewed Hugh as the "boy next door" and found him a congenial companion. A touch of romance crept into her memoir's description of their waltz to Strauss's "Blue Danube," as they sailed down the river from Vienna.[43] In her 1911 travel diary, she underlined her exclamation, "Waltzed the Blue Danube on the Blue Danube!"

Each stop on the trio's six-week tour followed the same routine: visits to historic sights, museums, and churches (they faithfully attended Mass each Sunday); meals at renowned restaurants, often with city officials; trips to theater performances; and shopping for jewelry and clothing. The Fitzgerald party returned to Berlin, recalling the girls' 1909 New Year's visit there, and then took a side trip to Potsdam. They stopped in Dresden, where Honey Fitz purchased some of the city's famous china, before heading to Prague in the Austro-Hungarian Empire. They toured the city by carriage and celebrated Rose's twenty-first birthday with a party, dancing, and dinner. Despite the revelry, Rose headed off to 8:30 Sunday Mass the next morning.

After stops in Nuremberg and Munich, the Fitzgeralds traveled by train to Vienna, visiting the Royal Palace at Schönbrunn, home of the Hapsburg monarchs. Rose expressed surprise at the coed Viennese public baths. She attended a dance at the Sacher Hotel, famous for its chocolate torte. During dinner there, she sat with the emperor's personal adviser. Honey Fitz and his daughters attended a High Mass at St. Stephen's Cathedral that featured a full orchestra and stunning stained-glass windows.

The Fitzgeralds headed west to Innsbruck and on to Zurich, where they caught the Paris train. Parisian customs officials frightened Rose, perhaps because she frequently tried to find ways to avoid declaring purchases. After shopping for hats, she and Agnes drove along the Champs Élysées and through the Bois de Boulogne in a horse-drawn carriage; they whiled away their final hours in Paris sipping champagne at Maxim's. No wonder Rose would always view the City of Light as an idyllic destination.

Back across the Channel, they arrived in London, where they caught a train to the port of Southampton and another cruise with Sir Thomas Lipton. Visiting with counts and duchesses on board, and spying the royal yachts of Spain's and Britain's kings, intrigued Rose. She happily collected more autographs before the tour's end in Ireland, and the trio sailed for home.

Barely a month later Rose accompanied her father to Chicago for an international meeting of city officials. They stopped at South

Bend, Indiana, for a tour of the University of Notre Dame, dinner with priests on its faculty, and meetings with nuns from nearby Saint Mary's College. In October she and her parents toured Massachusetts by automobile, giving Rose a foretaste of the campaigning she would undertake for her sons. The next summer Honey Fitz and Rose set off for Baltimore, to attend the 1912 Democratic Convention and watch the delegates select New Jersey governor Woodrow Wilson as their presidential candidate.

Rose's most exotic trip came in spring 1913, when Honey Fitz took another Chamber of Commerce junket, this time to Central and South America. They sailed first to Kingston, Jamaica, and Rose spotted Cuba en route. She sipped a "cola" that tasted "sweet like orangeade" and "bought Jippi Jappy hats and beads." On to Panama, they viewed the new canal. While the Boston delegation pondered the impact of the landmark shortcut on their city's trade, Rose toured Colón and declared a Spanish church that she visited "not nice." The delegation then sailed southeast to Cartagena, Colombia. Rose described Colombian ports as "Awful . . .—Squalid houses—naked children—Animals in houses and in streets." The city of Santa Marta also failed to meet Rose's high standards: "Very hot—lime and cement houses. Usually a garden or open space in center—No mattresses on bed—Marketplace very poor. Church being renovated . . . [Attended] reception by mayor in municipal [building] which was shabby and not overclean." After touring a United Fruit Company banana plantation, the Boston party sailed for home. Stopping again in Kingston, Rose was relieved to be back in Anglo territory. She loved the beautiful cathedral and thought the English barracks looked "very fine." Rose had obviously inherited her father's wanderlust. She thrived on seeing new sights, visiting historic landmarks, dining on foreign cuisine, and meeting interesting people, especially state officials and royalty. More perfect training for her subsequent duties as a diplomat's spouse and politicians' mother is hard to imagine.

As 1913 ended, Honey Fitz locked horns with his political protégé but now rival, James Michael Curley, over the impending mayoral race. Initially Fitzgerald indicated that he wouldn't seek another term, but he changed his mind and threw his hat into the ring. Retaliating, Curley planned a series of public lectures, focusing on graft in Honey Fitz's administration and the incumbent mayor's affair with "Toodles" Ryan, a cigarette girl of the same age as twenty-three-year-old Rose. To avoid additional scandal, the mayor left the campaign and completed his term in 1914.[44]

Josie Fitzgerald had once angrily told a newspaper reporter that her husband rarely spent time at home,[45] but the "Toodles" story was obviously more serious and embarrassing. Rose, too, had her own reasons for being annoyed at Honey Fitz. While trying to keep her perfectly legitimate romance with Joe Kennedy a secret from her disapproving father, he—a married fifty-year-old—cavorted with a floozy nearly half his age. Rose never publicly revealed her thoughts about her father's feet of clay. Instead, she wrote in her autobiography that "gossip and slander and denunciation and even vilification are part of the price one pays for being in public life." She warned her daughters-in-law that they might hear "scandalous gossip and accusations" about their husbands, but "they should understand . . . and be prepared from the beginning, otherwise they might be very unhappy."[46] Rising above the mudslinging, even if the muck contained more than a grain of truth, would be Rose's approach to three generations of philandering men in her life.

Whatever Rose's private musings about her father's indiscretions, he must have slipped from his pedestal in her eyes. She would no longer remain obsequious to his judgment on her matrimonial choice. Graduating from Harvard in 1912, Joe had become a Massachusetts bank examiner, allowing him to grasp banking's inner workings throughout the state. The experience made him a perfect candidate for president of East Boston's Columbia Trust, a small bank his father had founded.[47] At age twenty-five Joe Kennedy became the youngest bank president in the country, or, as Rose would say, the world.[48]

Like Hugh Nawn, Joe had a steady, well-paying job. Approaching age twenty-four, Rose could finally act on her feelings. "I had read all these books about your heart should rule your head. I was very romantic and [there] was no two ways about it." "I was just in

love with Joe Kennedy and that was it." In 1914 the Fitzgeralds
announced Rose's engagement to Joe. Years later she couldn't
remember the exact moment of proposal "because we were sort of
flirting with the other for a long time" and talking about marriage.
Saving enough money to buy a ring, Joe headed to New York to
purchase it from a Harvard classmate in the jewelry business.[49] The
pure clarity of the round, two-carat diamond impressed the bride-
to-be and must have symbolized to her the clear path to marital
happiness. Soon she would be Mrs. Joseph P. Kennedy, a title she
proudly used, indeed insisted upon, for the rest of her life.

❧

CHAPTER 3

Joe's Wife

Stepping into golden autumn sunlight, the newlyweds beamed for the *Boston Globe*. Rose Fitzgerald was the "talented and charming" daughter of the mayor; Joe Kennedy, Harvard '12, president of a local bank, was "prominent in social events among the younger Catholic people of the city."[1] On October 7, 1914, Mr. and Mrs. Joseph P. Kennedy exited William Cardinal O'Connell's Back Bay home, where he had performed the marriage ceremony in his private chapel. Instructing Honey Fitz not to send Rose to a secular college, O'Connell had thwarted Rose's wish to enroll at Wellesley years ago. Now he solemnized her most profound desire to marry her true love.

Attended by a small wedding party, a few friends, and immediate family, the ceremony's modesty evinced Honey Fitz's lack of enthusiasm for the union. An equally subdued reception for seventy-five guests followed at the Fitzgeralds' Dorchester home. What a contrast to Rose's lavish 1911 debut! Facing whiffs of scandal, Mayor Fitzgerald was also a lame duck. As an octogenarian, Rose would remark that she wished her nuptials had occurred in a large church so that she and her husband could have passed by peri-

odically and recalled their marital vows.[2] Perhaps she had longed
for a more concrete symbol of her marriage when rumors of Joe's
womanizing circulated.

Yet on their wedding day Joe and Rose were the picture of a
striking young couple—she aglow in her white satin gown trimmed
with lace, and a fashionable Normandy lace cap trailing a chapel-
length veil; he jauntily sporting a black top hat, morning coat, and
striped trousers. Their broad smiles radiated happiness and anticipa-
tion. Two decades later, after nine children, Rose speculated in her
diary, "When I look back now, I wonder at the size of the job & I
think that when we stood as a blushing radiant gay young bride &
groom we were not able to look ahead & see nine little helpless
infants with our responsibility to turn them into men & women
who were mentally morally & physically perfect, how we would
have felt—But as the pious old Irish nun in the Convent used to
say—Pray to our dear Lord & that is what we did—as that is all we
could do."[3]

The couple embarked on a carefree honeymoon. For three
weeks they traveled, first to New York, where they rode in a
"machine," the common name for early automobiles. After seeing a
play starring Douglas Fairbanks, they left for Philadelphia to attend
the 1914 World Series. An avid baseball fan, Joe brought his new
bride to see their hometown team, Boston's Braves, defeat the
favored Philadelphia Athletics, 7 to 1 and 1 to 0. Then they journeyed by train to West Virginia's White Sulphur Springs, where the
posh Greenbrier Hotel had just opened in 1913. During their ten
days there, the honeymooners rode horses every day and enjoyed
playing tennis and golf, pastimes that they would pursue throughout their married life, though often separately. From the Greenbrier, where they dined on pheasant with high-society patrons,
they traveled to kitschy Atlantic City. Then she and Joe returned to
New York City for another play, followed by dining and dancing at
the Biltmore. Returning home in late October, they moved into
their new house at 83 Beals Street in Boston's Brookline suburb.

Rose's lifelong pursuit of excellence and recognition now
coalesced with Joe's innate desire for money and power. They

immediately distinguished themselves from their relatives and peers
by moving to a middle-class Protestant enclave. Most of their newly
married friends were settling in apartments or received homes as
wedding gifts. The young Kennedys purchased a three-story clap-
board home for $6,500; Joe had borrowed a $2,000 down payment
two months before his marriage. Rose particularly liked the neighborhood's open feel, with empty lots on either side of her new
home and across the street. How far removed in atmosphere, if not
mileage, from her birthplace in the crowded North End, where
young Honey Fitz had lived cheek-by-jowl in immigrant tenements. Beals Street carried little traffic, yet shops and a neighborhood Catholic church, St. Aidan's, were only a few blocks away,
within easy walking distance. Joe had a short commute to his East
Boston office at Columbia Trust.[4]

Declining a wedding gift from her husband, Rose reasoned,
"[T]here wasn't anything I wanted especially, and I thought we
should reserve our resources for the immediate problems, which
were furnishing a house and getting settled."[5] From the beginning
of her married life, however, Rose hired household staff. A friend
sent her "a gay neat Irish girl" to cook and clean for $7 per week
and board on the house's third floor.[6] Taking for granted that "most
everyone has a decorator," Rose supervised the furnishing and
arrangement of her first marital abode. The room to the left of the
center hall contained a dining set purchased by the couple and
china hand-painted by Joe's sister. For tea they used cups and sau-
cers from Rose's admirer, Sir Thomas Lipton, stamped with the
Erin's emblem, reminding Rose of her visit aboard the Irish yacht.
Her large living room, with its cozy fireplace, accommodated a
baby-grand piano, a gift from Rose's uncles. The house's second
floor contained a master bedroom with twin beds for the couple, a
guestroom for visiting family and friends, and a small bedroom on
the back of the house. A tiny chamber that overlooked the roof of
the front porch became Rose's study, just big enough to hold a
mahogany desk and a Martha Washington sewing cabinet.[7] "I
should love to . . . show you my new little house," she wrote to an
old friend in Concord.[8]

.d Rose settled easily into married life. Rose continued
.g Ace of Clubs functions, and the newlyweds enjoyed
.zing with friends, going to symphony concerts, and cheering
larvard football team. The new bride soon discovered that she
, expecting her first child, due in July. Joe rented a summer cot-
.ge in Hull, near Rose's parents, who had acquired a Victorian
mansion at the historic beach resort. Rose and Joe (on the weekends) spent the first summer of their marriage in the sun, sand, and
surf, as they had as teenagers on Maine's beaches. Ocean breezes
refreshed Rose in her pregnancy's last trimester. The Kennedys
were happy to escape the stifling city, even more uncomfortable
prior to modern air conditioning.

Joseph Patrick Kennedy Jr. was born at Rose and Joe's Hull cottage on July 25, 1915, exactly nine months and eighteen days after
his parents' wedding. "Honeymoon babies" were common before
reliable, legal contraception. Since 1873's Comstock Act, Congress
had considered contraceptives obscene materials and banned their
movement in interstate commerce. Victorian crusaders viewed
birth control as an affront to Mother Nature and a means to promote promiscuity, asserting that the threat of pregnancy functioned
as birth control. Just one year before Rose's marriage, Margaret
Sanger had published the *Woman Rebel*, a monthly newspaper advocating family planning, and coined the term "birth control." Her
devoutly Roman Catholic mother had succumbed to tuberculosis
after producing eleven children. Federal authorities arrested Sanger
for violating the Comstock Act, but she escaped to Europe. Returning to the United States after the government dropped charges, she
opened a family-planning clinic in New York City's slums. There
she ran afoul of state bans on contraception and served a one-month
prison sentence.[9]

After World War I, the alarming spread of venereal disease
persuaded a New York court to legalize contraceptives if physicians
prescribed them for preventing sexually transmitted diseases. Relaxation of sexual mores in the Roaring Twenties coincided with
Sanger's 1923 establishment of New York City and Chicago institutes
to research women's reproductive needs and to distribute family

planning information.[10] Yet Connecticut's criminal statute proscrib-
ing the use of contraception, even by married couples, remained in
force until 1965, when the US Supreme Court invalidated it as a violation of constitutional privacy rights.[11]

Even if civil law had sanctioned birth control, Catholic couples
like Joe and Rose wouldn't have practiced contraception, in order to
comply with Church doctrine that declared it sinful. Catholicism
viewed production of children as the primary duty of marriage. A
spouse who refused to achieve this mandated goal, especially via arti-
ficial birth control, was guilty of an "unnatural and unchristian" act.[12]

Rose recalled how strict her father had been during her teenage
years, not allowing her to "dance with boys at the age of sixteen,"
when Joe invited her to a dance at the Boston Latin School. Victorian constraints of her youth forbade her from even kissing a beau
until she became engaged to marry him.[13] Yet her furtive, premar-
ital rendezvous with young Joe, their soulful walks, slipping into
the Christian Science Mother Church for privacy, and their dance-
card ruses all illustrate Rose's rebellious streak that might have
raised eyebrows among Blumenthal's nuns. Being a Child of Mary
obviously didn't preclude Rose's pursuit of Joe, even if that meant
circumventing her parents' attempts to limit her access to him.
Once married, she graduated from the "no kissing" rule to pregnancy in a matter of weeks.

As their firstborn, baby Joe immediately became his parents'
pride and joy. A youthful, athletic, rugged Joe Sr., clad in a bathing
suit, proudly holds the smiling Joe Jr. in a 1916 photograph.[14] The
baby settled into his nursery, and his parents hired a $3-per-week
trained nurse to care for him. Rose would now play the role of the
ever-pregnant matriarch, presiding over a growing and boisterous
Kennedy brood, the first five born in a mere six years, from 1915 to
1921. Her public life, so carefully practiced with Honey Fitz, came
a distant second to maternal obligations. Yet Boston's new mayor,
Andrew J. Peters, named her to his wife's reception committee for
Mrs. Woodrow Wilson's 1919 visit.[15]

Rose's second child, John Fitzgerald Kennedy, named for her
father, entered the world on May 29, 1917. She gave birth to the

future president in her Beals Street bedroom. Always the practical New Englander, Rose situated her bed next to the window so the doctor had plenty of light to deliver the baby, who arrived at three o'clock in the afternoon.

Unlike robust Joe Jr., young "Jack," as the family called him, was often scrawny and hollow-eyed. He caught nearly every childhood disease, including scarlet fever when he was only two-and-a-half. Caused by the same streptococcal bacteria that produces strep throat, potentially fatal scarlet fever provoked panic and fear before the 1940s advent of antibiotics. Doctors and the public dreaded its onset, marked by fever, sore throat, and characteristic red rash. Highly contagious through casual contact, it could also lead to complications like rheumatic fever. Typically, public-health officials quarantined patients in their homes.

Rose had just given birth to her fourth baby, Kathleen, on February 20, 1920, the day Jack developed his alarming symptoms. "If a baby had just been born [and] the [infected] child was in the house, [a] small house, they were afraid the new baby would get scarlet fever, I would get scarlet fever," Rose recalled. Using Honey Fitz's contacts, Joe managed to persuade Boston City Hospital to admit the desperately ill child for treatment (even though the Kennedys lived in Brookline) to protect Rose and the other children. Joe kept vigil at the toddler's side, while Rose remained at home with her new baby. Even in religious matters, the Kennedy patriarch employed deal-making. He begged God to spare young Jack. If so, Joe promised the Almighty, he would donate half his "fortune" to charity. The little boy survived, and his grateful father contributed $3,700 to the St. Apollonia Guild for a bus to transport disadvantaged children to doctors.[16] When Jack regained his strength a few weeks later, his parents sent him to a Poland Springs, Maine, sanitarium for two months, where he continued recuperating with a governess and visits from Boston relatives.[17]

Before inoculations limited the spread of potentially fatal childhood diseases, Rose fretted constantly about her children's health. She insisted on fresh air for them. Pushing the youngest in a baby carriage and bringing the others in tow, Rose took daily morning walks. Often they would toddle to a nearby shopping center. The live-in maid grocery-shopped, laundered mounds of diapers, sterilized baby bottles, and prepared formula. "[Diapers] never concerned me," Rose recalled.[18]

Only occasionally did she breast-feed her first several children, which made her more susceptible to pregnancy and them more prone to disease. Nursing mothers can usually prevent conception by having their babies suckle for all feedings during the first six to twelve months after birth. Yet Rose became pregnant with each of the four children after Joe Jr. on an average of every eight months. "If you got run down and you had to go away you stop[ped breast-feeding] at six months," she explained. "Unfortunately when Eunice was born she didn't get along very well because the bottle wasn't very well organized, and I couldn't nurse her at that time because I had breast abscess[es]. . . . Baby is just as well on a bottle, maybe better, it's more regular." Moreover, Rose found it "a little confining to be home every three hours to nurse the baby. . . . [A] baby is usually fed at 10 or 10:30 [P.M.]. You're at the theater, so what do you do?" Rushing home to nurse an infant didn't suit her schedule.[19]

During one of her morning walks with the children, Rose purchased index cards and a small wooden file box. She began meticulously, some might say compulsively, to record all of the children's religious milestones (baptism, First Communion, confirmation) and vital medical statistics—one card per child—much as parents now store such data on computers. In addition to maintaining a card catalog of childhood illnesses and medical treatments, Rose obsessively monitored her children's weight for years, not just when they were infants. "I used to weigh them every week and keep track and then give them more nourishment if they were losing weight, give them an extra glass of milk or cream in their milk. Jack, who was always thin, used to get the extra juice from the steak when it was carved, or the roast beef juice, which was an idea I had to build up his health because we didn't talk so much about vitamins then."[20]

Several of her nine children, perhaps because of their mother's constant worry over their being too thin, tended to add pounds, and then both Rose and Joe would chastise them for looking chubby. Rose's own "nervous tummy" caused her to have an adversarial relationship with food, and she focused single-mindedly on remaining petite. Later in life she adored receiving compliments on her svelte figure—especially after producing nine offspring. Twenty-first-century doctors might diagnose her with an eating disorder. Perfectionist women who strive to achieve unhealthfully thin physiques may suffer from anorexia nervosa. Rose linked her concern for the children's diet with creating perfect Kennedys: "I was usually home by lunchtime so as to see that the children ate properly. At suppertime I sat with them and then had my own dinner a little later. My great ambition was to have my children morally, physically, and mentally as perfect as possible."[21]

Yet Rose's third child was anything but perfect in her mother's eyes or by early twentieth-century standards. Her first daughter, christened Rose Marie, but also known as Rosemary or Rosie to her family, arrived on September 13, 1918, between older brother, Jack, and younger sister, Kathleen, known as Kick. In the midst of the worldwide Spanish flu pandemic, Rose archived a newspaper clipping about the latest Kennedy baby in her scrapbook: "[A] dainty daughter was added to the nursery which previously sheltered two sturdy sons. . . ."[22] Yet Rosemary's cherubic face and sweet smile initially masked what Rose gradually began to comprehend—the shy little girl couldn't keep up with her active, bright, and precocious older brothers and younger sister. Rose first noticed that Rosemary's motor and verbal skills developed more slowly than Joe's and Jack's. She began walking and speaking at a slower pace. As she grew older and tried to participate in sports with her competitive siblings, Rosemary couldn't steer her sled, ice skate, hit a tennis ball, or row a boat—all activities that the energetic Kennedy children performed as naturally as their athletic parents. More alarming to her mother, Rosemary scrawled her letters from the right side of the page to the left.

Joe Jr. and Jack began their formal education around the corner from Beals Street at the public Edward Devotion School. Joe Jr., Rose assumed, had the higher IQ of the two boys, but teachers reported that Jack scored above him. (Even years after his presidency, Rose continued to believe that Jack had a lower IQ than Joe Jr.)[23] Devotion School teachers told Rose that Rosemary had a low IQ and recommended that she repeat kindergarten. "I was puzzled by what all this might mean," Rose agonized. "I did not know where to send her to school or how to cope with the situation. I talked to our family doctor, to the head of the psychology department at Harvard, to a Catholic psychologist who was head of a school in Washington. Each of them told me she was retarded, but what to do about her, where to send her, how to help her seemed to be an unanswered question. . . . I had never heard of a retarded child."[24] Not knowing how to help Rosemary, Rose felt "very discouraged and really heartbroken."[25]

She eventually concluded that Rosemary's condition had resulted from a "genetic accident." Some children suffered brain damage at birth, but Rose believed that was not the case here. In many families "someone is brilliant and someone [is] slow," Rose reasoned.[26] Her view of Rosemary's intellect relative to the Kennedy family corresponds to the modern definition of mental retardation. It "describes how people with low intelligence function in society."[27]

In fact, the Kennedys' initial approach to Rosemary was quite enlightened. They engaged, at times, in what would now be called "mainstreaming." In the early twentieth century, authorities considered children with IQs under seventy to be "mentally retarded." Such "feebleminded" persons, as they were then labeled, faced years of horrific institutionalization, ridicule, and, during the eugenics movement, forced sterilization sanctioned by the government, including the US Supreme Court.[28] One hundred years later, the same IQ categorization (below seventy) still applies to individuals currently said to have an "intellectual disability," but intelligence tests are no longer viewed as infallible. The more commonly accepted paradigm of intellectual disability views it as a formula: "person x environment."[29] In other words, how do people with low IQs and social adaptability issues relate to others?

According to Rose, the Kennedy family wavered between two

equally imperfect options then available. If they tutored Rosemary at home, she would have no schoolmates, as her popular siblings did. If they sent her away to a school for "slow" children, Joe and Rose worried that she would be forever behind her peers. Even if they had decided on the latter course, very few schools existed in the 1920s for children with special mental and physical needs. They refused to institutionalize her. Instead, with their financial resources, her parents decided to homeschool Rosemary with hired tutors. She ultimately learned how to write but never advanced beyond block letters. Rose eschewed cursive handwriting in order to communicate by mail with Rosemary and avoided speaking French to her children for fear of making their slower sister feel inferior. When asked in 1972 if Rosemary demonstrated "any particular aptitude or interest," Rose starkly replied, "No. She was never capable, sometimes they [the mentally retarded] do, but she never showed any [aptitude]." On second thought, Rose added, "She swam well."[30]

Always promoting an active lifestyle, Rose hired physical-education instructors to teach Rosemary how to play tennis, dance, and swim. "I gave her a great deal of attention, thinking that I could circumvent this affliction that she had, or I could have her so educated that it wouldn't be noticed at all or she could still go on with the other children in a normal way. But it took a tremendous lot of time and thought and attention, and visits away from home to visit schools and to visit psychologists."[31] What did such pressure to fit in, albeit applied with loving intentions, impose on Rosemary and her siblings? Reminiscing about those demanding early days of motherhood, Rose wondered if she had neglected young Jack. In fact, she returned home one day from her travels to learn that he had accidentally sipped from an ammonia bottle. Fortunately, "he didn't swallow it so he was okay," Rose reported in her diary.[32] Clearly, the Kennedy household didn't always function perfectly.

Joe remained president of Columbia Trust until 1917, when he left to become assistant general manager of the Fore River Bethlehem Shipbuilding Corporation's plant, south of Boston. His draft board declared him eligible for military induction in World War I, but Joe explained to draft officials that he had resigned his bank presidency and "enter[ed] the ship-building business . . . prompted by a desire to feel that I was doing something worth while."[33] The draft board refused his deferment requests until influential friends intervened.[34]

Joe worked sixty-five-hour weeks to ensure the production of naval vessels for the US war effort, earning a $4,000 annual salary, plus a bonus of 1 percent of the plant's total profits. They were considerable, as Fore River produced thirty-six destroyers for the war. In addition to handsome bonuses, the war production's frenetic pace also brought Joe a case of nervous exhaustion. He would be prone to such stress-related ailments, including peptic ulcers, throughout his career. His drive and entrepreneurship led him to sign a lucrative contract to run the Fore River cafeteria. In addition, he made his first contacts with the young assistant secretary of the Navy, Franklin D. Roosevelt.[35]

When Armistice Day, November 11, 1918, ended the "Great War," Joe looked for his next professional challenge. To unload the Fore River shipyard's postbellum surplus, he attempted to negotiate a deal with Galen Stone, one of the founding partners in the brokerage firm Hayden, Stone. Though unsuccessful in that effort, Joe so impressed Stone that he hired Kennedy as a broker and manager of the firm's Boston office in the summer of 1920. Joe now acquired an effective professional mentor, as well as an office in Boston's downtown business district. His base salary ($10,000) represented more than twice what he had made annually at the shipyard. More important for his future career and financial status, he began to play the stock market systematically (with mixed success initially) in the precrash decade, before federal regulations. Joe's Wall Street maneuvers required numerous trips to New York City. On September 16, 1920, he narrowly escaped injury when a bomb exploded in front of J. P. Morgan & Co. during one of Kennedy's Wall Street visits. Authorities suspected anarchists of planting the lethal device, which killed forty and injured scores. Joe's harrowing brush with terrorism prompted him to consider joining the Republican Party to support its law-and-order stance. Rose, however, convinced her husband to maintain the Kennedy-Fitzgerald families' historic Democratic ties.[36]

As Joe increasingly turned his attention from home, Rose frequently had to perform her parental tasks alone. Once, while pregnant with Kathleen in 1920, she became so distraught that she moved back to her parents' Dorchester home. How could she face the unremitting pressures of motherhood with her husband focused on business concerns, not to mention chorus girls and actresses?[37] Later, Rose would remark that he had "an unusual [knack] for getting along with princes or paupers, chorus girls, society matrons, Catholic and Protestant, East Boston and Back Bay, businessmen or dilettantes. . . . He could talk to anybody."[38] Resigned to Joe's gregarious nature, Rose eventually decided to accept it as a benefit to her sons' future political careers.

Rose's 1920 absence lasted only several weeks. Her father told her bluntly that she had to resume her responsibilities as a wife and mother. Honey Fitz and Josie's prophecy, uttered when Rose begged them to let her attend Harvard's 1911 prom with Joe, had come to pass. Married life had overtaken her opportunities to think of herself first. After attending a religious retreat, Rose returned to Beals Street with renewed determination to fulfill her spousal and maternal duties.[39] Years later she scoffed at the suggestion that the Kennedys might have contemplated ending their marriage. "[Y]ou never heard a cross word, we always understood one another and trusted one another and that's it," Rose proclaimed with characteristic certainty. "All the world was wondering, watching and saying we were separated, one day; the next day we were going to have a baby. This was in our early married life. There's no reason ever to change or have any reason to doubt."[40] Rose would not likely have contemplated divorce, because the Catholic Church strictly forbids it. In fact, those Catholics who do divorce are denied the sacraments and may not remarry in the Church unless their previous union is annulled. Recognizing that spouses face "great trials," especially in rearing children, Catholicism preaches the need for self-sacrifice.[41] At least Rose could take comfort in knowing that her marital sacrifices constituted a noble vocation.

She never publicly conceded her temporary separation from Joe in 1920 or her knowledge of his womanizing. In fact, she squelched all such references as "gossip." Producing children confirmed a successful marriage in her worldview. Rose always insisted that she and Joe never quarreled during their fifty-five years as husband and wife because they had so much in common. That view of her marriage coincided perfectly with the Catholic Church's ideal. Its doctrine of parents' responsibility toward their spouses and children to maintain a "Christian family" became the sine qua non of Rose's life.

She described Joe's responsibilities primarily as being the breadwinner. Unlike her own mother, who told a newspaper reporter that Honey Fitz rarely spent time at home, Rose never chastised Joe publicly for his absences, even at the birth of their children.[42] She enjoyed describing how the first five Kennedy offspring enthusiastically greeted their father at the train station, after his two-month stay in New York, with the exclamation, "Daddy, Daddy, Daddy, we've got another baby!" He, in turn, recalled the bemused look on his fellow travelers' faces, as if to say, "What that fellow certainly does not *need* right now is *another baby*."[43]

Contrasting her view of childbirth with that of her adult daughters in the 1970s, Rose observed, "I think the modern idea is to have them [husbands] go through this trivia with the wives so they'll know, they will appreciate the child more, appreciate more what the wife does [in childbirth]. That wasn't my idea, the idea was it was something the woman had to do and the less bother she gave to anybody else, including her husband, the better it was, and the easier it was."[44] Remarkably, she described labor as "trivia." Of course, in that era, even when the majority of births occurred at home, not a hospital, most men didn't assist their wives in childbirth, but would await the postnatal news beyond the birthing chamber.

Rose explained that she saw no need to disrupt Joe's work if the baby wasn't expected for six or seven hours. In fact, her husband was in Florida when Kathleen was born. "[T]here was no need in keeping Joe around in the winter . . . so he went to Palm Beach." She conceded, however, that her acceptance of, indeed seeming preference for, her spouse's absence from the Kennedy nativity scene "might be misinterpreted."[45]

Clearly, Rose believed in a literal division of labor between husband and wife. The Catholic Church approved, and undoubtedly shaped, her view. "Being the provider of the family, and the superior of the wife both in physical strength and in those mental and moral qualities which are appropriate to the exercise of authority, the husband is naturally the family's head, even 'the head of the wife,' in the language of Saint Paul," proclaimed Catholicism's patriarchy. Still, the Church maintained that wives were equal to their husbands, except "when disagreement arises in matters" of household governance, then "as a rule," the woman was "to yield" to her spouse. Nevertheless, "care and management of the details of the household belong naturally to the wife, because she is better fitted for these tasks than the husband," Catholic dogma explained.[46]

To Rose, "the more children you had, the better developed would be your life. . . . [O]f course, it was a very strong teaching in the Catholic Church." In addition to having the satisfaction of conforming to her faith's edicts, Rose always received jewelry from Joe, of increasing value as his fortunes rose, after giving birth. By the last few children, Joe would ask his jeweler to lend him several diamond bracelets or pins. Rose would then choose the reward for delivering yet another Kennedy child.[47]

She saw herself as the manager of hearth and home, while Joe toiled in the business world. "I ran the house. I ran the children," Rose neatly summarized. "We were always busy in our department, and he [Joe] had his, a great deal to do, and I think that was the way [it was] most of our lives. I mean I didn't interfere, and he didn't interfere, . . . I would say I wanted all rubies and not all sapphires if he was buying jewelry. . . . [H]e loved to buy jewelry, and he wanted me to have everything everybody else had."[48]

In the earliest years, Joe would take the children to his parents' Winthrop home each Sunday in the Model T Ford he had purchased shortly after his marriage. Rose appreciated some quiet time, even if she had to care for the newest baby when the nurse took off every other Sunday. "Some people used to get substitute nurses to take care of their children when the regular nurse was away, but I always liked to take care of them myself because, if one does, one discovers little discrepancies or little leaks in the system." Rose periodically checked on the cook to see that she offered the children enough variety in their meals. She reported that the hired help sometimes cut corners and fed the youngsters the same soup every night if Rose failed to supervise mealtimes closely. "If you take care of [the children] yourself, or at least you're at home when they are eating, you would see that. Then you can make suggestions [that] the nursemaid doesn't want to do . . . because she doesn't want to get in wrong with the cook. So I think it's a good idea to be around quite often so that you know what's going on."[49]

Rose took most seriously the role assigned her by the Catholic Church—teaching the faith to her children. On their daily walks they visited St. Aidan's so that her offspring would associate praying in church with the other quotidian aspects of life, not just with attending Sunday Mass. By 1923 Joe Jr., at age seven, became an altar boy. Still, Rose's piety sometimes ran counter to her two bumptious boys. Explaining to young Jack that attendance at Mass on the first Friday of each month for nine straight months ensured a "happy death," she was alarmed that he would rather pray for "two dogs." Joe Jr.'s attendance at Stations of the Cross while "all dirty" mortified his mother.[50] No wonder that Rose wanted to send the boys to Catholic school to bolster their religious instruction. Joe countermanded her wish, however, contending that they would learn their religion at home, the way he and Rose had. Further, sending them to non-Catholic schools would prepare them to excel in a Protestant world.[51]

Four high-spirited children under one roof, with only three bedrooms and one bath, necessitated a move to larger quarters. In 1921 the Kennedys purchased a more commodious home a few blocks away. It featured three bathrooms, a large porch, and a private bedroom for Rose. Money "never was a big question," she observed. "I always had maids, [Joe] was president of a bank, there was very little money in the bank, but he had other assets and naturally as time went on I realized we had more money, because we had bigger houses and I was able to have more maids and more expensive clothes and more expensive fur coats."[52]

Joe and Rose's fifth child, Eunice, named for her mother's fatally ill sister, was born on July 10, 1921, shortly after the move from Beals Street. In addition to maids, cooks, and nurses for the new babies, Rose hired governesses to assist with the older children. "I always had a school teacher [to serve as governess] because I thought they spoke correctly, and they could interest the children in the proper books and proper reading." As a little boy, Jack "used to ask the Canadian governess why she would prefer to be under the king of England instead of under the president of the United States." His mother believed that Jack's question proved that the little boy had politics "in his roots."[53]

JOE'S MENTOR, GALEN STONE, retired in 1923, and Joe hung out his shingle as a solo banker and broker in Boston. He arranged for his assistant and confidante, Edward (Eddie) Moore, and his wife, Mary, to purchase the Beals Street house. Moore had served as Honey Fitz's secretary before dedicating his life to Joe Kennedy. A childless couple, the Moores became surrogate parents to Joe and Rose's brood. Edward was also Rosemary's godfather and helped supervise her care.

The Moores' complete devotion to the Kennedy family, and the presence of household staff, meant that Rose could travel, as she had while single. Sometimes she took the children. Just after Christmas 1922, Rose, Joe Jr., and Jack went to Poland Springs in Maine, where Jack had recuperated from scarlet fever. Mary Moore accompanied them, and the two women's husbands joined them a few days later. The three youngest children remained behind with household staff. Rose reported in her 1923 diary, which she vowed to keep each day, despite her busy lifestyle, that the New Year's crowd at Poland Springs consisted of numerous "college boys and girls." Her youthful, carefree days had ended, however, and the diary that year consisted of numerous references to mundane maternal duties—nursing sick children, curtailing thumb-sucking for

fear it would misalign their teeth, celebrating birthdays, supervising
the children's religious instruction. Joe Sr. and Eddie left Rose
behind in Maine and returned to Boston. Rose, in turn, left Jack
and Mary in Maine and went home with Joe Jr. This pattern of
splitting the family among a host of locales would mark the Kennedys' future, with the distances growing greater as the years progressed. On January 7, 1923, Rose's frustration leaps from the page
of her journal entry: "Took care of children. Miss Brooks, the governess, helped. Kathleen still has bronchitis and Joe sick in bed.
Great life."[54] Still, Rose continued a surprisingly active social life,
despite her family obligations. In 1923 she recorded attending an
Ace of Clubs dance as president of the organization she had founded,
spectating at the Harvard–Princeton hockey game, going to the
theater, and hearing a lecture by Hilaire Belloc, the Anglo-French
writer and historian. Her travels continued apace. Sometimes she
rewarded herself by leaving the kids behind altogether. When her
children were young, she would escape Boston's bitter cold winters
by returning to Palm Beach for a couple of weeks. "I did go to
[California in 1923] with my sister because I thought we'd been [to]
Palm Beach three or four years; we'd never been to California.
[W]e could see new places and faces and California. So we had
friends out there, . . . and had a glorious time. . . ." Jack, always a
precocious little boy, chastised Rose as she left on the California
trip: "Gee, you're a great mother to go away and leave your children all alone."[55] Assuaging her guilt, Rose reported later that when
she returned to the house to retrieve a forgotten item, the children
were happily showing no signs of abandonment.[56]

Joe Kennedy, known as the deal-maker in the family, found his
match in Rose when it came to arranging travel. She would allow
Joe to vacation with his friends in Palm Beach during the winter if
she could travel with companions. On the 1923 trip out west, she
left her home, husband, and children for more than six weeks. Her
sister Agnes accompanied her for their transcontinental adventure.
Rose would have adapted perfectly to Facebook and Twitter, using
her diary entries as daily postings. "I left for California at 10 A. M.
from South Station." "Arrived Chicago, 1 o'clock, shopped at Mar-

shall Fields." "Arrived Albuquerque. Visited Indian Museum. . . .
[C]ountry more interesting, hilly, red sand and muddy rivers shal-
low. Indian clay houses—adobes—oil fields." "At Grand Canyon. . . . I rode around rim. . . . Colors beautiful—purples, lavenders,
and reds and blues."[57] Agnes ventured into the canyon for a close-up
look. The difference in how they experienced nature's wonder
reflects Rose's approach to life: she often confined herself to the edge
of experience, preferring a more superficial view of even the most
profound sites.

From home Joe sent news of the children. Using his nickname
for her, "Rosa," in cables, Joe assured her that he was the "greatest
manager in the world" because the children were "fine." "I hope
you are having a real good time because you so richly deserve it.
Please do not think too much about us and spoil your party. I am
not lonesome because I find myself very happy in the thought that
you are enjoying yourself. Lots of love from us all."[58] Refusing to
worry her about an outbreak of measles among the children, he
kept the health report mum.[59] Likewise, she never reported bad
news from home when he traveled because, as she put it, "There
was little or nothing he could do to help the situation at a distance,
so why worry him?"[60]

As Rose explored California, from the missions to the orange
groves and Sunkist factory to Coronado Beach and La Jolla with a
detour across the Mexican border to Tijuana, Joe encouraged her
to write to him: "I like to know how you are." Meanwhile, Joe
met with teachers, took the children to parties, and treated them
to Friday night suppers. Rose traveled north to Los Angeles, where
she and Agnes stayed at the new Ambassador Hotel and dined at its
famed Coconut Grove nightclub, a hot spot for new film celebrities such as Louis B. Mayer, Charlie Chaplin, Douglas Fairbanks,
Mary Pickford, Howard Hughes, Clara Bow, Rudolph Valentino,
and Gloria Swanson. In Hollywood she lunched at a restaurant
frequented by actors and actresses and saw Gloria Swanson perform a film scene.[61] The next day Rose explored Santa Monica,
Venice, and San Pedro, and then sailed to Catalina Island, finding
the boat trip "tiresome" when she nearly became seasick. But she

enjoyed seeing the home of chewing-gum magnate William Wrigley Jr., who developed the picturesque island. She loved her hotel in Santa Barbara, describing her room's decor in detail. Taking an auto excursion to Miramar and Montecito over a "beautiful mountain road," she caught a glimpse of Douglas Fairbanks's property. The central California flora fascinated her, especially the eucalyptus trees, date palms, and cypress, as did the stunning topographical wonders of Yosemite. Moving north, she spent five days in San Francisco.

By now, Joe pined for her, writing, "I am looking forward to the nineteenth [of May, her return date] like I did for October seventh [their wedding day] some years ago. Everybody still fine but I think the help will welcome you back."[62] Rose returned by way of Salt Lake City, where she recorded Brigham Young's family statistics: "19 wives, 28 daughters, 24 sons." Colorado Springs and Denver were her last stops, and she marveled at the Rocky Mountains' splendor.

A few weeks after her mid-May return, the family moved to the South Shore for the summer. In 1920 they had begun to rent a house at Cohasset, a Protestant bastion. Finding the local golf club inhospitable, Joe was angry but not too surprised when its members blackballed him. The Kennedys celebrated Rose's thirty-third birthday with a trip to Hyannis on Cape Cod, where Joe presented his wife with a Cartier vanity case. While summering at the South Shore in 1923, Rose became pregnant with baby number six, Patricia. She sent Joe and Jack back to Boston to start school in September, while she stayed at the beach. The boys resided with the Moores in Brookline. Jack told Mary that "the cops are chasing me already," after he had teased a playmate who then complained to the police. Rose would stay on the South Shore until early October. By the time she returned home, the boys were playing more childish pranks, including shoplifting Halloween paraphernalia. Yet six-year-old Jack could be a charming "elf," as his mother described him. "Daddy has a sweet tooth, hasn't he? I wonder which one it is?" she reported he queried her. Rose's admonitions to buckle down at school met with his boyish response, "You know, I am getting on all right and if you study too much, you're liable to go crazy." Believing that both boys had too much time to conjure up mischief, she and Joe sent them to Dexter, a private, nonsectarian elementary school, with supervised play and sports in the afternoons.[63] Joe Jr. and Jack could walk to the exclusive school, which attracted boys from Boston's WASP elite. Joe Sr.'s plan to remove his sons from their socioeconomic roots was now under way.

Joe and Rose had more worries than the boys' antics in 1923. The first of their family tragedies began to befall them. Just after Rose returned from her California trip, Joe's mother, Mary Hickey Kennedy, died of stomach cancer at sixty-five. "It was just God's will," Joe wrote.[64] In September Rose's sister Eunice passed away at twenty-three from tuberculosis contracted while working for the Red Cross during World War I.

One bright spot for the Kennedys in the Roaring Twenties appeared in their improving financial position. By the middle of the decade, Joe's net worth approached $2 million.[65] Eventually Rose's household staff included four maids, a cook, a waitress, a nurse, and a governess. Honey Fitz advised her to hire as many servants as necessary to ease her maternal burdens. Joe, too, indulged his materialistic desires. One day he brought home two Rolls-Royces. Rose remembered, "I thought then he was going a little crazy and that I should talk to him tactfully because they say if you run afoul with your husband . . . perhaps he'll stop giving you presents. . . . I said, 'Well, really two Rolls Royces cost [a lot], and I don't think we need [them].' . . . [B]ut I never asked [Joe] how much money he had or where he was getting it or anything. . . . [H]e used to like my clothes. [But] [h]e didn't want to see the bills. . . ."[66]

Cooks constituted more than a luxury in Rose Kennedy's household. They represented an absolute necessity. She simply didn't know how to prepare meals for any size family, much less an army of young Kennedys. "I tried to learn [to cook as a young girl]," Rose asserted, "but my mother always had a cook for years, and she wasn't really very cooperative. She wanted to get the work done. She didn't want to stop and teach me, but I thought I should know how to cook because I thought it would be an advantage. But I never had to cook much."[67]

ATTEMPTING TO THWART a hostile investor pool engaged in driving down Yellow Cab stock to the detriment of a Honey Fitz crony, in 1924 Joe spent considerable time in New York. He and his associates manipulated the company's stock prices to counter the attack. Rose knew that her husband "was running a [stock] pool," although she admitted, "I don't understand the stock market. But [Joe] had two or three different things going, selling and buying at the same time, mixing everybody up."[68] Though a financial naïf, she actually grasped the primary aim of Joe's Wall Street machinations.

As Joe spent increasingly more time in New York, Rose considered moving the family there, but "I didn't want to change the children's schools. . . ."[69] Honey Fitz had switched Rose's school several times, including taking her from Concord to Boston for a few months during grammar school so that he could tell the electorate he lived in the city. She found the experience difficult and didn't want to treat her children similarly. While away from the family, Joe kept in touch by telephone, an invention he quickly adopted for personal and professional use. Rose labeled her husband "a great telephoner. He used to telephone before we were married every night and afterward nearly every night, which was a wonderful habit, and one which the children inherited, which was rather expensive. . . . I suppose every family has their pet economies and their pet extravagances."[70]

Perhaps Rose had another reason to stay in Boston and communicate with Joe by phone. During his many New York absences, she experienced the longest interval among her first seven children's births: three years between Eunice (1921) and Patricia, born May 6, 1924.

Joe's increasing wealth enabled him to indulge his passion for entertainment, especially live stage productions. Since his days at Hayden, Stone, he had dabbled in "moving pictures." As early as

1919, he likened them to the invention of another of his favorite electronic instruments, the telephone. "[W]e must get into this [movie] business," Joe declared to a friend. After trying unsuccessfully to do so throughout the first half of the 1920s, he finally completed a deal to purchase Film Booking Offices of America (FBOA) and became its president and chairman of the board in 1926.[71]

Working on the movie deal, Joe's weekly commute to New York grew tiresome. He wrote lovingly to Rose from New York's Harvard Club, just before sailing for Europe in the summer of 1925 to negotiate with English film moguls: "I just want you to know that going away on trips like this makes me realize just how little anything amounts to except you as years go on I just love you more than anything in the world and I always wonder whether I ever do half enough for you to show you how much I appreciate you. Well dear this is just a little love letter from a husband to wife married 11 years."[72]

Joe's letters to Rose from shipboard and Europe reflect warm affection for her and their family. Aboard Cunard's *Aquitania*, he penned, "Rosa dear, Well here I am two days out and already wishing I was home. . . . You were certainly a peach to think of your letters and have the pictures of Jack . . . and the little girls. I am looking forward to opening the rest of them." As the ship neared Cherbourg, Kennedy told Rose about his unrelenting homesickness and that he had received her photograph: "I was tickled to get it but you should have put it in the first envelope. You know that's where you belong and always will." From Paris he admitted, "I know it is terrible to tell you in every letter how homesick I am but it is terrible. I can't seem to shake it off at all. I think of you and the children all the time and almost go silly. . . . I have received one letter from you but I suppose the others are in England. It was just bread from heaven." Observing his First Friday duty, Joe "went to communion . . . and went to an English priest for confession. When I finished he asked me if I was a priest (how do you like that old darling[?]). . . . I can't get along without you, Rosa. It may be nice to travel but only with you. The complete success of your system is acknowledged. I admit absolute defeat and beg for terms. . . . I am crazy about you."[73] In later years Joe continued to express his love for Rose in letters during his many and lengthy absences, but none ever achieved the ardor or tenderness of the 1925 billets-doux.

After the FBOA purchase, Rose relented on moving to New York. She had occasionally visited Joe while he worked there and "found it a very exciting city." They would enjoy a "week of fun. We would go to theaters and see the life there. So I was very happy to go. Although some of my friends did not want to go to New York. Joe had two or three associates' wives who did not want to go at that time. But . . . I always was interested and joyous and happy about seeking new adventures."[74]

Joe's explanation of the family's 1927 move to Riverdale, in the Bronx, was less sentimental. Hoping to escape Boston's provincialism, he set his children on a course to avoid the Brahmins' religious and ethnic bigotry.[75] Once in New York, the Kennedys acquired "a bigger house and more servants" for their seven children, which now included a third son, Robert, born on November 20, 1925. The family bestowed the diminutive "Bobby" on the little boy. Rose's mother worried that he would become a "sissy" because he was surrounded by sisters and governesses.[76] When asked in 1969 to share anecdotes of his childhood, Rose wrote that his sisters might have more stories to offer "as Bobby was [the] youngest of seven children of whom [the] eldest was only ten years old, and I do not remember many details—Children were all grouped together. . . ."[77]

The thirteen-room Riverdale estate had once belonged to Republican Charles Evans Hughes, who would become chief justice of the United States in 1930. Rose admitted to acute homesickness for Massachusetts.[78] Maintaining their Bay State roots, Joe rented, and then in 1928 bought, a summer home at Hyannis Port that would become the nucleus of the family's Cape Cod compound.

Kennedy and Fitzgerald family associations continued to shadow Joe and Rose during the 1920s. Although an abstemious drinker because of his sensitive stomach and a desire to avoid the stereotype of the drunken Irish, Joe had access to the stored sherry, port, and spirits from P. J. Kennedy's days as a saloon owner. Joe sold his father's wine, and supplied alcohol for his tenth Harvard reunion in 1922, despite Prohibition. Yet the terms "bootlegger" and "rumrunner," often attached to Joseph Kennedy's legend, exaggerate his deals. Amanda Smith, Joe's granddaughter, found neither "confirmation nor denial" for the age-old rumor that he sometimes waited on Massachusetts's North Shore for nighttime deliveries of illicit alcohol. Even the federal government never discovered any illegalities in Joe's alcohol business prior to the repeal of Prohibition in 1933.[79]

Joe also assisted Honey Fitz's ongoing political ambitions although Rose's marriage and motherhood removed her from the campaign trail. In 1916, two years after he withdrew from the mayor's race in disgrace, Fitzgerald had won the Democratic Party's nomination for US Senate, but incumbent Senator Henry Cabot Lodge Sr. defeated him in the Bay State's first popular senatorial election. Vying for the US House of Representatives seat from the Tenth District two years later, Honey Fitz won and served seven months until a congressional investigation uncovered voter fraud. The House then voted to remove Fitzgerald. He never held public office again, though he tried unsuccessfully to win the governorship in 1922.[80]

Honey Fitz turned his attention to young Joe Jr. and Jack, delighting in taking them to parades, political rallies, Red Sox games, and Boston's historic sites. Waiting in the car with his Grandma Fitzgerald while Honey Fitz shook voters' hands at political rallies made Jack impatient. John Fitzgerald's namesake would never relish pressing the flesh as much as his grandfather. It would be another of Rose's sons whom Ted Sorensen would label the "reincarnation of Honey Fitz."[81]

CHAPTER 4

Mother of Nine

Rose HAD THOUGHT THE MOVE TO RIVERDALE WOULD REUNITE the family while Joe pursued his movie business in New York City. She had barely settled in, however, when Joe began spending most of his time in Hollywood, as he would until 1930.[1] At least Riverdale was a pleasant community. Prosperous nineteenth-century businessmen had built their mansions there to escape cramped urban life. The Kennedys' home sat across from an estate once rented by Teddy Roosevelt, then by Mark Twain.

Maintaining a flock of seven, ranging in age from twelve-year-old Joe Jr. to two-year-old Bobby, presented Rose with numerous challenges. First came the search for new schools. Joe Jr. and Jack enrolled in Riverdale Country Day, which proved more than adequate for scholastic and extracurricular activities. Established in 1907, it was among the nation's first country day schools. Wealthy parents had created these posh suburban enclaves so that their sons could have a prep-school experience without boarding away from home. RCD maintained high academic standards, fostered esprit de corps and character, and promoted sports, as well as other after-

school activities.[2] Rose knew her two animated oldest children
needed such supervised afternoon play and studies.

Only once—in spring 1927—did Rose visit Joe in Hollywood.
"I couldn't travel a whole lot on account of having all these young
children. . . . [T]he winters were quite severe in New England, and
the children had colds, and I stayed pretty close to home. And Hollywood was three days away on the train, or four days and three
nights. I went once, but a child could be dead and buried by the
time you would get back from Hollywood."[3] As we have seen,
Rose worried incessantly about her children's health, perhaps with
memories of Jack's scarlet fever preying on her mind. Or maybe her
method of handling Joe's infidelity, knowing that she had cast her
lot with him forever in 1920 (after a brief respite with her parents),
was simply staying home and protecting her children. When she
needed a break from single parenting, she could rely on Eddie and
Mary Moore, as well as household staff, to provide child care.

Rose's spring 1927 Los Angeles visit with Joe marked several
turning points. Her older children could now compose coherent
letters. Joe Jr. wrote, "Dearest Mother: I thank you and dad for the
lovely telegram. The most important thing I have to tell you [is]
that I was confirmed yesterday by Cardinal O'conell [sic]."[4] Rose
must have felt some guilt about missing her eldest son's confirmation in the Catholic Church. He reported that he had served early
Mass, received Communion, and returned to church later for the
confirmation ceremony, attended by the ever-present Moores,
Grandma and Grandpa Fitzgerald, sisters Eunice and Rosemary,
and Aunt Agnes. He dutifully thanked Joe and Rose for the prayer
book they had given him to mark his becoming a "Soldier of
Christ," and he reported that Grandma Fitzgerald and Aunt Agnes
presented him with a rosary. He also observed that his sister Kathleen would make her First Communion the next week, another
important religious milestone that Rose and Joe would miss. The
governess, Miss MacSwain, assured Mrs. Kennedy that Kathleen
would "look very sweet" for the holy occasion. Eunice, not quite
six, scrawled, "Dear Mother, I love you and Daddy. We all are
fine," and the governess attached an update on all of the children.

Rose had been gone so long that MacSwain commented, "When you come back, you will see quite a change in [Bobby]." "He says ever so many words now."[5]

While her children braved a rainy, cool Boston spring, Rose experienced Hollywood's sun-kissed life, including visits to movie stars' opulent homes. Although Beverly Hills extravagances shocked Rose's frugal New England sensibilities, she charmed her Los Angeles hosts. Meeting celebrities throughout her life had prepared her to hobnob with Joe's hospitable colleagues.[6] Asked years later, "Were you impressed by those people, kind of excited and thrilled. . . ?" Rose responded, "Well, I was, [but] . . . I didn't see them a lot. . . . I only went out there once. . . . [T]he people themselves, they were all very pleasant, I thought."[7] She took Joe's ascent from minor East Coast movie entrepreneur to Hollywood mogul "in my stride and tried to learn the names of the moving picture companies, and the actresses and the actors. . . ."[8]

From her sole California visit with Joe, Rose returned pregnant with their eighth child. Although already settled in New York by the baby's due date, Rose returned to Boston to be near her familiar obstetrician, Dr. Frederick Good. By 1928, medical protocols had changed, and Rose gave birth to Jean Ann Kennedy at a Dorchester hospital on February 20. Back in Riverdale, and attempting to keep meals orderly, Rose imposed a strict schedule on her octet of children: up to age six, they ate an hour earlier than the rest of the family. Rose sat with them and discussed simple topics of interest to toddlers and preschoolers. Then the older children dined together, and she would chat with them about more complicated subjects.[9] Through their early school years, Rose encouraged Joe, Jack, and Kathleen, then Eunice, Pat, and Bobby, to read daily newspapers. She posted articles or documents on a bulletin board, expecting the older children to read them and discuss the content at dinner. Even during summer vacations, they continued supper seminars. Every July 4, she celebrated Independence Day at Hyannis Port by displaying the Declaration of Independence and discussing its historic signers.[10] On Sundays and Holy Days she posed questions about the priest's sermon and Catholic symbolism.

Looking back, she believed the children felt no pressure to perform at mealtime. "[N]othing was stressed or strained. . . . If they wanted to do it fine, but if they didn't want to do it, they were more or less ignored. Not definitely, not deliberately, but, because they just were not interesting. . . . "[11] Visitors sometimes felt intimidated, especially when Joe was home and presided over the dining table. Rose's friend Mary Sanford admitted years later:

> It was an education to go to lunch with the whole family—it was a frightening experience. [Joe] would sit at the head of the table, and, if you didn't know what was happening—if you weren't au courant with all the politics of the day, you just felt like you were the most stupid person in the world. And each kid would get into the arguments and the conversation. It was very stimulating. And he was like a tyrant. I think they were always scared to death of him. You can see how interesting they are now [1972]—every one of them is interesting. Well, I think they've imbued them with this terrific drive and ambition—and certainly Rose has it. . . .[12]

Rose insisted on mealtime punctuality, even during the summer. "My husband was always on time. And I think it is rude to be late," she asserted. She attributed her ability to accomplish so much in life to running the household by strict rules.[13] Young Jack, however, chronically defied his mother. She would instruct the children to assemble at an appointed hour for their lunchtime trip home from the pool. Each day he missed the ride from the country club, found alternative transportation, and wandered in halfway through the noonday meal. Rose's rule decreed that a tardy diner must start with whatever course the cooks were serving. But she let Jack sneak to the kitchen afterward and charm the staff into feeding him. Decades later she still bemoaned Jack's recalcitrance. "[W]hat could you do if he was late everyday, and it was deliberate?" she wondered. "But he was so thin all the time that I couldn't really adhere to the original [rules]."[14]

Jack had a sweet, endearing side, too. When Rose gave birth to her last child on February 22, 1932, in Boston, fourteen-year-old Jack asked if he could serve as the baby's godfather. JFK waggishly wanted to name him "George Washington Kennedy," in recognition of the infant's historic birth date. Instead, his parents chose Edward Moore as the child's name, to honor their dear friend, but they nicknamed the robust infant "Teddy." Challenging two of her most cherished possessions—her girlish figure and devout faith—Rose's friends criticized her for having yet another child. "[P]eople said, 'Why do you want to have nine children? You have had eight. You are over forty-years-old, and you will be tired out, and you will lose your figure and looks. Why do you want to pay any attention to those priests?'" Obviously, her friends knew that Rose was following Catholic dictates. "I got rather indignant," she responded, "and made up my mind that neither Teddy nor I [was] going to suffer and were going to be independent and make it in superior fashion. [I] [w]asn't going to have any body feel sorry for us."[15] Rose declared, "[H]e *was* happy. . . . He would never get upset with anybody or anything."[16]

Teddy remembered her lovingly: "Mother was . . . our Pied Piper into the world of ideas. She led us on educational outings to museums and to concerts, to Concord and Bunker Hill and the Old North Church, rattling out improvised math challenges to us along the way. . . . She was moderator of our topical dinner table conversation, the topics—geography one night, the front-page headlines the next—announced in advance on cards that she wrote out and pinned to a billboard near the dining room."[17]

Admitting that "[Mother] was the disciplinarian of all our headstrong impulses, and was sometimes strict," Teddy recalled that "spankings and whacks with a coat hanger were in her arsenal, as were banishments to the closet. On one such expedition, I stood in the darkness feeling sorry for myself, until I realized I was not alone: Jean was standing beside me, serving out her own time for some infraction of the rules. But Mother was also the tender index-card archivist of the small moments, the letters, notes, and remarks that were the lifeblood of our family."[18]

Teddy earned a spanking *and* closet time for walking home alone from kindergarten. As Joe grew wealthier and more prominent, Rose worried that her children might be abducted for ransom.[19] The 1932 kidnapping and murder of toddler Charles A. Lindbergh Jr. stunned her and fixated the nation. Rose frequently mentioned the tragedy and her fears about the children's safety, especially Rosemary's, agonizing that without constant supervision, the retarded youngster might wander off.

Rose later dismissed Victorian discipline's potential ill effects on her children: "Well, I put them in the closet, but . . . they weren't scared of the dark. It would just get one or two of them out of the way for awhile. . . ."[20] Looking back, she admitted, "I spanked them with a ruler. Then I spanked them with a coat hanger as they grew older because there was always a closet near and there was always a coat hanger in the closet. And I couldn't be bothered, you know," throwing up her hands and smiling, "with nine children and all their friends in and making a lot of noise when you were telephoning or teasing one another. . . . I'd just give them a couple of [whacks]."[21]

Mary Sanford refused to criticize her friend's parenting: "All the time that Joe was in California making money, and with all these deals and things, she was home looking after the children and bringing them up."[22] "Shopping for eight or nine children takes a tremendously lot of time," Rose noted, though in truth she turned many duties over to the governess. After all, "I had a social life. I used to go to the opening of plays all the time. There were a lot of new openings then."[23] Daughter Pat recalled, "My room . . . was right next to my mother's, and I remember often when she'd go out at night with Daddy (maybe it's because she went out very infrequently). I remember her coming in to kiss me good-night. She was always so beautiful. My room was dark, and this vision just sort of came in, just smelling absolutely marvelous with her perfume."[24]

Rose continued her religious observances too: "I went to the convent; the first Friday [of the month] was always a day of prayer."[25] During summers in Hyannis, Rose attended daily Mass at St. Francis Xavier. Each morning she drove her blue coupe to church, although she could barely see over the steering wheel. "Unlike the rest of us, my mother would have been dressed in a way befitting respectable society, in a tilted broad-brimmed straw hat and floral dress, her earrings and pearls in place, a small purse held tightly in her two gloved hands," Teddy recalled. In the 1930s Rose "was named the best-dressed woman in public life by a poll of fashion designers."[26]

AFTER TWO YEARS in Riverdale, from 1927 to 1929, the Kennedys bought an estate at 294 Pondfield Road in Bronxville, about fifteen miles north of midtown Manhattan. The $250,000 mansion sat on six acres. Joe Jr., Jack, and eventually Bobby rode a bus to Riverdale Country Day School, and the girls attended the Bronxville School, described by Rose as "a very good public school, a progressive school," just down the street from the new house. "And then there was the golf course. We played golf. . . . We liked [Bronxville]. They were all happy at school. . . ." Rose invited the children's teachers to lunch each new school year and visited their classrooms.[27]

Teddy retained vivid memories of the Bronxville home. "The colonnaded house . . . stood in the village's leafy Sagamore Park neighborhood. Its three stories and twenty rooms occupied a crest of land, its red-tiled roof catching the sun above a thick scattering of tall old trees." "A curving third-floor balcony rested on top of three Ionic columns," Teddy remembered, "and a smaller balcony below it stretched above the front entrance. Inside, amid the master rooms, were such modern wonders as shower baths, an oil-burning hot water heater, and a number of enclosed porches. The basement held a billiard table, and the garage was big enough for five cars. . . . A driveway bordered by shrubbery arced downward along the terraced lawn until it reached the street."[28] In a mere dozen years, the Kennedys had moved from middle-class Brookline to Bronxville's opulence.

Despite Joe's many absences, Teddy insisted that his "father's voice" was "paramount."[29] When at home, Joe lavished attention on the children, treating them to lunches and Radio City Music

Hall movies. Eunice affirmed Joe's central role in the Kennedy universe: "I can remember Sunday lunches. My father was [the] personality that dominated. He dominated things always, although my mother was more articulate with everything when he wasn't there. But when he was home, she let him sort of take over." Yet Eunice recounted that her father seemed to be away "always" during her childhood. To her, Rose played the role of "presiding parent" only in her father's absence. "[A]s we got older, he made it possible for us to do things, but I think that the terrific drive and everything, to me, came much more from my mother, than my father," Eunice asserted. Rose's and Joe's influence on their children depended on their gender and birth order. As the fifth child, exactly in the middle of her eight siblings, Eunice thought her parents struck a "balance" in child rearing. "He didn't interfere with the girls as much as he did with the boys. He was more concerned about the boys' future than the girls'. Then she had more to do where we went to school."[30]

All children under Rose's supervision, including nieces and nephews, agreed on her exacting persona. "She was, I think, quite stern," Eunice remembered:

> She knew there were certain ways to behave. We went to dancing lessons once a week, we had our teeth straightened. I remember going five years with my sisters, five or six of us in a car. We'd go all the way into New York. She's a perfectionist. Instead of going to the local dentist, which I suppose we could have done, we had to hop into the car once every three weeks. We'd drive for an hour to New York. Go to the dentist and back we'd come. We'd wait our turn and then we'd go to the chair. Then we'd go to our dancing class, Arthur Murray's. She bought the lessons, and then I would have to go with my sisters. We'd go once a week. We were really organized. . . . She was a great believer in opening up many opportunities for all of us. And though some of those things were difficult, she would compensate by saying you ought to try them. Encourage my father all

the time to let us go. He'd say it was good, but she'd talk him
into it all the time. Saying "they should go abroad, take the
trips," and it started out with my sister Rosemary when I was
about sixteen. We went to Switzerland. . . . She [Rose] just
believed it; they ought to be exposed [to new experiences].[31]

The dazzling Kennedy smiles resulted from another of Rose's
perfectionist obsessions: oral health. Before dental hygiene became
an American craze after World War II, Rose set the standard by
insisting that her children brush their teeth before going to school,
play, and bed. She prided herself on asking if they had performed
their ablutions and instructed the governess to supervise. Rose's
request for goodnight kisses led to her inevitable follow-up:

> "Did you wash your teeth?" It's just habits. If they start when
> they're three years old, they go on. . . . I had nothing else to do,
> and I was interested. If the toothbrushes are right there in front
> of them, it's not very much of an effort. And they all had beau-
> tiful teeth. When they were straightened, it cost a lot of nervous
> energy. Doctors every . . . week. . . . New York to Bronxville
> was [a] little bit of a trot. They couldn't go alone all the way
> because they were too young sometimes. They were eight or
> ten years old. To get from the station to the dentist was another
> haul. I would bring them home if I were shopping, or some-
> body would have to put them on a train and telephone. Of
> course, we had all this help. It was mostly management [on
> Rose's part].[32]

Her children did not simply possess healthy teeth. Their smiles
radiated what became known in politics as "Kennedy charisma."
Even as young men, Joe and Jack impressed their peers and elders
with their pearly whites. The son of JFK's prep-school headmaster
explained, "When [Jack] flashed his smile, he could charm a bird
off a tree." And Joe Jr.'s crusty British tutor described the young
man's grin as "pure magic."[33]

IN 1929 JOE SR.'s career as a Hollywood producer neared its end. Combining two smaller movie businesses into RKO, he made more than $5 million (nearly $70 million in current dollars).[34] Joe also romanced silent-movie goddess, Gloria Swanson, the epitome of his penchant for exotic women of stage and screen. Rose found herself in the awkward position of accompanying Joe, Swanson, and her spouse, Henri Marquis de la Failaise de la Coudraye, to the 1929 Paris and London premieres of Swanson's first talking picture, *The Trespasser*. Swanson wondered how Rose could accept such humiliation: "Was she a fool, I asked myself . . . , or a saint? Or just a better actress than I was?"[35] If Rose kept a travel diary for the trip, as she did on most of her other European excursions, it didn't survive or isn't among her papers.

Years later Rose recalled a tense moment at Swanson's London premiere: "the people were disappointed when I got [out of the car] instead of Gloria. They could see me coming instead of Gloria. 'Who are you? What are you doing? We want to see Gloria.'"[36] How demeaning for Rose to accompany her husband's paramour to a public event and hear spectators clamoring for the "other woman." For a childhood friend from Concord, however, Rose put a positive spin on these matters: "I have had quite an interesting life. My husband was quite successful in the movies and we went out frequently with Gloria Swanson and other stars."[37]

Although Gloria was nine years Rose's junior, the two women looked strikingly similar in their flapper clothing, smiling broadly from under cloche hats. They were both petite and battled sensitive stomachs. Gloria followed a vegetarian diet and embraced macrobiotics. Rose ate birdlike portions of bland food. Their personalities and lifestyles, however, could not have been more divergent. Gloria's half-dozen marriages, countless liaisons, and several abortions represent the very antithesis of Rose's staunch Catholic mores. Indeed, her Victorian sensibilities starkly countered vampish Gloria, who, even in her seventies, reveled in double entendres when she appeared on talk shows wearing dramatic outfits—a contrast to Rose's conservative wardrobe. Gloria spoke in low, sultry, sexy tones; Rose's Boston accent, and somewhat brittle voice, occasionally grated.

Even more awkward for Rose were Swanson's visits with the Kennedys in Bronxville and Hyannis. Mary Sanford assumed Rose knew about the affair: "When I met Joe—I'd talked to him on the phone—I don't know if I should say this—he was stuck on Gloria Swanson—you remember that?" she queried Rose's memoirist. "[Rose] knows about that—and she went for a trip . . . with them, didn't she . . . ? I've never discussed it with her. Anyway, [Joe] was smitten with Gloria Swanson."[38]

Officially, Joe served as the actress's financial adviser and producer of several films. Behind the scenes, he pursued her ardently. Swanson's 1980 autobiography described a brief consummation of their affair in a Palm Beach hotel.[39] How many other assignations occurred over their several-year association remains unknown, but most biographers report that the affair was "common knowledge" in Hollywood.[40] Like numerous stars, Swanson believed in serial matrimony: she married six times and divorced all but the last spouse, who simply outlived her.[41]

Rose's 1972 comments reveal her complicated history with the screen siren who captivated Joe Kennedy. "Gloria Swanson was with us a lot," Rose observed. "And her daughter [Gloria]. My daughter [Pat] brought her to public school . . . , and nobody would believe that it was Gloria Swanson's daughter, because everyone wondered why would Gloria Swanson's daughter be in Bronxville, naturally. Because at that time we had just moved to Bronxville, and nobody knew us very well and the connections that we had with the movies or the connection that we had with Gloria."[42] Just prior to her ninth birthday in 1930, Kick wrote to her father, "Tell Gloria [Swanson's daughter] that I sent her a letter and ask her if she got it. Would you please get me a picture of Miss Swanson with her name on it."[43] Two months later, Kick asked of Joe, "How is little Gloria[?] Will you please ask her to write me a letter [?]"[44]

Rose explained her family's tie to the actress:

[Joe] managed Gloria Swanson because she had financial difficulties at the time. . . . So we traveled with her a good deal.
And the stories circulate, because . . . they had their pictures
taken and notice I wasn't in the movie picture. See, on the
ship [returning from England] I stepped aside, and afterwards
the story got around that Joe and Gloria had gone on a trip to
Europe together. A long story started, until they said the
child [Gloria's adopted son Joseph Patrick] was named after
him. But she contradicted that, I saw a month or two ago. In
fact, I cut it out. The [adopted] boy Joseph had been named
after her father. But, of course, the story got around that he
was Joe's son. . . .[45]

Eunice Kennedy Shriver insisted that Rose heard no gossip
about Joe and Gloria Swanson until the late 1960s and was not
bothered by an alleged, twenty-year-old romance.

Like Jacqueline Kennedy's attempt to mitigate scandalous stories about her husband by constructing the Camelot mythology,
Rose created an idealistic image of her marriage. "In my relations
with my husband, there was never any deceit. . . . He never said
he was going out on business; he would say he was going to a
show, and I would say, 'Fine.' Eddie Moore was usually always
with him. . . . He told me that he kept Eddie around when he was
signing contracts with some of these 'dames,' as he used to say,"
Rose laughed. "And then he'd, you know, get framed and get into
difficulties. Whatever business he was in, he always had Eddie
Moore with him as his private secretary at this country and
abroad."[46] But, she conceded, "[Joe] was meeting women all the
time that were well dressed, too, and working for him, so I found
no reason that I shouldn't be [well dressed]."[47] That resigned comment parallels Lady Bird Johnson's attitude toward her husband's
adultery. She adopted a philosophical approach to LBJ's infidelity,
deciding to glean beauty and fashion tips from the women to
whom he was attracted.

IN THE LATE 1920S, Rose's daily responsibilities decreased, when Joe Jr. and Jack enrolled in boarding schools. "I wanted to send them to a school in New York State so we might see them more often." Yet eventually she realized that when they were "in boarding school you don't see your children very much."[48] Nevertheless, the boys remained close by in neighboring Connecticut. She won, temporarily, the debate with her husband over secular versus parochial education, enrolling thirteen-year-old Jack in Canterbury School in New Milford, Connecticut. Letters to his mother focused on what he knew mattered to her—health and weight: "I hope you and Dad and all the little girls including Bobby and lastly Buddy and Pal [the family dogs] are feeling O.K. I was weighed yesterday and I have lost one pound and have not grown at all."[49] The rail-thin adolescent followed a routine his mother had recorded so assiduously on her index cards. Rose reported on Jack's file, "Oct., Nov., Dec. [1930] lost weight at Canterbury and went down to 95 ½ [pounds]. . . . Examined by Dr. Schloss on Tuesday, Dec. 30. Found to be in good general condition. Loss of weight attributed to lack of milk in diet, tonic prescribed."[50]

With Jack away, she couldn't supply the extra cream or steak juice that she administered to him at home to add pounds. Trying to alleviate his mother's worries, Jack reported, "I guess the only thing wrong with me is that I am pretty tired." To his father, however, he described a worrisome fainting spell suffered at Mass.[51] After expressing concern to Rose about his low grades, he included a postscript, "Am coming to Dentist I think on Wednesday."[52] At least his mother could take comfort in that! His weight began to tick upward that spring, exceeding 100 pounds for the first time, until an appendectomy felled him, causing the loss of several pounds.

While Jack suffered from illness and isolation at Canterbury, Joe Jr. excelled at Choate, and JFK asked to join his brother at the Wallingford, Connecticut, prep school the next year. "It was a good school and it was near Bronxville," Rose explained, only about a two-hour car drive from home.[53] It boasted the nation's largest school infirmary, important for chronically ill Jack. The school's formidable headmaster, Reverend George St. John, ruled the campus in stern English public-school tradition.

From Bronxville, Rose continued to track Jack's health and attempted to impose her dietary rules on him. To the headmaster's wife she wrote that Jack shouldn't be eating "sweets" at the school's "Tuck Shop." "Jack has no discretion," Rose criticized, "in fact, he has never eaten enough vegetables to satisfy me." "I do not want to bother you, but will someone please investigate this matter a little?" she asked Mrs. St. John. Rose noted that "Mr. Kennedy will probably be up next week, but I have not been well enough to visit Jack, and I do want him to go along the right track." Rose rarely admitted ill health, but she wrote this letter around Teddy's birth, which perhaps accounts for her indisposition. She added a postscript about Jack: "How is his weight?" Then she noted that he had weighed 114 ½ in September and 115 in January "after supper."[54]

In contrast to Rose's critiques of Jack, she took great pride in Joe Jr. Graduating from Choate in 1933, he received the Harvard Prize for scholastic and athletic achievement, which his mother kept proudly for decades.[55] Writing to Headmaster St. John, she thanked him "for your interest and patience in Jack. He has a very attractive personality, we think, but he is quite different from Joe for whom we feel you have done so much." Jack "hates routine work but loves History and English—subjects that fire his imagination."[56]

Even with Joe Jr. and Jack away, Rose's maternal duties continued. "Her role was a little different," Eunice explained. "She was there all the time. She organized our lives. . . . I guess the word is discipline. She had us out no matter what the weather was. . . . I can remember going ice skating in Bronxville. Mother would take us, and I remember her skating." Rarely described as warm or demonstrative, Rose's relationship with her children "wasn't a great emotional thing," offered Eunice. "She was more a teacher or an inspirer. She was more interested in whether you were reading or whether taking skating lessons. You just wouldn't go skating off into the blue yonder. She'd say, 'Use your right leg or use your left leg better.'"[57]

The same was true in academics. Rose wanted the children to do their best and never make excuses. "She'd say, 'You just get along there; don't be stupid about it,'" Eunice recalled. "Never, 'Oh, you poor thing, you may not feel very well today. You can't do Latin well. That's too bad. You drop Latin and take another subject.' No. [She would say] 'You go in there and you learn Latin.' . . . So she would do homework with me, and, if I couldn't do it, she'd get cross, [and] say, 'You just learn this, and sit here and learn that verb.' Instead of saying, 'Why don't you drop Latin.' Never." Rose sounded "sort of [like] an ogre," Eunice conceded, "but you never felt that she was. . . . You felt that she felt you had more in you than you thought you did. She never assumed that you didn't."[58]

Eunice once ran afoul of Rose's sense of propriety when the young girl tried to raise money for Catholic missions by selling apples on her Bronxville street. "[S]uddenly this low voice came up behind me and out popped my mother. She was absolutely enraged, told me to go right home. 'How dare [you] sell those apples. Never do that again. Go right to [your] room. See that you go. Stay 'til morning.' I thought it was one of the few times I saw her so angry. I guess she . . . [thought], living in Bronxville at that time, it was unseemly. I was about ten years old."[59]

Why was Rose so outraged, especially since her daughter simply wanted to earn money for Catholic charity? Perhaps, as Eunice surmised, Rose thought it inappropriate to hawk apples in an upscale neighborhood. Or maybe she thought it reflected poorly on their wealthy family to have the children asking for money. Did Rose not want to draw attention to the Kennedys' Catholicism in a WASP enclave? Maybe she believed Eunice evoked scenes of the unemployed, forced to sell apples on street corners during the Depression.

In 1933, while a quarter of the nation's workforce battled unemployment and many families faced homelessness, Joe Kennedy took some of the money he had made in films and the stock market, which he abandoned before its 1929 crash, and purchased a third home. "The crash in the stock market left me untouched; I was more fortunate this time than usual," Joe wrote to the attorney who handled his father's estate.[60] (P. J. Kennedy died of liver disease in 1929, just after his son had returned to California. Joe Jr. represented his father at the funeral.) With the collapse of the Florida real estate market, Joe negotiated a bargain price of $100,000 for a classic Mediterranean-style home designed by Addison Mizner. The white stucco, red-tile-roofed house, featuring seven bedrooms, a pool, decorative Spanish tile, and wrought iron, sat on two acres of prime oceanfront property.

Each winter Rose spent several weeks there with her family. When she returned to New York, Joe used the house as a refuge for himself and golfing buddies or business associates. Caring for children on the train to and from Florida presented logistical challenges. "Coming down in February, there were a lot of drafts in the trains, in the corners, and we would stuff [the openings] with towels and with papers. . . . And then we would have special milk for the baby, and we would have to feed the baby, and we would have to keep the milk hot, and we would have to keep something else cold, and we would have to have woolen nightgowns for the train, and books to read and games to play, and cough medicine and toothpaste and all those things."[61] Once more Rose had to manage the family "department" while Joe enjoyed another sunny venue.

The family continued summering at Cape Cod's Hyannis Port. Evoking *You Can't Take It with You*, the 1938 movie about a lively, eccentric family whose household is in constant motion and chaos, Teddy described the Kennedys in Hyannis: "[B]edlam would be pouring through the windows. . . . We would hear their raucous, contending voices and laughter, high-spirited insults and their tramping on the stairs, as telephones rang, dogs barked, radios blared, and some passing virtuoso banged out a few notes on the living room piano en route to somewhere else."[62]

The tumult literally drove Rose from her home. She ordered a small prefabricated cottage for the beach. "I had my bathing suit and my books down there, and the telephone ringing and the children were playing up . . . [at the main house]. I would just go down there to get away from the confusion, where I would[n't] hear any of that, and read my books or read my mail. And maybe put on my bathing suit and go in swimming, and take a rest afterwards." The refuge had a little desk and porch, where Rose could sit and enjoy the ocean view. She loved and craved the solitude "[b]ecause all my life I have had a great many people around me. With the children and . . . the household staff. And we had these big storms, which came up and washed away the first [cottage]. And it washed away the second one. And there were only two as I remember. Then I started going to Europe, and I didn't need it. . . ." Even the famed Kennedy touch-football games on the broad Hyannis lawn frazzled her nerves. She understood college football from attending Harvard games, but "whatever this game was, I didn't [understand]. Except it was noisy, so I'd go to my little house and try to rest."[63]

Explaining his mother's more definitive escape, Teddy wrote, "She became a familiar figure in international ports of call: after seventeen years of birthing and nurturing her nine children, Rose Kennedy in her forties resumed her girlhood penchant for travel, making several trips to Europe and to her beloved Paris in particular. Dad would arrange to be at home with us when Mother was rekindling her love of European art, languages, and cities."[64] Rose reportedly took seventeen trips to Europe in the mid-1930s.[65]

Before fame or public imagery intruded, the children wrote frank letters to absent Rose revealing how much they missed her. Nine-year-old Kathleen told her that she had brought home "puppet Snowwhite for you to see," but Rose had already left. Kick assured her that the puppet "was very cutely dressed. You will see her when you come home."[66] Perhaps because of her frail constitution, similar to Jack's, Eunice was the most heartsick during Rose's absences. At age seven Eunice printed, "I am sorry that you are away. I hope you will be home soon. I am getting along better at school. I am sorry that you will not be [here] to see the puppet show."[67] With Rose in Boston for Teddy's birth, Eunice, then ten, wrote, "I miss you verry [sic] much and wish you were home. I am nearly all better now and know [sic] body else has been sick." A few weeks later, she followed up woefully, "I miss you a[n] awful lot. . . ." "I love you lots and lots," Eunice concluded, underlining "love you" four times.[68] Eight-year-old Bobby seemed to take his mother's absence in stride, reporting that "Daddy took us to lunch at the Plaza. Then we saw 'Peck's Bad Boy.' . . ." He closed with "[m]uch love and kisses" for his globe-trotting mother.[69]

Rose chose to spend her twentieth wedding anniversary away from Joe and the family, sailing for France one week before the date. She and Joe took contrasting approaches to their anniversary. From the Ritz, Rose cabled, "Thank you. Twenty years rare happiness. All my love always, Rosa." Her economy of words may have reflected a worry about Western Union's charges.[70] Or maybe Joe's nearly two decades of infidelity diluted her devotion. Joe's felicitations to Rose were warmer and perhaps contained a veiled reference to the pain he had caused. "Darling: This is your twentieth anniversary. I cannot tell you how happy these years have been for me and what a marvelous person you have been through it all. The thing that makes this so true is proven by the fact that I love you more now than ever. . . . I wish I were with you in Paris today to celebrate our universary [sic?]. Love from all, Joe." Was the last sentence's final word a typo or a clever construction on Joe's part to describe their union? The word "person" seems so bland a term to label his spouse of two decades. Hadn't Rose been a "marvelous" wife or mother or soulmate? Like so much Kennedy correspondence, Joe's telegram updated Rose on the children's health. Thirteen-year-old Eunice, who often experienced stomach upsets, had gained 1 ½ pounds. Jack's worrisome low blood count had returned to normal and his eyes had strengthened. Rosemary "raised Cain" the first week in her new surroundings in Boston, where Joe had sent her to study with a tutor, but she had calmed down considerably.[71]

Joe had assumed primary responsibility for Rosemary's education and medical treatment, although he intended to discuss his findings with Rose when she returned from Europe. He began consulting endocrinologists about the possibility that a "gland situation" contributed to fourteen-year-old Rosemary's "backwardness." As we have seen, the Kennedys always urged their children to give maximum effort in studies and sports. Joe felt conflicted in trying to determine how much of Rosemary's problem might result from "her inherent backwardness" and how much "from her attitude." He visited her in Boston and "had a firm talk," telling "her that something must be done. . . ."[72] With her tutor's help, the teenager wrote a poignant letter to him after their visit in clear but childlike block script. "I would do anything to make you so happy. I hate to Disapoint [*sic*] you in anyway. Come to see me very soon. I get very lonesome everyday. . . . lots of love kisses, Your loving Daughter, Rosemary."[73]

As she traveled, Rose wrote tender letters to Rosemary. The determined mother, who had tried so hard to help her "slow" child achieve her potential, wrote in simple language: "We are here at a place called Cannes where people come in the summertime for bathing, and they also come here in the winter time like we go to Palm Beach. . . . We are leaving tomorrow and are going to Rome, where I expect to see the Pope. I shall ask him to pray for all of us. Much love from me my darling daughter, Mother." Rose encircled her signature with little x's to represent kisses to the daughter she struggled to make whole. Always the geography teacher, Rose added, "Find Rome on your map."[74]

WITH BUSINESS OPPORTUNITIES scarce during the Depression, Joe searched for new challenges. Deciding to support Democratic New York governor Franklin D. Roosevelt in his 1932 presidential campaign, Kennedy raised nearly $300,000 in donations and loans. He contributed $25,000 and loaned an additional $50,000. His funding earned Joe a spot on FDR's transcontinental campaign train. Kennedy attracted supporters from the movie industry, assisted with campaign speeches, and linked FDR's camp to the press corps. When Roosevelt defeated incumbent President Herbert Hoover, Joe sponsored a celebration for the president-elect's family and friends.[75] He hoped that President Roosevelt would offer him a government position. Joe coveted the treasury secretary position, but FDR awarded it to two other candidates in succession. Joe bided his time. Now Rose "had to learn who the people were in Washington."[76]

Meanwhile, having graduated from Choate, Joe Jr. set sail for

England to study with London School of Economics professor Harold Laski, a noted British socialist, who invited him on a trip to the Soviet Union. Rose wanted Joe and Jack to attend Oxford or Cambridge for a year after their prep-school graduations. Her husband thought they should learn about socialism and communism so that they would understand the challenges to capitalism in an uncertain, depression-ravaged world. Yet why not attend "Oxbridge"? Joe consulted his friend, Harvard Law professor and New Deal advocate Felix Frankfurter, who had an Oxford visiting professorship. Perhaps the Kennedy boys didn't make the grade for Oxford. In any case, Oxford and Cambridge didn't accept Americans for one-year courses.

In spring 1934 President Roosevelt invited Rose and Joe to stay with him. Rose proudly wrote letters to her children on White House stationery. To Eunice, in Palm Beach with the Moores, she reported that FDR, Joe, and the president's son Jimmy would attend the Gridiron Dinner that night, while she dined with Jimmy's wife and sister. Rose vowed to ask the president for an autographed photo "for us to have at home."[77]

Jack responded from Choate, "P.S. Got your White House letter. It must have been swell." His note focused on his weight loss and exam grades, which were passing, if not with "flying colors."[78] Rose continued to worry about his health and, in particular, his fallen arches, which she believed were "inherited" but worsened by Jack's choice of flimsy shoes. Writing again to Mrs. St. John, Rose alerted the headmaster's wife to Jack's foot condition and hoped that more supportive footwear would solve the problem.[79] Rose Kennedy was a "helicopter parent" long before the twenty-first-century term came to describe hovering mothers. Her letters about Jack echo the theme: he possessed certain weaknesses—physical or intellectual—that he aggravated by his own lack of responsible behavior, always a serious offense in his mother's ledger.

THREE MONTHS AFTER the Kennedys' White House visit, FDR appointed Joe chairman of the new Securities and Exchange Commission. What better person to rein in Wall Street's excesses than the very man who had skillfully maneuvered through them prior to the crash? The media launched the Kennedy family's public image with an International News Photography Service picture that appeared in newspapers, including the *New York American*, on July 9, 1934. With Joe Jr. still abroad, eight of the Kennedy children lined up in birth order. Two-year-old Teddy, in his Buster Brown haircut, stood at one end, and seventeen-year-old Jack, in a white double-breasted blazer, posed at the other, next to his mother and father. In a stairstep row, the Kennedy children produced a compelling image over the photo caption, "A New Deal Family." Three days later Hal Phyfe, photographer of stage and screen stars, sent the clipping to Rose, asking if he could photograph her family. He offered to construct bleachers, and even move to a roomier studio, to accommodate the large family in a pose "so that everybody's best camera angle" could be achieved—an improvement on the newspaper's less artistic lineup.[80] Rose accepted his offer, hiring him to create a classic portrait of her and her family at Hyannis. With his eight fashion and makeup tips for women to be photographed, he was the perfect match for Rose to enter her new public life.

Joe left Bronxville for Washington, moving to a 125-acre Maryland estate. It included a luxurious mansion, with a hundred-seat movie theater and a huge pool, where Joe entertained FDR, his Brain Trusters, and the president's secretaries/mistresses. Rose maintained that she didn't move to DC in order to avoid uprooting the children from their schools, orthodontists, and doctors.[81]

Meanwhile, Jack, noted for his leadership of student shenanigans but named "most likely to succeed," graduated from Choate in 1935. He hoped to copy Joe Jr.'s experience and study under Professor Laski at the London School of Economics. Rose and Joe Sr., who had resigned from the SEC after getting the commission under way, accompanied Jack and fifteen-year-old Kick abroad in late September. They dropped JFK in London and Kick at a Sacred Heart convent near Paris. (Rose worried that her attractive daughter was too interested in boys and initially sent her to a Sacred Heart girls boarding school in Connecticut.) Suffering once more from undiagnosed ailments, Jack returned home, after only a brief stay in

London, and enrolled at Princeton for the fall term of 1935. There he joined his prep-school buddy Lem Billings and began to chart a different course from Joe Jr. at Harvard. But ill health again intervened and landed Jack in Boston's Peter Bent Brigham Hospital, forcing him to withdraw from Princeton midway through his first semester. He wrote his parents that his blood count was less than half of brother Joe's. Yet he maintained his humor, noting that his hale and hearty older sibling, now on the Crimson football team, must be "twice as healthy."[82]

After two months' hospitalization, still with no definitive diagnosis, in the spring of 1936 Jack headed to Arizona for a dryer, warmer climate. In later years Rose was vague about this period of his life. She had cared so much about her young children's health, but once they matured and, in Jack's and Rosemary's cases, problems became more serious, Rose relinquished matters to her husband, much as she washed her hands of his business and extramarital affairs.[83] She simply let Joe coordinate Jack's and Rosemary's medical care and education. Although Rose's domestic "department" was shrinking, she soon undertook another role. When she and Joe returned to the States in fall 1935, Rose visited Boston and began the next phase of her life. Delivering a lecture about England and France to the Ace of Clubs, she marked the start of her public-speaking career about her travels.

Rose spoke admiringly of Winston Churchill, whom she and Joe had visited at his country estate, Chartwell. Not realizing the public service that still lay ahead of him, she wrote of the future prime minister, "[He is] almost seventy—a pleasant, talkative, country gentleman, probably the most versatile whom I have ever met."[84] She delighted in telling the Ace of Clubs that Churchill, in addition to being a statesman, politician, and writer, "feels that every man should use his hands and so for a pastime has laid many of the bricks in the wall surrounding his estate. He also has a small studio filled with his paintings and that day was working on a bowl of flowers."[85]

Keeping the lecture light, Rose added her impressions of Hollywood celebrities she encountered on the 1935 trip. She found Elsa

Maxwell "vibrant," Barbara Hutton "attractive," and Merle Oberon "pleasant, unspoiled." Charles Boyer didn't fare so well: He "was a great disappointment in his looks and should never make personal appearances." Rose's characteristic discretion quickly returned, however, when she described his wife, Scottish actress Pat Paterson, as "very petite" and "perfectly adorable, as the debs would say."[86] Like many American travelers to Europe, Rose complained about England's lack of central heat, France's dearth of "excellent milk," and the unreliability of foreign elevators. "And so, though it was immensely stimulating to visit foreign shores," Rose concluded, "still I am tremendously thankful that my little family and I are living in the United States."[87]

Yet she sailed again for Europe in April 1936 to rendezvous with Kathleen. While her sons gravitated toward Joe's supervision, Rose continued monitoring the education and travels of Kathleen and the younger girls. The era, however, and Rose's own conservative background limited her aspirations for them, at least in contrast to her hopes for the boys. "[W]hen my daughter [Kick] went abroad to school, . . . none of the girls whom she met had thought of going to college [or] had any associations with the girls who were in college. They expected to come out at the age of eighteen with a big party and travel, perhaps spend a year in France to familiarize themselves with the French language and then get married."[88]

Rose, however, could expand her and her daughters' horizons through travel beyond France. During Kick's year abroad, Rose planned a trip to "the Soviet," as she called the USSR. It was a courageous adventure for two refined Irish Catholic ladies. "Poor little Kathleen didn't know why we wanted to go to the Soviet because everybody was so shocked that two women were going alone to the Soviet . . . , and she finally said to me, 'But Mother, why are we going to Russia.' I said, 'We've been in Italy, been in Spain, now we are going to try [Russia].'" Joe Jr.'s trip to the USSR with Professor Laski the previous year had piqued Rose's curiosity. She breezily termed it a "marvelous country" with a "new political philosophy." Her husband thought traveling beyond the capital and Leningrad would be too difficult for women, but he knew US

Ambassador William C. Bullitt in Moscow and made arrangements for Rose and Kick to stay at the comfortable US embassy.[89]

They visited art museums, attended the theater and ballet, viewed Lenin's tomb, and saw the czars' palace, where Rose noted the icons of Russian Orthodox saints. Her understanding of the Soviet regime lacked nuance. She inaccurately assumed that "[b]allet artists are left alone to follow their professions and are not molested by political ideologies." Typical of her tendency to focus on fashion and propriety, she wrote about the Moscow ballet, "Of course, no one was suitably dressed for a ballet. The men were in shirts with no ties, and I was the only woman who wore a hat."[90]

Rose demanded that her Soviet guide take her to a Catholic church. There she discovered that the priest said Mass on Sunday evening because the Sabbath was not a day of rest. All of the congregants were very old or very young. "If working people went to Mass, they were apt to be demoted in the factory or some of their privileges taken away," she learned. Rose concluded that the Soviets had "great enthusiasm for the new regime as giving people opportunities never enjoyed under the Czars, but life provided far, far below the material comforts and luxuries and opportunities given in our country every day. . . ."[91] Despite seeing Soviet spies trailing their every move, Rose recalled the trip as enjoyable and "a very enlightening experience, as future events proved."[92]

Rose tried to keep up with headlines by, like her father, compulsively snipping newspaper articles. She meticulously preserved them in her "Black Book," along with information about "men, music, art people," as well as "quotations and definitions" she wanted to learn. For composing speeches, she consulted this vast archive of information. She always carried it with her while traveling so that she could refer to it while killing time. Self-improvement, discipline, responsibility: these were Rose's guiding principles— along with her religion. Although like many of her coreligionists she rarely read the Bible, Rose frequently studied modern Catholic treatises to renew her faith.[93]

Teddy credited his mother with bestowing "the gift of faith as the foundation of my life. It is the core factor in my understanding

of who I am. My own center of belief, as I matured and grew curi-
ous about these things, moved toward the great Gospel of Matthew,
chapter 25 especially, in which he calls us to care for the least of
these among us, and feed the hungry, clothe the naked, give drink
to the thirsty, welcome the stranger, visit the imprisoned."[94]

His sister Eunice listed Boston and religion, in that order, as the
two most potent influences on Rose's character. "We'd all have to
keep First Fridays, for example. . . . [W]hen [Jack] was president he
would say his prayers morning and . . . night. Now that doesn't
mean he was terribly religious . . . but the point is that [Rose's]
influence on saying prayers and doing sort of religious rituals [was]
so strong in her and she was successful in getting it in her children. . . . Jack was, he was always a little less convinced, but [Lem]
Billings can tell you, on trips and everything he went to Cathedrals
and used to go to mass on Sundays. . . . I lived with him a long
time while he was a congressman in Washington, and he always
hustled off to mass. . . . Bobby . . . was very really quite religious.
He was at Communion Sundays all the time."[95]

Rose conveyed her profound religiosity to her children by placing a rosary on each of their beds, hearing their prayers, and testing
their knowledge of the Catholic catechism. When fourteen-year-
old Pat suffered a severe post-appendectomy infection, Rose prayed
over her, holding a crucifix and telling her sick daughter, "Remember how Christ suffered and died on the cross."[96] Rose intended to
comfort her ill child, who had to endure a second abdominal surgery, by encouraging her to "offer up" her pain as a prayer for healing, a common practice among traditional Catholics.

To reinvigorate her faith, Rose also made annual religious
retreats. "I do think they are a very good practice because they
review your past actions and your past resolutions. They give them
new life and new fervor. . . . And then if you have any questions,
it's a good time to resolve them because it's a trained priest, philos-
opher there, [a] priest who is able to answer them," she explained.
"And if you are floundering, why you read these notes again. You
read these observations, and then you gain new strength, new
understanding, courage to go on."[97] With her staunch commitment

to Catholicism and self-discipline, Rose rarely admitted to "floundering" about anything, least of all, her religious faith. But the
many tragedies that befell her family provided numerous reasons to
question God and his priestly representatives.

Her husband's infidelity might have been an additional factor in
Rose's search for theological guidance. At a retreat or anonymously
in the confessional, if she had spoken to clerics about her husband's
philandering, they would have preached that she must make her
union with Joe successful, defined as having offspring and raising
them to become devout Catholics. Though Rose thought she was
old, almost forty-two, when Teddy was born, she was still a decade
short of menopause. Her numerous trips to Europe, often without
Joe, along with choosing to let him move to Maryland and take his
vacations without her, could have been her method of contraception in the final years of her fertility. About this time, the Catholic
Church began advocating the natural rhythm method of birth
control, but even when used fastidiously, it has a failure rate of 25
percent.[98] According to some authors, when at home, Rose insisted
on abstinence.[99]

Eunice, however, asserted that her mother, unlike Eleanor Roosevelt, maintained both "a very independent personality" *and* a
"marital relationship."[100] Nevertheless, Joe Kennedy resigned himself to the fact that he and Rose would have no more children. At
Christmas 1937, he wrote to a former Kennedy nanny, "Teddy is
growing big now and I am afraid that he has got out of the baby class
and I will have to look forward to grand-children to fill the void."[101]

BY 1936 BOTH Joe Jr. and Jack were attending their father's alma
mater, Harvard. (After his restorative stay in Arizona, Jack did not
return to Princeton.) Every Sunday they lunched with Honey Fitz
at the Bellevue Hotel, across the river from Cambridge. He regaled
them with stories of Boston politics and history, as well as tales of
his campaigns and Washington career. According to Rose, they
would laugh at and with him, enjoying visits with their colorful
grandfather.[102] "I guess some of his stories were a little risqué—they

told me since! But, of course, they wouldn't tell me that then, nor would he—it would have shocked me," she confessed.[103]

Rose's Victorian, indeed puritanical, nature developed a scheme that she convinced Joe to apply to their children. She wanted them to abjure smoking and drinking until age twenty-one, when, if they had succeeded, their father would reward them with a thousand dollars. She borrowed the idea from the Rockefellers. According to Rose, she and Joe drank milk at home to set a wholesome example, and she tried to instill discipline in her older children so the younger ones would imitate them. "[S]ometimes they'd think I was old-fashioned," Rose admitted. "I knew when I had problems what a great help my husband was as they grew older and as they had problems, which I couldn't really cope with. . . . I think, of course, boys are probably more difficult than girls at a certain age—teenagers probably."[104] She told journalist Robert MacNeil that they weren't always "angels."[105] In fact, she developed a protocol for dealing with unpleasant news from them. "[I]f the boys were going to tell their father anything that was difficult, I'd always say, 'Well, wait until the morning. . . .'"[106] She reasoned that nothing could be done at night about a "difficult" situation, and the news would only lead to unnecessary sleeplessness.

Just as Rose began to kick off the traces of motherhood in the mid-1930s, another family tragedy befell her, eventually bringing more responsibilities. Her sister, Agnes, Rose's stalwart convent roommate and loyal travel companion, died suddenly in 1936, at age forty-three, from an embolism. She had married Joseph Gargan in 1929 and given birth to three children, all under age six when their mother passed away. Though disconsolate, Rose tried to be attentive to her two nieces and a nephew two years Teddy's senior. She took on even more supervision of them and their education when their father died eight years later.

JOE SPENT CONSIDERABLE time, energy, and money working for FDR's 1936 reelection. After the president's landslide victory, Roosevelt hosted Eugenio Cardinal Pacelli, the Vatican's secretary of

state, at Hyde Park. Joe and Rose accompanied Pacelli by private
railcar to the president's Hudson River estate. Afterward, Pacelli
stopped in Bronxville for tea at the Kennedy home. Glowing with
pride, Rose watched four-year-old Teddy climb up on the prelate's
lap and examine his gold cross.[107] She preserved the couch where
they sat and placed a commemorative plaque on it when Pacelli
became Pope Pius XII in 1939.[108]

Shortly after his second inauguration, attended by the Kennedy
children, Roosevelt again asked Joe to join the administration, as
head of another new regulatory body, the United States Maritime
Commission. Kennedy's experience managing the Fore River shipyard during World War I served him well. Rose was proud of Joe's
high-ranking position among Catholics in the administration, yet
she knew that he coveted a more exalted job. She grew impatient
with FDR's hesitance to elevate Joe and hectored her husband about
when the president might issue the desired offer. She pointed out
that Joe had left his family numerous times to serve the chief executive and deserved a reward.[109] As 1937 drew to a close, FDR finally
issued a plum offer, the ambassadorship to the Court of St. James's.
Joe Kennedy would become the first Irish American to serve as the
United States representative to Great Britain. And Rose, the Boston colleen and daughter of Honey Fitz, would soon launch her
public career as the matriarch of a political dynasty.

❧

CHAPTER 5

Mater Admirabilis

"THE KENNEDY FAMILY: NINE CHILDREN AND NINE MILLION Dollars," *Life* proclaimed in December 1937. President Roosevelt had just named Joe as US ambassador to Great Britain, and the media loved it. Splashed across oversized pages, the Kennedy photo portrayed Joe, Rose, and nine offspring posed around their Bronx-ville hearth.[1]

"Big, rich, good-looking families always beguiled *Life*'s attention back in 1937 when the magazine was only a year old," explained editor Philip B. Kunhardt Jr.

The variety of their [the Kennedys'] activities and their sump-tuous settings and life-styles were ideal for pictures. In addition, the Kennedy children had a shrewd, outspoken father who wielded enormous power in financial circles, had a glamorous background in Hollywood filmmaking. . . . And there was mother Rose, the lovely daughter of a storied mayor of Boston— stylish, reverent, eloquent in her own cool way—the ideal mother. The four sons seemed dashing and athletic. The five daughters pretty and competitive. The settings were usually

Palm Beach or Cape Cod. Politics was on the horizon. How could a fledgling magazine ask for more![2]

In 1986, Teddy Kennedy pronounced *Life* "the scrapbook for our family."[3]

Joe wrote Christmas 1937 greetings to the Kennedys' former nanny: "I am delighted that you liked the picture and I think the one in *Life* was very cute. Of course, I am getting a bit fed up with hearing that my wife looks so very young, because to really understand that it means that I look like her father and that is a terrible state of affairs after all these years of struggling to keep my youthful figure, so I am going right back to chocolate ice cream and plenty of chocolate cake," he teased.[4]

The *Boston Post* caught Kennedy fever as well. One tabloid-style headline touted "The Real Story of Joseph P. Kennedy's Romance." Another described "Why He Turned His Sweetheart's Picture to the Wall" when Rose's father declared that he was seeing too much of his daughter. A third headline proclaimed, "And He Married His Childhood Sweetheart, Beautiful Rose Fitzgerald." Mrs. Kennedy appeared as "Slim, Girlish Looking at 47." Rose loved that caption. Yet the *Post* couldn't help poking fun at the Kennedy clan and its newfound prominence. One cartoon portrayed Joe bowing with Rose before the enthroned King George VI and Queen Elizabeth. The new ambassador looks a mite self-conscious in his knee britches (which in reality he refused to wear), but Rose ("Mrs. Joe," as the cartoon labels her) smiles like the poised public celebrity she had been most of her life. Behind them stand caricatures of "9 Little Kennedys," a riff on the popular children's book *Five Little Peppers and How They Grew*. Attempting to join the spectacle is pint-sized Honey Fitz, singing "Sweet Adeline."[5]

At the White House on February 18, 1938, Supreme Court justice Stanley Reed swore Joe in as ambassador to Great Britain. Smiling broadly, FDR shook Kennedy's hand; undoubtedly, the president relished the irony of appointing the first Irish Catholic, only two generations removed from Ireland's peat bogs, to represent the United States before the British. By doing so, Roosevelt was also sending to England a potential rival for the White House, should FDR try for an unprecedented third presidential term in 1940. The voluble new envoy, although at the pinnacle of his career, seemed uncharacteristically subdued in accepting the president's felicitations.

Recovering from an emergency appendectomy, Rose missed the ceremony as well as Joe's departure for England. She recuperated at Palm Beach, with nurse Luella Hennessey, who had cared for Pat when she had appendicitis and for Bobby when he had pneumonia the previous summer. Eight of the nine Kennedy children bid their now-famous father farewell at the pier. Suffering from a cold, Jack skipped the rain-dampened departure.[6]

By March Rose was well enough to ready five of her nine children for the voyage to join their father. Ambassador Kennedy joked with the press that such a large family would have to come across the Atlantic in installments, lest they cause a UK housing shortage. Joe Jr. and Jack stayed behind at Harvard. Attending convent schools in New York and Connecticut, Rosemary and Eunice would make the Atlantic crossing five weeks later. Eunice, though only sixteen, was adept at supervising her older sister. Sending Rosemary apart from the rest of the family also ensured that she would receive less media attention.

The night before Rose and five of her children set sail, the *New York Sun* featured the Kennedy matriarch and her family, using *Life* magazine's photo of the clan accompanied by a full-length portrait of stylish Mrs. Kennedy outside her Palm Beach home. This coverage of Rose launched many of the family's iconic images. Described as "an Irish beauty," whose petite figure and youthfulness belied her mother-of-nine status, Rose asserted, "In the case of such a large family as mine it is necessary to have absolute regularity and cooperation. The children are taught that they must be on time for meals, always help one another, be courteous and considerate of servants, and own up to any of their small faults, telling the truth no matter what the penalty." The article portrayed the children as accomplished swimmers and tennis players (on the Bronxville estate's grass court). Rose discussed her devotion to golf: "it does give me a chance to get away for a little time from the house and the children." Noting her knowledge of French and German from her days at Blumenthal, the paper cited Mrs. Kennedy's love of travel. The article described the Bronxville home as a center for music, with its grand piano in the drawing room, and reading, from the shelves of books in the sunroom.[7] "What a charming family!" inscribed the Associated Press's Mary Elizabeth Plummer on a clipping of the article that Rose kept in her diary.[8] Having climbed the ladder from Famine Irish to Lace Curtain Irish in parochial Boston, the Kennedys and Fitzgeralds had achieved money, power, and celebrity in New York. They would soon conquer the international scene in London.

Journalists surrounded Rose, Teddy, Jean, Bobby, Pat, and Kathleen, dressed in their Sunday best, on the deck of the USS *Washington*. Poised yet charmingly boyish, twelve-year-old Bobby stepped to the newsreel microphones, encouraged by his mother: "This is my first trip to Europe. I was so excited, I couldn't even sleep laaast night!" he exclaimed in his Boston accent. Around the world flashed the AP wire photo of the six voyagers.[9] Elizabeth Dunn, the children's governess, had signed on for duty in England, and Joe had persuaded Nurse Hennessey to accompany them "for a while to help out until we get settled."[10] (Hennessey stayed with the family for their entire tenure in England and for years after they returned.) Rose was transformed, from a mother obsessed with her children's health, once observing that she dared not leave them, to an eager player on the public stage of her husband's ambassadorship.

After six days of braving stormy seas, the ship made landfall in Cobh, Ireland. "Kathleen and [the] other children were besieged in the dining salon by a lot of reporters inquiring about her rumored engagement [to Peter Grace, of the Grace Steamship Company]," wrote Rose in her diary. For the next decade Kick's love life would prove an endless source of news fodder. Rose earnestly began her attempts at stage management in the world arena, which meant redoubling her legendary self-control, as well as her attempts to supervise the family's public image. The media gaggle insisted on photographs, "which it seems we must allow them to do—otherwise, they become very disagreeable and extremely annoying and take pictures in unconventional poses. They inquired about my Irish ancestry, about the number of the children—their whereabouts. . . ."[11] "Kathleen was [a] debutante at the time, and everyone was interested that she was going to marry" into the Grace family. "[She was] quite attractive. And every place that we would stop I would get questioned by people trying to find out about her romance or whether she was really hav[ing] a romance with Peter Grace [one of Kick's many beaux]. . . ," recalled Rose.[12]

Appropriately, on St. Patrick's Day this Kennedy contingent disembarked in Plymouth, on the Devon coast, about 190 miles southwest of London. "Jolly Joe," as the British had dubbed the American ambassador, bounded onto the ship to greet his children and Rose, swathed in her fur coat. Arriving in London, they proceeded directly to the embassy at 14 Princes Gate, near Kensington Gardens and Hyde Park. The seven Kennedys now in London marched arm in arm into the embassy's private garden. A scrum of some twenty photographers snapped away at Britain's newest media sensation. Six-year-old Teddy, in short pants and knee socks, looked particularly adorable. Rose's seventeen years of giving birth and nurturing nine children now reaped dividends. Simply having so many babies, yet appearing youthful and svelte, made Mrs. Joseph P. Kennedy an instant celebrity. "Joe and Rose Plus Nine" would be their reality TV show in the twenty-first century.

"When they arrived [in 1938] it caused a sensation in London," Deborah ("Debo") Mitford, the Dowager Duchess of Devonshire, declared decades later, "because no diplomat had ever arrived with nine children attached. And the chief thing that amazed [the British] was Rose—not any of the others—because she had such a marvelous figure. And she was so smartly dressed that all of the people of her age and anybody who had anything like nine children were incredibly jealous of her because she just looked so wonderful!"[13]

Comparing the family to Canada's celebrated Dionne quintuplets, *Life* covered the Kennedy invasion of Britain. Yet, the magazine proclaimed, "There are only five Dionne Quints and the

Kennedy kids are nine. . . ." It named Joe and Rose's brood "the most politically ingratiating family since Theodore Roosevelt's."[14] Rose later calculated her family's appeal: "One advantage our family had was there were plenty of us to photograph and that, I was told, was an asset. People are attracted by a group much more than by a single child, or even by two people. Also, it seems girls or women are more of an attraction than men and we had plenty of femininity too. Teddy was so young and unselfconscious that he would pose any time, but he alone was not enough, two or three girls must be along."[15]

If Joe reached the pinnacle of his short political career as US ambassador to Britain, Rose's experience created a bridge in her long public life—from the young daughter of Boston's mayor to a political matriarch. No longer was she simply a well-traveled Boston debutante. She had become a celebrated spouse on an international and historic stage. Honing her social skills in courtly prewar London, Rose's experiences would form the core of her initial campaign speeches for John F. Kennedy during his first forays into the political arena.

Until World War II's onset, Rose kept a meticulous daily diary that reflected the essence of her personality. No superficial detail eluded her observation. No notable persons—heads of state and government, lords and ladies, dukes and duchesses, ambassadors and their wives, star athletes, Hollywood stars—escaped her all-seeing eye. She noted clothing, hairstyle, makeup, facial characteristics, hair color (or lack of locks in the case of men), height, weight, posture, demeanor, accent, religion, and intellect. Her thoughts on places visited amount to a travel guide. Accounts of meals she supervised or attended list each course, sometimes the menus themselves, and occasionally the prices.

Rose also recorded her practical concerns about teeth, weight, and health. Was her family's milk pasteurized? Were the children too heavy or too thin? What about dental hygiene, never a priority in England? To her 1938–39 diary Rose attached society columns, news stories, and features. Craving the public spotlight, she especially enjoyed preserving press photos of herself at Epsom Downs and Winchester Cathedral or representing Americans in London at July 4 and Memorial Day commemorations.

Her new, fairy-tale life couldn't have been more spectacular and memorable. Only a day after reaching London, Rose rode to Buckingham Palace for her presentation to Queen Elizabeth, King George VI's charming and gracious wife. Rose curtsied and Joe bowed before the queen, who radiated a "happy natural smile."[16] Rose admired the queen's porcelain complexion, which "never came through in photographs." Indeed, newspaper portraits of Rose (as captured by Phyfe) and the queen reveal Mrs. Kennedy as the more attractive woman.[17]

As Rose and Joe embraced their diplomatic duties, their children began a whirlwind of London tours. Bobby, Jean, and Teddy eagerly photographed the changing of the guard at Buckingham Palace and listened intently as a kindly Beefeater explained the Tower of London's colorful history. Rose quickly enrolled Bobby and Teddy in a London day school, Gibbs, in nearby Kensington, and sent Eunice (once she and Rosemary joined the family in late April), Pat, and Jean to board at a Sacred Heart convent in Roehampton. Rosemary settled in with Assumption nuns and thrived under the tutelage of Mother Isabel.

The European fashion scene drew Rose's attention. Her annual trips to the Parisian couture houses, starting in the 1920s, gave her a head start on the latest styles. A compulsive shopper, she reportedly once told a Boston store clerk that she annually purchased two hundred suits and dresses.[18] Elsa Schiaparelli offered Rose discounts, but her clothes were "severe—plain—almost exaggeratedly so; they are not feminine enough for me," said Mrs. Kennedy. Schiaparelli's avant-garde creations, influenced by Salvador Dalí, violated Rose's utilitarian tastes. She described Schiaparelli's 1938 "circus" collection, with elephants, horses, and clowns on the clothing, as "fantastically embroidered" and rejected it for evening wear. Instead, her favorite designer was Britain's Edward Molyneux in Paris; his creations were "conservative, smart, supple, easy to wear."[19] That they were ubiquitous in London didn't stop her from purchasing one of his white lace gowns, trimmed in silver and gold beads, for the presentation of Rosemary and Kathleen to the king and queen at Buckingham Palace that May.

Luncheons, cocktail parties, and teas with British aristocracy abounded. Little did Rose know how tea-party etiquette would create a paradigm for her political work on behalf of her sons. She recorded that British socialites "looked conservative, little make-up, hardly any lipstick. All very cordial." They reminded her "of the Boston B[ack] Bay society." This was no compliment from Irish Catholic Rose, whom the Boston Brahmins had shunned. She later wrote that British people "do not look as well as in the U.S.A. Figures of older women are not as good and their clothes look dowdy not smart." And their teeth were bad, the ultimate hygienic sin for Rose.[20]

Mrs. Kennedy also expanded her political horizons. She met the editor of the *Catholic Herald* and discussed the ongoing Spanish Civil War. He "feels [the] only way to fight Communism is for Catholics to take some action to improve workers' condition rather than ignoring it as has been the attitude of the Church often in the past."[21]

A mere three weeks had passed before Joe and Rose were driven to Windsor Castle for a weekend with King George and Queen Elizabeth. The trip took less than an hour, but it represented a journey back through centuries of British history for the enthralled Kennedys. Arriving at 7 p.m. sharp, they were met by the "master of the household," a former army general, who clearly approved of their punctuality. Escorted to elaborate bedrooms in the castle's Lancaster Tower, they sipped sherry prior to dinner. Forever after, Rose loved to quote her husband's pithy summary of the royal scene: "Rose, this is a helluva long way from East Boston." In the reception room the Kennedys chatted with Prime Minister Neville Chamberlain and his wife, and at dinner Ambassador Kennedy sat next to the queen, while Rose took her place beside the king. What does one say to a king? Rose chose the subject she knew best and one that stirred no controversy: her children. When the gentlemen excused themselves for an after-dinner chat with the king, the ladies conversed with his wife, the former Lady Elizabeth Bowes-Lyon, mother of the future Queen Elizabeth II. "I must be dreaming that I, Rose Kennedy, a simple young matron from Boston, am really here at Windsor Castle, the guest of the queen and two little princesses," she thought to herself later that night.[22]

Beginning with her 1934 stay at the White House, Rose loved writing to her family and friends from historic homes. She reported to daughter Pat from the royal castle in Windsor, "We have just spent the most delightful day here after a very brilliant dinner party last night. I sat on the right of the King, and I was so thrilled. We shall be returning in the morning. Much love, Mother." Thinking ahead for history and posterity, Rose added, "Pat—Please keep this note, dear."[23]

The next day, Palm Sunday, the Kennedys attended Mass at a nearby church, followed by lunch with the king and queen and their two princesses and a walk around Windsor's manicured grounds and gardens. When, during tea, the queen's older sister suffered a heart attack, quick-thinking Rose escorted the young Princess Elizabeth (age eleven) and Princess Margaret (age seven) outside. Joe proudly observed that the king and queen expressed gratitude to his wife, who had "established a bond" with Queen Elizabeth.[24] To a friend back in Dorchester, Rose wrote on Windsor Castle stationery that the weekend had been "very brilliant" and the royal family "charming."[25] Of the top seven events in her life, Rose would rank the "weekend at Windsor Castle" at number five.[26]

The Kennedys were also getting to know the Chamberlains, lunching with them at 10 Downing Street. To Rose, the prime minister compared favorably to her husband. Both men possessed business backgrounds, enjoyed walks with their wives, and appreciated classical music. Rose shared her thoughts with Joe, but he cautioned her not to comment on these similarities in public.[27]

ROSE HOPED TO VISIT the Roehampton convent for Pat's birthday but had to cancel her trip because of a flu outbreak. She couldn't risk illness, for in a few days she, Rosemary, and Kathleen would be presented at court. When associating with English royalty, certain proprieties had to be observed. One was to wear a tiara. Rose liked jewelry—real, "brilliant" jewelry, not "paste." Always pragmatic, she considered buying a tiara with precious jewels and then converting it to a bracelet or clip. Instead, she borrowed a "gorgeous marquise diamond" tiara but had to have it enlarged to fit comfortably on her head. Ultimately she purchased her own tiara. She loved precious stones: "The most flattering jewels are, I think, pearls and diamonds. Pearls are especially very flattering, especially when you get older. Rubies with diamonds are very effective, and they are my birthstones."[28]

As the court presentation drew closer, so did photographers. *Vogue* snapped pictures of the Kennedy ladies, and Rose obliged press requests for interviews and photographs of the younger children at tea. Questions about the upcoming court presentation were off-limits, however. In order to decrease the embassy's burden of sponsorship, Joe had just cancelled the tradition for most American debutantes. Only those living in England—seven to be exact, including the two Kennedy girls—would be presented. "To enthuse too strongly about" the presentation wouldn't be tactful.[29] Rose's premature release of the seven names several days before the event stunned Buckingham Palace, which traditionally made such announcements. She had committed her first faux pas in England.

Meanwhile, Kathleen and Rosemary practiced curtsying. From her convent days, Rose had already mastered balancing on one foot, while bending slightly at the knee, before the reverend mother. Rosemary required extra training because of her poor coordination. Each lady had to display three feathers in her hair, a symbol for the Prince of Wales, and carry flowers. Rose's innate penchant for perfection and precision obviously served her well in rule-bound British aristocracy, as did her Prussian convent background. Dresses and trains worn by ladies presented to the king and queen had to be a prescribed length so that, according to Rose,

> the person behind you would not step on your dress because the curtsies for the king and queen were [in] perfect alignment. You take three steps and you curtsy, the lady by you takes three steps and then curtsies. Therefore, if her dress was so long, she'd

have to take four steps to curtsy. It would throw out the whole procession. . . . The procession is mathematically carefully thought out. Because there's a long line of curtsies. The whole court was watching each woman as she presented each embassy, and each embassy wants to make a good show. [T]here was a rehearsal at the embassy before we were presented. . . . Nobody wants to make a mistake because there were a good many people there who keep you in line. . . .[30]

May 11 finally arrived; Rose cleared her morning to relax and have her hair styled. Then she inspected the bouquets of roses and lilies of the valley that Rosemary and Kathleen would carry. An Elizabeth Arden makeup artist arrived for the Kennedy trio. Dressed in her new Molyneux gown, Rose joined her two daughters on the embassy's windy balcony for press photographers. Fretting that gusts were mussing her decorative feathers and tulle train, she happily moved indoors. There she discovered a Movietone News crew but didn't realize that microphones were recording "even our most casual conversation." (The next day Rose was embarrassed to hear on the film's soundtrack that she was "giving orders to everyone . . . fussing at the lights, and generally [being] more or less difficult.") At the appointed hour Joe and Rose motored to the palace, acknowledging the crowds along the route who waved and smiled. Kathleen and Rosemary followed in a separate car.[31]

The *Evening Standard* commented, "Miss Rosemary Kennedy, one of the daughters of the American Ambassador, looked particularly well in her picture dress of white tulle embroidered with silver."[32] That clipping went into Rose's diary. The *New York Times*, however, noted how few American debutantes were presented by Mrs. Kennedy to the king and queen. "Ambassador [Kennedy] Limited the List So Only One [Debutante] Was Not Relative of an Official," headlined the paper.[33] Fortunately, no one reported that Rosemary had tripped after her curtsy to the queen, and Rose never publicly acknowledged her daughter's literal faux pas.[34]

The social season remained in high gear. After a weekend at historic Blenheim Palace, near Oxford, Rose moved on to Epsom

Downs and the English Derby. She particularly enjoyed meeting
Lord Derby. He sent her a handwritten letter outlining the Derby's
history and its inspiration for America's Kentucky Derby. "Of course,
he was part of the Victorian–Edwardian era of good manners and
graceful living, in which personal correspondence was regarded as
important and almost as an art form," recorded Rose. "I have often
wished our society had retained more of that feeling: So much correspondence nowadays comes off a typewriter and lacks the personal
qualities of handwriting; and, of course, there is such a great deal of
telephoning now, instead of writing, and the words spoken are lost
forever."[35] Eventually, Rose embraced telephonic communication for
keeping up with her peripatetic family, but she also became the
chronicler of its activities through round-robin letters.

In early June, for their debut, Rosemary and Kathleen welcomed
eighty "close friends" for dinner. Afterward, two hundred additional guests joined the coming-out party and danced the night
away in the embassy's second-floor ballroom. Although the celebration focused on Kick, the Kennedys insisted that Rosemary be
included. Rose admitted to apprehensions over how she would
respond to so many unfamiliar people, in new surroundings made
more chaotic by the dancing, music, and frivolity. Apparently,
Rosemary committed no social errors.

The previous day Bobby and Teddy had presided "gracefully"
over the ribbon-cutting at the new Children's Zoo in Regent's Park,
according to a London magazine society column.[36] Bobby delivered
his maiden speech. "It gives me pleasure to be here today. My
brother—he is six—and I are enjoying ourselves enormously, and I
hope all the English children who come here will do so, too." A
Ministry of Education representative responded, "I think we have
just listened to a future president of the United States."[37] At the ele-
phant enclosure, Ba-Bar reached out his trunk to snatch a peanut
from a startled Teddy, and British photographers chronicled the playful incident. Meanwhile, after attending the Ascot races, Rose made
London's *Evening Standard* society column. Although it described the
queen's dress and those of the duchesses of Kent and Gloucester and
the Princess Royal, the paper ran only one photo. "Mrs. Kennedy,

wife of the American Ambassador, wore a short-skirted printed dress and a big hat for Ascot," announced the caption.[38]

JOE SAILED BACK to the States in mid-June for conversations with President Roosevelt and the State Department on European tensions, and ostensibly to celebrate Joe Jr.'s graduation from Harvard.[39] Rose stayed behind with the other children and maintained her busy social and media life. The *Ladies' Home Journal* wanted to feature the Kennedys' upcoming fall wardrobes. "Seems like a terrific chore," confided Rose, "as I am so particular about their clothes. [The reporter] says she can borrow things from shops here [and] pin them where they do not fit." But she happily admitted that pictures of Pat, Eunice, and Jean "developed into very attractive photographs." She especially liked the images of Rosemary, "who photographs extraordinarily well."[40]

In Joe's absence, Rose's parents visited. A veteran prankster, Honey Fitz mailed mock invitations on embassy stationery to his Boston cronies, asking them to tea. "[H]e thought [this was] amusing," but Joe thought it "disgraceful." "You know, different personalities, both strong personalities," Rose commented.[41] With some annoyance in her voice, she declared to her memoirist, "[My father] was an extrovert and Joe wasn't and that was it. . . . [Honey Fitz] liked to talk about the movies and talk about people . . . and Joe didn't. Joe was in the movies and he would just tell Father that and that was it."[42] Of Rose's four boys, Teddy was most like gregarious Honey Fitz. Conversely, Rose saw herself as a loner, although, like her husband, she welcomed the spotlight of public life. For Joe, the right kind of publicity afforded influence and power during his ambassadorship. Eventually, he became more like his father, P. J. Kennedy, content to serve behind the scenes as a power broker.

Rose and her mother attended Wimbledon's 1938 tennis championship, seated in the Royal Box with Queen Mary, the king's mother. There they watched American Helen Wills Moody defeat her countrywoman Helen Jacobs, hobbled by injury, in the ladies' final. It pleased Rose enormously that the queen had known Josie

Fitzgerald would be visiting, "which makes me realize how thoroughly conversant with or (au courant) with affairs the royal family is trained to be."[43] Mrs. Kennedy was quite au courant herself, having memorized the names of British Cabinet members to keep abreast of her husband's contacts and any officials she might meet.

On July 4, when Joe, Joe Jr., and Jack arrived in England, all of the Kennedys were together once again. That night, at the American Society's banquet in the Dorchester Hotel, Joe, as the society's honorary president, delivered the keynote address. Rose discovered a photo of herself chatting with Member of Parliament Anthony Eden in the next day's *Manchester Daily Dispatch*.[44] She requested three autographs from the future prime minister—one for herself and one each for Pat and Eunice.

The Kennedys had been in London fewer than six months when *Vogue* magazine made it official: "The American Ambassador and his family have swept like a conquering horde upon London, which has lowered its defenses and admitted itself stormed." Citing Rose's "youthful beauty," as well as the "transatlantic efficiency" of the index file on her nine children, the article concluded, "And so this remarkable woman stands, and London finds her responsible for much of that rare harmony and unity which is, as it were, both the central theme and leitmotif of the Kennedys. . . ."[45] Photos of Rose, Rosemary, Kick, Bobby, and Teddy covered three pages. In one, Rose served formal tea to her offspring gathered in the embassy's Pine Room. Each child had a separate photo; Rose and her two eldest daughters were featured on the opening page. Even Rosemary appeared relaxed and happy, just as photogenic as her siblings. The time hadn't yet arrived when the family would shield her from all publicity.

Not everyone in England, however, thought so highly of the Kennedy media blitz or the nine children. To Joe an irate British subject wrote:

Sir,
I am sick to death of seeing photographs of yourself and family in the newspapers. To be the father of nine children is nothing wonderful in

*this country though it may be in the U.S. and certainly does not merit
the publicity you get for yourself.*

A. Fraser[46]

Writing to her parents, Rose complained about intrusive press
coverage of her and the children, especially when they traveled. But
she appreciated American Catholics' support. Mother Grace Cowardin Dammann, president of Manhattanville College of the Sacred
Heart, wrote that the "whole Society of [the Sacred Heart of Jesus]
is calling down blessings on your dear husband for his great charity
in helping our nuns out of Spain [during the Spanish Civil War]."
Dammann added, "I hear such lovely things about your own personal and well-deserved popularity, the splendid impression the
children are making and the great work your husband is doing. It is
a joy to know that in the midst of all this, you, dearest Rose, keep
your unspoiled simplicity and straightness with God and man."[47]
Simple might not have been quite accurate concerning Rose's new
life abroad. Yet no words could have pleased her more.

IN LATE JULY the Kennedys embarked on a Riviera vacation. Rose
and several of the children left first, while Joe stayed in London
until Parliament adjourned. According to the press, "Kathleen,
who has been one of the most popular of the season's debutantes,
will join her mother at the end of the month."[48] In fact, Kathleen
spent several days at the Eastbourne estate of the Duke and Duchess of Devonshire, parents of her new friend Billy Hartington,
whom she had met at a Buckingham Palace garden party that summer. Kick attended the annual Goodwood horse races with the
Hartington clan, and Rose filed in her diary a newspaper photo of
Kathleen walking with Billy's younger brother, Lord Andrew
Cavendish, at the racecourse.[49] Andrew's future wife, Debo Mitford, recalled Kathleen's magnetism: "[E]veryone absolutely *loved*
Kick! I think girls of eighteen are often very jealous of each other,
but nobody ever said a word about Kick that wasn't nice. It was

extraordinary, actually." Yet Mitford, destined to become Kick's sister-in-law, did not succumb to all of the Kennedys' charm. About Jack, she wrote in her 1938 diary, "Danced with Jack Kennedy. Very nice but very dull."[50]

Rose and the children settled into their rented Cap d'Antibes villa. She planned their excursions and meals, even for twenty-one-year-old Jack. She thought him too thin and returned to her old tactics of bulking him up with dairy products. A part-time secretary was tasked with finding "fresh milk and cream. It is most urgent as Jack lost weight swimming at Harvard last spring, and the doctor was insistent on his having a quart daily."[51]

The family's villa was near the famed Hôtel du Cap-Eden-Roc, where they could sunbathe on the beach, swim in the Mediterranean's crystal-clear waters, or lounge around the pool. Tennis, swimming, golf, and sightseeing by day and summer balls and parties at night kept the energetic family occupied. Rose and her children encountered Marlene Dietrich walking on the beach and asked the German actress for her autograph. To Rose, Dietrich was "gracious, animated, pleasant to meet, seems to be taking a holiday with her hair thrown to the winds and no worry about make-up. Her daughter Maria, a child of fortune, well behaved, unspoiled, under the constant surveillance of an English governess."[52]

Despite, or perhaps because of, Dietrich's carefree appearance, the bisexual seductress caught Joe Sr.'s ever-roving eye after his arrival in early August. According to the actress's daughter Maria, Kennedy pursued a passionate affair with her mother during his beach holiday, often rendezvousing with Marlene at her cabana. Dietrich maintained a vast array of paramours, including many of her Hollywood costars, and preferred that her lovers not use condoms.[53]

Marlene's daughter, a somewhat awkward teenager, frequently found herself paired with Rosemary when she joined the family after a trip to Ireland with her caretaker, Dorothy Gibbs. Though nearly twenty, because of her developmental disabilities she could never travel or live alone. Rose observed that her eldest daughter had "[p]ut on about eight lbs, so we all razzed her about it, as well as Eunice [and] Pat, and she was rather upset. As they all are slimming, she started in, too, today." Rose admitted that she "almost [went] mad listening to discussions of diets as Jack is fattening. . . . Rosemary, Kick, and Eunice are slimming—Rosemary having put on pounds and pounds on her trips." Slender Bobby's vacation assignment from his mother was to improve his writing and spelling. His London school deemed him deficient in both, so Rose supervised his daily diary entries.[54] She delighted in pasting a comment in her own diary from a society column: "The American Ambassadress seems to find controlling and rounding up her family quite an important assignment. They have delightful manners, rarely squabble, . . ."[55]

IN MID-AUGUST Joe Jr., who planned to spend a year serving as his father's secretary, left for Paris. Joe Sr. thought his son should experience firsthand the impending currency crisis and visit the American embassy there. Perhaps after working informally with the US ambassador to France, William Bullitt, for several weeks, Joe Jr. would return with suggestions on how better to run the London embassy. By month's end, Rose and Joe Sr. departed for Paris, he by plane with Jack, she by train with Kathleen. Ambassador Kennedy then traveled to London and a meeting at 10 Downing Street with Prime Minister Chamberlain over Nazi Germany's aggressive move to annex Czechoslovakia's Sudetenland, home to a sizable German minority. A banner headline in the *New York Herald Tribune*'s Paris edition suggested that a proposed British compromise would divide the disputed Czech territory along the lines of the Swiss federal model. On the clipping Rose scribbled that she had shopped and met with Joe Jr. but had for the day "no special news."[56]

Always captivated by Paris, no matter what was happening elsewhere, Rose didn't recognize that these were the waning days of peace. "Hair shampooed and coiffeur arranged it on top of my head, which is the way a great many smart people are wearing it now. Makes me look very chic and Parisian but am not sure I like it." She bemoaned the fact that "the girls are not wearing any hats— most smart Americans lunch and pass in and out of Ritz not wear-

ing any—a very disastrous custom as far as milliners are concerned."
Rose attended Mass at La Madeleine. The French custom of standing, even during the most sacred part of the liturgy, perturbed the
devout Irish American. It was quite unlike Boston, where congregants knelt reverently. Considering a move for Rosemary, she visited a convent school outside Paris but discovered that most of its
girls were studying at the Sorbonne as part of their course, "so it
does not seem practical to leave her there."[57] Rose knew that her
daughter, whose writing skills were only those of a youngster half
her age, couldn't manage such academic rigor.

As her Paris trip drew to a close and she prepared a return to
Cannes to rejoin the younger children, Rose marveled once again
at the Arc de Triomphe "illuminated at night. It is so beautiful in
design, so perfect in its properties, so appropriate in its setting, so
exquisite in its detail, and when the upper part is lighted at night, it
is quite awe-inspiring in its beauty, silhouetted against the sky."
Perfection impressed Rose, but she didn't realize that soon the
lights of Paris and all of Europe would be extinguished. Before
departing for the Riviera, Rose paused to phone her husband in
London to wish him a happy fiftieth birthday, but the ambassador
was on his morning horseback ride. So she went to Cartier to buy
him cuff links. "They are baguette diamonds in a square link with
a small diamond at the corner. More elegant than anything in Paris
and still simple in design and especially right for him, as he would
not look right with a lot of *diamonds*, though these are terrifically
expensive. In fact, the man [at Cartier] said I had chosen the most
exclusive design in Paris."[58] Joe Jr. bid farewell to his mother as she
departed for the south of France again, looking forward to warm
Mediterranean sunshine. All seemed well. Joe Jr. was enjoying his
US embassy stint, and Rose concluded that his experience meeting
with important diplomats would serve him well in his next academic challenge—Harvard Law School.

With her husband in London, Joe Jr. in Paris, Jack preparing to
return to Harvard, and Kick heading back to the United Kingdom,
Rose moved the remaining Kennedys out of their rented villa and
into the Provençal Hotel in Cannes. She liked its modern rooms

with balconies, but the bathing facilities failed to meet her standards: "rather dirty looking and intensely crowded, air mattress laid closely to next and people sitting next to each other packed like sardines." The bathers weren't up to snuff either. "People mostly English, sprinkled with French, tall, lanky . . . women and girls with no particular look or figures. Suppose the trim, sleek figures at Eden Roc spoiled me forever."[59]

On September 10, 1938, Rose saved a newspaper photo of her husband arriving at yet another meeting with Prime Minister Chamberlain. In the picture, a black cat led the American ambassador into 10 Downing Street, an ominous omen for the superstitious. Joe's aversion to war began to attract rebukes from President Roosevelt and Secretary of State Cordell Hull.[60] A few days later, Hitler convened the annual Nazi Party conference in Nuremberg, featuring especially strident tirades against the Czechs.

Rose sent Teddy and Jean, along with Nurse Hennessey, back to London, where Teddy faced a tonsillectomy. The rest of the clan— Rosemary, Eunice, Pat, and Bobby—departed with Miss Dunn, the governess, for a two-week tour of Scotland and Ireland. Now the family matriarch could enjoy the sun-kissed Riviera alone. It lasted only a few days. Her husband phoned to report that "things were terribly agitated in London and perhaps I should leave in the [morning]." Rose's diary took on a more urgent tone when she found no available seat on the plane to Paris. Instead, she departed on the sleeper train to Paris and then caught a ferry across the Channel. She worried Joe might be shouldering too heavy a burden, with Teddy's surgery on his mind, along with "these crises in world politics. Everyone fearing war. The French all took part in the last war and are almost frantic at the specter of another one." Rose had a painful conversation with a French woman who had lost her grandfather in the Franco-Prussian War and her husband and brother in the Great War. The widow vowed that she would not send her son to yet another military conflict.[61]

Now Rose's diary turned, for the first time, to the dangerous state of international relations. Chamberlain, nearly seventy years old, was taking the first plane trip of his life to meet Hitler at

Berchtesgaden, near the führer's mountaintop retreat in the German Bavarian Alps. "Position much more acute and more urgent than P[rime] M[inister] realized. Hitler determined to march in [to Czechoslovakia] and risk a world war if Sudetenland Germans do not get the right of self-determination . . . ," Rose recorded. Several people had commented to her "that Joe [Sr.] has been on hand constantly and has aided [the British] by his presence. Feel that he has given great moral support." After Chamberlain's return, Rose concluded, "Everything looks as though it is moving to peaceful solution."[62] She wasted no time resuming her London routine, playing golf the day of her arrival and preparing for the return of Rosemary, Eunice, Pat, and Bobby.

From time to time, Rose felt the sting of a fickle British press. Now she resented stories that she would send the children to school in southern Ireland in case war broke out on the Continent. She traced these falsities to a phone call she had made to her parents on their forty-ninth wedding anniversary. She had told Honey Fitz that the children had just returned from a visit to the Emerald Isle, not that they were on their way there to find safety. Rose was convinced that someone was eavesdropping on her phone calls and informing the press.[63]

She was also surprised that England would be pilloried for sacrificing the Czechs to the Germans in order to preserve peace. She cited the "reproaches hurled at the English in the U.S.A. by the Jews who hate Hitler so desperately." The day that Rose recorded her views on the Czech crisis, she and Joe hosted Charles and Anne Lindbergh for lunch at the embassy. Rose found the charismatic aviator "rosy-cheeked, fresh-looking with wavy hair, which falls naturally without much combing." She admired his "wonderful smile, which comes easily and lights up his entire face." Anne was "small, gentle, terribly sweet in looks and manner with a wistful expression all of which makes you seethe to know that anyone had hurt her so tragically. She is always neatly, simply dressed and wears clothes of the latest fashion but always in a sort of subdued way. I should say no makeup or lipstick."[64]

As a mother, Rose empathized with the sorrow Mrs. Lindbergh

bore after her baby son's kidnapping and murder six years earlier. Contemplating the so-called crime of the century always sent a chill through Rose. "[W]hen we went to England, [the press] said that each [of the Kennedy children] had a million dollars. That was written up in *Life*. I remember protesting it to Henry Luce . . . because I said they'd be a prize for kidnappers, and if it hadn't been publicized nobody would have known if we had 1 million or 10 million but the fact that it was publicized might attract kidnappers and at that time kidnaping had been in the news considerably."[65]

Colonel Lindbergh's declaration that "Germany could turn out dozens of planes to England's one" startled Rose.[66] She didn't anticipate, however, that Joseph Kennedy's and Charles Lindbergh's intense efforts to keep the United States out of the next European war would indelibly stain their respective careers and provoke charges of anti-Semitism. While the charges against Lindbergh were true, it is harder to gauge Joe Kennedy's position. His "attitudes toward Jews are extremely complex, and any attempts to elucidate them are confounded by his diligent efforts to project a favorable political image and to use his memoirs to erase any stains on his ambassadorial tenure," writes psychologist Will Swift.[67]

Joe and Rose shared a strain of prejudice common in their religion, ethnicity, and social class. Rose simply had not socialized with Jews (or Protestants, for that matter) in her segregated life among well-heeled Irish Catholics. Meeting Jews occasionally among British aristocracy, she described them in stereotypes, but not malicious ones. At one formal dinner Rose sat next to Viscount Bearsted, whose father, Marcus Samuel, had founded Shell Transport and Trading Company, merged it with Dutch Petroleum, and formed Shell Oil. Bearsted "was interested in oil and, of course, in the . . . Jewish question in Jerusalem, also in art. Most Jews seem to be interested in the arts or intellectual pursuits," Rose commented.[68]

After Chamberlain's and Hitler's next round of negotiations, Rose bluntly wrote, "Hitler to occupy Czechoslovakia October first." Even so, she stuck to her habits, sending Teddy and Bobby back to their London day school and then leaving for Scotland.

Only five days had passed since her return from six weeks in France. She monitored the increasingly dire news coming from London. How sad she thought Prime Minister Chamberlain sounded on the radio, urging the British public to remain calm. In case war erupted over Czechoslovakia, "trenches were being dug in Hyde Park and sandbags were being put up around the air ministry building." Despite her children's vulnerability if war did erupt, Rose remained in Scotland. Joe, however, was alarmed. Phoning her on September 28, he told her to return to the embassy by evening "because war is imminent," but she ignored his edict. While Rose shopped for tweeds, she heard about the upcoming summit meeting at Munich to try to resolve the Sudentenland controversy. The news gave her hope and relief. She took a golf lesson, then played seven holes "on the Queen's course, which was wonderful."[69]

Joe called again the next day to tell her that the children were packed and ready to depart. Yet Rose still did not budge from her Scottish retreat. As other guests and staff (including her maid) left the hotel, she finally made preparations to leave but hoped to stay through the weekend (another four days). She pasted photos and articles in her diary about the distribution of gas masks throughout England, observing that they must be cared for properly in order to work. Another of her clippings detailed the British government's plan to evacuate some two million schoolchildren and adults from London's vulnerable sections.[70]

On September 30, 1938, after Chamberlain's return from Munich, declaring that he had achieved "peace in our time," Rose rejoiced: "We all feel that a new psychology for settling issues between difficult countries has been inaugurated and that henceforth war may be out of the question." Chamberlain's quote from Shakespeare's *Henry IV* particularly resonated with her: "Out of this nettle, danger, we pluck this flower, safety."[71]

Three days later Rose did end her Scottish fling and recorded that back in London she "did some shopping and got a report about Teddy, who had his tonsils taken out this [morning]." She did not mention whether she visited him at the London hospital, but she did report inspecting the newly dug trenches in Hyde Park, adjacent to the American embassy, and the blackened street lamps, "darkened as if for war." British gas masks concerned both Rose and Joe. They didn't fit children Bobby's age or younger, as American ones would have. Ambassador Kennedy warned the State Department that he was reporting it for refusing to spend $10 per US-manufactured mask for at-risk American citizens abroad. More disconcerting was Rose's report that when some Brits tested their masks at home by turning on their gas stoves, several died when the masks malfunctioned.[72]

Amid the growing crisis, Britain debated its next move on the diplomatic chessboard. In early October 1938, Rose began attending Parliament's sessions on Chamberlain's Munich pact with Germany, Italy, and France. Winston Churchill, firmly opposed to appeasement, fascinated her with his "delightful, easy to follow" rhetoric. "The past is no more," Churchill predicted. "We are in the presence of a disaster of the first magnitude which has befallen Great Britain and France. Do not let us blind ourselves to that." "It must now be expected that all countries of Central and Eastern Europe will make the best terms they can with the triumphant Nazi power," he warned.[73] Returning the next day to observe Parliament's confidence vote for the government, she referred to Clement Attlee, leader of the opposition Labour Party, as a Socialist who was bald, short, and aggressive. She found the Socialists' "method of speaking . . . decidedly less polished [than that of the Conservative Party majority], as the government is usually [alumni of] Oxford or Cambridge."[74] Ironically, Conservative prime minister Chamberlain, who impressed her with his "quiet, unhurried, deliberate way he addressed the House [of Commons]," held no university degree, much less one from Oxbridge.

Four days after six-year-old Teddy's tonsillectomy, Rose visited him in the "nursing home," where he was recovering from his surgery. His temperature had returned to normal, and she expected him home later that day. Rose was clearly relieved because she did "not like hospitals in Eng[land]. There is no heat, except an electric stove, there is no way of elevating or lowering the bed, which we have even in wards in [American hospitals]." She even critiqued the nurses' uniforms, especially their "shoes with a heel, which we think may allow them to fall."[75]

On October 7, 1938, Joe and Rose marked their twenty-fourth wedding anniversary with a play and late supper at the Savoy, packed with patrons calling each other "darling." Rose was unusually annoyed with the affectation: "Joe says it is the regular way to address one another. I was sick to death of it and worse I remember him using it to speak to someone on the phone occasionally." Not even his gift of a "gorgeous ruby necklace" placated her. "I am afraid [it] is too elaborate for the U.S.A. and . . . I feel constrained to return [it]."[76] This rare discordant note in Rose's journal may have revealed her usually sublimated anger over Joe's philandering.

DISCORD ON THE international scene was riling the British, who floated nearly a hundred barrage balloons over London. Steel cables tethering each balloon to the ground were intended to sheer off enemy aircraft wings. Rose carried on her maternal duties. Kathleen needed a college she could attend part time, one that offered courses in English literature and history. They visited the University of London's King's College, but it preferred full-time, degree-seeking students. Rose concluded that "most girls here do not go to college. Society girls stay in [the] country where they shoot or hunt and evidently not so much attention is given to education of young women as there is in the U.S.A." This observation was only half right. American college women had achieved numerical parity with men in the 1920s, only to lose ground during the Great Depression. Rose next tried Queen's College, surely perfect for Kathleen. Unfortunately, half of the students and instructors had fled to the countryside, and some of the girls had been called home because of war fears.[77]

Joe was obviously under severe pressure. Rose observed that he "at times . . . becomes restless and chafes at the restraint necessarily surrounding his position." To discuss "world affairs," he wanted to go to Berlin, but John Cudahy, the American minister in Dublin, "did not think the President would allow him to go, as the trip

would be thought at home and abroad to have political significance."[78] Rose felt most comfortable in her private, often solitary,
world. Even if she had yearned for a larger official role, women's
circumscribed opportunities at that time would have stymied her.
Yet, once, she found herself drawn into public debate over war and
peace by Joe, if only facetiously.

The occasion was a speech Joe delivered at the British Navy
League's Trafalgar Day dinner, where he quoted Rose several times.
Ambassador Kennedy observed to the audience of military veterans
and nobility that his wife had nixed several topics for his address:
arms reduction, dictatorships and democracies, and Prime Minister
Chamberlain—but only after he had told the audience just what he
wanted to say about each subject. His jocular rhetorical device kept
the speech light while allowing him to assert a serious position—
that an arms race would destroy nations' economies by diverting
them from peaceful productivity. Yet he conceded the dilemma
that *not* arming "may mean domination by a stronger Power or
group of Powers." Rose saved the London *Daily Herald*'s article on
Joe's speech, featuring her portrait with the caption, "Mrs. Kennedy warned her husband not to talk in his speech about" the trio
of controversial topics. The ambassador's picture appeared with the
notation, "Mr. Kennedy considered his wife's advice, then made a
speech about" the topics she supposedly told him to avoid. The
more staid London *Times* headlined, with tongue in cheek, "How
an Ambassador's Wife Makes His Speech." In her journal Rose
stated simply that Joe "[a]dopted a new technique in composing
[the speech], namely, submitting a few questions to me, which I
frowned [on], and finally returning to the original subject." Did he
literally consult her, or use Rose as a public-speaking contrivance?
The record is unclear. Kennedy men typically didn't view their
wives as professional equals, so it is unlikely that Joe genuinely
sought Rose's opinions. The day after the dinner she noted, "Reporters calling for interviews for me at Chancery and Embassy—as they
took speech seriously and believe I inspired it." Joe had run the text
of his remarks by the State Department in advance but had received
"hardly any recommendation."[79]

Apparently, State's Division of European Affairs felt safe in saying that the talk reflected Ambassador Kennedy's *personal* views, *not* those of the Roosevelt administration.[80] A few days after the Trafalgar Day dinner, Joe received a note from the State Department saying that if Rose was going to continue writing her husband's speeches, the department had some wisdom to impart to her. Rose observed that she "should like to send for [the suggestions]."[81] Accepting her limited role as Joe's sounding board, Rose drolly concluded years later, "That was the beginning and the end of my entire career in international politics."[82]

A few days later, Rose and her husband attended the funeral of a member of Parliament at Westminster Cathedral. She was "embarrassed by having a [purple and green] quill" in her hat when she should have displayed a black feather. "No other ambassadors' wives [were] there or one of them might have erred as I did."[83] Rose didn't wish for someone to have alerted her to proper attire but, rather, for someone to commit a faux pas with her.

Soon after, Rose paid Eunice, Pat, and Jean a visit at their Sacred Heart convent school. "They seem well," she observed, "altho[ugh] Pat never is as contented at any boarding school as are the others. She wept when I was leaving today."[84] Rose didn't note that she, too, had suffered homesickness during her first days at the Dutch convent before busying herself in studies and extracurricular activities. The Kennedy aversion to displays of negative emotion earned Pat a "stiff upper lip" letter from her mother: "I am a little worried about you, as you do not seem as happy as you should. Please do not let yourself get too depressed as really—darling—you know you will not be there too long. Everyone your age is away at school and in the long run you should be quite contented. So please cheer up my pet." Rose gave her a pass on cutting calories while at boarding school. "Please do not diet as you can get thin enough once you get out, and if you do not eat nourishing food you cannot study, etc. Well, lots of love, darling, and I shall see you all soon. Mother."[85]

Former US ambassador to Ireland Jean Kennedy Smith recalled in 2010, at age eighty-two, that she didn't suffer from loneliness at boarding school because her sisters were there. "My family were my

best friends." There was the slightest catch in Smith's voice when
she commented that her mother told her to live her life to the full-
est as Jean entered her college years. "Your father and I have lived
our lives," Rose told her youngest daughter. Tears welled in the
Irish eyes of Joe and Rose Kennedy's last surviving child, and she
clutched her heart. Reflexively, her interviewer reached out a hand
in sympathy, but the proud woman didn't grasp it and quickly
regained her composure.[86]

Rose observed that October 20, the day she visited the Roehampton convent, marked the feast of *Mater Admirabilis* ("mother most
admirable"). The title refers to a nineteenth-century fresco of the
Virgin Mary at the Trinità dei Monti in Rome. Catholic legend
maintains that a young French woman painted the portrait of Jesus's
Blessed Mother at the request of Sacred Heart nuns. When the
mother superior examined the woman's completed mural, she
decided the colors used by the painter were too bright and garish and
ordered it hidden from view behind a cloth. Pope Pius IX visited the
church on October 20, 1846, and instructed the mother superior to
remove the drape. The colors had faded, and the pope called the
painting *Mater Admirabilis*,[87] a title to which Rose surely aspired.

The fawning media might have bestowed such a label on Rose.
Her life as maternal teacher, booster, and wardrobe supervisor
appeared in the popular press with the publication of a *Ladies' Home
Journal* article soon after the Trafalgar Day speech, in October 1938.
It is among the earliest magazine features on the Kennedys, and it
supported many of the initial images and legends of the clan, especially of its matriarch, that would become so familiar to the American public. "Mrs. Kennedy might be mistaken for one of her
daughters. She is young, looks even younger, is slimmer than most
of the girls, hasn't a gray hair, prefers running up and down stairs to
taking the iron-gated lift, and is said to have the prettiest and best-
dressed feet at Ascot," the *LHJ*'s fashion editor gushed. She praised
Rose's camaraderie with the children: helping with homework,
dancing with them, attending their sporting events, joining their
meals at least once daily, encouraging hobbies, and offering advice
on wardrobe and hairstyles. All of the children, except Joe Jr. and

Jack, still at Harvard when the article's author arrived in London the previous spring, were photographed as young models. The girls wore sports attire, formals, and suits; Teddy and Bobby were pictured in their school clothes, which included coats and ties, and, for little Teddy, shorts and kneesocks. The largest photo depicted Rose, looking "so young, so right, in her gray-and-blue-plaid tweed suit," as she "helps Teddy with his lessons." Rose was delighted by how beautiful the children appeared, especially Rosemary, whom the article described as preparing to teach nursery school.[88] The article made no reference to Ambassador Kennedy, who was in the States when the magazine's fashion editor visited the embassy, or his role in the family.

Rose was also pleased with an article about Jack in October 1938. By then he was the only member of the immediate family in the United States. The *Boston Sunday Advertiser Green* magazine featured the twenty-one-year-old, including a photo of him dressed in coat and tie, unpacking at his Harvard dorm room. The article focused on his handsome looks punctuated by the "bluest of blue eyes made bluer by being framed in a sun-browned face." Rose was particularly gratified that, according to her hometown paper, Jack was "literally shown with polished cleanliness and the broad white smile typical of the Kennedys." Her efforts to produce perfect-looking children were reaping benefits. And her role as dinner-conversation moderator, when Joe was away, was producing results. In the Boston press, young Jack spoke intelligently about Europe's precarious situation and his impressions of the British response.[89]

As the tense fall of 1938 progressed, Rose continued her routine of daily golf, when England's fickle weather allowed. She reveled in the rare sunshine but felt slightly homesick one crisp autumn day, recalling Harvard football weekends. She grew weary of noisy construction next door to the embassy, which awakened her in the mornings, so she escaped to the country for a quiet break. Throughout her life, Rose remained sensitive to noise and disruption, and she frequently removed herself from her family to seek refuge. Whether retreating to the cottage that she kept on the Cape Cod beach (leaving her boisterous children to claim the Hyannis house and yard) or to the hotel rooms that she requested in the back of buildings (to shield herself from street hubbub), Rose simply craved solitude and peace.

Yet she was by no means a recluse, enjoying the high life of social seasons from New York to London to Palm Beach. In early November 1938 Rose and Joe attended a new play, *Dear Octopus*, by English playwright Dodie Smith, starring a young John Gielgud and Dame Marie Tempest, star of light opera and the British stage. The play took its title from the line, "The family—that dear octopus from whose tentacles we never quite escape, nor in our inmost hearts, ever quite wish to." No wonder Rose, so attached to her clan, adored the production, "built around a family of six grown-up children who have returned home to celebrate for two days the golden wedding of their parents." She explained that the play was a "[v]ery true portrayal, revealing the various vicissitudes through which the difficult members had passed, and the results in the characters of each of them through the years. There was just enough pathos with comedy to make the play one of the most absorbing which I have ever seen."[90]

Yet never too far from the mundane, Rose also commented that Nurse Hennessey returned "from her vacation in Ireland where she was shocked and distressed and rather annoyed at the squalor, the poverty there. A child barefoot winter and summer for four years runs the errands. Her relatives delighted at her strong regular white teeth, which they insist she show to all their neighbors."[91] How fortunate for Rose's family to have escaped the squalor of Irish poverty and American tenements. What a contrast between life in the Old Country and the Kennedys' new status among British aristocracy.

❧

CHAPTER 6

Ambassadress Extraordinaire

ROSE HAD REACHED THE PINNACLE OF HER LIFE AS SPOUSE OF
the American ambassador to England. "I might have been over-
awed by being the wife of the Ambassador," she admitted, "but I
had traveled widely and had visited two or three United States
Embassies where I had observed the manners and the attitudes of
the wives of the Ambassadors. I certainly felt that in education and
experience, I could fulfill the obligations creditably and I knew I
would give all my mind and heart to making the position a successful one."[1]

Her November 1938 calendar contained two historic ceremonies,
and, as usual, Rose wanted to look her best. The first was Parliament's annual opening. After two days of beauty treatments, she
donned her diamond tiara, as well as her ruby and diamond bracelet
and mink coat, for the short trip to Westminster. There she took her
seat in the Peeress' Bench and spotted the German ambassador,
whose countrymen would launch Kristallnacht a few hours later.
On "The Night of Broken Glass" ninety-one Jews perished, thirty
thousand Jewish men were incarcerated in concentration camps, and
nearly three hundred synagogues were ransacked and burned.[2]

The second major ceremony came on Armistice Day, when Rose attended a "very impressive ceremony at the Cenotaph, with the King laying a wreath at [the] Tomb of the Unknown Soldier."[3] Little did they know that "the war to end all wars" would be a colossal misnomer.

In mid-November, Rose, Joe, and Joe Jr., now back from his short stint at the Paris embassy, drove out of London for a dinner with colonial secretary Malcolm MacDonald, son of Ramsay Mac-Donald, Britain's first Labour Party prime minister who took office in 1924. Malcolm was focused on the deteriorating situation in British Palestine, where Arabs were mounting a rebellion to protest the immigration of Jews, thousands of whom were flocking to their historic Promised Land to escape Hitler's persecution.[4] Rose found the dinner discussions "[i]nteresting . . . especially one about the ultimate solution of the Jewish question about which there is constant agitation now. Joe feels that some countries like Australia, for instance, might offer territory, other countries, U.S.A., offer money and we might find a haven for them. Some concrete thing should be attempted, instead of everyone deploring the condition but nothing definite volunteered. If England put it up to each nation what they would do, then the responsibility would be theirs and not entirely hers in the disturbance in Palestine. [Joe] [a]lso said conditions had improved since Jews went to Palestine due to increase of money and capital brought there by them."[5] Joe, the capitalist, undoubtedly knew the financial landscape in Palestine, and Rose accepted her husband's stereotypes regarding Jews and money.

For Rose London life was quieter in the fall than the height of England's spring social season. In mid-November, however, she and Joe attended a reception and dinner given by King George and Queen Elizabeth in honor of Romania's King Carol. Rose slipped into a "glamorous" white satin dress and added her diamond and ruby accessories. Joe dined on bacon and eggs at the embassy before leaving for the palace, so as not to disrupt his bland diet. After the formal dinner, Rose tried surreptitiously to powder her nose and reapply her lipstick, a custom she had learned at home. She discovered, though, that the royals' guests didn't freshen their makeup, "especially in the presence of Queen Mary," the king's formidable mother.[6]

Just as Rose tried to redo her face, the Duchess of Northumberland summoned her for a tête-à-tête with Queen Elizabeth. Meanwhile, the Dowager Lady Airlie asked Rose to converse with Queen Mary. Referring to Kristallnacht, the widow of King George V "deplored conditions in Germany," where Jews now faced constant threats from Hitler's regime. Rose then chatted with Queen Elizabeth about her trip to the States, scheduled for the following spring. The queen remarked that "she would like to go to America as a simple visitor without people suspecting she was going there with the intention of forming a political alliance, which is the trend of the newspaper world at present."[7]

The next day Rose was photographed in her new gown for *The Sketch*, then flew to Paris for more shopping. While there, she learned that Queen Maud of Norway, King George VI's aunt, had died in London. "There is court mourning for six weeks, and I must wear black," Rose discovered. "Very difficult for me," she complained, "as I have three parties this week, including Thanksgiving." She then lunched at the Ritz with Schiaparelli's public relations agent, who wanted to include her in the World's Best Dressed Women competition. She later withdrew from consideration: "Less interested, as I was last year picked as Best Dressed Woman in Public Life in U.S.A." She returned to her quotidian quest for fresh milk and cream, always a struggle in France. "So I usually lose weight and feel less peppy," an unusual admission for the dynamic Rose.[8]

At age forty-eight, Rose could have entered menopause's early stages that sapped some of her normal vitality. Or her sensitive stomach, body-image issues, and abstemious diet may have led to weight loss. Her niece, Mary Jo Gargan Clasby, believes that Rose may have suffered from food sensitivities that produced chronic digestive upset.[9] If Rose was lactose intolerant, for example, dairy products would have been the last thing she should have ingested. Perhaps her physical problems were stress-related. She certainly faced tensions in her life—from international affairs to personal ones conducted by her husband. Rose's nervous response to environmental stimuli such as noise reflects a low tolerance for anything that upset her preference for quiet routines.

Nevertheless, back in London she mustered enough energy to host a tea and preside over a traditional Thanksgiving family meal, but she then sent her boisterous children to the cinema while she rested. That evening, the whole family attended the American Society's celebration at the Dorchester Hotel, where Rose sat with Lord Runciman, who had recently returned from Czechoslovakia. He told her that "Hitler was [a] fanatic and so could not be judged by ordinary standards."[10] Such an analysis couldn't have eased Rose's stress.

The next day Rose welcomed the archbishop of Canterbury to an embassy luncheon. Describing this social whirl to her well-preserved, seventy-three-year-old mother, Rose exclaimed, "No wonder I look young and beauteous with such a mother!" she confided that her London life could be difficult with the press hounding her: "They are still photographing us, and I wish they would stop."[11] "I do not mind having pictures when I am at leisure, when I can get my hair slightly waved and when I have the children's clothes partly unpacked," Rose explained. "But . . . there is a race and rivalry among newspaper men and the first one to arrive is the one who effects the coup for his paper and for himself."[12] Here was a dilemma that would confront Princess Diana five decades later. While both women reveled in media attention, each found it intrusive for herself and her children.

The press came under fire at a luncheon Rose attended at Lady Asquith's home in late November 1938. Rose diplomatically used the passive voice in her journal, refusing to assign the opinions she recorded to any particular guest. The Englishmen in attendance complained that "everything was blamed on England and Chamberlain, but . . . it was he who sent Runciman to Czecho[slovakia], and it was Chamberlain who made all agreements. Also the influence of the Jewish columnists in U.S.A. in forming public opinion was remarked and caused surprise. Comment was that until Munich, England had a good press in America but not since then.

Observation also made that the pros and cons regarding Munich were dividing English people into two camps almost as much so as the Dreyfus Case [and] the Irish question."[13] Indeed, the British aristocracy harbored anti-Jewish and anti-Irish sentiments similar to those Rose had been exposed to in parochial Boston.

AS DECEMBER DAWNED, Rose shopped for the family's Christmas trip to Saint Moritz. Ambassador Kennedy planned to leave for the States early in the month to spend the holidays with Jack in Palm Beach and take a two-month vacation. Joe would have to be back in time for his wife to travel in March to Egypt, which she wanted to see "while I am so near."[14]

On December 8 Rose attended Mass for the Feast of the Immaculate Conception. She and Joe then drove to the Roehampton convent for its celebration in the Blessed Mother's honor. Rose thrilled at the procession in which Eunice, Pat, Jean, and their classmates carried white lilies. Undoubtedly recalling her days at Blumenthal, Rose wrote that it "is always the most mystic, most beautiful, most inspiring ceremony in the [Society of the] S[acred] Heart [of Jesus]." She added that "Dad [Joe] lighted the candles on the altar as he told the [mother superior] he used to be an altar boy." The students then marched to a hall where Rose observed "the Blessed Virgin in a sort of grotto . . . like Lourdes."[15] Rose didn't write that she saw a *statue* of Jesus's mother; rather, she discussed the BVM as if she were really there. Catholic tradition holds that Mary appeared eighteen times in 1858 to an impoverished girl, Bernadette Soubirous, in Lourdes, France. On December 8, 1933, Pope Pius XI canonized Bernadette, naming her the patron saint of healing. A Catholic shrine to Our Lady of Lourdes, where the sick are said to be miraculously healed by the waters, now dominates the small French Pyrenees town and attracts five million believers annually.

Some days earlier Joe had reported that Eunice was "going wild as it becomes nearer to time for her to receive the Child of Mary Medal on December 8th."[16] This was the most prestigious honor conferred by the Sacred Heart nuns, and one that Rose had worked assiduously to attain at Blumenthal a quarter century earlier. Oddly, in this instance Rose's journal mentioned neither the award itself nor Eunice's reaction.

The next day, Joe and Rose welcomed Spain's former queen Ena to a luncheon at the American embassy. She and her husband, King Alfonso XIII, had gone into exile in 1931 when republicans came to power in Spain. During lunch, Rose sat next to the Duke of Devonshire, who was the undersecretary of dominions, "also father of Billy Hartignare [sic], one of Kathleen's beaux of the moment." Rose inaccurately recorded both the name of her future son-in-law (Billy Hartington) and his status with Kick. Also in attendance was John McCormack, the famous Irish tenor, whom the Kennedys had recently seen perform a farewell concert in the Royal Albert Hall. His lilting rendition of operatic classics and patriotic Irish ballads had brought Rose and her family nearly to tears.[17] Despite their newfound Anglophilia, the Kennedys remained nostalgic for their Irish heritage.

Three days before Christmas, the Kennedy clan (minus Joe Sr. and Jack) departed for Saint Moritz amid the glare of flashbulbs. A massive snowstorm struck as they traveled across England, the Channel, France, and Switzerland, delaying their arrival in Saint Moritz until Christmas Eve. Once again, the media awaited them. Ten photographers demanded pictures, and Rose bristled at the intrusion:

> Our trunks were delayed and my skiing costume, ordered especially from Schiaparelli, was missing and two children were minus ski pants. But, ting-ling-ling, along came the photographers ringing the phone for a picture early on our first day. I was saved because it was Sunday and I pleaded church, then the next day was Christmas. By that time we managed to fit up the nine [actually eight; Jack was in Florida] children to look properly clad for skiing. I borrowed the governess's cap which photographed remarkably well, though the color clashed horribly with my own. . . . An astonishing awakening comes to us when we believe we look particularly enchanting, only to see our

pictures and find that the hat which we thought very chic has turned out to be a complete failure in the photograph. It makes our heads look shapeless or perhaps huge.[18]

With photographs taken of her, Jean, and Teddy skating, as well as the family assembled for a sleigh ride, Rose could finally relax in the alpine splendor of Saint Moritz, eastern Switzerland's winter playground for the rich, not far from the Italian border. She particularly enjoyed accommodations at Suvretta House, the palatial luxury hotel opened in 1912. It featured stunning views of lakes Champfèr and Silvaplana, on the Chasellas plateau. "It is incredibly beautiful," she informed her mother. "From my window, I look across to the mountains covered with snow so white, so soft, so lovely. The fir trees are blanketed with the snow, of course, and when the sun comes up about 10:30 in the morning, everything glistens." She proudly reported that Bobby won the New Year's Day ski race for youngsters under sixteen. Joe Jr., however, enrolled in an advanced ski class, "was too daring, and ran into a rock and had to have four or five stitches in his arm, but he is at it again." Rose took skating lessons and mastered the figure-eight maneuver. Jean "will be a good fancy skater," her mother thought. Rose also embraced the opportunity to refresh her German language skills.[19] Yet the priest at Mass spoke too quickly, making it difficult for her to comprehend his sermon *auf Deutsch*. As always when she traveled, Rose made notes about the locals. "Swiss children, people and houses all look clean, healthy with fat red cheeks, pleasant and smiling. . . ." She was especially impressed by their "good strong teeth, probably because I am told they eat black bread considerably."[20]

From Palm Beach, where he and Jack were spending the holidays, Joe cabled Rose, "Associated Press today picked you as outstanding woman of the year for selling the world the American family. Jack and I are basking in your reflected glory. He has gained five pounds. My love to all, Joe."[21]

After three weeks of winter sports and shopping in Saint Moritz, Rose shepherded her brood back to London. She continued her solo golf rounds, even if she had to slog through the "slime and muck" of wet British courses. Visiting Eunice, Pat, and Jean at the convent, she treated them to cake and ice cream, giving them a break from dieting. Rose spoke occasionally with her husband, and let Teddy and Bobby catch up with their father, by phone. She worried about Bobby's studies. He had received low marks on an exam from his American school. Rose vowed to supervise his work "vigorously."[22] It was a daunting task. Like most of the young Kennedys, Bobby was orthographically and syntactically challenged: "I love allmost every thing, Cholcet," the thirteen-year-old wrote. "I don't like cricket very much I like baseball alot. . . . I can't dive very well, but like it to a cirten exstant."[23]

Despite her vow to oversee Bobby's schoolwork, Rose embarked on trips at the end of January 1939 that would absent her from London and her two children at the embassy for six weeks. Although Ambassador Kennedy remained in the States until he set sail for England with Jack on February 9, she departed for Paris on January 31. She stopped for the latest styles at her favorite couturier, Molyneux. Muted tweed became her fabric of choice after a Scottish hostess told her that bright colors, like royal blue, "draw the attention . . . in your direction."[24]

From the Ritz in Paris, Rose wrote to Joe, who was expected back in London soon, "Just to tell you how sorry I am not to be home to see you, and I am glad it will not be for long. I have enjoyed it here. . . . I saw Joe [Jr.] off to Spain. . . . I just keep on having fun and loving you. Devotedly, Rosa."[25] Like a number of adventuresome young Americans, Joe Jr. wanted to witness the Spanish Civil War at close range, causing his parents considerable anxiety. Young Kennedy indeed saw the ravages of war between Franco's fascists and Spanish republicans.[26] He didn't realize, however, that Spain's conflict was a dress rehearsal for the impending European war.

Rose simply couldn't bear returning to England's bleak midwinter weather, and from Paris she headed for the warmth of the Mediterranean sun, beginning in Cannes, then moving on to Italy, Greece, Turkey, Palestine, and Egypt. "I would love to see you people," Rose wrote to her mother, "but Joe will not stay here [in London] for a very long time and I may as well see all the places around here."[27] Traveling with her was a new friend, Marie Bruce, whom she had met at a Paris luncheon just after Joe's appointment as ambassador. Marie was rather stunned when Rose, a casual acquaintance, invited her to go along. Mrs. Bruce was recently widowed; perhaps her sadness had prompted Rose to reach out to her. "She is very perceptive to people's unhappiness and reacts to it, tries to help," Marie commented about her friend. "Young Joe was very much like her in this. . . . It is her humanity that is astonishing."[28]

In Italy Rose and Marie explored Pompeii's ruins, wrought by Mount Vesuvius's AD 79 eruption. They viewed the macabre plaster casts of victims, contorted at their moment of death from searing lava. Rose found the red and green murals in excavated homes "exquisite." "Wish I had seen them before I did the house at Palm Beach," Rose declared. She failed to record her reaction to Pompeii's infamous pornographic paintings. Then she was off to Greece, where she decried Lord Elgin's removal of marbles from the Acropolis to the British Museum in the early 1800s. "It seemed to me really almost an act of plunder to remove these art treasures which have come down through the ages and which belonged to their own particular setting in Greece." In Turkey Rose praised the reforms of President Mustafa Atatürk, who had died three months before her arrival. She particularly approved his promotion of Western dress, including abolishing fezzes for men and veils for women.[29]

Palestine was the most dangerous stop on the tour. Rose's cruise ship was the first to dock there in a year. Landing at Haifa, she was met by the American consul and ferried by car to Jerusalem, accompanied by two armored vehicles. Fearing guerrilla attacks, her convoy went by way of Tel Aviv instead of Nazareth, which was completely isolated from routine traffic. The consul explained, according to Rose, that "Jews have immigrated in overwhelming numbers and are now numbering one to every two Arabs. If this continues, Arabs will no longer have [a] foothold in the country and so are revolting. Arabs sell land to Jews, then spend money in town, then have neither land or money. Naturally, Jews buy only good land and as they are given huge sums from America, they now possess [the] best of land. Jews [are] not self-supporting but are helped [with] $2,000,000 from U.S.A," which may well be another example of Rose's Jewish stereotypes or at least acceptance of them.[30]

After lunching with the British governor, she explored Christendom's holiest shrines. Like many pilgrims to the Church of the Holy Sepulchre, Rose found the "whole effect of this church . . . rather confusing. . . . As different civilizations or sects had influence, they built chapels, also dark and difficult to see and distinguish." In fact, after visiting Bethlehem, she was "[r]ather disappointed and disillusioned in Holy Places." Devout travelers to the Holy Land often find that commercialism, as well as political and religious strife, taint the most sacred sites. Yet Rose understood her visit's symbolism in light of the ongoing struggle between fascism and freedom. Having her photograph taken in Jerusalem was important "because it is good propaganda now for Jerusalem to advertise it is safe for me to be there. Bad propaganda for England to be having all this trouble as totalitarian States say democracies cannot control [their people]."[31]

By February's end Rose and Marie had made their way to Egypt and toured, with an Antiquities Bureau guide, the ancient Temples of Karnak and Luxor, the Aswan Dam, and the Nile. Ancient magnificence and modern squalor collided, in Rose's judgment. Dust, dirt, and flies violated her dedication to cleanliness and hygiene. Even worse, she saw no evidence of efforts to improve living standards. Everything that Rose had done to move her family far beyond their Irish ancestors' peasant roots and the teeming tenements of Boston's North End clashed with the undeveloped world's poverty. Joe had made the Kennedys millionaires, but it was Rose who made them healthy and educated. In her Victorian worldview, to have done less would represent a weak character. As we have seen, responsibility and discipline were Rose's most prized traits. She simply could not comprehend the "utter lack of civilization" that she discovered along the Nile's banks. More disconcerting, even sickening to her, was that the Egyptian children "seem utterly indifferent" to flies that landed on their eyelids. Why didn't they brush them away? She focused on proper diets for her family; how could a country allow poor nutrition to cause blindness among its children? And why so little milk available for them, Rose wondered.[32]

After her month-long grand tour, Rose welcomed a return to Italy, where she would soon rendezvous with the entire Kennedy clan except for Joe Jr., still in Spain. The family gathered in Rome for the coronation of their friend, Eugenio Cardinal Pacelli, as Pope Pius XII, on March 12, 1939. Rose stunned the hotel clerk when she informed him that her family, along with their governess, nurse, maid, the Moores, and Joe's friend Arthur Houghton would be claiming sixteen rooms. She felt run down from insomnia and lack of potable milk on her Mediterranean trip, which she again blamed for weight loss.

But the Church, as it often did, would provide a welcome diversion. She had to assemble her eight children by 7 a.m. for their trip to St. Peter's Basilica. After inspecting her brood, she discovered that "Eunice's sleeve was ripped out of her dress in the back." No time for sewing repairs, they closed the torn seam with hairpins and covered it with a silver-fox scarf. As President Roosevelt's official representatives to the spectacle, Joe and Rose sat in the front row. Placed next to Eamon de Valera, the American-born leader of the Irish Free State, Rose listened politely to his version of the "trouble in North Ireland," where the British and Irish unionists refused to relinquish their Ulster counties.[33] She knew that an ambassador's spouse shouldn't discuss political topics, especially one as controversial as the "Irish question," at such occasions. Moreover, Rose must have experienced internal conflicts between her Irish heritage and her fervent desire to be accepted by British aristocracy.

The next day the entire Kennedy entourage returned to the Vatican for an audience with the new pope. Flanked by two Swiss guards, the family posed in their formal attire. Rose and the Holy Father reminisced about his 1936 trip as Cardinal Pacelli to Hyde Park and their Bronxville home. As Joe wrote later, "[The pope] talked to her so much and so kindly and intimately I thought she would faint."[34] Rose had achieved nirvana. From her childhood, she longed to be near famous and important people. From her days at the convent, she strove to be the most devout Catholic. Now she not only had witnessed the pope's coronation at St. Peter's Basilica, built on the bedrock of Roman Catholicism, but was conversing with her friend Pope Pius XII. Then Teddy became the first child to receive his First Communion from the new pontiff. Most Catholic children remember the pomp and solemnity of this sacramental ritual, but Teddy would recall with pride the extraordinary circumstances of his First Communion for the rest of his life.[35] And his mother would cite this holy achievement when campaigning for him.

From Rome, Rose headed back to Paris, where Joe caught up with her a few days later. He arrived at the Ritz to see her but discovered that she was at church. Searching for his devout wife in La Madeleine Church, he found her engrossed in prayer, her eyes closed and head bowed.[36] Starting at Blumenthal, where she rose earlier than the other students each morning to meditate, Rose found relaxation in quiet prayerfulness. The tactile and spiritual feel of rosary beads in her small hands brought peace and tranquility to her otherwise frenetic life. When maternal and spousal pressures impinged, she turned to the Blessed Virgin Mary, the rosary's patroness, for solace and strength.

Finally back in London, Rose plunged into the bustling spring social season: luncheons, teas, receptions, and dinners, interspersed with golf. First came a gala Buckingham Palace dinner for French president Albert Lebrun, a tense affair "because of the political unrest everyone felt" in Europe and its unpredictable impact on the futures of England and France. Despite noting this tension as the world inched closer to war, Rose continued to focus on superficialities. She would have loved the evening to be filmed so that viewers could see the palace's ornate rooms with their artistic masterpieces and the women guests, "very gorgeously gowned—tiaras and beautiful jewels. . . ." "[T]he men in their most elaborate uniforms with all their medals and decorations make a picture you wouldn't find a duplicate of anyplace else in the world. . . . But whenever I mention it [a film] to any Englishmen they always rather think it undignified."[37] Although Rose's preoccupation with such trivia seems misplaced in light of the impending war, she foreshadowed the British monarchy's eventual embrace of modern public relations in presenting its pomp and circumstance to large audiences. The BBC and American networks are replete with royal weddings, jubilee celebrations, and documentaries on the House of Windsor, all contributing to twenty-first-century increases in public approval for the royal family.

April 1939 dawned with Rose attending House of Commons debates on British foreign policy toward Hitler and Mussolini. She continued to admire Prime Minister Chamberlain's personal traits: "quiet, decisive, moderate in tone, never appealing to the dramatic or sensational, never raising his voice." But Rose worried about the physical toll that concern over Germany and Italy was taking on Britain's leader. During lunch at 10 Downing Street, she "asked him if Hitler died if he would be more confident about peace and [Chamberlain] said he would." Perhaps because of Lindbergh's alarming reports on the German air force, Rose wondered aloud if Britain had enough information on Germany's preparedness for war. Chamberlain assured her that he received such reports.[38]

On April 7 Joe and Rose played golf, but the ambassador grew tense upon receiving word that Italy had invaded Albania, seizing the strategic Balkan kingdom as a response to Germany's annexation of Austria and aggression toward Czechoslovakia. Joe Jr. returned from Spain with firsthand accounts of fascist victories, and the privations of civil war. In fact, Britain had already recognized Franco's regime in February.[39]

Ambassador and Mrs. Kennedy spent another weekend as guests of King George VI and Queen Elizabeth at Windsor Castle in mid-April. FDR had just declared his intentions to achieve peace with Germany and Italy, so Rose reported that "everyone was so appreciative of President Roosevelt's gesture and for us, being there at that particular time after the President's gesture—we could not have been more welcome. Everyone was particularly interested in America and happy and optimistic." Despite renewed optimism, the royals escorted their American guests to a display of barrage balloons in Surrey. Rose marveled that on "[o]ccasions like this the Queen always has a ready smile and a word for everyone, no matter how humble his position. It seems to me she must become tired and bored sometimes, but there is never any sign of flagging interest. The King of course is also very much interested, but for a woman it must be more difficult to go in for all sorts of mechanical things as she has had to do these last few months due to the war preparations."[40]

Over lunch the next day, Rose conversed again with a haggard Prime Minister Chamberlain, this time about the more restful topic of birds and gardens. She also discussed women's education, opining that more American coeds received schooling for careers than British girls did. The prime minister gently disagreed; his niece, for example, had attended lectures at London's Monkey Club, which tried to stimulate intellectual pursuits among well-to-do young ladies. "The name of the Club sounds as though it were a completely different sort of thing," Rose wryly observed.[41] Located in a row of houses along Pont Street, and named for the iconic Japanese carving of Three Wise Monkeys, it was one of the poshest finishing schools in London. Its founder had decided in 1923 that "there must be some mean between the bluestockings at the universities and the empty-headed young things of the [social] season."[42]

Meanwhile, Rosemary was thriving that spring, according to Mother Isabel. "We are very pleased, here, with Rosemary's remarkable progress. There is a great change in her lately. We are so glad to learn that your Excellency is pleased too," she wrote to Ambassador Kennedy.[43] The exact nature of this "progress" is unclear. It is unlikely that Rosemary's academics could improve beyond the developmental obstacles nature had placed in her way. The Kennedys' goal was to see her active and content. Mother Isabel simply may have thought that Rosemary had achieved her parents' modest expectations. Joe commended Rosemary: "You have worked very hard and I am very proud of you and I love you a lot."[44] In such a competitive family, his praise meant the world to her. Although Rose had spent considerable time with Rosemary during her childhood, Joe had now become her primary supervisor.

Rose was busy with her pursuits, including socializing with the royal family. After observing the two young princesses, she concluded that they were "natural, simple, solicitous of one another, and it does seem as though they have a difficult time always accompanying their parents now to some maneuver or public demonstration."[45] She also spent time with Lord and Lady Astor at their Buckinghamshire estate, Cliveden. Rose found the sometimes prickly American expatriate and member of Parliament Nancy Astor "inherently good." She admitted, however, that Nancy had been said to dominate her offspring "too much so it's difficult for them to be around her."[46]

Rose continued to burnish the public image of her family, explaining to *Reader's Digest* that Joe and she had decided "years ago . . . that our children were going to be our best friends and that we never could see too much of them. Since we couldn't do both, it was better to bring up our family than to go out to dinners. My husband's business often took him away from home, and when all of us had time to be together, we didn't want to share it with outsiders."[47]

ON APRIL 23 Joe informed Rose that Yugoslavia had signed a trade pact with the Axis powers. Nancy Astor considered the news disquieting, but Joe seemed "quite optimistic," observing that "Germany will need more customers to trade with and all is well."[48] Such a tolerant view of Germany's economic ambitions would soon run afoul of FDR's foreign policy.

A highlight of Rose's diplomatic spouse's career came on May 4, 1939. The king and queen were coming for dinner, and her whole life had been preparation for the perfection and precision of such an occasion. Rose especially loved the table arrangements: white and purple Phalaenopsis. (But she didn't utter the common name of the flower to the press, fearing that orchids "would sound too nouveau riche, or too extreme.") She imported strawberries for the shortcake dessert, hoping that they would prove tastier than London fruit. She had hoped to have American shad roe for the main course, but a delay in shipment forced her to serve English sole. One particularly nerve-racking logistical element included security for the royal couple to protect them from IRA terrorists. Rose assured Scotland Yard that the embassy's additional staff members had all served at Buckingham Palace. "Everyone seemed very calm and confident but I knew everyone in the house was terribly excited, including myself and the Ambassador." Promptly at 8:30 p.m. Joe and Rose assembled in the entrance hall to greet King George and Queen Elizabeth and accompany them up the grand staircase to shake hands with a receiving line, including all of the Kennedy children.[49]

At dinner's end, Rose and the queen adjourned upstairs to powder their noses and chat informally in Rose's bedroom. "She asked me if I got up in the morning to see the children off and I said I used to in what I called the good old days, but that now I was usually up late at nights and rested in the morning. To my astonishment and humiliation," wrote Rose "[the queen] said she usually got up, half-dressed, to see her children, and then went back to bed again."[50]

For entertainment the hosts screened the 1939 film *Goodbye, Mr. Chips*. Even the queen wasn't immune to Robert Donat's Academy Award–winning performance as beloved English schoolmaster Arthur Chipping, who loses his wife, played by radiant Greer Garson, and his son, but devotes his life to boys at fictional Brookfield School. "After it was finished," Rose observed, "it was very plain to see that the Queen had had a little weep, as had most of the people."[51] Mrs. Kennedy didn't include herself in that tearful group. When thank-you letters poured in from guests congratulating her and reporting how much they enjoyed dinner with the monarchs on the eve of their departure for the United States, Rose felt deep satisfaction.[52]

Moving from the head of state to the head of government, Rose and Joe spent several days with Neville Chamberlain at the prime minister's sixteenth-century mansion, Chequers. Located in Buckinghamshire, it had been the British premier's official country home since its owners, Lord and Lady Lee, donated it to the nation in 1921. Enthralled by the centuries of history that surrounded her, Rose particularly focused on the mansion's ties to Oliver Cromwell, whose grandson had lived there. Perhaps Puritan Cromwell's persecution of Irish Catholics during his 1648–1660 reign as the British Isles' lord protector drew her attention. Rose again turned to small talk about flowers, a relaxing subject for the "worn and tired" pre-

mier. She told Chamberlain about her trip to the Royal Botanic
Gardens at Kew in southwest London. Rose always took pride that,
as a diplomat's wife, she could find uncontroversial topics of mutual
interest to VIPs. "We did not discuss the international situation,"
Rose wrote, "because I know how loath Joe is to give his views, so,
much as I would have liked to have an expression of opinion, I never
introduce that particular subject. The prime minister also spoke
about the immorality and the changes for which a war is responsible
and cited the increase in divorce and the lack of morality following
the last war."[53] Given that Rose's religion banned divorce, she must
have agreed with Chamberlain's concerns.

On May 23 Rose hosted a lunch at the embassy "for people
whom we wished to see but whom we did not feel had to be fitted
into a dinner." These included the Egyptian ambassador, to whom
she spoke about blindness in his country. He reported that the condition was decreasing because of the country's efforts to alleviate
the ravages of sun, dust, and poor diet that Rose had seen firsthand.
She had a more difficult time with Lord Londonderry, the Conservative member of Parliament for Northern Ireland's County Down.
He thought that "the conflict between North and South Ireland is
kept alive by" Catholics and Protestants in the United States and
Canada. "As he had told me last year that Mickey Collins [the Irish
revolutionary leader, killed in 1922 during the Irish civil war] was a
murderer, I am always a bit resentful of his point of view."[54] Once
again Rose found herself caught between her Irish roots and her
desire to gain acceptance among Britain's elite and to exercise the
discretion required of a diplomatic spouse.

In late May Rose departed for a stay in the United States after
more than a year abroad. King George and Queen Elizabeth would
be there at the same time, on their first trip to America. Rose had
consulted with them and their staff regarding their itinerary, and
Ambassador Kennedy had talked to them and the State Department
about their visit.[55] Joe "was certain that the gracious and easy manners of the king and queen would break through the formalities" and
perhaps mitigate the Americans' reaction to Edward VII's 1936 shock-
ing abdication to marry American divorcée Wallis Simpson. After

all, the Anglo-American alliance was at a dangerous turning point as Hitler's bellicosity increased.[56] Rose didn't meet with the monarchs during their contemporaneous visits to the States, and the State Department wouldn't grant Joe the customary leave to welcome to his home country the head of state from his ambassadorial post, a sure sign of discord between Kennedy and the administration.[57]

From aboard the French Line's SS *Normandie*, during the voyage to America, Rose described to Joe her mundane activities, including that she ate "a baked potato everyday, but I am still underweight about twelve pounds, according to statistics." Because Rose usually erred on the side of thinness for herself, she didn't seem alarmed by the weight loss, even on her already petite frame, and in photos on board ship she doesn't appear gaunt or unwell. As always, she closed with warm wishes, "Much love to everyone and I miss you all terrific[ally]."[58]

According to writer Cari Beauchamp, Joe responded to his wife's absence by spending time with beautiful playwright Clare Boothe Luce, former editor of *Vogue* and *Vanity Fair.* Thirteen years Rose's junior, she was married to Henry Luce, publisher of *Life*, *Time*, and *Fortune.* A woman of sturdy libido, Clare, it was said, also included young Randolph Churchill (Winston's son) and elderly New Dealer Bernard Baruch among her conquests.[59] Her lovers' ages clearly mattered not.

Rose docked in New York City on May 29, 1939. As usual, a troop of newspaper photographers greeted her. Honey Fitz and Josie visited their daughter at the luxurious Waldorf-Astoria before Rose attended the newly opened World's Fair. Its theme, "the world of tomorrow," was best illustrated by the General Motors exhibition. There Rose rode a miniature train that wound through roads, gardens, and factories as they might appear in 1959. "[L]anes will be wide, crossings will be made safe by upper and lower ramps, cars will be so cheap and can run so fast that houses can be built away from factories, the home dwellers can have gardens and lawns," she reported. Rose really wanted to dine in the fair's most popular destination, the French Casino, "but it was impossible to get [a] table even for me," she lamented.[60] King George and Queen Elizabeth

also planned to visit the fair. Honey Fitz reported that the king's
Canada speech had gone well, with only one "almost imperceptible
hesitation" from his "impediment."[61] This was the first mention
Rose had ever made in her diary of George VI's stutter.

After stopping briefly at the family estate in Bronxville, she
headed to the Hyannis Port compound. Writing "Joe dear" that the
water was "super," she turned more serious: "All sorts of rumors
about your departure from England, and no one seems much surprised." Although First Lady Eleanor Roosevelt invited Rose to
attend events honoring the king and queen, she declined, "saying
Mother and Father would be too disappointed if I curtailed my
brief visit. . . ." Perhaps the real reason was that, if the State Department didn't want Joe to be part of the royals' visit, then Rose
wouldn't take part without him. "Good-bye, darling," Rose closed
her letter to Joe, "and all my love to the little darlings. Am having
a good rest—which is OK—for a while. Rosa."[62]

Back in New York, Rose bid farewell to her parents before setting sail on the SS *Washington*. Even as an inveterate traveler, fare-
wells could be painful for her: "Music playing furiously just before
we sail which seems to keep our spirits buoyed up and distract us."[63]
Perhaps the photographers in her cabin helped take her mind off
leaving Honey Fitz and Josie, now in their seventies.

Rose reached London to join Joe in welcoming the king and
queen home from their triumphant North American trip. They had
solidified Britain's alliance with the United States during a cordial
visit with the Roosevelts at Hyde Park. The Kennedys attended the
London Guildhall luncheon for the royal couple, where Rose ate a
bit of roast beef, although it was Friday, when the Catholic Church
required abstinence from meat. Chatting with the archbishop of
Canterbury, she was struck by the British focus on history. Americans looked ahead to the future, as she had witnessed at GM's
World's Fair exhibition. The king addressed the luncheon, "and
everybody said it was his finest speech," wrote Rose, adding that
"his stuttering was not at all noticeable and most people thought he
had gained such confidence from his visit to America from the
approval and applause which had been bestowed on both" him and

Queen Elizabeth. "[He] realized that he was much beloved and very much accepted for his own worth. . . . It was so delightful to see the charming smile of affection and approval the Queen gave him when he had finished speaking, as much as to say, 'Well done.'"[64]

Rose's social whirlwind continued with Eunice's coming-out party at the embassy, featuring dinner and dancing. "About half-past two they all started doing the 'big apple' and everybody got very gay. I was quite surprised and even a little shocked because I had never seen the people reach that state. However, I was assured by some of the chaperones that the party was a huge success. About a quarter of four I asked Ambrose [the orchestra leader] to play 'God Save the King' and everybody stood as straight as a ramrod and the party was over." The Big Apple dance craze peaked in 1939. With its roots in African-American jazz and religious circle dances, no wonder Rose felt somewhat shocked by the partyers' rhythmic gyrations.[65]

That summer, at the All England Club for the Wimbledon championships, Rose had tea with Princess Helena Victoria, who reported that she could no longer afford to donate money to charities. "The race in armaments is taxing us all, and the future looks even bleaker," Rose concluded, reflecting the opinion her husband had expressed in his controversial Trafalgar Day speech.[66] In early July Rose finally wrote of her concern about the impending hostilities: "This is a difficult time because the papers are full of war." Daily stories "about evacuation schemes and lists of supplies which should be stored at home. . . ." filled the British newspapers. Her friend Lady Astor began preparing Cliveden to become a military hospital, as it had been in the Great War, or to serve as an evacuation point for children. The Duchess of Marlborough took similar steps for Blenheim Palace.[67]

The Kennedys escaped London's gloom, taking off for what would be their last prewar holiday, again on the Côte d'Azur. Marlene Dietrich and her family also took their vacation at Eden-Roc, and Joe may have renewed his amorous adventures with her.[68] His audacity in doing so with his family nearby matched his brazenness in forcing Rose to associate with Gloria Swanson. Rose either didn't know about the Marlene-Joe relationship or chose to turn her usual blind eye. This was her marital arrangement. With divorce never an option, she seized all of the positive perks of being married to the man she had fallen desperately in love with as a teenager. Fame, fortune, and the lifestyle they facilitated were her rewards for accepting an unfaithful husband.

The Kennedys' vacation ended abruptly on August 24, when Germany and the Soviet Union signed a nonaggression treaty. It appeared that Hitler's next target would be Poland.[69] Ambassador Kennedy left Cannes for London, where he issued a dire press release advising "American travelers to leave England. We feel it is our duty to warn those Americans now in England that, by remaining any longer, they are running the risk of inconvenience and possibly danger. . . . All those who do not have any important reason for remaining are, therefore, urged to return to the United States without delay. Accommodations are now available on most vessels. The same may not be true in another day or two."[70]

Rose's journal, kept so faithfully during her eighteen months in Europe, now ended. "There was too much to think about, and too many plans to make."[71] She and the children truncated their Riviera holiday and raced back to the embassy after Joe phoned to say they were going home. Rose couldn't know how the magic of their interlude abroad would utterly disintegrate. She would spend the rest of her life trying to recapture it.

❧

CHAPTER 7

Pluperfect Rose

As expected, on Friday, September 1, 1939, Hitler invaded Poland. Joe and Rose, still planning the family's departure, were at the US ambassador's Hertfordshire home. They left on Sunday morning for London, where Rose attended Mass, while Joe hurried to the embassy and listened to Prime Minister Chamberlain's radio broadcast announcing that Britain was now at war. Ambassador Kennedy confided to his diary, "I almost cried. I had participated very closely in this struggle and I saw my hopes crash too." Rose's car arrived from church just as air-raid sirens began to wail. Joe ordered Joe Jr. and Jack to escort their mother across the street to the basement of Molyneux, Rose's favorite couturier. Fortunately, no bombs landed on London. Not recognizing the pun, Joe called the air raid a "dress rehearsal."[1]

Ambassador and Mrs. Kennedy, Joe Jr., Jack, and Kick set out on foot toward Westminster to witness the House of Commons' war declaration. Photographers captured a compelling portrait of the three Kennedy offspring: Joe and Jack handsomely attired in double-breasted suits, Kick in a smart black dress and hat, her pearls swinging to one side; the confident trio seems to stride off the page even seven decades later. Rose, however, suddenly looked all of her forty-nine years of age as she marched to Parliament. The sort of photo she detested, catching her in a bad pose, reveals her vulnerability. Her eyes are askew; the lace collar and cuffs of her dark suit seem matronly.[2]

"Everything I have worked for, everything that I have hoped for, everything that I have believed in during my public life has crashed in ruins," Neville Chamberlain confessed before the Commons.[3] "My heart sank, of course, and my whole world was shattered . . . ," Rose remembered.[4] She felt particularly distraught for the elderly prime minister whom she so admired and who she thought had spared the world from war in 1938. He and her husband had earned considerable enmity for their "appeasement" of the Germans. Now their best efforts to avoid war had come to nothing. In fact, worse than nothing; their policy of placating Hitler only emboldened him. Rose defended her husband, writing later that he was one of many statesmen who urged a peaceful solution to Hitler's aggression. She cited Joe's concerns about the United States' unpreparedness for war. He had, after all, secret knowledge of American naval resources from his tenure at the US Maritime Commission.[5] "Plus there was a great deal of anti-war sentiment in [the United States], and he didn't think it was right to promise help [to Britain] . . . when he knew a lot of people in this country felt the way they did. . . ."[6]

The British government urged parents to evacuate their children from London in case Germany bombed the city. Planning the Kennedys' departure, a nightmare scenario haunted Joe. On September 3 a German U-boat had torpedoed the British liner *Athenia*, bound for Canada with three hundred US citizens aboard. Though rescue efforts minimized the loss of life, Joe worked feverishly to book varied conveyances for his family, so that a German submarine attack on one ship wouldn't decimate the Kennedys. Rose, Kathleen, Eunice, and Bobby returned on the jam-packed American SS *Washington*. Joe Jr. sailed on Britain's *Mauretania*; Jack flew on the new Pan American Airways Yankee Clipper; Jean, Teddy, and Pat sailed with Miss Dunn, the governess, aboard the *United States*. By the end of the month, all but two of the Kennedys (Joe Sr. and Rosemary) were safely on American soil.

Rose and Joe thought it best for Rosemary to remain in England. She had been vacationing at Belmont House, a Catholic abbey, with her aide, Dorothy Gibbs. Located in Hereford, near the Welsh border, they were far away from danger. Yet war news reverberated even in Rosemary's cosseted world. "How is the situation coming along. How do you think about the war," she asked Joe.[7] On the eve of her twenty-first birthday, September 13, 1939, Rosemary wrote in her childlike printing and elementary narrative to her father, asking if she would be returning to the States or would study "in Montessori" at Hertfordshire's Boxmoor, with Mother Isabel.[8]

The Kennedys continued to perpetuate their wishful thinking, with the media and Rosemary herself, that she was taking vocational training to teach young children.[9] So little was understood about mental retardation at the time that the family had always hoped Rosemary could lead a productive life to the extent her abilities allowed. In that desire they actually foreshadowed modern theories of promoting meaningful lives for the disabled. In sometimes thinking that Rosemary wasn't trying hard enough, however, whether it was in her studies or maintaining her weight, Joe and Rose revealed a misunderstanding of her condition.

Joe, who for so many years had happily pursued his business and political careers away from his family, discovered that forced wartime solitude was less desirable. "Now darling, as to me," Joe wrote tenderly to Rose,

> [w]ith all of the family safe in America I have no worries. I will miss you terribly but that can't be helped. With the state of the world I doubt if I could be happy in business as long as I had any money to live on and support my family. . . . Get the children set in a way you will be happy and then take it easy. . . . Well, darling, drop me a line and tell me all the news, there ought to be a few laughs over there and remember you're still the most attractive woman in the world. All my love, always, Joe.[10]

Rose encouraged him to continue writing, in addition to his transatlantic phone calls. The sound of his voice soothed her. If he couldn't travel home, she intended to go back to London.[11] Perhaps because of the distance between them, and Joe's proximity to danger, the couple's letters became noticeably more loving.

Meanwhile, the Kennedy offspring scattered to their various educational institutions. Joe Jr. started law school at Harvard, where Jack returned to complete his undergraduate degree and write his senior thesis on Britain's failure to prepare for war, based on research he had gathered during his six months in Europe. In his Winthrop House suite he placed the Hal Phyfe portrait of Rose, looking beautiful but stern, on the bureau. Kathleen enrolled at Finch, a junior college, and Eunice at her mother's alma mater, Manhattanville College, both in New York. Bobby headed for St. Paul's, an Episcopalian prep school in New Hampshire, where a Harvard classmate of his father was rector. After only a few weeks, though, Bobby transferred to Portsmouth Priory, a Catholic school in Rhode Island. Rose preferred it, and Joe assured her from England, "Whatever you do will turn out OK, so don't worry."[12] Pat, Jean, and Teddy stayed with Rose in Bronxville; the girls returned to Maplehurst Convent, and Teddy enrolled in Lawrence Park Country Day School.

Rose settled into her sedate post-London life, relaxing in the garden, listening to the radio, playing golf, visiting the dentist, and shopping. Unlike her frenetic days as ambassadress, "I seem to have no desire to go to the theater or run around."[13] When she did go to a play, Rose became the object of autograph seekers. Occasionally, she spoke to women's groups about her "experiences as wife-hostess-consort of the American ambassador." Eunice and her mother traveled to Richmond, Virginia, in late September 1939, where Rose "made two marvelous speeches," according to her daughter. Rose had to learn, however, to avoid errors arising from her elite status, such as declaring, "Of course, you're all familiar with Windsor Castle. . . ." That presumptuous introduction to the story of her weekends with the royals prompted one women in a Boston Irish Catholic audience to stage whisper, "What does she mean, 'We're all familiar with Windsor Castle!'"[14] Such lessons about how to relate to the average woman would serve her well in future campaigns.

Joe decided that Rosemary should attend Boxmoor in Hertfordshire and continue working under Mother Isabel in a Montessori course. His daughter's presence north of London seemed to comfort him. "I told Rose[mary] on the phone," Joe wrote to Rose, "[that] she was going to be the one to keep me company, and as this house [also in Hertfordshire] is very handy to her new school, I would invite some of her girl friends and herself down to spend every other weekend with me and I would have a picture show at the house. That tickled her no end. So we will see how that works out. I think I will have the Moores stay over . . . until I see how serious this bombing turns out and then if it gets real bad they can take her home. And in the meantime the Moores can take Rose[mary] out every once in a while and between us all she will be really happy and enjoy herself," Ambassador Kennedy tried to reassure his wife. Although he supervised her care, Rose continued to worry about the small details of her daughter's health, especially her exercise regimen.[15]

Miss Gibbs thanked Ambassador Kennedy for "Rosemary's beautiful 21st birthday" presents, which the nuns had presented her at breakfast and lunch, "so again there was fresh excitement." She wanted to let Joe know that his daughter was "still perfectly happy and very, very well. . . . Everyone clapped her tremendously and she looked so very charming." Gibbs bolstered the Kennedys' hope for a miracle and prayed, "Please God that some day He will grant you all the joy of perfect healing for her."[16] But Joe knew that Rosemary was "not 100% of course. . . ."[17]

By October the ambassador was convinced that he had made the correct decision, to let Rosemary remain abroad. Spending weekends with her, Joe and Mary Moore both remarked on Rosemary's transformation in mind, body, and spirit. She looked "better than she ever did in her life," seemed completely happy to be working with Mother Isabel, and was relaxed. Her time with Joe at the ambassador's country home, with no mother or siblings to intervene, made her feel as though she was the "boss." What a boost to

her self-esteem after her frustrations over never feeling independent. "Mother says I am such a comfort to you," Rosemary reported
to her dad. She so wanted to please him. "Sorry. to think that I am
fat you.think—" Rosemary wrote to Joe in her fractured syntax.
She didn't seem to miss her family but loved "to get letters from the
children telling her how lucky she is to be over here, (tell them to
keep writing that way)," Joe urged Rose.[18]

The Kennedys always searched for ways to make Rosemary feel
special in a clan of celebrated children. Letting her remain in
England, which Rosemary desperately wanted to do, gave her a
sense of privilege. "I feel honor because you chose me to stay,"
wrote Rosemary to her father. She didn't have to compete with her
siblings for attention, and Rosemary thought they were "wild"
with envy.[19] "She is much happier when she sees the children just
casually," Joe concluded. "For everyone['s] peace of mind, particularly hers, she shouldn't go on vacation or anything else with them.
It certainly isn't a hardship when everyone, especially Rose[mary] is
1,000 times better off." Looking to the future, Joe speculated, "I'm
not sure she isn't better staying over here indefinitely with all of us
making our regular trips, as we will be doing, and seeing her then.
I have given her a lot of time and thought and I'm convinced that's
the answer. She must never be at home for her sake as well as everyone's else."[20]

Ambassador Kennedy thought he had discovered the perfect
solution to Rosemary's domestic disruptions, her upset over competition with active siblings, and her potential embarrassment for the
family if the truth about her condition found its way into the press.
Even as late as the 1950s, "[m]ental retardation was viewed as a hopeless, shameful disease, and those afflicted with it were shunned from
sight as soon as possible," writes historian Edward Shorter.[21] The
Kennedys had already resisted prevailing norms by giving Rosemary
a home life, as well as stimulating opportunities beyond it. Keeping
her active, happy, and fulfilled in the English countryside, far away
from prying British and American media, seemed to be the answer.
Rose's response to Joe's strategy remains unclear. Perhaps she and Joe
spoke of it by phone, but her surviving letters don't.

Far from his family and facing professional uncertainty as his differences with Roosevelt over the war became more pronounced, Joe reached out to his spouse: "I am sick of everybody [in England] and so I'm alone tonight by choice. It's funny that nobody in the world can be with me very long without boring me to death. I just can't help it. You are the only individual in the world that I love more every day. I'm sorry I'm not there for our 25th [anniversary;] to say they have been great years is [an] understatement. They've been the happy years that poets write about. I would like to live every day of them over again with you, but wouldn't want to live one more without you. So Darling, we'll celebrate when I get home. I love you devotedly. This job without you is comparable with a street cleaner's at home." In a funk, he told Rose, "I'm convinced more than ever that you, not I, made the 25 years a success."[22]

Joe rejoined his family for Christmas 1939, staying for several months in the States. Some American reporters still touted him as a potential 1940 presidential nominee. Publicly, Joe always claimed no interest, and Rose maintained that she and her husband never really discussed the possibility. In fact, she dismissed the idea years later: "I don't remember very much about that. The job he really wanted was secretary of the treasury, which he would have enjoyed. I know he didn't respond to making speeches . . . and a lot of things connected with the presidency. They didn't appeal to him as much as they did to Jack or my father, for instance. The financial situation all over the world, finances of the United States, that was more down his alley. . . . I never heard the presidential move talked about very much."[23]

HEADING BACK TO England by way of Italy and France in March 1940, Joe spent most of the voyage in bed with a fever. He reported to Rose that Clare Boothe Luce was aboard, bound for Europe to gather material about the war for a *Life* magazine feature, which eventually became the book *Europe in the Spring*. According to Clare's biographer, Sylvia Morris, Joe may have used a new country getaway, in Windsor, loaned to him by US car mogul Horace

Dodge, for trysts with Boothe Luce.[24] This was Joe's womanizing modus operandi: to be open about his "friendships"; even if Rose knew of his serial philandering, she could never divorce him.

While telling Rose, "I just need my family," he discouraged them from returning.[25] His expressed rationale was that they would be offended by the Brits' anti-Americanism, prompted by the United States' neutrality. Yet by April 1940 he missed Rose so much that he reevaluated his position on her visit. "[Y]ou could stop off in Paris for a few days before coming over to London," he suggested. Suffering from an upset "tummy," he bemoaned eating the "wrong things" in Paris. "Well, my darling I guess it's right [that] nothing is perfect in this life and I just don't like being so completely away from you. Yet knowing myself as I do when I've been home 6 months I'll want to get going again. Maybe old age and a bad stomach will change me. I don't know. I guess I'm a restless soul: Some people call it ambition. I guess I'm just *nuts*! Nevertheless, I love you so much. Joe."[26] At age fifty-one, the ambassador seemed to be suffering a delayed midlife crisis over his uncertain future.[27]

Rosemary, too, worried about her future, comprehending that her English adventure might be truncated because of the war. "I am dreadfully sorry about leaving. I will cry a lot," she told her father.[28] That was the wrong admission. Kennedys were raised under Joe's edict, "There'll be no crying in this house." Rose, too, usually displayed epic restraint, holding back tears in front of her family or household staff. Telling Joe about her tearfulness would earn Rosemary no sympathy. Joe's ban had "the force of moral law," according to Teddy. "[A]ll of us absorbed its import and molded our behavior to honor it. . . . To understand the profound authority of this charge to us is to understand much about my family."[29]

Rose searched for some way to see Joe, and bring Rosemary home, in May 1940. Trying to organize affairs in Bronxville while preparing the Kennedys' summer home at Hyannis was burdensome. Edward Moore, always a help with the children and logistics, remained in England with Rosemary. The children's governess had left, Nurse Hennessey had fallen ill, and Rose's secretary had taken another position. Even so, Rose prepared to leave for England on

May 10, the very day the Battle of France began, forcing the British retreat to Dunkirk's beaches. "It seemed like taking too many chances. I am still hoping I may go a little later, which will be better for me," she informed Joe.[30] Years later, Rose remembered this frightening time: "[W]e decided it was too dangerous because, if both of us were together in London and were bombed, it would have left nine orphans under the age of 25."[31]

"I'm heartbroken," Ambassador Kennedy replied to Rose's news, "but you just couldn't be here." As for the Nazi offensive on the Western Front, "I think the jig is up," Joe reported. "The situation is more than critical. It means a terrible finish for the Allies. I'm planning to get Rose[mary] and the Moores out either to Ireland or Lisbon. We will be in for a terrific bombing pretty soon and I'll do better if I just have myself to look after. The English will fight to the end but I don't think they can stand up to the bombing indefinitely." Joe had consistently given Britain long odds against Germany. He predicted a "dictated peace" in which the Nazis would get the British Navy, "and we will find ourselves in a terrible mess. My God how right I've been on my predictions. I wish I'd been wrong."[32] After cancelling her trip to England, Rose departed for West Virginia's Greenbrier Inn, where she and Joe had spent part of their 1914 honeymoon.

On June 1, 1940, Rose told Joe that she wished he had left with Rosemary and the Moores the previous week.

> I am hoping and praying that somehow or other, I shall see you soon. I suppose we are infinitely better off than thousands of other people. I do hope your tummie [*sic*] is not too awful—but of all places to be! There seems not much more to be said. It was such a wonderful experience, and as I said to the children . . . so few youngsters their age have seen the old Europe. But you are so important to me—my darling—so do take care of yourself the best way you can & we shall just keep on praying.

The short note crystallized Rose's essence. As the European war crept closer to her home and hearth, she continued to focus on the

details of her husband's health and her children's worldly opportunities, while placing her larger concerns in God's hands. "I believe
you said you had got to church all right. At this time of my life
there need be no mental reservations," Rose wrote to Joe.[33]

Ambassador Kennedy missed Jack's 1940 Harvard graduation,
but Rose, Eunice, Bobby, Rosemary, and Kathleen attended. Jack's
irresponsibility in failing to plan the family's visit rankled his
mother, but she was proud of his looks: "He was really very handsome in his cap and gown as he had a tan which made him look
healthy and he has got a wonderful smile."[34] The once indifferent
student had earned magna cum laude on his thesis, "Appeasement
at Munich," allowing him to graduate cum laude. With his father's
help, Jack had it published as a book, *Why England Slept*. Displaying
his wry humor, he inscribed Rose's copy: "To Mrs. K. Who in
spite of her many houses and many children manages to retain that
charm which causes us to echo John F. Fitzgerald's trumpet, 'Get a
girl like your mother!' Jack."[35] His inscription to the Kennedys'
longtime governess was equally witty: "To Kiko who was always
going to 'tell my father the moment he stepped into the house'—
but never did!—With love from 'that bold stump'—Jack Kennedy."[36] JFK biographers who suspect a distant relationship between
Rose and Jack could cite "With love," in his inscription to Kiko
and its absence in his mother's copy.[37]

WITH ROSEMARY BACK in the States, Edward Moore began investigating new places for her to study and receive supervision. An
Assumption convent outside Philadelphia seemed to be the perfect
spot. Its facilities and surroundings were more commodious than
those at Noroton, the Sacred Heart school in Connecticut that
Kathleen and Eunice attended. Several Assumption nuns had connections to the sisters Rosemary loved in England. Moore crypti-
cally suggested that "Miss Dunn [the Kennedys' governess] . . .
could discuss some of the more intimate matters [about Rosemary]
with the Reverend Mother. . . ."[38] As Rosemary moved into adulthood, desiring more freedom and male companionship, her parents

worried for her safety. They sent her to Camp Fernwood, in the Berkshires, for the summer of 1940, where she served as a junior counselor, teaching arts and crafts to young children.[39]

For the first time, Joe saw Rosemary as an adult and used more mature language in correspondence:

> It looks to me like all the rest of the Kennedys are still going to school, including the boys, while my eldest daughter is out working. I . . . have talked to Mother Isabel on the telephone and she is very anxious to have the war over soon so that you will be able to come back and take up your duties with her. . . . Mother Isabel is hoping that while you are waiting to come back to England to work with her, you will be going to the Assumption Convent in Philadelphia to continue your work, because she is very anxious to have you continue with the Assumption nuns since the other [Kennedy] girls are with Sacred Heart [nuns]. . . . Give my love to all and keep right on working and setting a good example for your brothers and sisters.[40]

Even with Nazi bombs raining down on Britain, Joe took time to encourage Rosemary to further her schooling "so that you may be able to do that teaching that you hope to do when you are over here." The next week he cabled, "You see, darling, with all the bombs I couldn't forget your birthday. My love to my oldest daughter and many happy returns."[41] Ultimately, the Kennedys decided to send Rosemary to St. Gertrude's School of Arts and Crafts in Washington to practice some of the basic teaching skills she had learned in England.

Joe's London life grew increasingly precarious. Dodging Luftwaffe bombs, marginalized by Prime Minister Winston Churchill's new Conservative government, "thoroughly disgusted" with FDR's approach to the war, and missing his family, Joe longed to leave. He kept Rose apprised of his medical condition, assuring her that he felt amazingly well and had even regained weight lost under stress. He was sticking to his bland diet and had stopped taking belladonna, a plant-based drug prescribed for peptic ulcers.

Only "occasionally" did he have to take an antispasmodic for gastrointestinal distress. Joe also found time for recreation, attending Clare Boothe Luce's new play, *Margin for Error*. On entering the theater, he received a round of applause from the British audience. Yet he knew that his popularity was fleeting at home and abroad. He wished he could simply depart. Most other American ambassadors in Europe had already gone. "[B]ut I don't want to do anything that would reflect [poorly] on the family," Joe reasoned. "After all that is why we went into this [ambassadorship], and I don't want to spoil it. . . ."[42]

For Joe's fifty-second birthday, Rose sent a recording of the children's musical greetings. He reported playing "it at least twenty times already. . . . And incidentally your piano touch was never better." German bombing raids intensified. One night a bomb hit 250 yards from his Windsor retreat, and the embassy had a closer call. From the roof of the US chancery, Joe could see St. Paul's Cathedral dome silhouetted against the burning sky. He shared his fatalism with Rose: "I don't think anything is going to happen to me, and for that reason it doesn't worry me the slightest bit." What did she think, he asked: should he stay at his dangerous post or come home?[43]

As the 1940 presidential election approached, and Roosevelt finally tossed his fedora in the ring for an unprecedented third term, Rose wrote an uncharacteristically political letter to her husband after consulting with his friend and attorney John Burns. Rose recognized that the president wanted to keep Joe in England, where his "explosive, defeatist point of view" would be less likely to "upset" FDR's reelection. Rose offered to go "to the W[hite] H[ouse] as a wife, say I am worried about your health, think you have done enough, guarantee to chloroform you until after the election and say you should be brought home."[44]

Finally, in mid-October 1940, FDR summoned Joe home for "some relief" and to learn his "last reactions with regard to the war in England."[45] Roosevelt invited him and Rose to spend the night at the White House, and they gathered for drinks in the president's study along with his secretary, Missy LeHand, and South Carolina senator Jimmy Byrnes and his wife. The president wielded his cocktail shaker and spoke informally, but Rose thought he looked pale and had a "habit of nervously snapping his eyes."[46]

After libations, the small party had a simple supper of scrambled eggs, sausage, toast, and rice pudding. Perhaps the White House chef knew of the Kennedys' preference for bland meals. Politics was on the agenda. Byrnes suggested that Joe deliver a radio address supporting FDR's bid for an unprecedented third term. At first Joe balked, complaining about how the administration had mistreated him. "The president worked very hard on Rose, whom I suspect he had come down [to Washington] because of her great influence on me," Joe thought.[47] FDR told her flattering stories about Honey Fitz. Rose recognized the manipulation, but she couldn't resist Roosevelt's charm. Both Joe and Rose agreed to endorse the president on radio just before the election.[48]

Using his own money to buy airtime on 114 CBS radio affiliates, Ambassador Kennedy expressed his pessimism about the European war. He and his wife had "given nine hostages to fortune. Our children and your children are more important than anything else in the world. The kind of America that they and their children will inherit is of grave concern to us all. In light of these considerations, I believe that Franklin D. Roosevelt should be reelected President of the United States."[49]

Rose's brief radio endorsement of the president started where Joe's had ended:

> I am the mother of nine children. Four are boys, Joe, Jack, Bobby, and Ted. I love those boys, although I have no monopoly on motherhood; I do have a big share of it. Like all of you other American mothers, I want to vote for a president, who will keep your boys and mine out of war, and who will make this country so strong in its defense, that never again will I have to see gas masks on my children, as I did in London. I shall never forget war torn London and England and the courage and spirit of its people. Nor will I forget the gallantry of those English lads. American youth, too, has devotion and gallantry

and bravery. It, too, is entitled to the best defense and training
in the world. Therefore, on next Tuesday I feel I have a solemn
duty to my sons and to all the sons of all the mothers of America to vote for Franklin Roosevelt and the road to peace.[50]

Rose's public image over the past two years had been entwined
with her nine children. Now she and her husband made them the
centerpiece of a "family values" argument to reelect FDR. Roosevelt embraced the theme, proclaiming at a pre-election Boston
Garden rally, attended by Honey Fitz and Jack, "Your boys will not
be sent into any foreign wars."[51]

Rose's files are silent about who wrote her endorsement, but it
appears that she deleted its last few lines from her radio broadcast:
"It is impossible for me to understand all of the issues of the campaign. I do feel confidence in Mr. Roosevelt because of his long
experience and because of the valiant efforts already launched for
our defense."[52] Perhaps she thought the first sentence offensive to
her and other women. She was no Eleanor Roosevelt, deeply
immersed in public policy, but she understood issues. And she certainly possessed a genetic feel for politics.

Joe submitted his resignation to President Roosevelt a day after
the election, but FDR asked him to keep the ambassadorial title
until the administration named his successor. As of February 1941,
Joe's tenure at the Court of St. James's officially ended. The war
years would stand in stark contrast to heady weekends at Windsor
Castle, dinners with kings and queens, audiences with the pope,
and Riviera family vacations. And through a self-inflicted wound,
Joe Kennedy banished himself to the political wilderness for the
rest of his life. Thinking that an interview with the *Boston Globe*
was off the record, Kennedy opined, "Democracy is finished in
England. It may be here, too."[53] That quote, and several derogatory
statements about Eleanor Roosevelt as well as the British cabinet,
appeared on the *Globe*'s front page and made its way into the
English press. Joe's undiplomatic comments permanently relegated
him to the political sidelines, where his wife joined him, at least for
a while.

The sidelines turned out to be literal. At the 1941 Foreign Service football game in Miami, Mrs. Kennedy sat with hoi polloi.

[I]t seemed so strange to sit with the rank and file of Americans again. Every possible type of person was around me. . . . A woman well and expensively dressed in summer clothes with a couple of children was next to me, all of whom were vigorously eating peanuts. Behind me were a half a dozen football fans, clad in flashy sport coats who were shrieking . . . at anything and everything long before the game commenced. . . . Girls and women were talking loudly, calling back and forth, men were bandying bets back and forth about the players and the game. . . .[54]

Hardly the royal box at Wimbledon.

Another of Joe's decisions further separated Rose and him from the centers of American political and social power. Joe no longer wanted to maintain three homes.[55] He sold the Bronxville estate in late 1941. Henceforth, the Kennedys would live in Palm Beach from Christmas through Easter and at Hyannis Port from late spring through Thanksgiving. Rose left Bronxville feeling rather nostalgic, telling her children, "[Y]ou all grew up there very happily. . . ." But she was a pragmatist: "I am relieved too to have one less house to worry about; with none of you there, the house was no longer a necessity. So today I feel quite relieved and very free with nothing on my mind except the shades of blue for my Palm Beach trousseau."[56]

Teddy suffered most as his parents followed the sun from Florida to Cape Cod and back. In the spring of 1941 Rose had decided to send him to boarding school although he was only nine, much younger than his three brothers had been when they went away to school. Because of his youth, Rose had Teddy join Bobby at Portsmouth Priory. It was an odd decision; the Rhode Island school started with seventh grade, four levels ahead of Teddy. Thus began Teddy's academic odyssey that "did not prove to be happy, joyous years," according to his memoir. All told, he attended nine schools prior to settling at Milton Academy, outside Boston, for high school. During these years, his cheerful disposition—for which his mother took credit—turned to loneliness and despair, often triggered by bullying and abuse at the hands of older students and dorm masters. Too ashamed to tell his mother, he rejoiced when she took him and Jean with her to Palm Beach each winter and enrolled them in day school there.[57] Peripatetic Rose admitted years later that Teddy had changed schools "too much."[58] She had drawn the line at taking the children to California in the 1920s or to Washington in the 1930s, when Joe's work took him away from Boston and New York. As noted previously, moving seven children to different doctors and orthodontists was her stated reason for not following; living separately from him also reduced her pregnancies. Now age fifty, however, Rose needed more rest, and she reduced her maternal duties by sending the youngest children away to school.

Rose struggled with a common parental tension. She had fond memories of early motherhood, but grown offspring in her home disrupted her preferred solitary routines. Yet she missed them after they departed. After their annual Palm Beach Christmas in 1940, she wrote,

Dear Children: We have missed you all very much since you left, although I must say while you were here it seemed a little more hectic than usual. When you all were little and I could regiment you and have you all come and leave at a certain time and at the same time, and when I was sure of what clothes you were going to wear and how you were going to have your hair cut (Kathleen) and what hat you were going to wear, it seemed to me much more simple. However, time marches on and I suppose I must get used to the new uncertainties and excitement.[59]

Now Rose faced her own midlife crisis, complicated by empty-nest syndrome as well as Rosemary's struggle in adjusting to life after England. "She started to deteriorate," Eunice explained years later, observing that Rosemary "was high strung and had quite a lot of temper tantrums all the time, and she had some epileptic attacks."

Doctors would rush to the house with injections to calm her. The family arrangements that Rose had made over twenty-one years for her retarded daughter were becoming unfeasible. Rose had spent considerable time with young Rosemary, but she also relied on Eunice, particularly, to help entertain her slower sister. "[S]he [would] say to me, 'Will you play tennis with Rosemary?' Eunice recalled. "She wasn't very good, Rosemary, but I played tennis with her. Or [Mother] would say, 'Would you take her sailing, racing?' I was quite good at racing in those days so I handled a boat all right by myself, so I would take Rosemary. Then I'd tell my mother she did well on the boat and she was pleased." Eunice emphasized, "Rosemary was never hidden away or anything. She was pushed right on. She would come with me. . . . And even though she was slow, she was always given every opportunity that everybody was given."[60] But now Rosemary was a woman of twenty-one, with a child's mental capacity. Planning tennis or sailing outings simply wouldn't solve Rosemary's deterioration.

Until 1941 or so, the family tried to "jolly Rosemary along, and she laughed, she was always rather jolly, not that we weren't terribly serious about her problem," Eunice explained. "Like Jack would be told to take her to a dance, and he would take her and kid with [his friend] LeMoyne Billings, and they [would] take turns dancing with her. She'd come home at mid-night, and he'd go back to the dance."[61] "Why don't other boys ask me to dance?" Rosemary would inquire from the time she was a teenager.[62] Instead, she had to attend dances with her popular brother and his gay friend, who would then bring her home and return to the party without her. How frustrated would Rosemary have felt, after the excitement and semblance of independence during her life in England, to be patronized by her parents and siblings—no matter how well intentioned their efforts?

According to Billings, Rosemary "became aggressively unhappy, irritable," even physically and verbally abusive upon returning from Britain. Of most concern to the family, she would wander away from caretakers, especially at night. As we have seen, since the Lindbergh baby kidnapping and murder, Rose had worried about the safety of her children. The possibility that men would take advantage of Rosemary added to Rose and Joe's fears.[63] As Catholics, they presumably wouldn't have sterilized their daughter, a common procedure for the "feeble-minded."

Rose's pattern of removing herself from stress now returned in full force. In April 1941 she decided to explore South America. Distracting herself from the impending entrance of the United States into the war and worries over Rosemary, Rose prepared to leave for a five-week trip in two hemispheres that would require clothing for two different seasons. She and Eunice, who would accompany her, also had to receive vaccinations for smallpox and typhoid. "I must be a gypsy at heart," Rose told Joe, "because I get such a thrill out of it all no matter how uncomfortable I may be—which was the case yesterday when I felt the reaction from my typhoid inoculation."[64]

Thus began another of Rose's anthropological observations about the people, clothing, food, topography, religion, and sights encountered on her travels. Yet Rose's comments reveal more about her than about the people she observed. For instance, the Latin American passengers bidding farewell to their families on shore "were much more demonstrative and more unashamed of their tears," so different from the Kennedys' Yankee stoicism. The small ship compared poorly with the "trans-Atlantic deluxe steamers" that Rose preferred. She was pleased, however, when a Dominican priest on board told her that Argentina's constitution required its president to be a Catholic. That "evened things up," because in New York she had heard so often that a Catholic couldn't become president of the United States.[65]

In Barbados, Rose and Eunice were surprised to see "colored and white children sitting together" at an Ursuline convent school. "The nun said the sisters took them because one could not discriminate and they seemed to get on quite happily together, the children making their own friends as they chose. . . . Was struck by the cleanliness of all the children. They looked so scrubbed and immaculate, and I blushed when I though of my little Teddy when he rushed to school some days." She discovered several children saying their prayers. "I have seldom been so moved; to see that group of dark skinned, little faces, with those immense, trustful, gentle brown eyes raised in prayer, convinced me for all time that there must be angels with dark faces as well as light ones, although I have never thought of them before."[66]

In Rio, Jack, who had left Stanford Business School after just one term, joined his mother and Eunice for a few days of sightseeing and took in the famous Christ the Redeemer statue overlooking Rio and a funicular ride to the top of Sugar Loaf Mountain. Yet, Rose concluded, "Not anything of special historical interest in South America compared with all the multitude of things in Europe and those monuments which there are mean little to us, since we are unacquainted with history while in England or Italy we are familiar with most of the landmarks through study and experience of our friends."[67] Eurocentric, to be sure, yet at least Rose now added Hispanic and indigenous cultures to her experiences.

Eunice and her mother pressed on to Buenos Aires, where Rose found the Argentines "not a well-proportioned, handsome, virile looking race." They seemed "short, pudgy, and once they reach maturity, they seem to be heavy, coarse-looking, fat." In contrast, she had thought the women in Rio "were quite chic and smart," as in Biarritz or Cannes. After crossing the "dreary and bleak" Andes and spending a few days in Chile, they proceeded up the west coast of South America to Peru and Ecuador. When fog stranded them just outside Lima, Rose and Eunice explored a small village. "Never saw such poverty," Rose wrote. "[C]hildren barefooted—dressed in dirty rags, living in shacks without roofs made of reeds, with goats and mules living alongside. Still they seemed happy. . . . They had small Indian faces—broad, brown and patient." Rose's determination never wavered, despite delays, snowy weather, and primitive airports. She displayed an adventurous streak that differentiated her from most women of her age and background. Rather than return by ship, Rose and Eunice caught a flight in Quito for the United States and went straight to Cape Cod "just in time to get almost the full benefit of a Cape Cod summer."[68]

IN THE LAST few months before Pearl Harbor, the older Kennedy children scattered again. After two years at Harvard Law School, Joe Jr. headed to the US Naval Air Station in Jacksonville, Florida, for pilot training and to earn his officer's commission.[69] Ambassador Kennedy, pulling strings with an American naval attaché whom he had known in London, enabled Jack to bypass medical requirements and become a Navy ensign with an intelligence assignment in Washington. Rose could take pride that her "republican motherhood" had produced two sons now in service to their country. As for the girls, Kick served on the staff of the *Washington Times-Herald*, a position arranged by another of her father's friends.[70] She pined for her days in England and Billy Hartington, with whom she had fallen deeply in love. Eunice transferred to Stanford University in hopes that the warmer California weather would prove more healthful. Like her parents and Jack, Eunice suffered from digestive upsets and a tendency to lose weight.

That fall Joe Sr. made a decision that would haunt the Kennedys forever. He had heard of a new psychosurgical procedure, first used by Portuguese physician António Egas Moniz, that severed neural connections in the brain's prefrontal lobes. The surgery, called a leucotomy (from the leucotome instrument used in the procedure), and, later, lobotomy, reportedly might relieve patients of psychiatric illnesses, especially "agitated depression." By 1936 two American doctors, Walter Freeman and James Watts, began performing leucotomies, with alarmingly variable effects, at George Washington University Hospital in Washington, DC. The American Medical Association warned in 1941 that mutilating a part of the brain by definition couldn't "restore the person concerned to a wholly normal state." Yet at the time no other medical governing body questioned the procedure. Moreover, Freeman, a neurologist and psychiatrist, and Watts, a neurosurgeon, never claimed that lobotomies would produce restorative results. They simply promoted it as the final resort for seemingly hopeless cases of mental illness. Pharmaceutical therapies were, of course, decades away. British neurosurgeons, typically more conservative than their American counterparts, began using the procedure in 1941.[71]

In the fall of that year Joe Kennedy, without Rose's approval, subjected Rosemary to the psychosurgery hoping that it would provide a cure for her agitation and violent outbursts. It failed and undid all of the progress she had made with the family's loving support and attention. Reduced by it to a childlike state, Rosemary now required constant custodial care. The one thing that Joe had vowed never to do—institutionalize Rosemary—he now had to force upon her. She disappeared from the family and, for most of the 1940s, lived at Craig House, a psychiatric hospital in Beacon, New York. In 1949 Joe, with Boston Archbishop Richard Cushing's guidance, quietly sent her to reside at St. Coletta School for Exceptional Children, in Jefferson, Wisconsin, where nuns cared for her.[72]

The story about Rosemary that the Kennedys had offered while in England—that she would be a teacher—simply continued. When she disappeared from view, they told the press that she was continuing her studies. Such a secret could never be maintained in today's ubiquitous media culture, but, amazingly, it worked in the 1940s and '50s. More heartbreaking was Joe's ban on visits with Rosemary. He told the family that she had to be institutionalized because they could no longer care for her. Even Rose couldn't see her, he said, because Rosemary had to get used to her surroundings without disruptions from home.[73]

Only in 1962 did Eunice admit, in a *Saturday Evening Post* article on mental retardation, that her sister had been institutionalized twenty-one years earlier. No mention was made of the surgery.[74] Dr. Moniz won a 1949 Nobel Prize for pioneering the procedure, but by 1955 it had fallen into disrepute. Twelve years after Eunice's article, Rose publically acknowledged that Rosemary had undergone "a certain form of neurosurgery" for "tantrums, or rages" and "convulsive episodes." She wrote that she and Joe had "brought into consultation the most eminent medical specialists," who had recommended the operation. Rose didn't elaborate, however, on her husband's ultimate decision. Kennedy biographer Laurence

Leamer believes that Rose had asked Kathleen to investigate the surgery and that they both decided it wasn't appropriate for Rosemary.[75] Comments to Doris Kearns Goodwin reveal Rose's unvarnished feelings: "I will never forgive Joe for that awful operation he had performed on Rosemary. It is the only thing I have ever felt bitter towards him about."[76]

Rose's 1972 comments to Robert Coughlan, her memoirist, are also revealing. She described Rosemary's having had "an accident . . . in which her brain was further damaged, and so [it] was found expedient and necessary, really better, for her to go to this home in Wisconsin where she is very well taken care of with the nuns of St. Coletta." Coughlan gently pressed: "You don't want to say anything about the accident." "No," Rose replied. "Her mind is gone completely."[77] When Coughlan followed up with Eunice several weeks later, she used the same term, "accident," to describe the reason Rosemary had to be institutionalized. The Kennedy Library's interview transcript blacked out Mrs. Shriver's forty-year-old response and her reference to Rosemary's "labadomy," which, she said, doctors had recommended. Granting a scholar's 2011 request, the library finally removed the redaction, allowing Eunice, now deceased, to confirm the surgery that ended any hope of Rosemary leading a productive life. "We couldn't dream of letting her live alone; she couldn't function at all in the outside world," including "in a workshop," Eunice had sadly explained.[78]

Not commenting directly about Joe's decision to lobotomize Rosemary, but about his dominant role in the family, Rose explained in 1972 why she accepted her husband's influence in a very traditional marriage:

I married a man who I felt made very good decisions. Who was almost infallible. My sons thought he was almost infallible. Because over the years his judgment was so perfect that what he foretold did happen. And in finance and in people and so I relied on that more or less, because I was brought up that way. Your husband worked hard, and he had a good many difficulties during his business day and when he came home he wanted to have comfort and peace and love and affection. He didn't want to be bothered, and he didn't want a cocky wife or a complaining wife. And I had all day to rest and enjoy myself outside, and, if he wanted to stay in or if he wanted to do something I was ready and expected that was my role. And as I said when the children were ill or I was ill and he was in California working [in the 1920s] I never told him.[79]

This obsequious posture, typical of many women in Rose's era, would only have encouraged Joe to wield familial power without reservation. Moreover, although Rose typically kept track of the young children's basic medical records and illnesses (through her famous card file), her husband clearly managed the more complex health issues as they matured. When Jack fell ill with mysterious gastrointestinal problems and a low blood count during college, Joe handled the physicians and supervised JFK's care. He also helped Jack finesse his physical handicaps, including back injuries from football, to enter the Navy. No evidence from Rose exists, at least in written form, to indicate that she questioned Joe's decisions to keep Rosemary in England or to remove her from most family gatherings and vacations. Moreover, Rose and her husband participated in efforts to protect one another from bad news. She didn't even want to bother her husband when she gave birth to their children.

WHAT REMAINED OF Joe's public life consisted primarily of commencement speeches, where he began to soften the anti-interventionist rhetoric that had cost him a future political career. Just after the Japanese attack on Pearl Harbor, he wired FDR: "Name the Battle Post, I'm Yours to Command," but the president offered nothing that appealed to the ex-ambassador.[80]

With Eunice studying sociology at Stanford, and the world at war, Rose began to explore the American West, reachable from Florida in less than a day by air. At age fifty-one, Rose told her children that the easier mode of travel "would be less tiring for me, as I seem to tire easily now."[81] In the spring of 1942 she fell in love with Palo Alto's Spanish architecture, Stanford's date palm trees, and northern California's temperate climate. "I feel much peppier than in the South. It is also much less expensive than in N.Y.—so come the Revolution—I know just where to go," she quipped. Always pursuing self-improvement, Rose attended courses with Eunice and began contemplating an autobiography: "I am thinking of a name for my memoirs and as [actress] Ilka Chase named hers *Past Imperfect* I thought mine might be *Past Pluperfect*."[82] The title, with its play on a verb tense, may have been an inside joke with her children, whose grammar she frequently corrected. But how absolutely essential that she described her life as "more than perfect; supremely accomplished; ideal," according to pluperfect's other denotation.[83]

During the war, as her children went their separate ways, Rose became, more than ever, the central family correspondent, writing round-robin letters to all of the Kennedys. Jack, now a best-selling author, could not help needling his mother over her famous efficiency: "I am saving [the letters] to publish—that style of yours will net us millions . . . it's enough to make a man get down on his knees and thank God for the Dorchester High Latin School which gave you that very sound grammar basis which shines through every slightly mixed metaphor and each somewhat split infinitive." Knowing that his mother would want a medical report, even from a grown man in the US Navy, he closed, "My health is excellent—I look like hell, but my stomach is a thing of beauty—as are you, Ma,—and you, unlike my stomach—will be a joy forever."[84]

Bobby, now sixteen, received special attention from his mother for earning poor grades, especially in Christian Doctrine. After all, why had she sent him to Catholic school except to learn about his religious faith? Rose also urged him to take dance lessons because they would boost his confidence, although he loathed them.[85] Joe Jr., approaching his late twenties, received advice regarding his Lenten observance. He had told Honey Fitz that he planned to give up candy for the pre-Easter season of self-denial, but Mother thought that a bad idea: he had lost too much weight, it would put

candy-makers out of work (according to the Catholic Church), and
it would be better to do something positive, such as "say a Rosary
occasionally." If he had to abjure a treat, she suggested Coca-Cola:
"[Y]ou know that I am thinking about you and always hoping that
you are having the best possible break whether it is worldly or spiritual."[86] Young Joe wrote his mother faithfully, ending one letter,
"There is nothing new in the girl situation, but I'm still hopin to
find a gal like you."[87] Though using a teasing vernacular, both Joe
Jr. and Jack demonstrated a gallant devotion to their mother that
must have pleased Rose.

On the home front she tried to do her small part for the war
effort, taking a first-aid course in Palm Beach. A letter written in
early 1942 reveals her tendency to become involved in the mundane
details of her children's lives, her sense of entitlement, and her frustration at playing second fiddle to her husband. She reported to her
children that young Joe had received "five hours' marching and ten
demerits for having a dirty wastebasket" at the Naval Air Station. "I
think it is very unfair myself and I wanted to write a letter to the
Navy Department and the War Board and some Commanders—
and maybe Mr. Roosevelt himself. . . . [B]ut your father has again
restricted my activities and thinks the little woman should confine
herself to the home. Personally, I think it shows [an] antiquated system with emphasis made on the unessentials, and after all, there are
times when a woman should show initiative, even to the extent of
counseling the Navy Department to use common sense in disci-
plinary methods." Parenthetically, Rose added, "This, of course, is
all in fun, and don't discuss it outside of the family circle."[88]

But perhaps more than fun was involved here. Joe Jr. was her
perfect firstborn. How could the Navy treat him so inequitably?
Didn't her husband's position as former ambassador to England
count for something? Did Rose believe that she could not seriously
critique the role of women in American households, especially her
own? She made these private comments only a few short months
after her husband's unilateral decision to lobotomize Rosemary. As
we have seen, Rose expressed a very different image of her marriage for public consumption in her 1972 interview with Robert

Coughlan, describing her husband as "almost infallible." (That view also absolved her of any complicity in Joe's treatment of Rosemary.) Many years later, in a lighthearted exchange with granddaughter Caroline Kennedy about marital differences, Rose claimed that she and Joe didn't quarrel. "I would just say, 'Yes, dear,' and then I'd go to Paris."[89]

Rose soon had an opportunity to apply her first-aid lessons. In 1942 ten-year-old Teddy, now at Riverdale School, contracted whooping cough and pneumonia. From a New York hospital, she brought him to Hyannis Port for recuperation. "This was the first time since infancy that I really had my mother to myself," Teddy recalled, "and the first time I enjoyed such close attention from her, and I basked in it. We took long walks on the nearly deserted beach together . . . and in the evenings she would read to me: books on science, history, geography, and the occasional adventure from Jack London or Sir Walter Scott. . . . But more than any specific activity, it was my mother's constant tenderness and attention that I cherished." He concluded, "As sick as I was, those days were a tonic for me. And they cemented a special bond between my mother and me that survived until her death. . . ."[90] Such devoted caretaking showed Rose at her maternal best.

As for Kathleen, who had been promoted from her *Times-Herald* secretarial position to society columnist, Rose wrote to her in fall 1942 from Los Angeles, "I can see improvement in your column, . . . so you are certainly to be congratulated." Nevertheless, Rose had found errors that "were probably typographical, but as people notice your English now, I want to be sure they are familiar to you." Interspersed were Hollywood tidbits. Rose had taken tea with Mary Pickford and seen Joan Crawford, Robert Montgomery, and William Powell at MGM's studio. She would spend Christmas with Eunice at Sun Valley but longed for a family holiday in Palm Beach. "Now that I am rested, I have a strange nostalgia for all the excitement and confusion and turmoil [at home]." "Much love to you, dear Kathleen and do keep writing. . . . I am planning to see you in Washington on my return. Love again, darling, Mother."[91]

As the United States sank deeper into war across two theaters,

Rose worried about her sons' spiritual lives. Jack wrote to her from his new post in Charleston, South Carolina, that the Navy Yard had given him an extracurricular religious assignment that he asked Rose to review. Always less formal in tone than Joe Jr., who only referred to Rose as "Mother," Jack began, "Dear Ma: Thank you for your latest chapter on the '9 Little Kennedys and How They Grew,' by Rose of Old Boston. Never in history have so many owed so much to such a one—or is that quite correct," Jack teased. He joked that she might want to verify the quotation in her book of sayings under "Churchill, Winston." "You now really have the obligations of Motherhood—with none of the pleasures (the pleasures that is of seeing all of us and [Lem] Billings.)" Although she took her maternal role very seriously and knew that her brood of nine added to her celebrity, Jack used it as a humorous foil. Was his following discussion of Catholicism, the most profound element of Rose's life, another way to tweak her? "They want me to conduct Bible class here every other Sunday for about ½ hour with the sailors. Would you say that is un-Catholic? I have a feeling that dogma might say it was—but don't good works come under our obligations to the Catholic Church? We're not a completely ritualistic, formalistic, hierarchical structure in which the Word, the truth, must only come down from the very top—a structure that allows for no individual interpretation—or are we. [The Catholic Church was exactly as Jack described it.] However, don't worry about this—just send me Father Conway's Question Box as I would like to look through it. . . . Love from your Lt. son, John."[92]

In February 1943 Rose wrote to Joe Jr., now stationed in Puerto Rico, with a simple request: "I hope you are still saying your prayers when you are hopping about in all those different countries. I got Jack a medal while he was here but I expect Father Sheehy [Joe's Jacksonville priest] fixed you up. If not, please let me know as I think you should have a medal on saying that you are a Catholic in case of an accident." Rose had developed the religious equivalent of a mother telling her son to wear clean underwear. She didn't know, it seems, that military dog tags list a wearer's religious affiliation. Or maybe she merely wanted Joe to emphasize that aspect of his identity. "Jack would like to get into and see a little fighting and of course would prefer to go straight to whatever point the Japs are fighting furiously," she reported. "I guess the plans of the whole T.P. [P.T.] boats are rather up in the air." "I am sure, dear Joe, that I do not hear all that is going on as they fear it will worry me," she admitted.[93] Two months later Jack arrived in the Solomon Islands to command PT 109.[94]

From the South Pacific, Jack reported, "[G]ot to Church Easter—they had in a native hut—and aside from having a condition red 'enemy aircraft in the vicinity'—it went on as well as St. Pat's," and later that "you will be pleased to know that their [sic] is a priest nearby who has let all the natives go and is devoting all his energies to my salvation. I'm stringing along with him, but I'm not giving over to[o] easy—as I want him to work a bit—so he'll appreciate it more when he finally has me in the front row every morning screaming halleluyah [sic]."[95]

As Jack settled in overseas, Kathleen sailed for England as a Red Cross volunteer. She couldn't have been happier to return, after four years, to her London friends, especially the love of her life, the Marquess of Hartington. She went out with him a few weeks after arriving, prompting gossip about what the future could possibly hold for this couple. Kick, after all, hailed from the world's most prominent Irish Catholic clan, while Billy's titled family represented pillars of the Anglican faith.

One morning in early August 1943, Rose received a confusing phone call at Hyannis Port, informing her that Jack had been found. "I didn't know he was missing," Rose later explained. "Somebody called his father. It was early in the morning about 8 o'clock, and I answered the phone. His father had left to go riding, so I got his father at the stable on the farm, which was perhaps fifteen to twenty minutes from our house at Hyannis and that was the first time [I heard about it]."[96] The explanation was simple—Joe had not told Rose or the children that Jack had been declared "missing in action," after a Japanese destroyer sliced his PT boat in two during a night patrol of Blackett Strait in the Solomons. The collision had slammed Jack into the cockpit, reinjuring his back, already unstable from sports injuries. Nevertheless, Kennedy swam with his eleven surviving crew members to nearby islands, as he towed a badly burned sailor. After a desperate week of scavenging for food and water, and eluding the Japanese, PT 109's crew encountered a friendly native on Olasana Island. He led Jack to an Australian coast watcher and ultimate rescue of the crew. In a letter home after his harrowing experience, Jack wrote that he survived thanks to Saint Christopher, Saint Elmo, and Saint Clair. "One of them was working overtime."[97] As Rose would write about Jack's exploits, "[W]e are more proud and thankful than words can tell to have him such a hero and still safe and sound."[98]

Joe and Rose were less pleased about Joe Jr.'s behavior after Jack's heroic story made the papers. "We were considerably upset that during those few days after the news of Jack's rescue we had no word from you," Joe Sr. chastised him. "I thought that you would very likely call up to see whether we had had any news as to how Jack was."[99] They hoped that Joe would head to Hyannis Port prior to leaving for his next post, in England, later in September. All was forgiven, however, when Joe Jr. arrived at the Cape for his father's birthday. "Joe Darling: It was wonderful last week to have seen you looking so well and feeling so full of pep . . . ," Rose wrote to her cherished son. She concentrated on finding a gold religious medal, with a gold chain, to send him for protection overseas. Complications ensued, Rose explained to him, "until in desperation I mailed along a simple silver one bought and blessed down here [at the Cape]."[100] She hoped that it would protect him as well as the gold version. By September's end, Joe had reached England, where he visited Kick in London occasionally and reconnected with old friends. "Mother, there is no need in worrying about me over here," he assured her. "If I can keep my feet dry, the greatest hazard will be overcome."[101]

❧

CHAPTER 8

Gold Star Mother

IN JANUARY 1944 ROSE'S RESERVE VANISHED MOMENTARILY when Jack returned safely home. The mere feel of his coat brought her joy. Incredulous at his homecoming, she touched his arms to convince herself that he was really there. Even she could hardly believe that her prayers had been answered: "What a sense of gratitude to God to have spared him." While Jack was at war, Rose's normally sparkling eyes would dim at the mere mention of his name, as fears for his safety gripped her. Nightmares that he had died would rouse her from fitful sleep, and she would awake clutching her heart. Now he was safe, but Jack had changed. His once boyish face looked thin and drawn. South Pacific sun and combat had etched it with lines and fatigue. Jack's ordeal had played havoc with his delicate digestive system, and he ate sparingly back in Palm Beach, even of his favorite meals. As it had when he was a boy, his weight loss concerned Rose. More worrisome was how nervous and skittish he had become after his brush with death in the Solomons. But other habits had not changed: "He still is late at meals— He still is vague on his plans—he still overflows his bathtub and ruins my bedroom rug," Rose complained.[1]

While Joe planned how to attract media attention to Jack's heroism, Rose reverted to her usual concern with detail, focusing on a relic of his miraculous escape from the Japanese—a coconut. It had been Jack's only means of communicating with the Australian coast watcher who then alerted the US Navy to the stranded PT 109 crew's location. With no paper or writing implements, Kennedy had used his service knife to carve a message on the nut's smooth skin: "NAURO ISL . . . COMMANDER . . . NATIVE KNOWS POS'IT . . . HE CAN PILOT . . . 11 ALIVE . . . NEED SMALL BOAT . . . KENNEDY." Then handing it to the non-English-speaking native who had discovered him and his crew on a deserted island, Jack prayed that the SOS would fall into friendly hands. Rose now urged him to preserve it before shrinkage obliterated Jack's printing.[2] Following his mother's suggestion, he had it placed on a wooden base and encased in plastic as a permanent symbol of his wartime exploits.[3]

With Jack home, and Joe Jr.'s reassuring letters from England, where he was safe at his English countryside airfield, Rose turned her attention to Kathleen, who was attempting to remove the religious obstacles to marrying Billy Hartington. His parents, the Duke and Duchess of Devonshire, adored Kathleen, and they asked King George VI's chaplain to describe how she might find spiritual parity as a convert to Anglicanism. In turn, Kick explained that Catholicism's centrality in her life made her reluctant to embrace "a substitute." Likewise, she knew that Billy wouldn't renounce his religious duties, about which he was fanatical, according to Kathleen. Flattering Joe and Rose, Kick wrote that they had "been wonderful and a great strength" in the midst of her crisis. She especially appreciated her mother's prayers.[4]

Joe, always less doctrinaire than Rose, wired Kick a supportive message: "I feel terribly unhappy you have to face your biggest crisis without Mother or me. . . . With your faith in God you can't make a mistake. Remember you are still and always will be tops with me."[5] Three weeks later, Kick informed her family that she would marry Billy. Rose followed her usual pattern when worries inundated her—she left home. Retreating to The Homestead, a luxury hotel spa in Hot Springs, Virginia, Rose felt "horrified—heartbroken" at Kick's news. How could she plan to marry Billy Hartington, the heir to the Duchy of Devonshire, in a London registry office? Despite Joe's more pragmatic outlook, he was sleepless after hearing Kick's intentions. Joe and Rose felt guilt-ridden for allowing Kathleen to "drift into this dilemma." Perhaps it wasn't too late "to extricate her" from a life-altering mistake. They cabled Kick, instructing her to seek advice from a colleague of their friend New York archbishop Francis Spellman. Rose's advice consisted primarily of religious platitudes: "Anything done for Our Lord will be rewarded hundredfold."[6]

Rose thought it unfair for Kathleen to make all the sacrifices to marry Billy. Would he consider some "concessions?"[7] Agonizing over the repercussions of Kick's actions, Rose combined religious fears with concerns for her family's reputation. Everyone took such pride in the Kennedys, Rose thought, and now their prestige would be ruined. She wondered why no one worried as much as she about *that* result. The perfect family image that Rose had worked diligently to create would now be destroyed. She prayed fervently for a different outcome, trying to protect herself from "emotional upset." Perhaps Kick could continue her Red Cross work as Lady Hartington.[8] But Rose literally made herself so ill with worry that she spent several days in New England Baptist Hospital.[9]

How could this have happened? The plan had been to spirit Kathleen away from boys by depositing her in Catholic boarding schools, but now she was a determined woman of twenty-four, preparing to marry the man she loved, despite her parents' disapproval. Rose's own matrimonial history was repeating itself. She had married Joe without the Fitzgeralds' enthusiastic support. They wanted her to marry Hugh Nawn. But Rose had been adamant: she loved Joe, "and that was that!"

Moreover, in London Rose had been utterly starstruck by the English aristocracy. Could it really seem inconceivable to her that Kathleen might marry a member of that class? Billy wrote to Rose directly, trying to change her mind: "I could not believe . . . that

God could really intend two loving [?] people, both of whom wanted to do the right thing, and both of whom were Christians, to miss the opportunity of being happy, and perhaps even useful, together because of the religious squabbles of His human servants several hundred years ago." But he refused to budge on his faith or its edict that the marriage's children be raised Anglican.[10] Kick cabled her father, "Religion everything to us both. Will always live according to Catholic teaching. Praying that time will heal all wounds. Your support in this as in everything else means so much. Please beseech Mother not to worry. Am very happy and quite convinced have taken the right step."[11] Rose remained obdurate. In the eyes of the Roman Catholic church, Kathleen's marriage wouldn't be valid.

On May 6, 1944, with the Duke and Duchess of Devonshire, Nancy Astor, and Marie Bruce in attendance, along with Joe Jr., Kathleen Agnes Kennedy became the Marchioness of Hartington. The civil ceremony at London's Chelsea Register Office lasted ten minutes. Debo Mitford Cavendish, Kick's friend and new sister-in-law, remembers that the vows were said only after "a long tussle with two archbishops and goodness knows who else because the Catholic and Protestant trouble that there was at that time between religious people of that day, and it's extraordinary to think of it now, to think what a barrier it was, but it was. . . ."[12]

Rose's friends, Lady Astor and Marie Bruce, cabled that she "would rejoice in their [Billy and Kick's] young happiness. Only grief your sorrow. Kathleen looked lovely. Pale pink [dress]."[13] Now it was Joe Jr.'s turn to take his parents to task: "The power of silence is great," he wrote in a terse wire.[14] On her honeymoon, the new Mrs. Kathleen Kennedy Hartington took time to cable her father, expressing distress over Rose's upset and urging her not to worry.[15]

Joe Jr. now played the responsible role that his mother had prepared him to assume. Presenting a tableau of Kick's rise to marchioness, he tried to convince his parents to accept the marriage. "Billy is crazy about Kick, and I know they are very much in love. . . . As far as Kick's soul is concerned, I wish I had half her chance of seeing the pearly gates. As far as what people will say, the hell with them. I think we can all take it. It will be hardest on Mother, and I do know how you feel Mother, but I do think it will be all right."[16]

Kathleen was relieved to hear from Joe Sr. that her mother was not seriously ill, as the papers had indicated. But on both sides of the Atlantic, the press accurately reflected the historic British Anglican v. Irish Catholic rifts reopened by the merging of two such prominent families.[17] Indeed, irate Catholics wrote to Kick, accusing her of selling her soul for a British title. Trying to assuage Rose's guilt, Kick assured her that she had performed her "duty as a Roman Catholic mother."[18]

As the summer of 1944 wore on, marked by the Allies' D-Day invasion of Europe, Rose seemed to rethink her position. She told Kathleen that the Kennedy clan was looking forward to Joe Jr.'s return to Hyannis Port on leave. "We only wish you and Billy were going to be along too." The Duchess of Devonshire, Billy's mother, had written warmly to Rose, expressing heartfelt love for Kathleen. That prompted Rose to tell Kick, "I hope Billy felt we were giving him an equally warm welcome into our family." She began to regret having written to Billy when she was still in shock over the nuptials. "However, that is all over now, dear Kathleen, and as long as you love Billy so dearly, you may be sure that we will receive him with open arms. I guess I told you that Joe [Jr.] liked him better every time he saw him, which was a great satisfaction to all of us."[19] Rose's change of heart revealed the better nature of her Christian faith—forgiveness.

NEARING THE ONE-YEAR anniversary of PT 109's sinking, Jack faced ongoing health problems, including malaria. Even worse, his colitis medication may have caused spinal deterioration. In midsummer 1944 he underwent surgery at Boston's New England Baptist Hospital for relief of chronic back pain, and Rose noted that "[h]is tummy was a bit upset yesterday, but I am sure that he will get that straightened out." Unfortunately, both his back and gastrointestinal ailments would flare up periodically throughout his life.[20]

Meanwhile, Rose was relaxing at Hyannis Port, nursing her own stomach problems and reading books all day at her small beach cottage.[21]

Despite the thaw in Rose and Kathleen's relationship, Kick contrived to campaign for her mother's approval. Praising Rose's maternal skills was both genuine and strategic: "First, . . . you are the most unselfish woman in the world. Any house where we have all been has been difficult to run and you have always put us before any of your own desires or pleasures. We all have happy personalities and get along with people far easier than most people—This is due to the happy atmosphere which has always surrounded us. When I see homes I marvel at you more and more. Certain qualities I have—people admire. They are all traits that you have instilled in me."[22] Years later Marie Bruce confirmed Kick's feelings about her mother. Taking shelter one day during an air raid on London, "clutching our possessions and waiting for the next bomb," Marie recalled, "Kick looked at one of her [jeweled] clips and said, 'Dad was wonderful to us. He gave us lovely things, but it is Mother who gave us our character.'"[23]

Rose now seemed much more at peace with herself and her children. Kathleen adored married life, although Billy had to leave for the Continent just five weeks after their wedding to join the attack on Hitler's Fortress Europe. Jack was home, safe, if not quite sound, but was receiving medical attention for his ailments. The Kennedys awaited Joe Jr.'s arrival on leave. He wrote in late July, however, that he had decided to extend his stay in England. For every extra month overseas, he would earn nearly three more days of R & R stateside, before his next assignment that he might not like as well. With the invasion of Europe under way, and the Germans on the defensive, his antisubmarine patrols over the English Channel were more like training exercises, he explained. Joe also told his parents that he had spent his twenty-ninth birthday with Pat Wilson. He didn't mention that a romance had developed; the Australian woman was married to a British soldier stationed in Libya. Kick joined the birthday celebration and welcomed a break in the peaceful countryside, after harrowing experiences with German buzz bombs dropping on London.[24] The German weapons, used as a form of terrorism against the British population, were part of Joe's decision to stay in England. In letters to both his parents and Jack, he mentioned that he was working on a "quite secret" project. "Don't get worried about it, as there is practically no danger," he wrote Joe and Rose on August 4.[25]

A little more than a week later, two Navy chaplains appeared at the Kennedys' Hyannis Port doorstep. Joe was napping upstairs; Rose sat reading the Sunday newspaper. She assumed that the priests wanted to see Joe on routine business, so she invited them in and asked if they might wait for her husband. "No," the clergymen replied, "the matter is urgent." Joe Jr. was missing. Rose stumbled upstairs to tell her husband, who raced down to the priests. They relayed the stark report that the Kennedys' son had perished. The former ambassador, who had tried so hard to avoid war for fear of losing his sons, then repeated the unbearable news to Jack, Teddy, Eunice, and Jean. The usually stoic family, including Rose, dissolved into tears. "Our first born who had shown such promise and had always been such a joy to us and the other children" was gone, Rose thought to herself. Some of the children wailed in grief, Teddy remembered. Joe, his face twisted in pain, disappeared upstairs to hide his sobs. Rose later claimed that the Kennedy patriarch told them, "We must carry on like everyone else. We must continue our regular work and take care of the living, because there is a lot of work to be done."[26] Teddy only recalled that Jack, now the head of the Kennedy brood, declared, "Joe wouldn't want us sitting here crying. He would want us to go sailing. Let's go sailing."[27] And they did.

Joe Jr.'s last mission had been designed to attack sites along the French coast where Nazi troops were launching buzz bombs and were preparing a "super gun" to shoot 300-pound projectiles at London. Joe had volunteered to pilot his PB4I-1 Liberator bomber, packed with 22,000 pounds of explosives, toward a predetermined German target and bail out with his crewmate over the English countryside. By remote control, the plane would then cross the Channel and crash like an unmanned drone into the site at

Mary Josephine (Josie) Hannon Fitzgerald,
Rose's mother, c. 1889.

John Francis (Honey Fitz) Fitzgerald, Rose's
father, c. 1894.

Rose Fitzgerald (on right) with her siblings, Agnes and Thomas, c. 1900.

Rose, second from right, and her classmates from Dorchester High School, c. 1906.

Rose christening the *Bunker Hill*, Philadelphia, March 26, 1907.

Mayor John F. Fitzgerald (with hat over heart) and Rose (to his left), at Boston parade, c. 1910.

Rose and Joseph P. (Joe) Kennedy on their wedding day, Boston, October 7, 1914.

Rose's first three children (left to right) Rosemary, John (Jack), and Joseph (Joe) Jr., Nantasket, c. 1922.

Rose's card file with her nine children's medical and religious milestones.

(Left to right) Joe Sr., Rose, Joe Jr., Jack, Buddy (the dog), Rosemary, Kathleen (Kick), Eunice, Patricia, Robert, and Jean, Hyannis Port, September 4, 1931. Rose was three months pregnant with her ninth and last child, Edward (Teddy).

Rose's only visit to California during Joe's Hollywood career as producer, c. 1927.

(Left to right) Jack's friend, K. LeMoyne (Lem) Billings, Kiko (the family governess), and Jack, Palm Beach, spring 1936.

(Left to right) Kick, Rose, Rosemary, US Embassy Residence, London, May 11, 1938. Rose keeps an eye on Rosemary before they all leave for Buckingham Palace.

Rose oversees a family portrait on the Cannes beach, summer 1938.

Rose, Jack, and Eunice on Mount Corcovado,
Rio de Janeiro, Brazil, spring 1941.

Last known formal photo of Rosemary (far left) before her lobotomy. Bobby, Pat, Jean, Teddy, and Rose are all dressed in white for the launching of the USS *President Polk*, June 29, 1941.

Joe Jr. escorts Kick to her wedding, London, May 6, 1944.

Rose accepts the Navy Cross for Joe Jr. posthumously, June 27, 1945.

Rose, at far left on stage, campaigns for Jack, at microphone, in his first campaign, the 1946 Democratic primary for Massachusetts's Eleventh District, US House of Representatives.

Jack, a newly elected congressman, poses with former congressman John F. Fitzgerald, his grandfather and namesake. Rose carefully captioned the photo.

Bobby with his first child, Kathleen Hartington Kennedy, Josie Fitzgerald, and Rose, beaming over four generations, Hyannis Port, 1951.

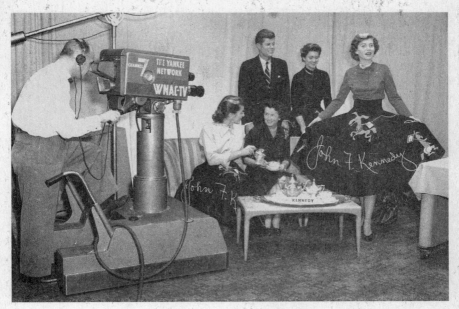

Jack and Jean (back row); Pat and Rose (seated); Eunice models JFK skirt on televised tea for Jack's 1952 US Senate campaign.

Pope Pius XII and Rose at the Vatican in the 1950s.

Rose campaigning for Jack, date unknown.

Rose with Jack and Lyndon Johnson on stage at the Democratic Convention, Los Angeles, July 15, 1960.

Joe greets Rose at the airport as she arrives for the Christmas holidays, 1960.

Rose with President Kennedy, First Lady Jacqueline Kennedy, Vice President Lyndon Johnson, and Lady Bird Johnson at Inaugural Ball, January 20, 1961.

Pablo Casals kisses Jackie Kennedy's hand after his White House concert, as Rose applauds, November 13, 1961.

Rose subs for the First Lady at a state dinner for Ethiopia's Emperor Haile Selassie (to President Kennedy's right), White House, September 23, 1963.

Rose with twenty-one of her grandchildren, Hyannis Port, August 3, 1963.

Rose receives an honorary degree from Sister Rosemary Pfaff, president of St. Joseph's College (to Rose's left), Emmitsburg, MD, October 5, 1963.

Rose at President Kennedy's Arlington gravesite, with Pat and Eunice (to her right); Bobby, Jackie, and Teddy (to her left), for JFK's interment, November 25, 1963.

Rose chats with artist Marc Chagall on the Riviera, September 1964.

At the groundbreaking for the Rose Fitzgerald Kennedy Center, Albert Einstein College of Medicine, Rose lifts a spade of dirt with son Bobby (to her left) and Yeshiva University President Samuel Belkin (to her right), New York, May 2, 1966.

Rose appears on the *Mike Douglas Show* with its host, Philadelphia, July 8, 1967. © Michael Leshnov.

Rose and Teddy at Lt. Joseph P. Kennedy Jr. Memorial Skating Rink, Hyannis, c. November 1967.

Rose campaigning for Bobby in Indiana's Democratic presidential primary, Michigan City, IN, April 27, 1968. A fan inscribed the photo to Mrs. Kennedy, "a great mother."

To a national TV audience, Rose reads her brief eulogy for Bobby, with Teddy (to her right) and Joe (to her left), Hyannis Port, June 10, 1968.

Curtseying to Emperor Haile Selassie on her July 1970 visit with him in Ethiopia, where Rose celebrated her eightieth birthday.

In Teddy's 1970 reelection campaign for Senate, Rose and his wife Joan join him to portray a stable family after his 1969 Chappaquiddick accident.

Rose is greeted at the Westbrook, Maine, Special Olympics, May 1971.

With uncharacteristic animation, Rose stumps for Teddy in the 1980 Iowa presidential caucuses, which he would lose to incumbent President Jimmy Carter.

Rose waves to a crowd on her Hyannis Port lawn with (left to right) Eunice, Jean, and Teddy, celebrating her ninety-second birthday and campaigning for his 1982 Senate reelection.

Mimoyecques, France, near Calais. Just after Joe affirmed that the plane was flying by remote, and a few minutes before he was to exit, it exploded in midair. Flaming wreckage scattered across a wooded area just south of Blythburgh, a small British coastal village in Suffolk.[28] Lt. Kennedy and his crewmate died instantly. It didn't matter if Joe's religious medal was silver or gold. No trace of him was ever found. And now Rose was a Gold Star Mother. That fall she would accept for her son the Navy Cross, the service's premier medal. Surrounded by her husband and Pat, Bobby, Jean, and Teddy, Rose and her family never looked so grim.

Clara St. John, wife of Choate's headmaster, summed up Rose's agony in a poignant condolence letter that she kept for the rest of her life:

> *August 25, 1944*
> *Dear Mrs. Kennedy:*
> *"There is no anodyne for pain*
> *But just the shock of it."*
> *I wish I could have some word of comfort for you in your overwhelming grief. All one's children are equally dear, but there is something about the first born that sets him a little apart—he is always a bit of a miracle and never quite cut off from his mother's heart.*
>
> *And Joe was such a son as any mother would pray for—with charm and integrity and responsibility and rare power of mind and character. Even to a stranger it must seem a tragedy that such a life should be cut short. But "honorable age is not that which standeth in lengthe of days, nor that is measured by number of years, having fulfilled his course in a short time, he fulfilled long years. For his soul was well-pleasing unto the Lord." Solomon knew! But for the loneliness and the continuing sorrow and the beautiful unfinished promise, our hearts go out to you all in deepest sympathy. We too loved Joe—and love him always. Faithfully yours, Clara St. John.*[29]

Mary Jo Gargan Clasby, Rose's niece, remembers that her aunt would disappear for hours each afternoon to mourn alone in her little beach cottage. "It was so hard for her," Mrs. Clasby recalls.[30]

Kathleen flew home for a memorial service, bringing comfort to her parents. She made sure she would be notified if Billy received a leave and could return to England. In that case, Kick would join him in London immediately. On September 4 Billy wrote to his bride from "a great city" on the Continent, which he could not identify for security reasons. (Later she discovered it was Brussels.) Major Lord Hartington's Coldstream Guard's battalion had helped to liberate the populace, and Billy was overcome by their gratitude. "I long for you to be here as it is a[n] experience which few can have, and which I would love to share with you," he told Kick. "Such Germans as we find, and there are quite a lot, are quite exhausted and demoralized and I cannot believe that they can go on much longer."[31] A few days later, as Kick shopped in New York City, she received word to come to her father's suite in the Waldorf-Astoria. There Joe told her that Billy was dead, the victim of a German sniper in Belgium. Quickly returning by plane to England, Kathleen wrote to her parents about the irony of her mixed marriage: "Remember I told you that [Billy] got holier after we married. Now he is the one to bring me closer to God—what a funny world."[32]

Bolstered by her own religious faith, Rose responded immediately to Kathleen:

> I have been thinking about you day and night ever since you left and praying for you and loving you more and more. . . . I have been to Mass for Billy frequently. In fact, I am on my way now (7:15 a.m.). After I heard you talk about him and I began to hear about his likes and dislikes, his ideas and ideals, I realized what a wonderful man he was and what happiness would have been yours had God willed that you spend your life with him. A first love—young love—is so wonderful, my dear Kathleen, but, my dearest daughter, I feel we must dry our tears as best we can and bow our heads to God's wisdom and goodness. We must place our hand in His and trust Him.

In such sorrow, Rose's sense of her personal relationship with God felt most comforting, and she hoped Kathleen would also find spiritual solace. Emphasizing corporal works of mercy, Rose urged her to support Billy's mother because then Kick would focus less on her own grief. Only one month removed from Joe Jr.'s death, Rose knew how much support Kathleen's mother-in-law would need. Rose even arranged for Masses to be offered in Billy's honor.[33] That gesture itself was significant. Catholics rarely request Masses to be said for those outside the faith. Rose must have thought her prayers answered when Kick informed her mother that she had begun receiving Communion again.[34] No longer would her invalid marriage prove a barrier to that sacrament in the eyes of the Catholic Church. Kathleen was again a Roman Catholic in good standing, much to her mother's relief.

BY 1944 ROSE took on more responsibilities for her late sister Agnes's three growing children, Joey, Mary Jo, and Ann Gargan. The Kennedys invited them to spend part of their summers at Hyannis and paid for their schooling. (In fact, they offered college tuition to all of their more than forty nieces and nephews.) "[I]t was a tragedy . . . leaving three little children . . . ," Rose remembered about the Gargan trio, left without their mother, and then their father, at such young ages.[35]

Rose treated the Gargans with the same "tough love" that she applied to her own children, yet Joey and Mary Jo described their aunt with genuine fondness. Joey recalled that every summer Rose drilled him on religion, current events, table manners, and wardrobe rules. Imposing strict curfews when he began dating, Rose warned, "I don't want one of those girl's mothers calling here wondering where they are."[36] Rose sent Mary Jo Gargan to her alma maters, the Sacred Heart Convent and Manhattanville College. The young girl would receive a letter, phone call, or other communication at least every two weeks from Aunt Rose.[37] "She always had a sense of responsibility for us," Mary Jo remembers.[38] Rose modeled the behavior she expected from her charges.

Both Joe Jr. and Billy had died less than a year before the war in Europe ended with Germany's surrender on May 7, 1945. Joe Sr.

wrote to Kick, "Mother is feeling a little better, but after reading
your letters has made up her mind that she doesn't think you'll
come back very soon, and she thinks she'll probably just move over
there. I think she can hardly wait to get back to London and
Paris."[39] As for himself, he admitted to Cissy Patterson, "I find it
very difficult to get over Joe's death. . . . I don't think that the older
people ever get over the death of the younger ones."[40] Even so, he
negotiated a deal that would expand the Kennedys' postwar business empire and become the basis of their charitable work. On July
21, 1945, Joe purchased Chicago's Merchandise Mart, the world's
largest commercial space, for $13 million. Experts predicted the
investment would reap profits of 23 percent a year. Three months
later he created the Joseph P. Kennedy, Jr. Foundation. Buying one-
fourth of the Merchandise Mart, the foundation received a quarter
of its profits tax free.[41]

The US Navy honored Joe Jr.'s memory. Two days before his
thirty-first birthday, the Kennedy family gathered at Bethlehem
Steel's Quincy, Massachusetts, shipyard to launch the USS *Joseph P.
Kennedy, Jr.*, a Navy destroyer. Rose, Joe, Pat, Eunice, Teddy, and
Honey Fitz gathered around as Jean, Joe Jr.'s sister and goddaughter,
christened the ship. In Joe's memory, the Kennedys donated the
central altar to St. Francis Xavier Church, their summer parish in
Hyannis. On the second anniversary of his death, they contributed
$600,000 in his name to Franciscan nuns. The donation was to
establish a convalescent home "for crippled children and mentally
deficient ones."[42] Rosemary's experiences were beginning to shape
the family's charitable mission.

Joe Kennedy also turned his energies to twenty-eight-year-old
Jack's future political career. "I think it extremely likely that he will
run for Congress . . . ," Joe wrote to the editor of the *Washington
Times-Herald* in late 1945. "With his background, brains, and his
courage, he would do a good job if anybody could. I hope, for his
peace of mind, that he does."[43] The Kennedy legend, revised and
re-created by the clan, absorbed Joe Jr.'s death and moved forward.
"Jack originally intended to be a writer, editor or something in the
literary field," Rose explained. "[W]e lost our oldest son, and Jack

assumed his mantle in a way because I noticed it not in politics only. . . . But his attitude toward the younger children and his attitude toward me. He took on more responsibility, and I spoke of him to his father, and his father agreed." Jack's change in attitude occurred spontaneously, according to his mother.[44] Finally, Rose could apply the adjective "responsible" to her second son. Had he truly become so, or did she simply bestow that characteristic on him as a means of replacing Joe Jr.?

John Kennedy's own description of his decision to choose a political career reveals more complexity:

I was at loose ends at the end of the war; I was reluctant to begin law school again. I was not very interested in following a business career. I was vitally interested in national and international life and I was the descendant of three generations, on both sides of my family, of men who had followed the political profession. In my early life, the conversation was nearly always about politics. My father, who had directed much of his energy into business, nevertheless, as the son of a Massachusetts state senator, was himself interested in politics. My mother, also, shared the interest. Her father had been mayor and a United States congressman, and both my great uncles were state senators and my father's first cousin was mayor of Brockton, Massachusetts. . . .

But I never thought at school and college that I would ever run for office myself. One politician was enough in the family and my brother Joe was obviously going to be that politician. I hadn't considered myself a political type and he filled all the requirements for political success. When he was 24 he was elected as a delegate to the Democratic convention in 1940 and I think his political success would have been assured. . . .

My brother Joe was killed in Europe as a flyer in August 1944, and that ended our hopes for him. But I didn't even start to think about a political profession until more than a year later. When the war came I didn't know what I was going to do, and in those days . . . and for those few months after the [war] . . . I didn't find it oppressive that I didn't know. In '44 and '45 I had been in the hospital for about a year recovering from some injuries I received in the Pacific. Then I worked as a reporter covering the San Francisco [United Nations] conference, the British election, and the Potsdam meeting—all in 1945.

So there never was a moment of truth for me when I saw my whole political career unfold. I came back in the fall of '55 [*sic*— it was 1945] after Potsdam, at loose ends, and the head of the Boston Community Fund asked me to help him during the drive . . . [which] meant making speeches for the first time in my life, and they seemed to be acceptable. The first speech I ever gave was on "England, Ireland, and Germany: Victor, Neutral, and Vanquished." It took me three weeks to write and was given at an American Legion Post. Now, the speech went rather well. A politician came up to me afterwards and said that I should go into politics, that I might be governor of Massachusetts in ten years. Then I began to think about a political career. I hadn't even considered it up [un]'til then. Later in the fall, James M. Curley was elected mayor of Boston and a congressional seat became vacant. This was the Eleventh Congressional District, which my grandfather had once represented in Congress 50 years before.

Suddenly, the time, the occasion, and I all met. I moved into the Bellevue Hotel with my grandfather [Honey Fitz] and I began to run. . . .[45]

By Rose's own admission, she played no direct role in Jack's decision to run for Congress in 1946. Joe would talk by phone with him regularly, but the Kennedy men simply didn't consult Rose about their political decisions.[46] She was relegated to household management and assumed another task, destined to last for decades—tracking bills incurred by her grown children. "I still have a lot of trouble with bills down here [at Palm Beach]," she declared in one of her round-robin letters, listing purchases from New York, Boston, and Florida that she couldn't identify. She and her secretary had to phone stores asking which Kennedy had charged this item of clothing or that piece of jewelry. Rose warned, "I am afraid it is going to be embarrassing [for the children] from now on as I have just told them I would not be responsible [for the bills]."[47]

Rose had begun leading an even more solitary life, with her adult children out on their own and the younger ones (along with the Gargans) away at school. She wrote in early June 1946 to Kathleen, who had settled in England, that she was back at the Hyannis Port house, now "very quiet with little excitement." Perhaps she had achieved her dream, a home all to herself, but Rose sounded rather lonely, rattling around in a large, "very damp" house. Despite the isolation, she remained "cheerful," but hoped that warmer weather might attract "somebody" to join her. Instead, Jack was now the family beacon. Eunice was with him in Boston, working on his primary campaign. Rose still worried about Jack's health. She thought him too thin, and she was right—photographs revealed a haggard candidate. Believing that he worked too hard, Rose wished that he could spend a few days each week at the Cape, where she could supervise his diet.[48]

But she had become an empty nester. If only her son would return, she could care for him. Despite craving solitude when her house had been filled with rowdy children, these were difficult days for her: Rosemary institutionalized, Joe Jr. dead, Kick living in London, Joe Sr. relegated to the political sidelines. "Your father has kept out of it [Jack's campaign]," she wrote to Kathleen, "and is only doing a little work behind the scenes so whatever success there is will be due entirely to Jack and the younger group."[49]

Rose didn't mention that Joe's controversial career had also forced her out of the spotlight. In the past, travel would have banished her boredom, but in the immediate postwar years, she couldn't escape to devastated Europe, and shortages meant that she couldn't shop for wardrobes at home or abroad. "I am hoping to see you soon," Rose told Kick, "although I am afraid it will not be this summer [of 1946]."[50]

About this time, a wave of uncharacteristic sentimentality swept over Rose, making her nostalgic for the days of early motherhood in Brookline, as she chose to remember them: "Life indeed was busy but how absorbing and there was no mental hazards. Just take care of 3 or 4 wonderful active bouncing offspring, feed them, air them and make them rest, read books on child psychology, discuss your problems with other young mothers and with the young teachers and always carry on with the conviction that your children were always the loveliest, the brightest and the ones with the rosiest futures."[51]

Now even her youngest children, Jean, eighteen, and Teddy, fourteen, had been bitten by the political bug and were anxious to join the all-consuming family business—politics. Jean had just completed her first year at Manhattanville College. Instead of going to Hyannis for the summer, she headed to Boston and Jack's campaign. "Teddy is chafing a bit and wants to go up and be with the gang," Rose told Kick, "but I think I have prevailed on him to stay the weekend here. Possibly, we may all go up next week."[52]

Rose applied her attention to detail in helping with Jack's campaign. She encouraged his staff to record the names of everyone who attended Kennedy rallies. According to Jack's campaign operative Dave Powers, "She didn't do a lot of speaking. We used her just at special times where it could count most, like with the Veterans of Foreign Wars. . . . Each time she was the star of the show. She must have been about fifty-six then, but she looked more like thirty-five." Rose relied on her tried-and-true subjects—raising nine children, managing her household (including the famous index cards), her tenure in London before the war, and life at the embassy. "When she finished she got a standing ovation. Then she introduced her son, the candidate for the nomination in the Eleventh Congressional District."[53] Rose confined her advice for Jack to tips on public speaking. Slow down, she told him.[54]

While Rose played only a small role in Jack's first congressional campaign, she supplied a very large asset—the Fitzgerald name. Both she and her father had been born in the Eleventh District, also encompassing the Kennedy enclave of East Boston. "I had in politics, to begin with, the great advantage of having a well-known name and that served me in good stead," Jack later commented. "Beyond that, however, I was a stranger in Boston. . . . I was an outsider, really. I was living in a hotel. I had never lived very much in the district. My family roots were there, but I had lived in New York for ten years, and on top of that I had gone to Harvard, not a particularly popular institution at that time in the Eleventh Congressional District."[55] As a novice public speaker, with Rose's somewhat reserved nature, Jack needed all of the advantages he could find to boost his candidacy. One day, speaking to Gold Star mothers at an American Legion hall, he inserted an impromptu remark that struck an emotional chord among the ladies. "I think I know how all you mothers feel because my mother is a Gold Star Mother, too," Jack confided.[56] The women grew misty-eyed and swarmed around the young war veteran.[57]

In fact, they wanted to take care of him. Jack's wan appearance, resulting from malaria, chronic digestive ailments, and undiagnosed Addison's disease, ironically became something of a benefit. His mother agreed: "[Women] used to have this sympathetic feeling toward him because [of his appearance]. And some of the younger women—of course he was a bachelor. So romantic. . . ."[58] Nearly fifteen hundred women of all ages turned out in their best finery (some even rented formals) to meet Jack, the war hero, and his celebrated family, including Rose, at a "tea" just three days prior to the June 1946 Democratic primary. Having received engraved invitations, Irish American ladies flocked to the unique political event at Cambridge's Hotel Commander.[59] Rose's days as hostess for Mayor Fitzgerald and as wife of the ambassador to the Court of St. James's provided perfect preparation for meeting and greeting Jack's future constituents. On primary election day, Jack cast his ballot with proud maternal grandparents, Josie and Honey Fitz, at his side. That night Joe and Rose stood arm and arm with their son, so lanky (at six feet tall and 120 pounds) that he looked like a teenager. All three Kennedys beamed with joy, as a crowd of well-wishers gathered around them.[60]

Jack attributed his nearly eleven-thousand-vote victory margin to his early start and "long, long, long labor."[61] His father's strategic planning, unlimited funds, and public relations resources (including distribution of the PT 109 story) also contributed to Jack's success.

In a solidly Democratic district, he won decisively that November. John F. Fitzgerald's namesake, following in his grandfather's footsteps, now sat in the US House of Representatives.

With Jack in Congress and Europe rapidly rebuilding, Rose made her way back to England. This time she took twenty-four-year-old Pat, "my 6th child." "That's another advantage of having a large family," Rose explained. Taking "a trip with a different offspring every time" takes us out of our "grooves."[62] Recovering from Billy's death, Kathleen had bought a town house in London's Smith Square, near Parliament. The brick building reminded Rose of the posh homes in Boston's Louisburg Square on Beacon Hill. "It has been done up very attractively and she has all her friends (all of whom I like) dropping in and so it is very pleasant," Rose wrote home to Joe. She seemed a bit homesick, however. "I shall be glad to get home in spite of all the gaiety, but I shall come again and hope you will the next time at least for a quick look."[63]

Kathleen welcomed her mother to Lismore Castle, the Cavendish estate in County Waterford, Ireland. Acquired by Billy's family in the eighteenth century, the Gothic edifice recalled to Rose "a picture-book castle, with the grey walls covered in moss—green and soft—and ivy on the other turning red now in the autumn." She loved the surrounding pastoral scenes of Eire. "It is beautiful here beyond words, quiet, peaceful, secluded," she wrote to "Joe dearest."[64] Rose seemed rather disappointed, though, to learn that Glocca Morra didn't exist, "like in the play *Finian's Rainbow*."[65] The fictional town had appeared in a song from the 1947 Broadway play about an Irishman and his daughter who come to America to turn a pot of gold into a massive fortune, and reminisce about the Old Country.[66] The play's romanticism matched Rose's description of the magical time spent with Kathleen exploring County Waterford. "I feel *perfect*," Rose proclaimed.[67]

Rose might have felt less perfect had she known of Kathleen's new love interest. In mid-1946, she had begun to see wealthy Lord Peter Fitzwilliam, a war hero but inveterate womanizer ten years her senior. If Billy Hartington's religious affiliation had been vexing to Rose, how would she respond to the fact that Peter was not only a Protestant, but also married and the father of a young daughter? Kick didn't want to find out. She spared her parents the truth about her romantic pursuits until she moved closer to marrying Peter, which she planned to do as soon as his divorce was final.[68]

Within the family, only Jack knew about Kick's romance. She had told him on his 1947 visit to Lismore, and he approved, seeing how happy the relationship made her.[69] On that trip, Jack had fallen ill, and Kathleen's friend Pamela Churchill, former daughter-in-law of Winston, had arranged for his medical care in London. The doctor issued a dire diagnosis—a chronic adrenal deficiency, Addison's disease, was the cause of Jack's perpetual brownish skin tone, gastrointestinal distress, low blood pressure, and weight loss. "That American friend of yours, he hasn't got a year to live," the London physician reported to an alarmed Pamela. The Kennedys sent a nurse to accompany Jack on the ship back to the States, where he received the Catholic Church's sacrament of extreme unction.[70] Once again, Jack defied the odds and survived.

Years later, Rose spoke of her role, or lack of it, in her adult son's illnesses: "Jack was ill so long that he [Joe] was so involved because he sort of took over that responsibility, talking to the doctors and deciding where he would go and what he'd do with his physical ailments—. . . rather than have me do it." At times it seems that Rose continued to view her son's serious health problems as if they were a minor stomach ache. "Jack inherited the same thing [Rose's "tummy" problems]. Eunice has it. My father had it. It's just a personal thing, as I said."[71]

The development of effective cortisone treatment for Addison's gave JFK the more robust appearance he presented to the world in the 1960s. He worried, however, that the medication sometimes made his face puffy, and he thought he looked overweight, a sin in the Kennedy family.[72] When pressed about Jack's medical condition in later years, Rose grew testy: "I don't know why he happened to be sick. How does anyone happen to be sick? I don't know the answers. I didn't follow Mr. Kennedy, that was his department. He decided whether Jack should go to the hospital. He talked to the doctors whether he had something which makes your face all brown. Jaundice or whatever it was he had. Then he was . . . in England and he almost died in England they said."[73] That's as far as Rose would go in discussing her second son's complex medical problems. Even as late as the 1970s, she labeled his illness as "tummy problems," couldn't admit his Addison diagnosis (Eunice also had the disease), and absolved herself from decisions about his care.[74] As with Rosemary's lobotomy, it appears that Joe Kennedy called the shots for his son's medical care without his wife's input.

In February 1948 Kick returned to the United States knowing that she had to tell Joe and Rose of her plans to marry Peter. But two months elapsed in Palm Beach and Washington, and still she couldn't do it. When she finally did in April, at a Greenbrier resort family gathering a few days before her departure for England, Rose responded more vehemently than she had to Kick's first marriage, threatening to disown her daughter for marrying a divorced man, strictly forbidden in the Roman Catholic Church. For his part, Joe offered none of the you "always will be tops with me" pep talks of 1944. He may, however, have consulted with his Vatican contact, seeking some way to validate a future union between Kathleen and Fitzwilliam.[75] Kick held out hope that her father might approve of her choice if only he could meet Peter. Joe had business to conduct in France and England that spring, so he agreed to meet the pair in Paris three weeks later. The couple decided to spend a few days relaxing on the Riviera before the tense summit with Joe. Fitzwilliam chartered a plane for the trip. After a refueling stop at Le Bourget, the pilot informed him of stormy weather between Paris and Cannes, recommending the flight's postponement. Fitzwilliam, a well-known risk taker, ordered the two-man crew to take off.[76]

1948 May 14 11:07
Washington DC Via Hyannisport Mass
Urgent Joseph Kennedy
Department of State regrets to inform you that according to a message received from the American Consulate at Lyon France that Katheline [sic] Hartington bearer of Passport 40507 showing birth Brookline Mas-

sachusetts February 20 1920 has been identified as one of the four per-
sons killed in an airplane crash near Privas France

Edward E. Hunt Chief of Protective Services
Department of State

No family members were in Hyannis Port to receive the Western Union telegram. Rather, news reached Joe the morning after the accident, at his Paris hotel, where he had planned to meet Peter and Kathleen. Then came the excruciating task of traveling to the Rhone Valley in order to identify his daughter's body. Searchers had retrieved it from the side of a mountain where the plane had crashed in a violent thunderstorm. In Washington, Jack initially received unconfirmed media reports about Kick's death at the apartment he shared with Eunice, who was working in the Justice Department. As they awaited the dreaded follow-up call, Jack listened to the haunting strains of "How Are Things in Glocca Morra?" about the Irish lass with the twinkling eyes. When confirmation arrived, he broke the Kennedy rule, shedding tears for Kick.[77]

"It is a terrible thing . . . she was a beautiful girl. Please don't disturb her mother," a bereft Honey Fitz implored the *Boston Traveler*.[78] Jack called Rose at Virginia's Homestead spa, where four years earlier she had agonized over Kick's marriage to Billy. Now her daughter and both loves of Kathleen's life were gone, all victims of violent death. Everyone but Joe gathered at Hyannis Port. Where so many happy summers had transpired, the Cape Cod retreat was becoming the family's grief shelter. Joe accompanied Kathleen's body back to England, where Billy's mother, the Duchess of Devonshire, offered the family plot in Edensor, near the Cavendish ancestral home, Chatsworth. No other member of the Kennedy family saw Kick to her final resting place.[79]

Andrew Cavendish, Kick's brother-in-law, asked London newspapers to say only that a chance meeting caused Kick and Peter to be passengers on the doomed plane.[80] American papers followed suit, portraying Kathleen as the beautiful but star-crossed Kennedy daughter. Eunice requested that her boyfriend, Sargent Shriver, who managed the Merchandise Mart for Joe, gather the newspaper stories about Kick's death and send them to her parents. "Merely looking at these clippings is not pleasant for me, so I know what poignant unhappiness they must bring to you. Please accept once again my deepest sympathy," Shriver wrote to his future in-laws.[81] At least Rose didn't have to read that her daughter had died on route to a Riviera assignation with a married man.

A devastated Joe Kennedy made his way back to Hyannis Port, where he wrote an effusive and frank thank-you letter to the Duchess of Devonshire for her many kindnesses during "the whole sad affair. I would like to be able to tell you that I am very much better," he wrote, "but I just can't." He simply couldn't expunge memories of Kick from his mind. The thought of never seeing her again, never experiencing her effervescence, plunged him into a dark depression. Like all the Kennedys, he tried to hide his pain, not even revealing it to Rose. She was "ten thousand per-cent better than I am," he told Billy's mother. "Her terrifically strong faith has been a great help to her, along with her very strong will and determination not to give way."[82]

Rose's own thoughts from that dreadful time are conspicuously absent from her records, but she had a telling exchange about the accident in a 1972 interview with Robert Coughlan. He conversed routinely about Fitzwilliam: "As it happens, one of those small coincidences, I knew _____, the man who was flying back [sic] with Kick." "Oh, yes," Rose replied. Coughlan added, "He was a very pleasant guy," to which Rose replied, "Yes, he was nice. I didn't know him." "I was in England in '48 _____," Coughlan continued. "Oh, when he was killed," commented Rose. The interviewer clarified, "Very soon afterwards." Rose recalled, "In the spring—because her father was over there." Then Coughlan switched the subject to Rose's thoughts about her daughter: "And Kick was the one you feel resembled you the most of all the girls?" "Well, she was, of course, nearer—she was the oldest one practically— in fact—and she traveled with me more, and of course—and the others were much younger during that period—and she made her debut in England, and, of course, I was much younger then—you know, interested. . . . She was lots of fun and very gay," Rose summed up Kick's personality.[83]

The next theme of the Kennedy legend was taking shape. Rose had persevered to perfect the nine children she had produced, scripted, and directed. She had taken the media at home and abroad by storm with her large clan of smiling Kennedys and her own youthful looks. Now the fates seemed to conspire against her. One by one, almost in birth order, they were disappearing. "Kathleen's Death Is Third Tragedy in Kennedy Family," ran the *Boston Globe*.[84] Joe's description of his wife created another public role for her: stoic mother relying on religious faith for support in times of sorrow. And yet, ironically, the next dozen years would bring success and happiness to Rose Kennedy as her children achieved unprecedented fame and produced the next generation of the Fitzgerald-Kennedy dynasty.

CHAPTER 9

Matriarch of a Political Dynasty

As the 1950s dawned, two landmark events began to reshape the evolving Fitzgerald–Kennedy dynasty. In June 1950 Bobby married Ethel Skakel, Jean Kennedy's former roommate at Manhattanville College and a wealthy Catholic dynamo who fit seamlessly into the active Kennedy clan. Unable to attend Kathleen's wartime wedding in England, Rose happily splurged on this one. Writing to her confidante, the fashion icon Hélène Arpels, wife of the famous jeweler, Rose boasted, "I cannot tell you what a great success I had with my dress. Everyone said I stole the show and I was really quite embarrassed because I was standing next to Mr. Skakel and so many Boston people rhapsodized over it that I finally started to say hush hush before they spoke too loudly. Really, dearest Hélène, it was a great success."[1] Clearly, Rose was back in the social spotlight, this time with her children the catalysts, instead of her father or husband.

Additional etiquette rituals now occupied Rose. She asked the newlyweds for a list of their wedding gifts in case she met friends in Boston who had sent them.[2] Rose wanted to comment knowledgeably about each present and thank the bestower. Perhaps this was also a way of checking Ethel's diligence regarding thank-you notes.

That fall Rose left for her annual trip to Paris and London in search of the latest fashions. She went knowing that Honey Fitz's chronic circulatory problems had confined him to bed. "In the summer when I was in Hyannis, if [Honey Fitz and Josie] were not down there, if my father was ill, I used to go up [to Boston] at least once a week and spend the day with them."[3] A few days into her trip, on October 2, 1950, Honey Fitz died, at age eighty-seven, attended by his wife and their two surviving sons. Rose had been the apple of his eye, but she couldn't return from France in time for the funeral.[4] More than thirty-five hundred mourners jammed the Cathedral of the Holy Cross, the mother church of Boston's Roman Catholics. About to win his third term, Congressman John Fitzgerald Kennedy, along with Eunice, Pat, Jean, and Teddy, represented their mother at the funeral Mass.[5] Teddy had grown especially close to "Granpa." During his nomadic school-boy years, Teddy had visited Honey Fitz regularly on Sundays when enrolled at Fessenden, just outside of Boston. The jolly Irish pol loved exploring Boston's historic sites with his grandson, introducing him to old friends throughout the city. "There's no question that I inherited this joy of people from him. I inherited the whole way I approach politics," wrote Kennedy about his maternal grandfather.[6]

In 1951 Rose received an honor that couldn't have pleased her more. Starting in the Middle Ages, popes sometimes bestowed royal titles on their religious subjects. The tradition had largely fallen into disuse by the twentieth century. Only six American women have ever received the title of papal countess. Pope Pius XII honored just one woman during his nineteen-year pontificate, Rose Kennedy, "[i]n recognition of her exemplary motherhood and many charitable works."[7] Rose proudly used her new title in Cath-olic circles, a world that recognized her feats of motherhood and unstinting devotion to her faith, though her most significant chari-table work lay ahead.

———

THE KENNEDYS' FIRST grandchild arrived July 4, 1951, when Ethel gave birth to a girl, whom she and Bobby named Kathleen Hartington, after Kick. The baby, baptized on Rose's sixty-first birthday, wore a new Parisian christening robe from her Grandma Kennedy. Rose was delighted to have received orchids for her birthday with a card from the baby enclosed. In turn, the new grandmother gave Kathleen a blue locket that had belonged to baby Kick.[8]

Rose's next adventure would bring her back into the political arena with a more active and significant role than she had played in Jack's 1946 congressional race. He had run unopposed in 1948 and faced minimal opposition in 1950.[9] By December 1951 Jack had decided to challenge Henry Cabot Lodge Jr. for his US Senate seat, held since 1937 with a three-year hiatus while he was on active military duty during World War II. The race would once again pit the Lodges, national Republican icons, against the Fitzgeralds. In 1916 Brahmin Henry Cabot Lodge Sr. had defeated Honey Fitz for the US Senate. Now Henry Jr. was preoccupied with General Dwight Eisenhower's 1952 presidential campaign, having persuaded the war hero to run as the GOP candidate. The Kennedys mounted a statewide juggernaut in Lodge's absence. "In 1952 I worked a year and a half ahead of the November election, a year and a half before Senator Lodge did," JFK recalled in 1960:

I believe most aspirants for public office start much too late. When you think of the money that Coca-Cola and Lucky Strike put into advertising day after day, even though they have well-known brand names, you can realize how difficult it is to become an identifiable political figure. The idea that people can get to know you well enough to support you in two months or three months is wholly wrong. Most of us do not follow politics and politicians. We become interested only around election time. For the politician to make a dent in the consciousness of the great majority of the people is a long and laborious job. . . .[10]

Helping to make that "dent," Rose anchored "coffee hours" at private homes. Gathering ladies around the hearth, while they balanced coffee cups and petit fours on their laps, she spoke of her father's service in Congress, its inspiration for Jack's government career, and how the family's prewar London years tutored him in world affairs. Colorful anecdotes abounded: Buckingham Palace dinners, the trials and joys of raising nine children, and the importance of religion in her life. The script, prepared by Rose, skillfully wove the family's story with current political issues. The Korean War was raging, and Rose told the women that she knew a mother's heartbreak of losing her son and son-in-law in World War II, adding that Jack had recently visited Korea. "I promise you that he will work . . . his utmost to put an end to this war and bring your boys back to you as soon as possible." For television, Eunice interviewed her mother at their Hyannis Port home, and Rose displayed the desk her father had used in Congress.[11]

Sometimes Jack would appear and bedazzle women of all ages, who gathered around to see the handsome congressman. Soon no home was big enough to accommodate the crowds, so the Kennedys moved to larger venues, hosting formal receptions or teas—thirty-three in all—throughout the state at premier hotels. The first, held at Worcester's Bancroft Hotel, was expected to draw a thousand women. Five times that number came.[12] "Often Rose was as big a draw as her son. . . ."[13] Obviously, Jack's campaign hoped these ladies would create a ripple effect, reporting favorably on the candidate to family and friends. They did. Thus, the tea party paradigm, first used in JFK's 1946 campaign, became a powerful staple of Kennedy political tactics.

Rose related particularly well to people in small groups. "She's very interested in individuals. And I think this is a very important aspect of her success. I think people feel the interest that she [has in them]," remembered Teddy many years later.[14] As Rose explained, "[I]f you started in small groups, it's, of course, much easier because they don't know whether you are logical in your thoughts or whether you're pronouncing every word if you're confused or confounded. If you're in a small group of thirty or forty people . . . in some obscure part of the city, then gradually you advance to a more prestigious post of a larger group, in my case came gradually and naturally and more or less easily. Then, of course, we did a little television and then we did more television. . . ." It took awhile for her to feel comfortable in the new medium, but "I've been having this [public] exposure for a long time in England [and] from the time I was very young," she recalled.[15]

Rose honed her speeches for larger groups. "Sometimes [I] had friends in the audience who would hear people say she talks too fast or what does she want to talk about that for?" She learned early in her speaking career to tailor her topics to audiences' socioeconomic levels and to take informal surveys of their reactions to determine what they wanted to hear.[16] Her lifelong attention to detail, and an abiding interest in knowing what people thought of her, perfectly suited the world of politics. In a way, Rose ran an early version of the modern focus group to determine her effectiveness on the campaign trail.[17]

As she began speaking in bigger auditoriums, Rose took note of how her voice sounded through a microphone. And she learned that it was different in an empty auditorium while testing the amplifier, in contrast to when she appeared before a packed house. In addition, Rose continued to worry about how she looked in pictures and tried to direct photographers to capture her best image.[18] Candid shots were her least favorite.

In May, before the fall campaign, Rose traveled to Paris. Teddy, now a twenty-year-old private first class in the US Army's military police, was stationed near Versailles. A year earlier Harvard had suspended Kennedy, known around campus as a popular, privileged slacker, for recruiting a friend to take his final exam in Spanish.[19] He could be reinstated if he devoted a year to a worthy endeavor. Joe, livid at Teddy's behavior, decided that the discipline of military service was in order, so Teddy had enlisted for two years. PFC Kennedy's rendezvous with his mother wasn't exactly typical of his fellow soldiers. Renting a limousine to collect Rose at the Ritz in Paris, they motored to Deauville on the Normandy coast. There Teddy borrowed a dinner jacket and dress shoes to attend a black-tie event preceding the ballet. After his three-day furlough, Teddy and Rose returned, by way of Versailles, and the limo dropped him off some distance from the base's entrance so no one would see him arrive with his mother in such luxury. "I'd walked through the gate and was headed for the barracks, when I heard rapid, tiny footsteps and a familiar voice behind me, calling, 'Teddy, dear! Teddy, dear! Oh, *Teddy*, dear!' . . . Mother's bell-like voice was loud enough to wake the guards. 'Teddy, dear! You forgot your *dancing shoes!*'" He turned toward his mother. "I watched her hurrying toward me, her small hands clutching two shiny objects. She spent a minute or two catching her breath. 'Here are your dancing shoes!'" Teddy didn't have the heart to tell Rose that he had borrowed the shoes in Deauville and had neglected to return them. So he thanked her and turned around to see his mates staring at the spectacle. From then on, "Teddy dear!" rang in Kennedy's ears as soldiers greeted him with his mother's exclamation, followed by a mocking, "Do you have your dancing shoes?"[20]

Rose's many years spent studying and practicing French paid dividends in Jack's 1952 Senate campaign. She traveled to Massachusetts towns such as New Bedford, with significant numbers of French-speaking residents, and addressed them in their native tongue. Her speeches, written in Rose's high-school French, mentioned only briefly her visits to the Parisian fashion houses of Balenciaga and Dior. Focusing on her family's connections to France through study and travel, she described her visits to French Catholic shrines, including Lourdes. She also noted that Jack had visited Indochina, supported textile workers in New England, and would work hard for the interests of French Canadians who had settled in Massachusetts.[21]

Rose spent time in Boston too, reminiscing with voters about her childhood there. She didn't speak Italian but told Italian audiences about her youth in the North End, where many of them were born. She described her travels in Italy and her love of Italian art, music, and architecture. Recalling the thrill of accompanying Cardinal Pacelli to Hyde Park for his 1936 meeting with FDR, she emphasized that "we have had the honor and pleasure of knowing the most famous living Italian, our Holy Father Pope Pius XII. How proud you must be of your great inheritance—you people of Italian blood." She reminded the listeners that she named her son John Fitzgerald Kennedy after Honey Fitz, who represented Boston in Congress at the turn of the century. Rose added references to public policy issues of special interest to Italian Americans: US immigration quotas that discriminated against emigrants from Italy, and the World War II peace treaty that prohibited Italy from maintaining an army. Rose reported that her son had voted to revise that treaty so Italy could protect itself from "Communist aggression." In the midst of the Red Scare, Rose briefly cited the Communist menace, offering eyewitness accounts of "secret police" and desecration of churches from her 1937 trip to the Soviet Union. "My son, John, has been fighting Communism in this country for a long while. . . . [A]s a United States senator he will continue more effectively than ever this fight," she added. When Rose needed more "data," she called on James A. Fayne, Joe's financial advisor and ghostwriter of his unpublished diplomatic memoir.[22]

JFK's stunning win over the venerable Lodges, despite Ike's landslide defeat of Democrat Adlai Stevenson (including in Massachusetts), was by a slim 70,737-vote margin. Ethnic voters, who accounted for increased turnout, probably cast decisive ballots for Kennedy. Rose believed that "those extra votes [garnered from towns where she spoke to ethnic audiences] gave us the victory."[23] As in 1946, Joe Kennedy remained offstage, but he played a crucial role by writing checks, drafting twenty-six-year-old Bobby as campaign manager, and promoting journalistic support for Jack.[24] Rose maintained that her husband kept a low profile because he didn't care about getting "plaudits" from crowds, preferring to work behind the scenes while his sons learned the trade and earned the glory. Seeing her sons' relationship to her husband uncritically, she concluded, "They were so lucky to have [Joe], and he was lucky to have them because they did respond and it's a great joy to him to have them ready and . . . adequate and competent enough to accept these responsibilities and to accept these governmental tasks and to be able to do them and like to do them, of course."[25] Missing from this assessment was the disastrous end to Joe's ambassadorship twelve years previously. As for Joe, he gave Rose due credit for her expanded participation in the family's campaign machine. "[Y]ou would have been very much surprised and pleased to have seen the wonderful television programs that Rose and the girls put on for Jack and the remarkable speeches Rose made," he wrote to a British friend.[26] But perhaps most persuasive was Lodge's view, labeling "those damn tea parties" as the reason for his defeat.[27]

Rose played a particularly crucial role in reaching women voters because Jack remained unmarried even as he approached his midthirties. "I don't think he ever had anyone too serious around him among his friends," Rose remembered of that time. "He didn't have any bookworms or any people who were deeply concerned with the affairs of the world. On the contrary, he liked to know what was going on, where the beautiful women were, how he could manage to do things without his father finding out, which . . . was . . . impossible."[28] So while Jack's bachelor status might attract young female votes, in the 1950s' family-centered culture he needed a spouse and children to remain a viable political figure. Indeed, an unmarried man might prompt a whispering campaign about his sexual preference.[29] Jack's longtime friendship with prep-school mate Lem Billings, a confirmed bachelor, didn't help.[30]

Journalist and Kennedy friend Charles Bartlett, playing match-maker, had introduced Jack to Jacqueline Bouvier, a budding *Washington Times-Herald* columnist and photographer, in 1951. But no romantic sparks flew until Bartlett and his wife invited them to another dinner a year later.[31] Rose knew nothing of these machinations. She first became aware of Jackie Bouvier in the winter of 1952, when she visited the Kennedys' Palm Beach home. Rose was away, and when she received a thank-you note from Jackie, she thought the sender was a boy. Once Jack and Jacqueline began dating that spring, Rose approved. Then she read about a Bouvier engagement and, assuming it was Jackie, expressed disappointment: "I thought, 'What a pity.' Everybody said she was such a nice girl. She's Catholic, the right age, and she's been well educated, so that Jack would find her [a] helpful mate in that category and now he's gone and lost her." When it turned out that it was Jackie's sister, Lee, whose engagement was announced, Rose was relieved.[32]

The Kennedys welcomed Jackie to Hyannis Port in the summer of 1952, and she charmed them with her beauty, grace, and wit. Rose loved her refined manners, style, and appreciation of all things French. These traits might not mesh with Jack's interests, but the courtship survived his Senate campaign, and he asked Jackie to attend a presidential inaugural ball with him in January 1953. When she left for London that spring to cover Queen Elizabeth's coronation, Jack missed her. On her return he presented Jackie with a two-carat diamond-and-emerald engagement ring.[33]

Jackie certainly knew the key to Rose's heart. "As I met every Kennedy one by one, I liked them all so much. I don't think I ever knew you well until this weekend. Now I think I'm so lucky to have you as a mother-in-law," Miss Bouvier wrote to Mrs. Kennedy two months before the wedding.

> It seems to me that very few people have been able to create what you have—a family built on love and loyalty and gaiety. If I can even come close to building that with Jack I will be very happy. If you ever see me going wrong I hope you will tell me—because I know you would never find fault unless fault was there. I do mean to thank you for this weekend too. It was such a perfect one—and I would have made a terrible mess of it if you hadn't told me how to hold my arms for photographers. . . .[34]

Now Rose had in-laws to shape. For Jackie's family, molding their lives around the Kennedy media machine was much harder. Her mother wanted no reporters at Jackie's wedding. According to Rose, Mrs. Auchincloss, Jackie's mother, who had remarried after divorcing Jackie's father, thought that a media presence would be "demeaning and vulgar." That position never stood a chance against Joe's decree that "in our case they'll [sic] have to be reporters at the wedding because he [Jack] is a public figure," Rose explained.[35] St. Mary's Catholic Church in Newport, Rhode Island, posed a problem. It only held 750 congregants. But Hammersmith Farm, home of Jackie's wealthy stepfather, and site of the reception, was plenty spacious; Joe supervised invitations for fourteen hundred. Another three thousand spectators surrounded the church to catch a glimpse of America's newest celebrity couple on September 12, 1953.[36] From their Acapulco honeymoon Jack cabled Joe and Rose, "At last I know the true meaning of rapture. Jackie is enshrined forever in my heart. Thanks mom and dad for making me worthy of her. Your loving son, Jack."[37]

Future in-laws praised the job Rose and Joe had done in raising their children. Sargent Shriver thanked the Kennedys for producing his wife-to-be, Eunice. Upon their engagement, Shriver wired Joe and Rose, "Am furious at you know who. Typically she did not allow me to be present when she told you the news. Despite this and other peculiar ideas and actions I love her more than any telegram could say. Thank you both for making her possible for me. Affectionately, Sargent."[38] After a seven-year courtship, Eunice and Sarge married in May 1953.[39]

Rose resumed her overseas travels in earnest during the 1950s, making up for the war years. Now back in Paris, she wrote to Joe revealing thoughts about their relationship, along with details of life on the road and her preoccupation with the home she left behind. "I hope, dearest, you are feeling well. I could write you another long letter just telling you how deeply I love you and how happy you make me every moment. But I am sure you feel it."[40] From Salzburg Rose reported that she and longtime travel companion Marie Bruce were attending the opera and concerts during the annual summer music festival. "So all is well for us. But you certainly would not like it—I have thought of you all the time, especially when I was pushed and being pushed plenty getting aboard the train [to Austria]. And here there is no water except Gastein water, which tastes worse than Apollinaris [sparkling German spring water], so my medicine tastes obnoxious, like poison."[41]

Now in her midsixties, Rose packed an impressive personal pharmacy for trips abroad. On a three-page typed "Travel List," with her handwritten additions, she listed Bufferin, Vitamin B,

Vick's Nose Drops, throat lozenges, back plasters, cramp lotion, toothache treatments, "heat for rheumatism," collyrium (eye wash), Oculine (medicated eye products), Argyrol, and paregoric. For overseas trips, she added whiskey, which she may have used medicinally or to mask the taste of medicine. (Rose avoided most alcohol because it upset her sensitive stomach and represented empty calories.) She also packed a heating pad and enema bag.[42] The Kennedy Library's version of Rose's list redacted sleeping pills, Progynon (estrogen), and Dr. Fordan #6 Powder until a scholar requested their release in 2011.

The "obnoxious" medicine that Rose mentioned to Joe may have been the paregoric, a bitter-tasting liquid, sometimes mixed with water for ingestion. An opiate-based drug, commonly used up to the 1960s to relieve diarrhea, it was also a staple of many household medicine cabinets for treating digestive ailments, coughs, and painful teething. Its calming effect prompted some doctors to prescribe it for "hysterical" menopausal women. Like all opiates, if taken too often, paregoric could become addictive and cause uncomfortable withdrawal symptoms.[43] By the 1950s doctors had a new label, irritable bowel syndrome, for Rose's "tummy troubles." In addition, IBS could have accounted for the fatigue that she occasionally described in her journal as far back as the 1930s, and the disease's symptoms (alternating diarrhea and constipation) may have been exacerbated by stress and anxiety. Over the years, doctors eventually prescribed for Rose Lomotil (antidiarrheal), Bentyl (smooth-muscle relaxant), and Tagamet (acid reducer) for her gastrointestinal problems. Lomotil also eases symptoms of opiate withdrawal.[44]

Argyrol, developed at the turn of the twentieth century by Philadelphia eccentric Dr. Albert C. Barnes, is a silver compound, marketed until the 1960s as an antimicrobial agent to prevent or cure eye, nose, and throat infections. It was commonly used to treat gonorrhea in adults and prevent its spread to newborn infants' eyes. Before the development of more effective antibiotics, Argyrol made Barnes a millionaire and funded his renowned private collection of Impressionist art.[45]

Sleeping pills that Rose added to her 1957 list may have been Seconal (one of her prescriptions), a barbiturate available since the 1930s. Though highly addictive, it was used to treat insomnia, another of Rose's complaints through the years, especially when she traveled. Always a light sleeper, she would awaken at even the softest noise in her hotel room. And we have seen that she admitted to fitful sleep when nightmares about Jack abruptly awakened her in a panic during the war. Placidyl, also among her prescriptions, was another popular sedative in the 1950s.[46]

Estrogen use suggests that Rose might have been an early candidate for hormone replacement therapy, before the practice was widespread. Ironically, the common side effects of Progynon include hoarseness, cramps, stomach upset, and joint pain—all maladies that Rose mentioned having over the years.[47] She may well have been taking medicaments to counter the side effects of other drugs. Rose's health records and medical bills aren't readily available in her archives, so the portrait of her illnesses and drugs taken for them remains incomplete.

Perhaps as penance for leaving Joe yet again, or to let him know that she didn't experience a perfect life on the road, Rose sometimes shared travel travails: European electrical current caused her radio to "blow up" so she was afraid to use her heating pad; it rained constantly and her room was cold; her opera tickets went missing; rocky paths made walking impossible; she found no nearby golf courses; and foul weather prevented swimming. Despite these privations, Rose loved her stay in Salzburg. Mozart's birthplace intrigued her, but she thought that Marie knew too much about the precocious composer's "love life." They traveled to a stunning mountaintop overlooking the city, where they sipped hot chocolate and listened to Viennese waltzes. Rose didn't mention whether the sound of the music transported her back to her youth, when she cruised down the Danube, dancing with Hugh Nawn to similar strains. "Hope life is not too difficult with me away," she told Joe, then signed her letter "Gypsy Rose."[48] Her life was as peripatetic as a gypsy's, but how ironic that the prim papal countess should facetiously choose the title of American stripper Gypsy Rose Lee, especially in light of her husband's fondness for showgirls.

In another missive to Joe she continued to tease, "Drank hot choc[olate]—whipped cream every A.M.—Vienna patisserie every afternoon—If you ever divorce me—there I will live and get fatter." That seems to be the only time Rose used the "D" word in writing, presumably in jest.[49] It is remarkable that she would threaten to lose her girlish figure, which she highly prized, in the same context. Did she undergo the rigors of strict diets and manic exercise in an attempt to turn Joe's roving eye? Or was it her way of countering what she hadn't been able to control completely as a Catholic wife—numerous pregnancies and the resultant weight gain?

As Rose gallivanted through Europe, she pondered how Joe could simplify life and economize at home. "I suppose you still have all the help which seems ridiculous. You should let the kitchen maid go . . . close maid's dining room. Let parlor maid go and have Marguerite close upstairs rooms," Rose ordered. "Then get a cleaning woman in the village [of Hyannis] to clean entire house two days a week. Even if I am home in November there is no need of such a big staff." Rose left Joe—the business-man extraordinaire, ambassador, and movie mogul—explicit instructions on routine housework: "Tell the [maids] to go over all the bathing suits and pick over putting in buttons and mending—also have curtains taken down in my room and other upstairs rooms except yours. They probably could be washed at home by Marg and Betty and mended instead of paying Louisa to do them. Much—much—love—darling—Rosa." "[P.S.] Tell Marguerite initials on sheets can be done on machine if it looks like handwork. If question wait till my return."[50]

Money was never far from Rose's mind, even as she spent it on traveling and clothes. If she exceeded the balance in her account, supervised by Joe's New York business office, she simply called and asked for additional funds. Nevertheless, she repeated her financial mantra—New Englanders should be "sensible" and not show off their wealth—and worried that her daughters and in-laws were too extravagant. They had read press reports of Joe's "millions" and so didn't fret about the difference between $100 and $100,000.[51]

IN JUNE 1953 Manhattanville College awarded Rose an honorary degree. She and Eunice had attended the school; Jean and Ethel had received undergraduate degrees there. The honor particularly pleased Rose because Honey Fitz had denied her a Wellesley education. When she had attended the Academy of the Sacred Heart (forerunner of Manhattanville College), after returning from the European convent in 1909, it wasn't a degree-granting institution.

Between political campaigns, Catholic charities and institutions were the primary venues for Rose's speaking engagements. In October 1953 she spoke to the Christ Child Society at the Harvard Club in Boston on her favorite topic: "Experiences at the Court of Saint James's."[52] During a lecture on the same subject at Hyannis, she had been asked a handful of audience questions that she couldn't answer. So she contacted the British Consulate in Boston, seeking accurate responses to such queries as "Why did the late King George sign his name 'George R.I.'?" and "Do men still wear knee breeches in presence of the Queen?"[53] The consulate produced detailed answers within three days, and Rose incorporated them into her speech.[54]

These talks painted a pristine tableau of the Kennedys' London: "My two eldest sons worked at the Embassy and derived a great deal of pleasure and knowledge from their experience. My daughters made their debut and one of them fell in love and married an Englishman. Three others went to the Sacred Heart Convent at Roehampton and adjusted themselves to the school life easily and were happy. The youngest two boys went to day school. And so our family life was ideal."[55] The coming of the war and the unhappy end to Joe's ambassadorship were conspicuously absent, as were the facts that Rosemary had utterly disappeared from the family narrative, Kathleen had broken her mother's heart by marrying an Anglican, Pat suffered homesickness at boarding school, and Ted-

dy's classmates bullied him. Rose saw the world through Rose-
colored glasses, and the audience loved it. One member wrote to
say that the ladies "could have listened for another two hours." And
they netted $1,000 (more than $8,000 in current dollars) to serve
underprivileged children at Christ Child House. "I am sure the
Christ Child will bless you for your generosity," declared a society
member to Rose.[56]

Invitations to speak poured in. Rose accepted Trinity College
alumnae's invitation for 1954 and added to her engagement calendar
the Twentieth Century Club of Lynn, Massachusetts; the Ladies of
Charity Communion Breakfast in New York; St. Edward's Wom-
en's Club in Brockton, Massachusetts; and Elmhurst Convent in
Providence, Rhode Island.[57] In a more ecumenical setting, Rose
spoke at a fund-raising tea in Wellesley, Massachusetts, for the Children to Palestine Committee. The Judeo-Christian organization
rescued Jewish refugee children and resettled them in Palestine.
The committee's executive director told Rose that her "presentation was like a fine cut gem in its clarity and beauty. It certainly
gave character to our whole affair."[58] Joe's financial adviser, James
Fayne, suggested that Rose's speaking engagements to charitable
and religious organizations "be considered as contributions for
income tax purposes. . . . [T]hey will amount up to a sufficient sum
to be considered as contributions."[59]

Even as she aged, Rose continued striving to maintain a youthful appearance. In 1954 John Robert Powers, of the famous New
York modeling agency, named her one of America's eight most
beautiful women over forty, along with First Lady Mamie Eisenhower and actress Rosalind Russell.[60] A few months later, Rose
returned to the society columns when the New York *Daily News*
announced, "That large and far-reaching Kennedy clan is very
much in the news again. And only a few days after handsome Patricia, marrying British actor Peter Lawford, gave society its third
brilliant Kennedy wedding in less than twelve months. Now it's
Mrs. Joseph P. Kennedy, wife of the former U. S. Ambassador to
Great Britain, and mother of the seven Kennedy children, on whom
the spotlight has swung." The occasion was her selection to receive

the Club of Champions Award, a gold medal, from the Catholic Youth Organization of the Archdiocese of New York, for her "record of accomplishment in the field of youth work." Rose became the first woman to receive the award since its inception eighteen years earlier. (Previous recipients included FBI Director J. Edgar Hoover, Admiral Chester W. Nimitz, and Francis Cardinal Spellman.)[61] The CYO cited Rose's support for the Lt. Joseph P. Kennedy, Jr. homes for underprivileged children in New York and Boston, and her "effective community consciousness" for children's projects in Chicago, Palm Beach, and Worcester. The award's citation also praised "Countess Rose Kennedy" for "admirably fulfilling her role as mother to her own family" and serving as a surrogate mother "to countless children whose lives might have been blighted by the shadow of neglect."[62]

Like her papal countess citation, this encomium was more predictive than current in describing Rose's charitable work. As always, the family's male members were in the forefront, representing the Joseph P. Kennedy, Jr. Foundation's support of homes for disadvantaged children. Rose and Eunice, who would eventually become much more involved, were still on the sidelines. Yet Joe also stayed behind the scenes out of a sense that philanthropy shouldn't be self-aggrandizing. He didn't mind, however, aggrandizing his sons' political careers through the foundation's work. The family still had not acknowledged Rosemary's condition or made mental retardation its primary focus. That would come in the late 1950s, with Rose's and Eunice's enthusiastic participation.[63] In 1954 Rose was really being recognized for the donations her husband made under the foundation's name and for her famous maternal achievements.

The acceptance speech unmasks Rose's sentiments concerning her place in the male hierarchies of the Roman Catholic Church and the Kennedy clan. She humbly described her "small part" in helping Catholic youth but seized "this opportunity [to say a few words] although I am not the orator of the Kennedy family. The reason is because the men have never given me a chance, and I am sure the women in the audience will appreciate my dilemma when I have told my story." She explained that her late father, the congressman and mayor, "did all the talking for the [Fitzgerald] family." Then she married her husband, "a quiet, young man in his twenties—soon he became interested in politics and was afterwards ambassador to the Court of St. James's and then he made all the speeches. And now I have two sons in Washington and naturally everyone wants to listen to them—not to me." As for her motherhood, using the third person, not wishing to speak publicly about Rosemary, she said, "Sometimes a mother finds in her midst a handicapped child, one child who is abnormal mentally or physically. Then, a whole new set of baffling difficulties presents themselves, and then fervently she prays and how diligently she searches every avenue to find an answer to that child's problems." Rose praised priests and nuns devoting their lives to caring for such children, but she couldn't disclose that Franciscan sisters at St. Coletta now looked after her brain-damaged daughter in Wisconsin. "I have seen women who own famous racing stables, when they have won the Derby here, or in England—I have seen the faces of beautiful women dressed in the latest Parisian clothes and fabulous jewels at the Court of St. James's when they have made their curtsies to the king and queen, but I am sure there was not one-half of the ecstasy in their hearts in those moments" as when we look at the faces of children we have "rescued from a life of neglect and tragedy. . . ."[64]

Perhaps Rose struggled more than anyone knew to understand the meaning of life. Her reference to "Parisian clothes and fabulous jewels" as inadequate for happiness is telling. Did her own life of luxury and escapes from the family seem by the 1950s failed efforts to alleviate her marriage's disappointments and the tragedies that befell her children? Do they explain her increased charitable work? Was it her road to personal fulfillment, as well as an effort to find her own voice? As always, Rose returned to religion for explanations: "On the last day when we stand before the judgment seat of God—I am sure we shall be surrounded, not only by our own children and friends, but by thousands of the youth of today" helped by the Church's charitable works.[65]

By the mid-1950s, Rose was in need of fresh material for her lectures. How better to find it than by traveling around the world.

This time she took her niece, Mary Jo Gargan, as her companion, a few months before the young woman married Teddy Kennedy's Harvard football teammate, Richard Clasby, an All-American tailback. Mary Jo believes that having a personality similar to her late mother, Agnes, Rose's favorite travel partner, made her especially compatible with "Aunt Rose."[66]

They began with a California stop to visit Pat and her new baby, Christopher, born nine and a half months after she had married Peter Lawford. Rose, never low on advice, cautioned Pat about a baby's effect on health and love life. She should contact Boston's Lahey Clinic about taking high-potency vitamins to "get built up." Rose also warned Pat not to "wear falsies that are too prominent as they are not only cheap but tempt you know whom [Peter]." As Christopher wrote years later in his memoir, Grandma Kennedy's suggestion must have failed because his parents had three more children over the next six years (before Pat divorced Peter in 1966).[67]

After a bon-voyage party, Rose and Mary Jo embarked for the Far East, stopping in Hawaii for a week's stay in the Royal Hawaiian Resort on Waikiki Beach. They always had separate rooms. But Rose changed hers several times, looking for the quietest, so Mary Jo had to search for her each morning. In Japan Rose remarked on schoolchildren visiting historical sites. Honey Fitz had taken her to the places in and around Boston where American history occurred, and she did the same for her own children. Once home, Rose hoped to encourage more such activity in the United States. In Tokyo she met with Shigemitsu Mamoru, whom she had known during his stint as Japan's ambassador to Britain. She observed a session of the Diet and attended a party at the American embassy. Rose still loved dressing in evening attire and attending gala dinners.[68]

In India abject poverty shocked the genteel travelers. After meals, Rose collected leftovers and gave them to street beggars.[69] American ambassador John Sherman Cooper and his wife Lorraine entertained Rose and Mary Jo with an embassy tea. Cooper, former Republican senator from Kentucky, knew Jack from their days on Capitol Hill. Meeting Prime Minister Jawaharlal Nehru was a high point for Rose, who was impressed by his "great charm and . . .

obvious devotion he inspires among the Indian people." The Taj
Mahal, Rose thought, was the "loveliest place" they saw. Purchasing
colorful Indian saris, along with brocades in Hong Kong and Japan,
she intended to display them for American audiences. Rose also
snapped photos and purchased color slides to illustrate future talks.

She and Mary Jo circumnavigated the globe, returning through
Western Europe. Rose stopped in Paris to see Joe before leaving for
Boston and catching up with her mother in Hyannis. Then Rose
intended to fly back to France for July and August with Joe on the
Riviera. Upon returning to Logan Airport, the "slender and girlish" Rose, after clearing customs, asked for a glass of milk: "I hav-
en't had any in ever so long."[70]

From Hyannis Port Rose wrote to Joe that Bobby, now a graduate of Harvard and the University of Virginia School of Law, was
attracting significant press coverage for his staff work on the Senate's Permanent Subcommittee on Investigations. "Bob got two
very good notices in the *N.Y. Times*, which Ethel sent to me to
read—but I could not find anything in the *Herald Tribune*. Something should be put in the Boston papers & I am going to call Frank
Morrissey [Joe's former assistant] today." Rose also pondered ways
to attract media on her growing number of grandchildren. "I am
also thinking of having Grandma's [Josie Fitzgerald's] photo taken
with me, Bob & the 4 great-grandchildren. It would be a good
excuse for some good publicity & until I announced on my arrival
that Bob had another son, no one in Boston knew it."[71]

JACK'S HEALTH AND diet were always on Rose's mind. In 1951 she
wrote that he had "devoured caviar, sour cream, duck with all the
sauces and a strawberry soufflé" at dinner with her in Paris. "[He]
should have needed a few pills before he ever hit the Orient, I
should think."[72] In fact, Jack had fallen ill in Japan, his fever spiking
to 106 degrees. In 1953 his chronic back pain flared so badly that he
could barely walk. Apparently, the corticosteroids that he took for
his digestive ailments and Addison's had caused his fifth lumbar
vertebra to collapse. Following the best medical advice available, in

October 1954 Jack decided to undergo a delicate procedure at New York's Hospital for Special Surgery to fuse his lumbar and sacroiliac vertebrae. The doctors' prognosis was blunt. If the operation failed, Senator Kennedy might be confined to a wheelchair. At the very least, his Addison's made him vulnerable to life-threatening postoperative infections. "Jack was determined to have the operation," Rose remembered. "He told his father that even if the risks were fifty-fifty, he would rather be dead than spend the rest of his life hobbling on crutches and paralyzed by pain."[73]

Fearing the loss of another son, Joe tried to talk him out of the procedure, but Jack was adamant. The surgery went badly from the start; an infection set in, nearly killing him. Joe sobbed over his comatose son, but Jack rallied, and two months later his physicians released him to be flown to Palm Beach for Christmas. Still barely able to sit, stand, or walk, he spent much of his time confined to bed. His gaping surgical wound, around the steel plate implanted in his back, simply would not heal.[74] Jackie assumed the gruesome task of changing the dressings on the open incision.

By February 1955 so little progress had been made in Jack's condition that he decided to undergo yet another surgical procedure in New York—this time a spinal bone graft and removal of the troublesome metal plate. The third incision on his vertebrae finally healed, providing some relief. Even so, all winter and spring Jack convalesced at Palm Beach, where he began his second book, *Profiles in Courage*, aided by a battery of researchers and writers.[75]

As with Rosemary's lobotomy, Rose played no role in managing Jack's medical status. "[Joe] [k]ept encouraging him, too, although his father was heartbroken at different times when he was ill. There again he was with him," Rose remembered. "He went to the doctors, he made the decisions or he gave him the advice or he decided what he would do or where he would go. A good many times I was not consulted about because I didn't know enough of all the circumstances. . . ."[76]

Jack returned to the Senate in May 1955 and, although still underweight, he was well enough by the summer of 1956 to seek the Democratic vice-presidential nomination at the Chicago convention. He burst onto the national political scene with new charisma, not unlike that of Barack Obama forty-eight years later. JFK narrated the convention's film on the Democratic Party's history and delivered a stirring nomination speech for Adlai Stevenson. The *New York Times* captured Kennedy's essence: "Senator Kennedy came before the convention tonight as a photogenic movie star."[77] Rose's commitment to dazzling smiles was beginning to reap rewards on a national stage. Of course, neither Jack nor Joe consulted her about the vice-presidential candidacy. In fact, Joe opposed it, reasoning that if Stevenson lost, Jack's Catholicism would be blamed, barring him from a future presidential run. Rose and Joe listened to coverage of the convention on the radio in France and were relieved when the vice-presidential slot went to Tennessee senator Estes Kefauver.[78] Jack then joined his parents on the Riviera before embarking on a cruise with Senate buddy George Smathers (D-FL), rendezvousing with women in Mediterranean ports.

In late pregnancy, Jackie had stayed behind with her mother and stepfather in Newport. She had already experienced a miscarriage the previous year and was taking every precaution, but Jack apparently felt no obligation to be with her. Or perhaps Jackie had sent him on his way, as Rose did with Joe, when her due dates neared. This time Jackie delivered a stillborn daughter. Initially unaware of it, Jack continued his sailing vacation; his brother Bobby revealed the heartbreaking news to Jackie when she emerged from anesthesia and stayed with her in the Newport hospital until Jack finally returned. Smathers had persuaded him that ignoring his wife under such circumstances might produce negative publicity.[79]

For the public record, Rose, of course, denied any problems in Jack and Jackie's marriage. "As far as I know, she was perfectly happy and got along with everyone. There was no outward sign of distress or discomfort or annoyance or anything. As far as I was concerned, as far as the family was concerned. We made our adjustment, too, of course." When asked about rumors of discord in the marriage, Rose replied to her memoirist that she tried to explain to her daughters-in-law that they would hear and read "all sorts of stories. . . . I tried to alleviate or explain to them as soon as they were married or as soon as they were thinking of getting married. It would happen; it would continue to happen. . . . I didn't tell my daughters, they grew up with it. . . . It's my daughters-in-law that I warned. They were in a complete new atmosphere. Jackie, Ethel, and Joan [had] never been touched by politics."[80]

Rose believed that her husband had done his paternal duty by telling their sons to behave in public: "'Don't go out to the New York nightclubs because people will think you are a playboy. Don't drink because they will say "you're a drunk." If you don't want to go in [to politics], then I don't care what the hell you do, but if you want to go into politics. . . . And if you get into a scrape, come clean and I'll try and get you out of it or I'll try to help you. But if you lie in the beginning, then I'm licked.'" Of course, her sons got into "scrapes." Then they would determine who would tell their dad. Usually, they chose Teddy because Joe would be easier on the young boy.[81]

If the boys or their friends wrecked Joe's car, he didn't stop speaking to them, Rose recalled. "The car was fixed and there were no repercussions."[82] Traveling in Europe after his first year of law school, Teddy had an auto accident. Joe wrote to him from the Riviera, "I am sure that the insurance man will fix everything up."[83] So, although Rose always preached the importance of "responsibility," her husband became the fixer and, therefore, enabler of irresponsibility. Perhaps if the children had paid the price for poor choices, they might have been more prudent. Teddy's only genuine punishment followed a violation outside the family, when Harvard expelled him for cheating. Undoubtedly, Rose never saw the 1955 letter Joe sent to twenty-three-year-old Teddy, advising him to share his "beautiful women at Cape Cod" with his "oldest [and married] brother." "I'll leave this matter entirely in your hands and trust you will settle it to your mutual satisfaction," Joe wrote, tongue in cheek.[84] Even as he turned sixty-seven, Joe's libido remained intact. From the Riviera, he flirted by mail with daughter-in-law Jackie. "The only two things that keep me from carrying out my commitments to a young and beautiful girl are old age and running out of money. At the present writing I don't feel the impact of either." He encouraged her to buy the best horse she could find and send him the bill. About her husband, he wrote, "Remember I've always said he's a child of fate, and if he fell in a puddle of mud in a white suit he'd come up ready for a Newport ball. . . . Love and kisses, Joseph P. Kennedy."[85] Not only did Joe undermine Rose's "responsibility" lessons, he modeled the very sort of immoral behavior that Jack and Teddy embraced.

Even so, Jack continued to rise on the national political stage. Now was the time to solidify the image Rose had worked so hard to produce. Joe, however, worried that the family risked overexposure, at least in the print media. "I have one serious question in my mind as to whether people just don't get sick of reading about the Kennedys time and time and time again," he responded to a *Boston Globe* reporter, contacted by *Collier's* to write a feature on the family. "I didn't think Mrs. Kennedy would be very comfortable writing an article extolling her children," Joe declared.[86]

Not true. Rose loved to explain how *she* raised her children. She genuinely believed in her mission to help other mothers in child-rearing. It also gave her an opportunity to justify her life as wife and mother. So in 1956 she partnered with James Fayne in writing an article they submitted to *Reader's Digest*. After all, it had published "Nine Kennedys and How They Grew" in 1939 and had reprinted the *New Yorker* feature about Jack's naval exploits in the South Pacific. Rose's core list of maternal philosophy might have been aptly called "Rose's Rules for Raising Rambunctious Yet Responsible Children."

Rule One: "We felt they should be taught to take on responsibility not dodge it."

Rule Two: "Meal time is a good time to talk to children."

Rule Three: The Founding Fathers "are the people to be emulated— not gang busters."

Rule Four: "Show them lions at the zoo and explain how they consumed the early Christians—and so interest children."

Rule Five: "We who have been given this privilege of religious inspiration have a motive for every thought and deed—that is the one of working for God."

Rule Six: "In an atmosphere where everyone is talking 'books,' the children will read."

Rule Seven: "One [child] may be smart in studies, one dull—one may be over-confident, another shy—and so a different approach must be made."

Rule Eight: "Try to prepare them to have good judgment in emergencies or in circumstances where we cannot always be with them."

Rule Nine: "Try to stimulate interest in . . . civic or national undertakings and . . . have a responsibility and a real interest as they get older."[87]

From these fundamental precepts, Rose and Fayne created a longer piece, which began, "I have been thinking of writing this article for some time. All through my life people have evinced interest and curiosity in my family because there were so many children." Yet Rose described how she eventually kept the number of her children secret when she traveled, so she could discuss other subjects with people she met on the journey. "Not that I was not interested, but when I left my children and their problems at home, I wanted to tuck them aside mentally for a while and talk and hear about something new and different in order to refresh my mind." "For hours at a time I used to listen to the crack of croquet balls, to the arguments about the game until I yearned for the peace and quiet of a career woman's life." Such honesty about why she had to travel called for some balance regarding the life she had chosen or had thrust upon her: "Bringing up a family must be viewed as great fun and a great challenge. It is not always easy, it is not always interesting, but it is the natural way in which God intended most women to live, and it is the most satisfying." Rose described "career women" as secretaries or shop clerks. Without children, they save the best years of their lives for themselves and keep their figures. "[Yet] what thrill in a profession compares with the ecstasy and joy of a mother when she first holds her own baby in her arms . . . ?" Rose asked. Focusing on her children's health, she recalled the necessity of being home by late afternoon to observe early symp-

toms of colds, and she made the usual reference to her method of
tracking childhood medical events. The manuscript roamed from
how to choose a boarding school to the importance of study abroad
to religious training to making "a boy understand that he must be
truthful."[88] Perhaps the article seemed too rife with platitudes even
for *Reader's Digest*. Or maybe Rose's advice about boarding schools
and study abroad struck an elitist note. In any case, *Reader's Digest*
rejected it.

BY 1957, HAD ROSE taken stock, she would have found much to
please her. Jackie and Jack, despite his womanizing, had their first
child, Caroline, late that year, and were settled in Georgetown,
with Jack anticipating his 1958 Senate reelection campaign. Eunice
and Sarge had created a happy home in Chicago, where he continued to manage the Merchandise Mart. The Shrivers now had two
children. Eunice, the most career-oriented of Rose's daughters,
continued to apply her Stanford degree, working at a women's shelter and with juvenile delinquents. She and Sarge, both devout
Catholics, were a perfectly matched couple. Pat and Peter Lawford,
who also had two children, were living the Hollywood high life at
their Santa Monica beach house, palling around with Judy Garland
and Frank Sinatra. Before her marriage Pat had been a production
assistant for singer Kate Smith and for a Catholic television show.
While Rose always corresponded pleasantly with Peter, his alcohol
and drug problems would cause tension early in his marriage to Pat,
who also turned to drinking. Bobby and Ethel had purchased historic Hickory Hill estate in northern Virginia from Jack and Jackie
when it became clear that they wouldn't have a large family. The
Robert Kennedys filled it with five children by 1957. Ethel's
philosophy—"If you're obeying all the rules, you're missing all the
fun"—made her home chaotic, but she got on well with Rose
despite their differences on family discipline.[89] Meanwhile, Bobby
was making a name for himself as a hard-nosed Senate committee
staff lawyer, and he strategized with Joe on Jack's steps toward the
presidency. Jean had wed businessman Stephen Smith in 1956, and

they produced their first child the next year. Like Sargent Shriver, Smith worked for Joe. Based in the New York business office, Steve's understanding of the family's finances would make him a valuable asset in future campaigns. Joe and Rose now counted eleven grandchildren, and Grandma Kennedy freely dispensed her advice on child rearing.

Only Teddy remained single, but not for long. In late 1957 he visited Manhattanville College for the dedication of the Kennedy Physical Education Building, donated in Kick's memory. After the ceremony he met a stunningly beautiful and musically talented student, Joan Bennett. Her piano virtuosity "earned her a lot of points with Mother," Teddy remembered. Joan and Rose even played duets together. After a yearlong courtship, Joan and Teddy married. He gave her a clover-shaped pin that had belonged to Rose, and, after a brief honeymoon, Teddy and his bride moved to Charlottesville so that he could complete his law degree at UVA.[90]

As Jack moved toward his 1958 Senate reelection campaign and developed plans to run nationally in 1960, Rose's speaking engagements increased, sometimes as a stand-in for her son. In December 1956 Monsignor Newman Flanagan invited Senator Kennedy to speak to the Sons and Daughters of St. Patrick in Sioux City, Iowa, two years hence. A Boston native, Flanagan reflected the tactical savvy of an Irish Catholic pol: "Sioux City is at the junction of Iowa, Nebraska, South Dakota with western Minnesota eighty miles to the north (but out here we think nothing of 80 miles). I feel we could secure a large audience, and, with ample time to prepare, arrange for local Democrats to assemble. . . . The town is one of the larger stock yard centers and a good springboard for agricultural contacts." He raised the possibility of Rose's coming, too:

It has also been suggested to me that your charming mother might be interested in making an address here sometime. I understand she has a very interesting lecture on her experiences at the Court of St. James. We have recently organized the Council of Catholic Women from the 24 counties of northwestern Iowa—a thousand came to our September meeting. It could be arranged that an invitation be sent her if you thought well of her. Further I think, if you feel we should emphasize the public service of the family rather than the Church affiliation, we might suggest to some non-Catholic friends that she be invited to address the non-sectarian Woman's Club.[91]

Rose responded in early February 1957 with gratitude for the monsignor's invitation: "I was very flattered that you asked me and I should like very much to go, but during the last year I have had to decline all speaking engagements due to the fact that I have found it very exhausting to travel long distances. I hope to take a long rest this winter and if I regain some of that old Fitzgerald energy and gusto, I shall certainly contact you." Even though Rose was now sixty-six, her reason for declining rings rather hollow in light of her globe-trotting. She remarked that Jack would be visiting her and Joe in a few days at Palm Beach.[92]

Flanagan responded to Rose immediately, explaining that he hoped to organize coffee parties for Jack "in the Corn Belt," similar to those the Kennedy women had executed in Massachusetts. He regretted "that the Fitzgerald energy was temporarily run down. . . . However if the young vigor returns and it appears that we can ever be helpful to your son, whatever his decisions, please let me know and I am sure we can rearrange schedules and gather some good propagandists for ground work in an almost G.O.P. territory."[93]

Eleven days after Rose sent regrets, and after Jack had begun his visit with her and Joe in Palm Beach, she notified Flanagan of a change of heart. "It is very flattering to be invited to your city." When might she visit? Describing her lecture, "An Ambassador's Wife at the Court of St. James's," she offered to meet women over tea or coffee afterward. Within a week of Jack's Palm Beach visit, Rose had provided a date to Flanagan for her talk.[94] Clearly, Joe and Jack, understanding the importance of such events for JFK's presidential run, had reversed Rose's demurral. If Joe was the coach and Jack the quarterback, she was the head cheerleader.

The Iowa trip became a model for Rose Kennedy's appearances

in her sons' national campaigns. Her October 1957 speech before the Sioux City Diocesan Council of Catholic Women was followed by engagements at Mount Mercy College in Cedar Rapids and Marycrest College in Davenport. Press reception was warm. "I am writing to thank you for the interview," she told a "very cooperative" Cedar Rapids feature writer. "I thought it was one of the best articles which I have seen and Mr. Kennedy agreed with me."[95] "C.R. Audience Charmed by Mrs. Kennedy," proclaimed the headline in the women's section of the *Cedar Rapids Gazette.* "Mrs. Joseph P. Kennedy is a gracious, petite woman whose youthful trimness belies the role she enjoys most—mother of nine children and grandmother of ten." Noting her secondary role in a family of powerful men, she repeated her CYO speech themes: "I am not the speaker in the Kennedy family. The reason is, I've never had a chance." Well, she had it now, and she made the most of it. The paper pictured her with one of the ostrich-feather fans she had carried when presented at the British court, and her Parisian dress and hat received detailed descriptions. "[B]ut much of the audience was even more interested in getting a glimpse of the woman whose son, John, to whom she referred as 'The Senator,' has been mentioned as a possible presidential candidate for 1960," reported the paper. Rose eschewed public policy but commented on child-rearing and "handicapped children."[96] Rosemary's story remained under wraps.

Yet it was during this period that Rose began to influence Joe about moving the Joseph P. Kennedy, Jr. Foundation toward supporting research on mental retardation and concentrating less on underprivileged children. She left no archival material regarding that effort, and she never had executive power in the Foundation. Teddy insisted, however, that his mother's role should not be overlooked. Eunice and Sarge, along with Cardinal Cushing, ultimately convinced Joe Kennedy that the family's fortune should fund the study of why intellectual disabilities occurred in the first place.[97]

Rose kept meticulous notes on the people she met in Iowa. Her whole life had prepared her for this new political role. Traveling with her father, creating a large and celebrated family, entertaining (and being entertained) in London, speaking at charities, promoting her son, observing human nature, wearing couture fashions: all coalesced in a perfect education for the campaign trail. And Iowa was the first stop on the national map. Names, addresses, and comments—nothing escaped her. She even noted that one woman, who drove her to a tea, was "non-Catholic." Rose saw to it that each of those gracious Iowans received an autographed copy of Jack's 1955 Pulitzer Prize–winning *Profiles in Courage* for Christmas 1957.[98] The biggest campaign of Rose the Matriarch's life had begun.

CHAPTER 10

Mother of the President

AFTER ROSE'S 1957 IOWA TRIP, SHE BEGAN SPEAKING IN STATES crucial to Jack's presidential candidacy. The 1960 Democratic nomination contest featured only sixteen primaries, in contrast to 2008's forty. Jack Kennedy decided to focus on New Hampshire, Wisconsin, Indiana, West Virginia, Nebraska, Maryland, and Oregon. He couldn't secure the nomination by winning those states, but victories in most of them could demonstrate his electability.[1] New Hampshire, traditionally the first presidential primary, warranted Rose's attention in early 1958. She spoke to Catholic organizations in Concord (the capital), Manchester (the largest city), and Nashua (the second largest city). A letter, probably from Rose's secretary, informed one of the New Hampshire organizers that Rose did "not want to make her appearance in New Hampshire a political issue. We believe, therefore, she would not want to say 'hello' to the Governor as she doesn't want any publicity about it, other than what comes from the people to whom she is going to talk."[2] This arrangement suited Rose perfectly; she could fly under the political radar while raising money for charity *and* spreading the Kennedy name among potential voters.

Always fastidious, Rose asked for a quiet room, not a suite, at the back of hotels, and a second room for her maid or secretary.[3] In Nashua, her first stop, she spoke to five hundred faculty, students, and their guests at Rivier College, a Catholic institution founded by the Sisters of the Presentation of Mary. Next came Concord where six hundred Catholic Daughters of America turned out, followed by a capacity crowd of two hundred and sixty at a meeting of the Manchester Diocesan Council of Catholic Women.[4]

Rose's engagements, like her 1957 Iowa events, reflected Joe's strategic imprint and Jack's undoubted concurrence. She declined some Massachusetts charity functions, telling organizations that 1958 would be devoted to campaigning for Jack's Senate reelection. In reality, he seemed so likely to maintain his seat that the family didn't even have to call on Rose until late in the campaign.[5] The family was obviously looking ahead to 1960 when Rose wrote to James Cardinal McIntyre, "Joe has told me that your Eminence has graciously offered to get in touch with various groups in Los Angeles and in other parts of California to whom I might speak. I have been doing this kind of work for some time in Massachusetts and I have found it very stimulating." Her offered topics varied from the tried and true "An Ambassador's Wife in London" to her newly crafted "My Trip to Japan." She also reminded McIntyre that she accepted no honoraria; all proceeds would be donated to charities organizing her visit. Planning to see Pat in L.A. during April and May 1958, Rose could deliver her talks then or later.[6]

The cardinal arranged an invitation for her to speak at an Archdiocesan Council of Catholic Women meeting. Contacting Reverend Mother Mulqueen at Manhattanville College, Rose asked her to facilitate a talk at Sacred Heart College in Los Angeles. "To be frank," Rose confessed to Mulqueen, "we Kennedys want very much to spread our acquaintances in California which is very important during the [1960 Democratic] National Convention [in L.A.], since it has a large number of delegates."[7] A lecture to the nuns, students, parents, and friends at the college would be just the way to add new supporters to the Kennedy bandwagon.

While in Los Angeles Rose did an interview on "The Ten-Fifteen File," with KTTV television talk-show personality Paul Coates. Such appearances would become a public-relations staple for her in the 1960s and '70s, but this engagement must have been among her first television interviews. Remarkably, after an absence of nearly two decades, Rosemary now reentered her mother's litany of the Kennedy children. In a gentle and rather deceptive reference, Rosemary was described as "working for [a] retarded children school." Never mind that she was actually one of the patients at St. Coletta's. Rose resurrected the family's previous story that Rosemary was a teacher. Why lift the veil now? Perhaps the family's redefinition of the Joseph P. Kennedy, Jr. Foundation's mission, to fund research on mental retardation, gave Rose courage to mention Rosemary again and move closer to the truth. Or perhaps Joe and Jack had looked ahead two years to the Wisconsin primary. Rosemary had lived there since 1949. It wouldn't do to have that fact revealed in the midst of a presidential campaign. Paul Coates asked Rose, "You've often been called a matriarch. Does that mean you—rather than your husband—were the boss of your home?" "I'm called matriarch merely to distinguish me from the other well-known Mrs. Kennedys—the wives of my sons. I don't think it would be correct to call me the boss," Rose responded. Coates then cut to the heart of Rose's visit to L.A.: "You've asked me not to ask you any questions about politics, and I think I have stuck by my bargain pretty well. But I can't help wondering: How much have you and your husband thought about the idea that one of your children would someday become president?" "Naturally it entered our minds . . . ," Rose had to admit. So Coates pressed, "Your son, Senator John Kennedy, seems to be the most likely of the clan to make the White House. Now, I know it's impossible for you to be impartial but try to be as objective as you can and tell me what kind of president you think John would make." Describing him as "very conscientious, straightforward in his thinking, experienced, well-equipped in affairs of state," Rose added, "because, as a very young man, when others were swimming or golfing in the summer, he used to be traveling in

Europe studying there and so at a very young age, he had a knowledge of international events. . . ." As the '6os approached, the times
they were a-changin', not only in Rose's use of media but in the
kinds of questions she fielded. Coates, a member of her children's
generation and a leader in investigative journalism, asked her why
she had never gone into politics herself. "You're not opposed to the
idea of women holding public office, are you?" he challenged. "No.
It's simply that I've always been too busy raising nine children,"
Rose demurred with her stock answer. But Coates pointed out that
her children were now grown. Hadn't she become more active in
public life? "Yes, I lecture about my experiences as an ambassador's
wife, with proceeds to charity. And I work with the Joseph P. Kennedy, Jr. Foundation for retarded children. We have established
about ten schools in different cities for this group."[8] The discussion
of the topic went no further.

RESTING DURING THE summer before Jack's reelection campaign,
Rose wrote from the south of France, "Shall await the big
putsch—1960."[9] Back in Massachusetts by midfall, she finally
turned her attention to Jack's Senate reelection campaign. "At
Home with the Kennedys," a live thirty-minute television program, aired a week prior to the November 4 election. Joining her
around a cozy living room set were Jackie, Eunice, and Jean, who
debuted her toddler Steve Jr. The elder Mrs. Kennedy led a discussion among the women that by today's standards seems quite stilted.
She quizzed Jackie about her role in Jack's campaign, and the young
wife talked about traveling throughout Massachusetts with him.
Rose mentioned the many historic sites in the Bay State, encouraging parents to visit them so that their children would emulate
American heroes. When Jackie ventured that her mother-in-law
campaigned as a young child with Honey Fitz, Rose corrected her,
saying that girls didn't campaign in those days before women's suffrage. Jackie handled the correction with aplomb and observed that
Teddy was serving as Jack's campaign manager when he could spare

time from his final year at UVA's law school. Rose then introduced and narrated a video featuring Eunice, Bobby, and Pat with their spouses and children. Senator Kennedy joined the midmorning show and asked women viewers for their vote. If they called in, his sisters and his wife would field questions and pass them along to him. Jack displayed a firm command of policy details and a ready wit. When a teenaged boy phoned, JFK teased, "Why aren't you in school?" Then he thanked his sisters and his mother, particularly, for her support of Honey Fitz's and Joe's public service. As a warm denouement, Jack joined Jackie on the couch and introduced their one-year-old daughter Caroline.[10] Here was a vintage Kennedy performance in a new medium that brought three generations of the famous family into voters' living rooms. Just as Joe and Rose had captured print and newsreels to present their young brood, now television would launch Jack and Jackie as political celebrities.

One caller had remarked that JFK was a "shoo-in" for reelection. Why should voters even go to the polls? Jack responded that he had no votes prior to election day and that he would like to have as many as possible to show his Senate colleagues the strong support he garnered in Massachusetts.[11] Left unstated was his desire to demonstrate overwhelming popularity as he prepared for a bold run at the Democratic presidential nomination two years later, when he would be just forty-two years old. No Roman Catholic had run for president since Al Smith's 1928 shellacking by Herbert Hoover. Jack's final poll results didn't disappoint. He won 73.6 percent of the votes, the largest winning margin in Massachusetts history and the second-largest among all 1958 Senate candidates.[12]

As Jack crisscrossed the country, sometimes with Jackie, more often with alter ego Ted Sorensen, Rose continued to deliver speeches on her own. In October 1959 she received the Trinity Award, named for the Washington, DC, Catholic women's college. Its citation read:

In recognition of one who has contributed in a marked manner to the spiritual and physical well-being of so many exceptional

children, of a Catholic mother of charm and wisdom, whose
everlasting influence is dramatically apparent in terms of front
page news from New York to Moscow, of a woman whose
influence has direct bearing on the destiny of America and perhaps of the world, Trinity College is pleased to present the
Trinity Award . . . to a gracious lady who stands for the signal
virtues of motherhood, womanhood and for the influence of
women for GOOD—Mrs. Joseph P. Kennedy.[13]

Clearly, Rose's star was rising with Jack's. Her motherhood now
attracted attention and honors not simply for its numerical novelty,
but because, as she began stating in the 1950s, a mother influences
her child "not for one day, one month, one year, but for time and
for eternity."[14]

She also spoke with pride about Eunice's childhood tendency to
care for her siblings and now her outreach to "the mentally retarded
and . . . delinquent children." "Be with your children when they
are young and this applies to fathers as well as mothers," Rose proclaimed. She and Joe hadn't always followed that edict consistently.
Looking back, she may have wished otherwise. Somewhat wistful,
Rose revealed that the "greatest privilege" a mother could experience would be seeing her son join the priesthood. As we have seen,
Joe insisted that the Kennedy boys attend non-Catholic schools, an
unlikely route to religious vocations.[15]

Rose still took her maternal responsibilities seriously. Jack was
now forty-two and a US senator, but she wrote to Jackie, "Will you
please remind Jack about his Easter duty; I am sure that he could go
to confession some morning in Washington as the church is quite
near." The Catholic Church requires that all members receive Communion during the Easter season. Rose probably thought that meant
receiving the sacrament of confession, too. Technically, it didn't, but
the Church forbids Communion for those who have committed
grave sins and not confessed them to a priest. Rose also microman-
aged his wardrobe, asking Jackie to find "some old socks for Jack—
for him to wear playing golf or walking in the rain, as he did not
have any the other day when he was down here [at Hyannis]."[16]

IN CAMPAIGNING, ROSE enjoyed sparring with the common man. Taxi drivers proved a fertile source of opinion, especially about Jack. On her way to LaGuardia Airport in mid-1959, she grilled the cabdriver about the upcoming presidential race, keeping her identity secret.

> [H]e was a different ilk than usual. Born in Brooklyn of Jewish parents . . . he was strong for Stevenson—thought he was a great man—thought Kennedy too young and said his chances were nil because he was Catholic. I, of course, adopted my regular technique, saying I was from Mass[achusetts]—we all were ecstatic about him up here. His youth was an advantage as we wanted no more old men like Eisenhower–Dulles, and Kennedy was experienced and well versed in the rudiments of politics in spite of his youth—due to his exposure to it from his babyhood.[17]

Unlike current presidential campaigns that officially begin more than a year before election day, John Kennedy announced his candidacy in Washington on January 2, 1960. Rose, billed as "mother of the presidential candidate," continued her charity speaking engagements. In Fort Lauderdale she spoke to raise money for the Leukemia Research Fund. The talk on prewar London now included color slides of the late King George VI, the Queen Mother, and the Kennedy girls in debutante gowns. The women's section of the *Fort Lauderdale News* proclaimed that Mrs. Kennedy "looked the part of an ambassador's wife down to the tip of her elegant Italian shoes." She shared a comedic, and somewhat embellished, version of her conversation with the queen about whether Rose saw her children off to school each morning. Her poker-faced retort in Fort Lauderdale: "I did that for the first six . . . after that, I figured this would go on forever, so I quit!" Leaving behind a hint of her Chanel No. 5, Rose stepped into a chauffeured limousine. She was off to campaign for Jack. Her exit line—"With nine children, your job as a mother is never done."[18]

Nothing could have drawn Rose away from balmy Palm Beach other than Jack's first primary, in frigid New Hampshire. "She is still a top campaigner," thought Joe, again watching from the sidelines.[19] Rose now had a genuine campaign speech, not her England or Japan travelogues. Even if campaign staff supplied its gist, she added her thoughts and personal touches that made her son more human. Joined by daughter Jean Smith, Rose made a two-day swing through the Granite State, starting at Keene Teachers College with a speech to faculty and students. After lunch at the local Lion's Club, it was on to Manchester for an afternoon tea with women Democrats, then an evening reception in Exeter. The exhausting daily schedule would have challenged a youthful campaigner. Rose was sixty-nine, yet her "Fitzgerald energy" came in bursts for such trips. Up before dawn the next day, the Kennedy ladies were off to Laconia for a midmorning coffee hour and reception, then a student–faculty luncheon and public reception at Plymouth State Teachers College. One more tea, in Manchester, then it was back to New York.[20] Ultimately, Jack received 85 percent of the New Hampshire vote.

Wisconsin was next, and Rose spent a grueling week stumping for Jack there. JFK was battling regional favorite Minnesota senator Hubert Humphrey. Except for enclaves of Catholic voters in a few large cities, Jack faced Protestant strongholds. A credible showing might weaken the religion argument against his candidacy. Flying to La Crosse, anthropologist Rose noted that the male passengers were "more stalwart looking" and the "women more hardy and robust looking, less refined looking than [in the] East." Their "clothes [were] sensible, practical, bought for long use." An announcement by the stewardess that the "mother of Senator Kennedy was aboard" elicited no reaction that Rose could discern. Clearly, she was no longer in Massachusetts. Jack's old friend Lem Billings collected her at the airport, reporting that "the religious question was rampant." He "seemed very nervous" to Rose, but she attributed that to his wanting to have a large turnout and successful visit for her. Rose had come to Wisconsin to repeat the successful Kennedy teas; women, she explained, were more likely to come to a tea than a political rally. She decided to call the gathering a "coffee klatch," which sounded less formal in the Midwest than a tea. And the Wisconsin ladies, with German backgrounds, were more likely to drink coffee, as Rose remembered from her days at Blumenthal and her travels in Germanic countries.[21]

Whenever given the chance, Rose proudly elaborated on Jack's war record, noting in her diary that "Humphrey had not gone to war on account of [a] hernia." Questions of how Jack became interested in politics were right in her strike zone, and she offered the same stories about Honey Fitz that she included in her campaign speech. In addition, she invoked the New Deal and Jack's opportunities to meet principals from FDR's administration, as well as Winston Churchill, Anthony Eden, and Neville Chamberlain.[22]

La Crosse's Bishop John Treacy, a Massachusetts native whom Rose had met at Palm Beach, offered to help Jack, but he telephoned to say that "he was afraid to come to my tea on account of anti-Catholic literature which had been circulated. We secretly agreed it was better that way as people are saying Catholics will vote for Jack [anyway], and they [the Kennedy campaign] are trying to get Protestants [to vote for him]. . . ."[23]

Rose collected materials about Catholicism and its impact on the election. An article by Boston's Cardinal Cushing argued that "[f]rom the very beginning of the Republic Catholics have played active and significant roles." Roger Taney and Edward White, for example, had served as chief justices of the US Supreme Court. "The presidential oath is similar to that taken by members of Congress and the federal judges. Is there something peculiarly distinct in the office and powers of an American president which seems to disqualify a Catholic?" Cushing asked.[24] His answer, of course, was "no."

Rose also kept an article from the Catholic magazine *Jubilee* containing disquieting news about Jack's candidacy among her coreligionists. Ninety-seven percent of subscribers interviewed were concerned about anti-Catholicism in the United States and thought that Kennedy's run for the presidency would increase it. Only one-third of those polled believed JFK could win, although 57 percent reported that they would vote for him. Sixty-seven percent, however, indicated that they would vote for a Catholic other than Kennedy.[25]

From La Crosse to Viroqua to Richland Center to Prairie du Chien to Superior to Eau Claire to Milwaukee to Madison—Rose visited three of Wisconsin's ten congressional districts, including the tenth, which was "heavily Lutheran and [for] Humphrey."[26] In Milwaukee, the state's largest city, with more than seven hundred thousand people and a sizable black population, Rose provided another TV interview and then attended a small coffee hour "in a colored woman's apartment. She was an alderman—small neat flat." "Afterwards drove to a horticulture show to be photographed with colored representative." Rose seemed a bit peeved that the photographer was late, "so I had to sit in car with two other colored friends and wait for him and then take him to hall for photo."[27] Starting with FDR in 1932, Democrats could count on receiving at least two-thirds of the nation's black vote in presidential elections. Energizing Milwaukee's black residents for Kennedy over Humphrey would help Jack's primary contest with his Minnesota rival. Yet Humphrey had compiled a much stronger record on civil rights than JFK. At least Rose had drawn more voters to her La Crosse event than Humphrey had to his appearance.

At any rate, Jack did win Wisconsin's April 5, 1960, primary, carrying 56 percent of the votes and six out of ten congressional districts—no knockout punch to be sure, but a harbinger. For his part, Humphrey would fight on to the May 10 West Virginia primary.[28] As the primary season progressed, Rose listed "recommendations" for Jack's political team that she wanted "sent to all headquarters":

1. Bobby and Jack's books and photographs should be in all the headquarters; War pictures of Jack and Caroline on display in the windows.
2. Mrs. Kennedy and the girls should not cover the same groups, if at all possible.
3. There should be a few night meetings, because not every

woman can come during the day, particularly if she has children.

4. There should be adequate distribution of material to the various campaign headquarters.

5. There should be advance publicity pictures to stimulate interest.[29]

Leaving the grand strategy to Joe, Jack, and Bobby, Rose focused, as usual, on tactics that reached the grass roots, especially women.

Between the Wisconsin and West Virginia primaries, the Kennedys gathered at Palm Beach for Easter. Jack decided not to campaign during Holy Week, which pleased his devout mother. Rose took the opportunity to write in her journal about Jackie's response to a national campaign: "Jackie [is] in gay spirits, talks animatedly and gaily about campaign experiences." She fretted that Jackie "is more inclined to show her hates and be rude to newspaper people than Jack, who, according to the press and to his father, maintains a pretty level, unruffled front, never deviating from role of natural, inbred courtesy." Jackie "is constantly telling us what she would like to do or say to those people who have cast aspersions on Jack—Doris Fleeson, for instance, a columnist has constantly abused Jack." Fleeson, the first woman syndicated columnist, based at the New York *Daily News*, wrote scathing critiques of politicians. She invited Joe and Rose to the Press Club, and Joe wanted to accept, in hopes that it would "mollify Fleeson's resentments or criticisms, but Jackie bristled at the idea of Fleeson having satisfaction of producing me at Press Club. At any rate, I did not want to go and wrote her I was busy campaigning," Rose recorded.[30] Fleeson eventually defended Jackie against her critics, prompting Jack's wife to write a thank-you note to the journalist.[31]

Rose reveled in the excitement centered on her Palm Beach home. She loved the lively discussions of editorials, opinions, and rumors, as well as the incoming calls from all over the country. How fortunate, she thought, to have her sons and sons-in-law united in a common cause to secure the nomination for Jack and then elect him president. She didn't mention her daughters and

daughters-in-law, though they worked as hard as maternal obligations allowed.[32]

Jack scored a major victory over Humphrey in West Virginia,
proving that a Catholic could carry an overwhelmingly Protestant
state. It also eliminated one of his key opponents for the nomination. Short on money and organization, Humphrey couldn't mount
a viable response to the Kennedy family machine. Meanwhile,
Adlai Stevenson and Lyndon Johnson waited in the wings, refusing
to participate in the primaries. Jack's campaign now moved on to
Maryland and Nebraska, where Rose joined the Kennedy team
again. She did a three-day swing through Baltimore and nearby
towns. Mayor J. Harold Grady presented her with the key to Maryland's largest city before Rose arrived at Notre Dame of Maryland,
the nation's oldest Catholic women's college. When she spoke to
women, Rose observed that they didn't have the right to vote when
she was young. In fact, Rose was thirty before women earned the
franchise with passage of the Nineteenth Amendment in 1920. She
exhorted modern women to "get out and vote and urge our friends
to vote and urge our mother and grandmothers—like me." Rose
added that she now had sixteen grandchildren: her progeny were
still a point of emphasis and pride. But the days of simply chatting
about her family's London embassy experiences were over. Momentum was on Jack's side, as she cited his victories in New Hampshire,
Wisconsin, and West Virginia. She called for a "tremendous vote as
it will give Jack a tremendous boost in Los Angeles. . . . Thus we
have a chance to help select the next President of the United States.
Otherwise a few men in a smoke-filled room in Los Angeles will
have that privilege." Then she was off to two more receptions at
local Democratic clubs, and she stopped by a Baltimore hotel to
greet Jack's campaign workers.[33]

While in Baltimore, Rose attended a tea given in her honor by
the Colored Women's Democratic Campaign Committee of Maryland and then toured Morgan State University, Maryland's largest
historically black college.[34] As one women's-column writer noted,
"Wealthy beyond belief, she could have leisurely ordered breakfast
in bed. Instead, she was out on the political stump by 8:30 a.m.,

delivering at least six campaign speeches a day before women's clubs, college groups, and TV microphones."[35] Rose continued this whirlwind in Nebraska prior to its May 10 primary. In Lincoln she met with the state's first lady and welcomed the American Association of University Women to the governor's mansion. Rose offered a special greeting to Manhattanville College alums at the gathering.

By June, Rose could relax, knowing that Jack had won the Nebraska primary with 89 percent of the vote and Maryland's contest with 70 percent. She had campaigned for him in four of the seven primaries he entered, and he had won them all. Her weeklong marathon for Jack in Wisconsin might well have been the most crucial of her trips. He carried that contest with little room to spare. Had he lost, his momentum into the decisive West Virginia primary would have slowed. Even worse, his Catholicism would have received more—and very negative—attention.

Settling in at Hyannis Port for the summer, Rose was "confident that Jack will win because his father says so, and through the years I have seen his predictions and judgments vindicated, almost without exception." Joe also predicted that Jack would defeat Vice President Richard Nixon for the presidency. She doubted that her husband would ever receive credit for the "overall strategy" and "unremitting labor day and night, which he had devoted to making his son president." Then Rose turned to her usual concern: Jack's eating habits. She watched him down lobster and corn on the cob, New England favorites. Instead of feeling relief that he had a robust appetite after years of weight loss, Rose recalled that Dr. Sara Jordan of the Lahey Clinic at Tufts University had warned that such foods "are the worse things for a tummy like I have and Jack has."[36]

One of Rose's most triumphant moments neared as the family headed to Los Angeles for the Democratic Convention. Jack had compiled seven primary victories across the country. Yet the nomination was not assured. Some delegates supported Adlai Stevenson, the unsuccessful nominee in 1952 and 1956, who had the backing of Eleanor Roosevelt, no admirer of Jack or his father. Texas senator Lyndon Johnson, who detested the thought of young Jack Kennedy coming out on top, was launching a last-minute effort to rally support. His camp spread the word about Jack's Addison's disease, which the Kennedys, of course, had not publicized.

Jackie, now four months pregnant, stayed behind in Hyannis with two-year-old Caroline. From L.A. Rose penned a humorous and sweet note to her daughter-in-law, though she never sent it. Rose's feet hurt from so many appearances in high heels. While she soaked her "sore instep in hot water and Epsom salts," she told Jackie, "I am thinking of you and missing you. The conqueror's [Jack's] first words to Eunice after he had been pushed and jostled through the exulting, cheering crowd were, 'I wish I were back at the Cape.' . . . [I]t showed where his heart was." Rose complimented Jackie's "good judgment" for staying home "because the girls said the crowds were really almost rough in their enthusiasm and would have crushed you and worried everybody."[37]

While Joe continued to shun the spotlight, Rose welcomed it. Holding a news conference for women writers, she answered dozens of questions. The *New York Times* described her as a "strikingly dressed . . . soft-spoken New England matron." Most important, she announced that she would campaign for JFK that fall. "I'll go wherever they want me to go, and do whatever they want me to do during the campaign. I love to travel and will enjoy campaigning with Jack." Initially, she tried to duck the religious issue, not wanting to discuss its relation to politics. But she asserted that "religion is a wonderful thing regardless of what the faith. It gives a person stability and confidence which is so badly needed by us all. Our religion has certainly not been a handicap politically," Rose concluded.[38] Regarding JFK's youth, she observed, "Jack, incidentally, is only four years younger that Nixon. Older men have had their chance at the White House. I feel that younger men have a great deal of the vigor, enthusiasm, and idealism, which we need now." About Jack's health, Rose admitted that it took her son "a long time to recover from his World War II injuries in the Pacific (when his PT boat was rammed by a Japanese destroyer). Now I think he is in very good health and he has been for some time. His capacity for traveling and campaigning is the best evidence." Only a seasoned campaigner could so nimbly mingle Jack's war record with his robust health during the strenuous primary season. She even took one for the team, letting a reporter describe her as a "size 10," when she had remained a perfect size-8 figure after nine pregnancies. When asked her age, Rose noted that the press claimed she was seventy, even though she would not be for six more weeks. "It wouldn't look good for Jack if I were too young," Rose quipped. Also using humor to deflect queries about Joe's reported fortune, she joked, "When I first read in the papers that he had $100 million dollars, I went to him and asked, 'Why didn't you tell me you had that much money?'"[39] But, more seriously, she observed, "You all know that he's been rather a controversial figure all his life. He thinks it's easier for his sons if he does not appear."[40] The press was utterly charmed: "Today, Rose was the undisputed queen of the Kennedy campaign, handling press conference questions with the agility of a pro."[41]

Before the balloting began, Rose, Joe, and their niece Ann Gargan watched Stevenson's televised address to the delegates. The Kennedys were "furious with him as he will not say he is a candidate, but he does take delegates away from us, and California is strong for him." Joe was uncharacteristically quiet, but he perked up immediately when Jack came by appearing nervous about the outcome. The Kennedy patriarch tried to put his son at ease, and Rose admired how he became a "haven" for Jack "to drop all his cares, his problems, his misgivings in [his] Dad's lap."[42]

Soon the day they had all worked so hard for arrived, and they all gathered around the TV to watch the nomination process, while a barber trimmed Jack's shock of thick auburn hair. His mother was amused that he, apparently as vain as she, "held a large mirror in front of him and told the barber, 'A little more here on this side, a little more there,'" as he watched the convention proceedings. Rose tried to reach Jackie at the Cape, only to be told by the family chauffeur that she wanted no phone calls. Her mother and stepfather had traveled from Newport to be with her. Eventually everyone but Joe went to the arena to watch Jack defeat Johnson on the first ballot, 806 to 409. Rose felt "relieved, encouraged."[43] Jack would choose Johnson for the vice-presidential slot to secure Texas's twenty-four electoral votes and remove Lyndon from his Senate power base.

When JFK decided to make an informal appearance before the cheering delegates, he summoned his mother and his sister Pat, a California delegate, to join him on the platform. "I suppose that it was one of the proudest moments of my life," the new nominee's mother reflected.[44] An Associated Press photo of radiant Rose, bowing and waving to the throngs with Jack at her side, was captioned "Mother's Day."[45] Once again, with Joe sequestered, it was Rose, the matriarch, who represented the Kennedy clan in public. The next evening she sat with Jack on stage at the Los Angeles Coliseum and cheered his "New Frontier" acceptance speech.

With Jack's nomination secured, Rose and Joe flew to the Riviera for a late-summer holiday and, they hoped, a respite from press attention. But that was not to be. Throughout their vacation, the Kennedys were besieged for interviews and photographs. Rose agreed to grant an interview in Paris, *en français*. She planned to stay abroad until late September, looking forward to a stop in Vienna. As it turned out, she was needed at home: "Plans changed as Bob [Kennedy] says I am in great demand as a speaker—so home early."[46]

Soon she was back on the campaign trail, spending nearly seven weeks in fourteen states for Jack and his running mate. Her appearances took on added value because Jackie's pregnancy had curtailed her travel. Rose, however, was willing to go the proverbial extra mile. In Kentucky, for example, she attended a luncheon for the state's Democratic Woman's Club, held at Cumberland Falls State Park, in the state's rural, southeastern region. "Everybody realized it was quite a sacrifice for you to come down to such a remote place," wrote the club's president. She pointed out that nearly half of the state's 120 counties had been represented at the luncheon. "We were very much impressed with your informative speech, and you endeared yourself to us with your radiance and warmth. We are looking forward to your return trip to Kentucky. The women will carry this state for your son."[47]

Soloing suited Rose, although she usually had a maid or secretary in tow for assistance. "I used to campaign a lot alone because I could do it. That's why there are not a lot of photographs of Jack and me campaigning because I could carry a women's audience myself and my daughters were apt to be with him. . . ." Her typical schedule included three days on the road, followed by two days of rest. After her Cumberland Falls visit, she flew over the mountains of West Virginia to The Homestead, in Hot Springs, Virginia, a stop coinciding with the first debate between her son and Vice President Nixon on September 28. Jack, she worried, lacked debate experience, whereas Nixon had captained his college debate team. Rose prayed "all day" for Jack to turn in a winning performance. She sympathized with Nixon's mother, who must have been nervous, too. Rose was also concerned that almost everyone she encountered at the elite Hot Springs resort was Republican. Though it was the first televised presidential debate in US history, Rose inexplicably listened to the debate on the radio, and, like many listeners, thought "Nixon was smoother." Inheriting her rapid speaking style, Jack spoke too fast, Rose believed. Yet she maintained that her son had "more new ideas, more initiative" on the debate's topic: domestic policy.[48] His platform promoted civil and economic rights, including aid to farmers and the unemployed, health care for seniors, housing for the poor, and aid to education. Rose would have loved Jack's television persona—tanned, fit, and relaxed—in contrast to the haggard, jittery, and perspiring Nixon, with his infamous five-o'clock shadow. She needn't have fretted. Television viewers judged Jack the winner; Rose's prayers had been answered.

Occasionally the campaign paired Rose with Johnson's wife, Lady Bird. Rose had initially been dubious about Mrs. Johnson's campaign style. Lady Bird, for instance, used the southern expression "in tall cotton" when she appeared with Rose, which to Mrs. Kennedy meant "not quite up to me." This interpretation was, of course, too literal. In the South, the higher the cotton, the better the crop, and Lady Bird merely meant that being with Rose was special. Rose thought Lady Bird's gracious handling of campaign volunteers served her well, but "her speech is not so appealing because I can tell women so many simple incidents about Jack and family, which appeal to their hearts but [Lady Bird] does make the supreme effort."[49]

Fortunately Rose liked Kentucky, for Jack's team sent her back there, to Louisville and Lexington, just ahead of Jack's visit there on October 5. Although the birthplace of Abraham Lincoln, the state had been reliably Democratic in all but three presidential elections since the Civil War. With two Republican senators and a victory for Eisenhower in 1956, however, the Bluegrass State wouldn't be an easy win for Kennedy. Yet it did have a Democratic governor and a sizable Catholic population in Louisville, which supported a Catholic Democrat for Congress. Those factors might help. Again, Rose and Lady Bird worked in tandem. Rose read that the Republicans were making a pitch for women voters, but she felt the Kennedy campaign machine had perfected such outreach.[50]

Rose's female audiences usually ranged between five hundred and two thousand attendees. Marveling that they would often wait up to two hours just to see her, Rose wrote,

> There was always the same cross current of people, the modestly dressed young mother perhaps with a little girl or boy in tow; the middle-class matron of forty, ample in proportion, well dressed; the conservative-looking, middle-aged woman, usually attired in grey or beige and wearing a fur piece to show her affluence, who shook hands politely and wished my son luck; the jubilant voter who stepped briskly and smiled broadly and who said, "I just know he will win"; the quiet-mannered woman who whispered as she went by, "I have been saying a novena [a special Catholic prayer] every day and I am sure he will be our next president"; the light-hearted teenager who said, "[Jack] is a doll and you are, too"; and the shy ones who would smile quietly and say, "I am keeping my fingers crossed." Sometimes a Republican would step along . . . [and say], "I am one of those Republicans who is going to vote for your son this year."[51]

Some women "seem to regard Jack almost like a new Lincoln, saying 'Thank you for giving us someone like your son' or . . . 'I just know that he is going to save this country.'" Now Rose could thrill to the compliments of the masses as they thanked her for producing a Lincolnesque savior. Occasionally ethnic voters, Italian women particularly, Rose noted, expressed their gratitude to her with embraces and kisses. A reserved Yankee, Rose thought these voters "over-enthusiastic." She took special pleasure when Protestants told her that they would vote for Jack.[52]

Perfecting her reception routine, Roe preferred to speak "when we first arrive, then have women form a line, instruct them to shake hands without any conversation and then move on. That is maximum of accomplishment with minimum effort. They can drink their coffee while we pass on to something else." Lady Bird's attempt to repeat each attendee's name seemed too time-consuming and tiring, but Rose admired Mrs. Johnson's knowledge of each state and how she made a personal connection with the people. In Kentucky, she mentioned her friendship with Bluegrass heroes, the late senator and vice president Alben Barkley and the late US Supreme Court chief justice Fred Vinson.[53]

On her forty-sixth wedding anniversary, Rose found herself stranded in Jacksonville by a Florida thunderstorm. The rain, tropical humidity, and television lights matted her hair, which, along with her "flat shoes and tweed coat," she worried would look unattractive for photographs. She was so preoccupied with her appearance that she almost forgot to wish Joe "happy anniversary" when they talked by phone.[54] In fact, Rose's marriage to Joe, nearly five decades before, came a distant third to her appearance and Jack's second debate, scheduled for that evening. Once again, she turned to prayer, asking the Almighty to grant Jack a successful performance. Watching on television, "praying through every sentence," she thought that her son "looked much more assured than Nixon and looked better physically. Jack seemed to have all the initiative and again Jack rose to inspiring heights of oratory once or twice. . . ." His proud mother couldn't help proclaiming, "Jack really looks, sounds, and acts like young Lincoln."[55]

The 1960 election would be close, the narrowest contest in presidential electoral history until surpassed in 2000 by the razor-thin electoral college vote (won by George W. Bush, despite Al Gore's more than half-million-ballot margin in the popular vote). For much of the night and well into the wee hours of the morning, the Kennedys and their team huddled around televisions at the Hyannis Port compound, which now included the main house and separate homes for Jack and Bobby. Rose and Joe spoke very little on that momentous night, as her husband checked the returns from around the country. At Jack's house Rose visited with Jackie, who was expecting the baby in six weeks or so, to keep her company, while most of the work occurred at Bobby's home. Finally, Rose went to bed, not knowing what the morning would bring.

As the sun rose over Hyannis Port, the Kennedy compound began to absorb the bracing news that John Fitzgerald Kennedy was now the president-elect. His margin of victory over Vice President Nixon was only a little more than 118,000 votes of the nearly 70 million cast, one-tenth of one percent. Yet Kennedy had won electoral-vote-rich states, amassing a 303–219 edge (34 more votes than the 269 needed for election in 1960).[56] Eight of the fourteen states where Rose had campaigned for her son (New York, Pennsylvania, Massachusetts, Illinois, Michigan, North Carolina, South Carolina, and Louisiana) fell into the Kennedy column, accounting for 172 of his electoral votes.[57] Kentucky went Republican; so did Tennessee and Ohio, where Rose had visited ten cities. California, Nixon's home, and Iowa, where Joe Kennedy had sent his wife to start campaigning as early as 1957, also went for the GOP, along with Florida.

Rose beamed as all of her surviving children (except Rosemary), their spouses, and her husband gathered around the hearth for a family photo marking the historic occasion. Jack rightfully took the most prominent spot. His mother, wearing a bright red dress, perched on an armchair in front, her legs demurely tucked at an angle. The *Life* photograph marked the first time since before the convention that Joe made a media appearance with Jack. The gold-framed mirror behind them emanated an exquisite glow surrounding the Kennedys that happy morning.[58]

They would soon adjourn to the Hyannis Armory for Jack's

brief acceptance speech. He guided Jackie to stand at his side; Rose assumed the spot next to her. Shuffling her feet, seeking just the right angle, Rose posed with her arms behind her. But this event was all about Jack. He would now take center stage. Rose made the cover of *Life* but couldn't have been pleased—her eyelids had drooped, just as the photographer caught Jack looking straight at him, flashing a radiant smile.[59]

The arduous campaign behind them, Jack presented Rose a map marked with all forty-six of her campaign appearances, inscribed, "To Mother—With Thanks." Now it was time for her to travel again, this time for relaxation and closer to home—New York City—for several weeks of theater, opera, and Christmas shopping.[60] Then she was off to Palm Beach for Thanksgiving. Jack remained in Georgetown so Jackie wouldn't have to travel so near her due date. But as JFK headed down to Palm Beach the day after Thanksgiving, his wife went into labor prematurely, and by the time his plane returned to Washington she had given birth by caesarean section to a baby boy they named John Fitzgerald Kennedy Jr.[61] Rose's late father, Honey Fitz, had another namesake.

Two weeks later, mother and baby left Georgetown Hospital and traveled to Palm Beach for Christmas. The president-elect continued to organize his administration from his parents' ocean-side villa. Although the house swirled with "happy chaos," which upset Rose's routines, she enjoyed meeting the VIPs visiting Jack. Senator J. William Fulbright spent an entire day with him. The segregationist Arkansan had hoped to be secretary of state under Kennedy, according to Rose, "but was not chosen because colored people do not like him and now the colored, or non-whites, which I am told has a better connotation, are beginning to have a strong influence in the United Nations. And, if they side against us, and line themselves up with the USSR, then we are lost." Even so, Rose found Fulbright "charming, relaxed, easy to talk to, and very interesting because he has studied at Oxford for three years [as a Rhodes Scholar]." She neglected to mention that his devotion to scholarly exchanges had led to his establishment of the Fulbright Fellowships in 1946.[62]

Rose also liked Mrs. Fulbright, who joined them for dinner. She was "pleasant, natural, and contributed to the conversation without intruding, which after all is the proper role for a wife, I believe." Born in the nineteenth century, Rose was no feminist: "Men have had the experience and have the knowledge, and people want to know what they think, and not the opinion of their wives." She disapproved of Mrs. Douglas Dillon, wife of Jack's secretary of treasury, for angry outbursts "when her husband is criticized." Of more interest to Rose was Douglas Dillon's father, "a Jew who visited a Boston family when at school and fell in love with the sister of a classmate. . . . He changed his name, sent his son to Groton, Harvard, and severed all connections with the Jews."[63] Rose didn't reveal her viewpoint on this anecdote, but it corresponded to her lifelong fascination with people outside her social and religious circle.

Franklin D. Roosevelt Jr., a popular campaigner for Jack in West Virginia's primary, visited the president-elect in Palm Beach, hoping to be appointed secretary of the Navy. FDR had been assistant secretary of the Navy for Woodrow Wilson. Rose observed that JFK's incoming secretary of defense, Robert McNamara, nixed the idea. "Jack was a bit nonplused [about] exactly what to say [to FDR Jr.]," but Joe intervened and told Roosevelt to follow his father's footsteps by becoming governor of New York, then president. In the interim, he should show the public "that he was a hard-working, serious young man." JFK named him undersecretary of commerce and chair of the president's Appalachian Regional Commission. In 1966 FDR Jr. did run for New York governor but lost to Nelson Rockefeller. His eventual five marriages likely diminished Franklin's "serious" label among voters.[64]

Equally exciting for Rose was the arrival of a retinue to photograph Jack, Jackie, and their children. *Harper's Bazaar* and *Look* sent renowned portraitist Richard Avedon to capture the new first family. Avedon posed the stunning Jackie, only thirty-one, wearing an Oleg Cassini gown in front of a white backdrop in Rose's living room. Then Jackie slipped into a Hubert de Givenchy hostess gown for a portrait with her infant, John Jr. Rose worried about the premature baby, who had suffered from undeveloped lungs at birth but "looked infinitely adorable as he lay cuddled in his mother's arms." Grandma Kennedy's health obsession caused her to fret: "As it was a rather cool day, I worried that he would get cold, because his head was exposed for a long time in the living room, which has no heat and which may be drafty, although the photographer's big screen probably cut off a lot of the draft." Jackie had chosen for Caroline "an adorable white organdy dress and a pink ribbon in her hair." Good choices, thought Rose.[65]

After all of the photographic commotion, Rose heard Jack tell Lem Billings, "Well, that was certainly a morning wasted."[66] For others in this image-conscious family, it was anything but. Avedon's portraits appeared in *Harper's Bazaar* in February 1961, and *Look* ran more informal and candid shots as its cover story, "Our New First Family." Several of Avedon's photos became instant classics. The *Washington Post* published them, as did papers in Los Angeles, Chicago, and New Orleans.[67] Rose had produced another "perfect" family for the baby boom–centered America of the 1960s.

Having a son become president-elect utterly transformed Rose's Palm Beach life. Outsiders were now in charge. Secret Service agents prowled the beach, police guarded the front entrance, and crowds of onlookers strained to catch a glimpse of Jack and his family. Sometimes she felt like a stranger in her own home, for as soon as she stepped outside, the front door would be locked behind her, and the back entrance was always locked. "I am a bit confused as to where I should enter or exit." Trying to avoid the crowds, she once started out through the servants' quarters in the back of the house. There she discovered a local hairdresser having lunch. "I was dumbfounded, and she was doubly so at seeing me" as Rose came through the maid's quarters. The hairdresser just "threw up her hands and I gave a laugh and she gave a laugh and out I went."[68] Actually, Secret Service agents weren't there needlessly. A would-be assassin planned to blow up the president-elect with a carful of dynamite but decided not to murder JFK in front of his wife and children.[69]

Without a doubt, Rose liked Jackie, but she thought her daughter-in-law was taking too long to recover from John Jr.'s birth. Rose never underwent a caesarean, so the need for more than six weeks of bed rest after childbirth was unfamiliar to her. She wrote in her journal about the weeks preceding the inauguration: "Jackie had the bedroom downstairs in the extreme corner of the house, which is Jack's old room. She likes to be alone, read French, or books and articles on the arts or antiques or fashion. Often she does not come to meals, so I do not see her, alas . . . she does not make it a point to notify me when people are coming." Ten years later, for Rose's memoir, Jackie rewrote her mother-in-law's passage to say, "Jack and Jackie have the bedroom downstairs. . . ." In reality Jack had bunked in the same room with his friend Lem, a fact which neither woman bothered to remove from Rose's journal entry. Jackie deleted the remark that she read French and about antiques or fashion, as well as her mother-in-law's comment that she didn't inform her when guests were arriving. Instead, Jackie added that she ordered books about White House history from the Library of Congress and that she planned "the moving of her young family" to Washington.[70] Clearly Jackie matched Rose's image creation prowess. In the early 1970s, responding to Rose's request to review her memoir materials, Jackie wanted the world to believe that she and Jack had shared a bedroom at Palm Beach in the weeks leading up to the inauguration. She thought that her interest in French, antiques, and fashion were too elitist; instead, she focused on the more popular accomplishments of her White House years— refurbishing the White House and maintaining her family.

Eventually the Palm Beach house calmed when Jack returned to Washington. Rose, Joe, and Ann Gargan prepared to leave for the inauguration. They rented a home in Georgetown for, in Rose's view, an outrageous weekly charge of $1,000 ($7,500 in 2012 dollars). The cost-conscious Rose wrote, "It seemed very steep to me, but the hotels were demanding that people take rooms for that number of days; and with the hotel food and service so expensive I suppose we wouldn't have saved much." Joan and Teddy, who had managed his brother's campaign in the western states, joined them.[71]

In some ways the inauguration of the thirty-fifth president of the United States seemed to go by in an exciting blur for Rose, but certain aspects remained distinct. The historic snowstorm that paralyzed the nation's capital; sliding through the streets of Washington to attend the inaugural-eve gala that featured a galaxy of Hollywood stars; the man who rode with her and Joe and jumped out of the car periodically to dig them out of drifts and slush; Joe's attempt to remove his overcoat, taking his formal cutaway along with it, in the inaugural ball's presidential box, as everyone joined in the laughter: these random snapshots made their way into Rose's memoir.

On inauguration day Rose trudged through the snow to Mass at Georgetown's Holy Trinity Church. Once there, she realized that Jack, soon to be sworn in as president, would be arriving. "I was really very happy at the thought, because I had not mentioned the idea to him. I knew that Jackie was too weak to accompany him, so I realized that he had come from his own volition and without any outside influence." Indeed, as the first Catholic president of the United States, who had faced religious discrimination in his run for the office, JFK might have had every reason to worship privately, if at all. Moreover, he had stayed out until 4 a.m., partying with his family and Hollywood friends, so even Rose might not have begrudged a decision to sleep late that morning. Much to her joy, Rose explained, Jack "wanted to start his four years in the presidency by offering his mind and heart, with all his hopes and fears, to Almighty God, and he wanted to ask for His blessing before beginning his awesome duties." Not wanting to be photographed in her informal winter attire, Rose sat incognito on a side aisle.[72] How sad that she couldn't share her joy with Jack for fear of being photographed in her snow togs.

At the inauguration ceremony on the Capitol's east side, Rose once more had to watch from the wings. She and Joe were in the front row, but at the far end, while the Eisenhowers, Jackie, Lady Bird Johnson, and Pat Nixon sat closer to the podium. "[S]ince the photographers were focusing on the middle, we were left out of everything except the panoramic pictures. I have never seen one in which I am recognizable; in fact, some friends asked me later where I had been during the ceremonies. I had always wished I had a picture of me with my son when he was being inaugurated president."[73] (Actually, Rose stands out in the wide-angle shot because she wore a white fur hat, sunglasses, and a fur cape to ward off the cold. And *Life* did capture her peering at John Fitzgerald Kennedy as he raised his right hand to swear the presidential oath.)[74] "It was quite magnificent, an overwhelming feeling," she recalled of seeing her son become president of the United States: "I was quite emotional about it because to be the one who was fortunate enough or blessed [with] . . . that great distinction, that great joy and responsibility. . . . That my son was chosen of all the men in the U.S., all the people in the world. . . . It's something you never really expect. . . . Overwhelming in its importance and its magnificence and responsibility. . . . Everybody was so enthusiastic about Jack and Jacqueline, . . . who was beautiful, so talented, so perfect."[75] Watching her son deliver his stirring inaugural address, sans hat and overcoat, on such a bitterly cold day flashed her back to memories of how, as a youngster, he would forget his sweaters. Rose couldn't help noticing how healthy her once sickly boy now looked. "He had lost that lean, Lincolnesque look that I liked," she conceded, but she willingly accepted his new robust physique.[76]

On the inaugural parade reviewing stand, Rose's bright head cover was as recognizable as Jackie's famous beige pillbox hat. Yet the two ladies didn't last long in the bitter cold. Rose, capitulating to age, and Jackie to her recent difficult childbirth, left the platform in front of the White House, where their husbands reveled in the triumphant moments of the Kennedy clan's dream come true. That night, at one of the inaugural balls, Rose wore the same 1938-vintage gold and silver Molyneux gown that she had bought for presentation to King George VI at Buckingham Palace. She even brought her ostrich-feather fan. Recalling that she wore this classic dress, Rose was delighted at the press's observation that her figure hadn't shifted an inch from those days in London so long ago.[77]

CHAPTER II

Mater Dolorosa

JOE KENNEDY CONTINUED TO KEEP A LOW PUBLIC PROFILE
during Jack's first year as president, not wanting to provide ammu-
nition to those who feared his influence. As former president Harry
Truman had exclaimed about JFK during the campaign, "It's not
the pope I'm afraid of, it's the pop!"[1] Rose, however, "suffered no
such strictures." She would play "queen mother" in Camelot.[2]
Appropriately, when visiting the White House, she stayed in the
Queens' Bedroom. Five European monarchs had slept in the suite,
including Britain's queen mother and her daughter, Queen Elizabeth II.[3] It featured an elegant four-poster bed and comfortable sitting room, yet Rose found the view of Pennsylvania Avenue
"drab." She preferred the Lincoln Bedroom's spectacular panorama
of the Washington Monument. Unfortunately, though historic,
the room was drafty in winter and stuffy in summer. Rose wasn't
strong enough to lift the heavy window sashes for fresh air or tall
enough to climb into the high Victorian bed without a stool.
Furthermore—and not trivial to Rose—the dressing table lights
were so dim that she couldn't apply her makeup properly or choose
which jewelry to wear.[4]

At age seventy, Rose carried an array of cosmetics and other items to maintain her polished and youthful appearance. Eyebrow pencils, eyelash liquid, eye shadow, false eyelashes, foundation, face powder, rouge, hair lacquer and spray, curlers, and a wig were her travel-kit staples. Before appearing in the spotlight, Rose reminded herself to put her "hair over her ears, darken eyebrows, make up hands" to hide age spots from years of swimming and golfing in the Cape Cod, Palm Beach, and Riviera sun.[5]

Very few presidential mothers live long enough to see their sons inaugurated or to participate in their presidencies. When the White House Protocol Office determined that Rose's position at state functions was behind all government officials, military officers, diplomats, *and* their spouses, Rose felt rather disappointed. In April 1961 she happened to be at the White House when the Bay of Pigs invasion went terribly wrong. Joe, who once again remained at home, told Rose that he had been on the phone most of the day with Jack and Bobby in the aftermath of the disastrous attempt to overthrow Castro. Asking how Joe felt, Rose heard his one-word response: "Dying." Even so, Joe tried to bolster Jack's spirits, comprehending the disaster's impact on the new chief executive. Two days after the invasion debacle began, Rose accompanied the president and first lady to a dinner at the Greek embassy, hosted by visiting Prime Minister Constantine Karamanlis. Despite the week's serious developments, Rose was pleased that she chose to wear "a pink chiffon dress made by Greek designer Dessess in Paris," which "everyone seemed to like." Impatient with the diplomatic small talk, President Kennedy left early and, accompanied by Jackie and Rose, returned to the White House, bid them a quick "good night," and hurried to the West Wing, only to learn that Castro's forces had captured more than a thousand Cuban exile–invaders trained by the United States. More than a hundred of them had been killed. "Jackie walked upstairs with me and said [Jack] was so upset all day and had practically been in tears—felt he had been misinformed by [the] CIA [about the invasion]. . . ," Rose reported in her diary. "[I] [f]elt so sorry for him—Jackie seemed so sympathetic and said she had stayed with him until he had lain down as she had never seen him so depressed except once at the time of his [back] operation." Nevertheless, Rose had shopping to do in New York and left the next morning without seeing Jack. She browsed for furs, particularly "a Russian sable cape for wear in cool weather and fall and perhaps Austria and a white mink for festive occasions when Jack visits de Gaul [sic]."[6]

ROSE WAS ALREADY looking forward to accompanying Jack and Jackie on their first state visit beyond North America, starting on May 31 in Paris, where JFK had three days of talks scheduled with French president Charles de Gaulle. Then it was on to Vienna for the president's momentous summit with Soviet premier Nikita Khrushchev. Rose went to Paris a few days before the official delegation to purchase an evening gown for the state event at Versailles. As a private citizen, she stayed at the Ritz. "[I]t was rather difficult to make plans as I did not want to impose my presence or insist on invitations for my friends. Not having a man with me or anyone in the family, I had to telephone a few times and gradually learn what protocol permitted."[7]

Initially, Rose heard that she might not be included in the official welcoming party for Jack at Orly Airport, but, she said, "I wanted to go and just wait in the car somewhere near to see and hear the welcome and the reception of my son. Then, I was invited to go to the pavilion where the other guests had assembled." There Rose met President de Gaulle and his wife. Rose sat for a few minutes with Mme de Gaulle and spoke in French about President Kennedy's visit. She told France's first lady how excited and pleased she was about her son's arrival, and they discussed their children, "always a safe topic" on state occasions.[8] Their conversation was too short and too public for these remarkable women, both married to powerful men, to discuss their most poignant commonality. Each had a retarded daughter. Anne de Gaulle, born in 1928, suffered from Down syndrome. Though her parents kept her with the family and gave her the best care available, she died of pneumonia at age twenty. General de Gaulle, who had demonstrated uncharacteristic warmth toward his disabled child, comforted his wife at Anne's burial: "Maintenant, elle est comme les autres" ("Now, she is like the others").[9] On a later occasion, Rose had an opportunity to tell Mme de Gaulle "that we did work for retarded children, and she said they had one, as I told her we had one." She liked Mme de Gaulle's "charming, quiet manners" and her "unobtrusive, self-effacing" persona.[10]

After Air Force One landed, Rose received a place of honor with the American and French first ladies for the media photographs. A motorcade drove President and Mrs. Kennedy into Paris. Rose rode with the wives of the American and French ambassadors, a fitting assignment for the spouse of a former ambassador.[11] The trip was going well, Rose reported to Joe—"All the shops and newspapers have been wild in praise of Jack [and] Jackie. . . ."[12] Versailles's Hall of Mirrors was replete with "splendors and beauty." But in retrospect Rose questioned the need for such extravagant and prolonged occasions. Should heads of state, "who have such weighty questions on their minds," have to devote "hours at state luncheons or banquets exchanging polite pleasantries with the wife of some state functionary or listening to long-winded speeches?"[13] Perhaps her lifetime of serving as the daughter, wife, and mother of government officials was wearing thin. Or did her newest role, relegated to the bottom of the protocol list without the legitimizing presence of her ambassador-husband, offer so much less to Rose than that of her days in London two decades earlier?

Still, Vienna beckoned. She remembered going there with Honey Fitz and sister Agnes nearly a half century ago and the thrill "when I went on a small steamer one night down the Blue Danube and joyfully waltzed to the strains of the orchestra playing Strauss's beautiful Blue Danube Waltz. I wonder to myself . . . if the young man [Hugh Nawn] with whom I danced has ever come back and if he too remembered the night in 1911 when, young and gay and carefree, we danced the hours away." Rose seemed to long for her unencumbered youth and perhaps for a man who might have offered her fidelity, if not celebrity. From her convent days and Boston University courses, she could converse in German with her table partner, a government official, at the state dinner for JFK and Khrushchev at Schönbrunn Palace. She had hoped that Mrs. Khrushchev might speak German too, but the Russian knew rudimentary English. Their small talk centered on children and daughters-in-law. The Soviet first lady was interested in Rose's "beauty secrets" and watched as Mrs. Kennedy reapplied her makeup. In truth, Mrs. Khrushchev needed a complete makeover in fashion, hairstyle, and cosmetics. Drab gray suits and a severe hairdo only accented Mrs. Khrushchev's "strong, sturdy" figure, "capable of extreme physical exertion."[14]

Even so, Rose liked the wife of America's archenemy; she was a pleasant, kindly woman who had read a recent feature story on Rose in *McCall's*. In fact, the May 1961 edition of the women's magazine had pictured both wives on its cover. The article, an early profile of the Kennedy matriarch after Jack's election, lauded her as the family's scholar, musician, and linguist, noting that her husband and Jack were less than star students at Harvard. "When the children were little," the magazine observed, "it was primarily Mrs. Kennedy who whetted their appetites for knowledge of current affairs and faraway places and great books, and who generally provided the emotional balance necessary in a clan of alert, lively, questioning youngsters."[15]

On Sunday, while marching up the aisle for Mass at St. Stephen's Cathedral in the heart of old Vienna, the Kennedys were greeted by Viennese worshippers waving white handkerchiefs to honor the young American president and his wife.[16] Jackie had charmed Premier Khrushchev at the state dinner in Vienna, and Jack had hoped to do so in his summit with the Soviet leader. Unfortunately, Khrushchev's bellicosity, especially his threats over Berlin, where American and Soviet tanks were poised barrel to barrel in the divided city, stunned JFK.

After President and Mrs. Kennedy left the Continent, Rose flew on to Florence and Rome, meeting at the Vatican with Pope John XXIII, who had replaced her friend, Pius XII, in 1958. Joe joined Rose for the remainder of the summer in their favorite Riviera hideaway, the Vista Bella at Cap d'Antibes, with its panoramic views of Garoupe Bay's azure waters. Rose wrote to Bobby, "I think you should work hard and become president after Jack—It will be good for the country and for you. . . . Ever your affectionate and peripatetic Mother."[17]

Summers in Hyannis Port now held little charm for Rose. "The scene had been noisy enough with the children and grandchildren without tourist traffic," she wrote. With Jack president, Bobby attorney general, Ted running for Jack's old Senate seat, Jackie a celebrity in her own right, Sarge Shriver directing the president's Peace Corps, and Pat married to a Hollywood movie star, gawkers descended upon the tiny Cape Cod village. Tourist boats cruised by the Kennedy compound, and Rose could hear their guides' amplified patter. "I had always needed times of peace and quiet and by then had reached a stage in life when I needed them more . . . ," Rose declared.[18] Her niece, Mary Jo Clasby, saw the paradox in these opposing Fitzgerald traits. Honey Fitz, the ultimate ebullient extrovert, loved the spotlight and craved public attention, while Rose's quiet mother had displayed a classic introvert's behavior.[19]

Back in the States, Rose returned to her lifelong hobby of autograph collecting. She wanted a signed picture of Nikita Khrushchev. Gathering photos of Jack and the Soviet leader taken in Vienna, the president's mother sent them to Khrushchev for his signature. In turn, she asked Jack to sign the photos so that she could send the president's signature to his Soviet counterpart. What was a little cold war, not to mention Berlin and Cuba, between two world leaders? JFK was less than amused, writing to Rose just two weeks after the Cuban Missile Crisis:

Dear Mother:
I have signed today the pictures from Kruschev [sic].
　　Would you be sure to let me know in the future any contacts you have with heads of state, etc. concerning requests for pictures, signatures, etc. Requests of this nature are subject to interpretations and therefore I would like to have you clear them before they are sent.
　　Needless to say the picture is most interesting and will be highly regarded.

Love, Jack[20]

Although the president's letter to his stickler mother included a misspelling, uncharacteristically, she didn't point it out to him. But she did get his point. Her return letter expressed contrition and embodied the Catholic requirement to amend her life and sin no more.

Dear Jack,

I understand very well your letter, although I had not thought of it before. There were two menus which were autographed by Khrushchev at the dinner in Vienna, at the same time he signed one for Jackie. However, we did obtain the photographs from "Match" magazine, or a similar one, last winter, and afterwards sent them to be autographed. I can see that it was probably an error, and it will not happen again.

As you know, Chancellor Adenauer and President Eisenhower autographed books for you last Christmas, and I have asked General de Gaulle to do so for this Christmas. I guess this clarifies the situation.

Adding a humorous touch, Rose signaled that she hadn't taken offense at her son's chastisement: "When I ask for Castro's autograph, I shall let you know in advance."[21]

Throughout these days, Rose held tight to a remainder of parental authority, bolstered by knowledge of Jack's mischievous boyhood: "In looking over my old diary, I found that you were urged on one occasion, when you were five years old, to wish for a happy death. But you turned down this suggestion and said that you would like to wish for two dogs instead. So do not blame the Bouviers if John [Jr.] has similar ideas. Much love, dear Jack."[22]

During the 1961 fall social season, Indian prime minister Jawaharlal Nehru visited Washington after Jack and Jackie had entertained him and his daughter, Indira Gandhi, in Newport. Rose had met Nehru on her 1955 visit to India, and he now invited her to a dinner at the Indian embassy in honor of President and Mrs. Kennedy. Afterward, Rose extended her White House stay to attend Pablo Casals's historic concert there. The renowned cellist had moved to Puerto Rico after the Spanish Civil War and vowed never to perform in a country that recognized Spain's fascist Franco regime. Yet Casals, now eighty-four, so admired President Kennedy that he made an exception to his moratorium and came to Washington to play on the occasion of Puerto Rican governor Luis Muñoz Marín's visit to the White House.[23] Rose sat in the front row at the East Room concert, next to Marta Casals, the virtuoso's wife, sixty years his junior. The president's mother noted that Mrs. Casals "was one of his pupils . . . and was married after a short courtship." Adjourning to the Blue Room for an intimate supper in the cellist's honor, Rose appreciated Jackie's remark that her mother-in-law "knew more about music and musicians than she did," as well as the first lady's observation that "Belle Mère" had "added immeasurable lustre" to the event.[24]

THE FIRST THANKSGIVING of JFK's presidency brought the family to Hyannis Port. Jack's vigor pleased Rose. "[He] [h]as good color (uses sun lamp if necessary) and, of course, has filled out considerably and looks in good form—Actually he has no exercise so his face looks almost chubby." Ted's bulky physique also caught her eye. "Jack gets a great kick out of seeing Ted dance as Ted has great sense of rhythm, but he is so big and has such a big derrière it is funny to see him throw himself around." Rose was also amused as her children and their spouses tried the latest dance craze, the Twist. Rose described it as "Throw your hips around." "No one knew much about [the Twist]," the prim Mrs. Kennedy admitted, "but Jackie . . . in a Schiaparelli pink slack suit gave a three-minute performance to the jungling-rumbling music of Joan [on the piano]. Jack sits with his cigar (small ones usually) just looking on and smiling. . . ."[25]

Jack's ever-present friend, Lem Billings, arrived the day after Thanksgiving. "Jackie never has LeMoyne stay at [her] house. . . . Suppose she is sick of having someone always around, but I am surprised that she has nerve enough to say so. She looks well, and both she and Jack seem happy together," Rose was undoubtedly relieved to observe. While at Hyannis, the president met with Khrushchev's son-in-law, Aleksei Adzhubei, editor of the newspaper *Izvestia*. The interview later prompted a discussion among the Kennedys about bomb shelters. "[W]e have done nothing yet nor discussed it at home," Rose wrote, but she seemed unworried about an atomic attack on the Cape. More interesting to her was domestic politics, especially Joe's suggestion to Bobby that "he should move to Maryland and become governor—then president [in] 1968, but he hates to start in a new state, and Ethel hates to move [from Virginia]."[26]

Rose had just completed a speaking engagement at the Guild of the Infant Saviour, a Catholic organization supporting "the care of the unfortunate and destitute mothers and their infants." The Guild announced, "Mrs. Joseph P. Kennedy, Mother of President Kennedy," above a painting of the Blessed Virgin Mary holding the infant Jesus. "Rose Kennedy is far more than the wife of Joseph P. Kennedy, Washington veteran of many top-level appointments, or the mother of the youngest elected president of the United States," noted the program. "She is the mother of nine, a renowned beauty, intrepid traveler, accomplished speech-maker, pianist, honor student and devotee of both political and fine arts."[27] Rose showed slides from the White House, including Khrushchev's signature on the Vienna dinner menus, Jackie at Versailles, and the Oval Office, along with her standard lecture about England. She reported her "reactions to my first visit at the White House." "I, out of millions of women in the United States of America, had been lucky enough to be the mother of the thirty-fifth president." Now some months removed from her initial feelings about not being the center of attention, she decided that taking part in the festivities with none of the worries gratified her. It was much easier than when she had "been at the opposite end of the pole with the burdens and responsibilities" of an ambassador's wife. "I was overwhelmed with the joy, the wonder, the glory of it all. The climax of my life as I approached my 71st birthday."[28]

Describing her Infant Saviour Guild lecture as having gone "very successfully," Rose began planning how she could present her experiences in Paris with Jack and Jackie to French-speaking audiences around Massachusetts. "This idea especially useful now with view to interesting people for Ted's campaign who hopes to be candidate for Senate next fall 1962." As Joe's vigor ebbed, Rose seized the initiative in orchestrating a role for herself in Teddy's run for Jack's Senate seat. "For the first time—I have noticed [Joe] has grown old—Sargent noticed and said it was plain he was not himself. Doctor [Janet] Travell here with Jack and says cold wind and air bad for Joe but he keeps going out." Rose worried about an "attack" that Joe had suffered, which she described as "not at all himself but quiet—complains about a lack of taste in his mouth and feels blah. . . ."[29]

Perhaps Florida sunshine would be just the tonic for the seventy-three-year-old ex-ambassador. Following family tradition, they headed to Palm Beach for Christmas. Jack and Jackie joined them on their way back from a triumphant trip to South America, but JFK had to return to Washington on December 19. Joe accompanied him to the airport, and they stood on the tarmac for a brief farewell chat. It would be their last conversation.

Joe returned to his beachfront estate and then left for the golf course with niece Ann Gargan. Ann had studied nursing and planned to become a nun. Before taking her vows in 1959, however, she had received a multiple-sclerosis diagnosis. Needing a place to live, she had moved in with Joe and Rose.[30] With Rose away so often, Joe particularly liked her company. (His womanizing, most recently with his secretary for a decade up to the late 1950s, had come to an end.)[31] Ann provided loyal companionship and basic medical care for her aging uncle.

On the golf course, Joe suddenly felt faint and had trouble walking. Ann called for a golf cart to transport him to the car; back home, she thought he seemed better. He even wanted to take a swim with Jackie and Caroline. In light of the golf-course episode, Ann encouraged him to take a nap instead. Rose soon returned from daily Mass and shopping. Not terribly alarmed by Ann's report of Joe's indisposition, she went about her usual routine, but when Ann discovered that Joe had awakened coughing and unable to speak, they called a physician. One look at Joe and the doctor rushed him to the nearest hospital. He had suffered a massive stroke. The blood clot had struck the left side of Joe's brain, paralyzed the right side of his body, and robbed him of speech. President Kennedy flew back to Palm Beach on Air Force One with Bobby and Eunice. Pat, Jean, and Teddy followed soon after. Jackie joined them all at the hospital for a vigil at the patriarch's bedside. Rose remembered "praying, praying" at the hospital chapel. Immobilized, Joe developed pneumonia and received the last rites. Miraculously, he rallied, and, after several weeks, returned home. But the stalwart head of the Kennedy clan could not walk or speak intelligibly.[32] Nurse Luella Hennessey arrived to assist, and the family also hired Nurse Rita Dallas to help Ann look after her debilitated uncle.[33]

With matters well in hand at Palm Beach, Rose went ahead with her speaking engagements in Boston, New Bedford, and Fall River, raising money for scholarships and hospital charities and redoubling her efforts to add new material to her lectures. Just three weeks after Joe's stroke, Rose asked the French consulate's press secretary in New York to answer eight questions resulting from her June 1961 trip to France during President Kennedy's state visit. She wanted a primer on French politics and government, especially women's roles. Rose also requested information on Mme de Gaulle's political activities and her personal interests. Finally, she queried, "Does President de Gaulle speak English?"[34] She then prepared her speech in English, hired a translator to produce the French version, and asked her to provide a language lesson and practice session.[35]

She sent similar queries to the Austrian embassy in Washington. What percentage of Austrians were Roman Catholics? Was there "an organized Communist Party in the country and what is the percentage of the people belonging to it?" The Austrian embassy's secretary responded that 90 percent of Austrians were Roman Catholics and that only 3 percent of the populace belonged to the Communist Party: after the 1956 Hungarian Revolution, so brutally crushed by the Soviet Union, the party "lost its last seat in the [Austrian] Parliament."[36] For the first time in her life, Rose was performing substantive research, asking meaningful questions, and not simply focusing on superficial aspects of the countries she visited. With her husband now speechless, Rose's voice strengthened. Dining in Versailles's Hall of Mirrors might be wasted time, but its impact needn't be. A new day was dawning in her lifelong effort at self-improvement and public outreach. Rose was "a great success" in New Bedford and Fall River, according to her friend Charles Lewin, editor of the *Standard-Times* newspaper. She raised nearly $2,000 at each benefit, as well as earning local headlines and photos.[37]

Teddy's campaign for the Senate was going well and, as an aide reported, "A great many notices have come to us from all over the state; they all joined in saying how effective you were on TV, radio and in particular in securing the French vote in the Commonwealth. At least fifty French leaders in the state have called me up to assure me of this—you were tremendous!" "As you so well know," he continued, "the French people are a sentimental and nationalistic group, and your speaking in their native tongue and the graciousness that you showed clinched this vote for Ted. I have made a very careful check of reporters, newspapermen, and top French leaders throughout the state, and each one has assured me that you have been one of the most outstanding personalities ever to appear before them, and there is no question that you were helpful to Ted."[38]

In March 1962 Rose had to attend to her own health. Secretly entering Boston's St. Elizabeth's Hospital for hernia surgery, she took great delight in keeping the paparazzi at bay. She didn't want to alarm Joe with media reports. "Because I got into the hospital without any of them knowing about it, . . . they [journalists] told Teddy [that] when he wanted to have publicity about something else . . . , he might find it difficult. So when I was leaving the hospital, they were all there!"[39] Feeling invigorated after returning to Palm Beach, she threatened to jump off the diving board.

Later that spring, Joe had improved enough to be placed on a stretcher and flown with Rose and Ann to New York's Institute of Rehabilitation for intense speech and physical therapy. Dr. Henry Betts, a young physician specializing in physical disabilities, became his attending doctor. The responsibilities, medical and nonmedical, that the Kennedys imposed on him meant that he could attend no other patients but Mr. Kennedy. According to Betts, the family had to determine who would interpret Joe's desires and needs, an especially difficult task because he could only articulate the word "no."[40]

"I'm sure he would have given up every arm and every leg to be able to talk," reported Dr. Betts. Of course, as Joe's spouse, Rose had the final say; her forty-seven-year marriage to him should have enabled her to determine even his unspoken thoughts.[41]

"My impression was that she adored him," Dr. Betts asserted. When Rose visited with Joe at the rehab center, usually in the evening, they would watch TV "just like any elderly couple you might see." In Betts's view, Joe "was very content" with his wife and "liked having her around." But he also knew that their children claimed Rose made Joe nervous "before his stroke" because "she was always upset about something. . . ." Betts begged to differ: "[S]he didn't make him nervous when I knew him. [H]e loved having her. . . ." Simply sitting quietly with Rose seemed to make Joe happy. It couldn't have been easy for her, always on the move and often alone, suddenly to spend more time with her invalid husband. Yet Betts observed not only Rose's sense of obligation but her genuine love for her spouse.[42]

Because of her active lifestyle, however, Rose wasn't always with Joe. She also didn't want to make all of his health-care decisions. As noted previously, Rose eschewed decisions about serious medical matters regarding her adult children. Neither did she want to manage all the household problems in later years. The White House would fly Dr. Betts to the Cape because the pool needed fixing. "It's funny. I would explain it that she wanted somebody else to do what she didn't want to do—whatever it was. . . . [S]he would always just say, 'Get the doctor.' And I'd be called up then," Betts recalled.[43]

Once Rose phoned him to ask if she should stay in New York with Joe or go to the Cape and let Ann return from Michigan to care for her uncle. The doctor refused to get involved in a family power struggle. He simply replied each of the three times that Rose called him, "I think your husband is most happy when you're there [with him]." Nevertheless, Rose went to Hyannis Port, and Ann came back from Detroit to be with Joe. Dr. Betts believed that Joe eventually accepted his dependent role. "I personally think that he would have been much happier to just settle down and be content with his wife for all those years." But his children and Ann tried to make him feel as though nothing had changed. Joe's doctor thought this typical Kennedy approach to misfortune counterproductive: "You cannot always just repress everything, but with their sense of destiny and feeling that they are different—they made a stronger effort at repression than anybody I've ever seen."[44] The habit of repression, acquired in Rose's Victorian childhood, so antithetical to modern therapeutic culture, had placed its stamp on her children. Others saw compassion, rather than repression, in how the Kennedys dealt with their latest tragedy. When family friend Ben Bradlee observed them, especially Jackie, gathering around Joe at a White House dinner, Bradlee believed they were bolstering the former ambassador with their respect, good humor, and dignity.[45]

Rose's desire and preference for solitude struck Dr. Betts as quite remarkable, especially when he reflected on it in 1972: "[S]he can select the things she wants to do and be alone. That's the time she can be very happy. She has no fears of being alone, and I'm not sure [that is] true of anyone else in the family—I don't think any of the rest like to be alone—but she's perfectly willing to be alone and read and think and rest, play golf alone, sleep alone, swim alone—and that, if you are able to live with solitude and like it (and I think she does) and be able to select anybody else in the world—those other times you do want someone around—that's a pretty good deal, and she's got probably the deal she's most happy with."[46]

Rose's quest for isolation actually seemed compulsive to Dr. Betts:

[S]he demanded her solitude—she had to have a rest—she had to have her walk—she had to have her golf—she was very organized and those things were sacred. But it was all alone—she was alone all of the time—in Hyannis Port, in Palm Beach—all of the time. She met with her secretary in the morning and that was about it. I think her contact with the servants was very casual. She would go in and out of Mr. Kennedy's room occasionally, and she would sit with him in the evening briefly when he was in Hyannis Port, but she was essentially alone all of the time. She talked to him—and, I thought, very quietly and nicely and unnervously. It's my guess that prior to this stroke, she was so [like a] butterfly in her conversation (and maybe brought up things that upset him) that it got on his nerves. She didn't do that when he was sick. They watched television and she talked very placidly—not even as nervously as she talks to most people. . . . And she amused him. She's terribly amusing—I adore her and her company—she's very good company to me, particularly now [1972].[47]

Dr. Betts explained why he thought Rose's children found her difficult: "I think she made them all very nervous." His own interactions with Rose explain why: "In the days when I lived in the house, when I'd run into her, she would usually bring up some problem, in a quick, rather irritated way, so that you got so that you were trying to avoid her. She'd say things like, 'Why did you take the white towels on the boat—you know you're supposed to take the yellow ones'; or 'You're eating too many cookies'; or 'That pool cost too much.' . . ."[48]

A sure sign of controlling personalities is their attempt to dictate life's minutiae, especially if they have no control over its major components. And Rose rarely experienced such autonomy during the first three-quarters of her life. Honey Fitz dominated Rose's youth, particularly concerning her education, though Rose did defy him to marry the love of her life. Then she largely ceded control to Joe and couldn't always manage, to her high standards, her nine growing children. She was unable to make young Jack obey her rules or to solve his health crises, despite her index-card system. Nor could she mold her marriage as she and the Church had envisioned it. As a Catholic, she couldn't completely control her childbearing until after Teddy's birth, and only then by absence and abstinence, apparently. Retreating to solitude gave her command over her own world, but too often world events overwhelmed her. First, they took her beloved Joe Jr. Next, unable to govern the love life, or religion, of her most beautiful and charismatic daughter, she watched Kathleen's unwise decisions lead to her tragic death. Failure to superintend Rosemary's diminished destiny, after trying desperately to make her appear "normal," made Rose a helpless bystander. Ultimately, the doctor's swipe of a scalpel through Rosemary's brain, ordered by Joe, destroyed all of Rose's work. And now, forty-seven years into a difficult marriage, Rose watched her spouse slip from patriarch to infantilism.

And yet, Joe's disappearance allowed Rose to blossom more fully than ever. Working for Teddy's first election in 1962, she could make her own decisions. Teddy, the child she tried to make happy by vowing to be joyous about his birth, in turn accepted her love. Over time he had come to appreciate her religious faith and strengthen his own Catholic beliefs. He had also learned not to be annoyed by her controlling nature. Equally important, he knew just how much to tease "Mother" about her obsessions without raising her ire.[49]

As the summer of 1962 wore on and Joe failed to regain either mobility or speech, Rose's letters to her children and in-laws reflected frustration, although directed toward other matters. To the attorney general, with carbon copies to Eunice, Jean, and Teddy (only the president was spared), she wrote a lengthy description of how all of the cars at the Hyannis Port compound were to be used and by whom. Joe's car would now be for Rose's occasional trips to Boston; Ann's auto would be reserved for her and Joe; Rose's would be for her local trips; and the station wagon she assigned for staff errands. Two weeks before her seventy-second birthday, Rose concluded, "I think that completes the story of the cars. This is the way they are to be used. I do not want to be bothered this way at my age, and I do not think it is fair. Please give this to Ethel to read, so every one will understand."[50]

Ethel received a separate missive, signed by Rose's secretary, about linens at the Hyannis Port homes. "Mrs. Kennedy is very anxious that you have your linen at the Cape marked this year. A lot of her linen seems to be missing, and, as Mrs. Kennedy will be there herself this year [not in the south of France because of Joe's condition], she would like to keep track of her own. The fact that hers [sic] and Bobby's initials are the same make it more difficult."

Then came the inventory: "Mrs. Kennedy had six blue wash cloths initialed RFK, none of which can be found, and so with your permission, she is going to have Evelyn look through your linen." Lest Ethel think her mother-in-law unreasonable, the secretary concluded, "She asked me to tell you that she knows it is difficult to keep things straight among the houses, and she is not complaining."[51]

That fall Rose sent tips to Jackie at the White House and Ethel at Hickory Hill: "I would suggest that after your houses [at the Hyannis Port compound] are cleaned, a note be posted to the effect that the curtains be drawn." Otherwise, the sun would fade their furniture, Rose reasoned, and she might not think to inform the cleaners. "I am trying to rest my brain," she told her daughters-in-law. Before she did, however, she reminded them to distribute their perishable food to the maids "as it is a shame to waste it. Love, G.Ma."[52] Undoubtedly, having to superintend two large estates, visited by hordes of children and grandchildren, grew more burdensome as Rose aged. Yet the desire to control all of the details in order to perfect each home's maintenance added to the toll on her tired brain.

For the president, Rose broached more important issues of Joe's medical care. In the same letter where she tepidly apologized for nearly causing an international incident with her request for Khrushchev's autographs, Rose asked Jack for assistance in arranging Joe's nursing staff. She and Ann thought that a Dr. Wapman understood Joe's situation better than any of the other physicians who had examined him. Perhaps recognizing the contest between Nurses Hennessey and Dallas for power over her husband, Rose told JFK: "I sometimes think we could find a good man for your father, instead of two female nurses. From the doctor's letter, it appears as though it will be a long convalescence, and I really think your father would be happy with a man, as this doctor also speaks of the merit of having some male companion. However, I suppose we shall not make any change until we get to Palm Beach. You might keep this in mind, though, as it seems to be difficult to find a man."[53]

As Rose grew more impatient with life's details, her two absent daughters, Kathleen and Rosemary, returned to her thoughts. After attending a three-day religious retreat at Noroton, the Sacred Heart boarding school where she had sent teenaged Kick to remove her from social temptations, Rose, who rarely commented on unhappy memories, wrote a heartfelt diary passage. It "was sad for me in a way" to visit Noroton after so many years, she admitted. "I heard the grandfather clock chime in the hall—the clock which we had given to the convent when we moved to Bronxville probably. The two grandparents had given us the clock for the hall at 131 Naples Road when we moved there."[54] Perhaps its chimes took her back to Brookline, where she had borne the first seven of her children. Did she hear their laughter, their crying? Did she see them racing through the house on a rainy day or playing in the sunny yard?

When Rose spied Noroton's tennis court, donated by her and Joe to the school, it "brought back memories of Kathleen who had gone to Noroton perhaps for the longest period. I had sent her early because she was exceedingly popular with girls and boys as a young-ster and spent hours at night on the phone. Eunice did not have that problem so I never felt it expedient to ship Eunice off. So Kathleen went about age 12–13. She was happy there, I know." Kathleen had been dead for fourteen years, but now her life played over again in Rose's mind: "[L]ife presented so many problems to her later. Fall-ing in love with Billie [sic]. Both young people knew it would be difficult if not impossible to marry—both were young—deeply in love—admirably suited to one another with age, education, inter-ests, family antecedents quite different so romance was extraordi-nary in a way. . . ." These were far different thoughts from the angry diary entry she had composed at The Homestead on learning that Kick and Billy, in defiance of her and Joe, would marry outside the Catholic Church.

Also around this time, Rose began to visit Rosemary at St. Coletta's in Wisconsin, and both she and Eunice lobbied JFK to make mental retardation a signature policy program. On October 11, 1961, they succeeded, when President Kennedy announced "a national plan in mental retardation." The program was to feature a national commission on how to treat and prevent intellectual disabilities.[55] A year later Eunice published her pathbreaking article, "Hope for Retarded Children," in the *Saturday Evening Post*. She began by telling how her mother "took Rosemary to psychologists and to dozens of doctors" when she deteriorated after the family returned from England. "All of them said her condition would not get better and that she would be far happier in an institution. . . . It fills me with sadness to think this change might not have been necessary if we [had] known then what we know today."[56] She didn't define "this change" as the lobotomy that had made institutionalization necessary. Now it was Joe whose name disappeared from part of the family narrative.

With Rosemary now publicly resurrected, both Eunice and Rose began talking about her frequently in interviews. By 1963, when asked how she became interested in retarded children, Rose could finally give a truthful response. "Well, you see the answer to that question is a very simple one. We had a retarded child, born about a year and a half after the birth of our second son, Jack. . . ." She described the family's construction of "seventeen or eighteen" homes for disabled children in cities where her offspring lived, and how the Joseph P. Kennedy, Jr. Foundation changed its mission to support research for preventing mental retardation. "Sometimes it is a question of drugs, sometimes the expectant mother is taking the wrong kind of drugs, sometimes she needs drugs. . . ." Could Rose have been thinking about paregoric, the opiate-based medicine so common in American households during the era of her pregnancies? Might she innocently have ingested it for her "nervous tummy" while pregnant? Could it have caused Rosemary's developmental disabilities, as opium can do? In her interview, Rose spoke of voters approaching her during the 1960 campaign, asking for help to get their children into special homes for the disabled. "One woman said to me one day, 'I feel that my child and I are like the Infant Jesus and His mother. No one will take us in. There is no place for him to lay his head.'" This comment must have jarred Rose and triggered her religious sympathies. She was thrilled with the president's commission and its successful lobbying of Congress. Rose was equally proud that Eunice had started a summer camp for retarded children at her Maryland estate.[57] It would become the forerunner of Special Olympics, established with Eunice's inspiration in 1968 to promote physical fitness and healthy competition among the mentally retarded.[58]

WITH TEDDY'S SENATE campaign to fill his brother's seat in full swing by the fall of 1962, Rose took to the airwaves, as she had for Jack. Her fifteen-minute segment, "Coffee with the Kennedys," opened with a narrated drive through quaint Hyannis, arriving at the Kennedy compound, where, the voice-over explained, Rose and Joe had lived for more than three decades, raising their nine children. (Their homes in New York and Florida went unmentioned.) Rose, in coat and scarf to protect her hairdo, waved from the front porch—a "warm Kennedy welcome," declared the narrator. Then she quickly entered the house to greet the viewing audience. Wearing a dark dress and three-strand pearls, with three diamond pins at her beltline, Rose looked twenty years younger than her seventy-two years. The television production and her performance were more polished than "At Home with the Kennedys," aired for Jack's Senate campaign four years earlier. Still, Rose appeared a bit nervous as she mentioned that her living-room sofa was the same one on which four-year-old Teddy had sat with Pope Pius XII (then Cardinal Pacelli) in 1936, when he visited the Kennedys in Bronxville. Yet the anecdote offered an opportunity to display photos of other famous people involved with the Kennedys over the years. She showcased the picture of her family at the Vatican, where Teddy received his First Communion from the new pope in 1938, "the first American child so honored," Rose emphasized. She seemed particularly proud of an FDR photo that he had inscribed to her. In her excitement, she forgot to point out the desk used by her father as a US congressman, but she turned back to explain its history. Returning to the living room, she realized that she had left her reading glasses near Honey Fitz's desk, and called out in an unscripted moment, "Will someone bring me my glaaaaasses!" But no one did. So she simply circled back to the topic of her late father and his theme song, "Sweet Adeline," sitting at the piano to play a few bars. She used her father's memory as a segue to implore women to go to the polls. Only once had a Lodge defeated the family (John F. Fitzgerald in the 1916 Senate race), Rose announced, and that was before women could vote. Suddenly, Teddy's wife Joan appeared with their two adorable children, Kara and Teddy Jr. The visit was meant to be informal, but the children were dressed perfectly and on their best behavior. Rose asked two-year-old Kara, "Are you going to read with Grandma?" The beguiling blonde toddler reached for the microphone, but Rose turned Kara's attention back to *Peter Rabbit*. When little Teddy, seated on his mother's lap, clapping to "patty-cake" on cue, began to fidget, Joan ended the visit but promised to return later in the day to "see Grandpa." With that, Rose drew "Coffee with the Kennedys" to a close.[59]

Teddy handily defeated Republican George Lodge and took a US Senate seat in January 1963, having barely attained the constitutionally mandated age of thirty. Rose proudly attended Teddy's swearing-in ceremony, and now, as the mother of the president, the attorney general, and a senator, went to a dinner at the French embassy honoring the *Mona Lisa*, which had just arrived from Paris for display at the National Gallery of Art. From the White House she sent notes to nieces and nephews telling them that "Bob is going to make a speech before the members of the Supreme Court on Thursday so that is the special reason for my arrival here." She probably meant that the attorney general would argue as counsel in a case before the justices. Traditionally, attorneys general make a token appearance before the US Supreme Court. Robert Kennedy chose a voting-rights case to make his court debut. "I am sleeping in the Lincoln Bedroom, and occasionally I walk down the hall to see the president in his bedroom, so it is very thrilling," his mother related.[60]

Rose was equally thrilled to receive a laudatory letter about Bobby from Manhattanville College's president, Eleanor O'Byrne. Attorney General Kennedy had delivered a lecture on Southeast Asia to an audience of more than seven hundred students. His mother underlined O'Byrne's praise for his "intelligence, humor and directness and honesty." "Bob was excellent, also in the question and answer period . . . ," wrote O'Byrne. "It is one thing to know a great deal, which he does. It enhances discussion, too, when the speaker is forthright and when he is also able to laugh." Rose scribbled across the top, "Thrilled to read this letter, dear Bob—*Please return* as I wish to keep—Love to all, G.Ma."[61]

Bobby couldn't resist tweaking his proud mother. On his "Attorney General" letterhead, his secretary typed, "Dear Mother: I'm sure you had no doubt your favorite child would turn out this way. Love, Bobby." In his adolescent penmanship, he scrawled an additional tease: "I called to wish you a happy Easter—I hope you brought me home some presents from Paris—I love you now but if you brought me home something huge and expensive I shall love you even more. Waiting expectantly, I am your favorite."[62]

Rose now had a new reason to escape. She had gone to Paris "for a short rest, as I had never been so tired and nervous due to my preoccupation with Joe, not that he was in greater danger of death, but it was so sad and nerve-wracking to see him try to tell me something which I could not understand, or complain about something which I could not fathom. He is still very vital and vigorous about expressing his wishes and gets cross and impatient if we cannot understand him and if he is not handled properly. He uses his arm or leg to push or whack the nurses." One evening a nurse accidentally lodged his wheelchair in the elevator, and, according to Rose, "Joe sat there for five or six minutes frothing with rage at her [the nurse's] stupidity. Naturally, all these times fill me with annoyance and sadness for his sake, and frustrations because I can do so little about them." How different he was from her mother. Approaching the century mark in Boston, Josie Fitzgerald, her health diminished, sat "always in the same chair and weeping a little when she sees me, but Joe wants and tries to do things like he did in the past. I keep thinking what a pity that a superior mind dedicated to goodness and efficiency should be so destroyed, and rendered useless—incompetent through no fault of his own."[63] It must have been difficult for Rose to watch her mother and husband slipping away from her.

Once back in the States, Rose wrote a long letter to Bobby, seeking to fill the image-making void left after Joe's stroke. "This is just to review a few of the ideas we discussed over the weekend. I think Ethel's interest in charity could be stressed, because every one seems to be motivated by a charitable impulse these days. . . . And her interest in the Kennedy home, of course, could be mentioned." Bobby and Ethel now had seven children. Why not have them tout their large family, as Rose had done her own? "I do not think it is necessary to emphasize the fact that you are both tone deaf or that cultural things do not play such a large part in your life," she advised, "but rather the fact that you are both interested in history and that for years you have both collected autographs and letters of men famous in American history." Stress that the children play current-events games, she urged. "You can even say that this interest in history stemmed from your early years and that Ethel shared this with you, and even bring in the books that I have given you at Christmas time." As for the family's famous touch-football games, they were old news, and mention of them could "be eliminated for awhile." Ditto the repetition of animal anecdotes. Hickory Hill high jinks, as when Arthur Schlesinger Jr. landed in the pool fully clothed, should be nixed. That story "went to Paris and London," Rose noted with disapproval, "and I feel we should get away from this kind of publicity. I know you agree. It sounds harmless when you are talking about it, but repercussions are not always favorable." To soften her critique, she wrote, "It was wonderful to see you for the weekend. Ann and I, as well as your father, got a tremendous lift out of your visit." Yet she couldn't resist making a jocular reference to Bobby's undisciplined kids. "I can hardly wait to see you and the little darlings at the Cape—although I am afraid I shall have to take a trip to Europe!"[64]

Just as Rose had to escape her own offspring, she now found some of her grandchildren much too boisterous. Better to relate her child-rearing suggestions to Ethel from long distance. "Just heard on the radio that fruit juice not strained has lots more vitamins than strained," she advised her daughter-in-law.[65] Bobby's irrepressible wife took Rose's edicts in stride and, like her husband, with good humor. Ethel always threw in a soupçon of flattery when dealing with her mother-in-law. "You looked great at the benefit, and I have heard lots of men talk about that lovely figure and face. G-r-r-r-h," wrote Mrs. Robert Kennedy with feigned envy. "Love and kisses and I'm ordering my parchment gloves so at least my hands will be fashionable. Bearhugs from Ethel."[66]

Twice during JFK's presidency Rose substituted as White House hostess. In July 1962 Jackie decided to stay in Hyannis Port, vacationing with her children, so Jack asked his mother to pinch-hit for the first lady during the visit of Ecuador's president Carlos Arosemena. "I was thrilled but a little tired, as I have so much to do this summer with the added chores due to Joe's illness," Rose complained. The grief and pity she felt for him sometimes overwhelmed her, but "I'm glad I came," she recorded on White House stationery.[67]

The next summer, in August 1963, Jackie gave birth prematurely to a son, Patrick Bouvier Kennedy, at the Cape. Suffering from hyaline membrane disease, the infant survived only two days. As the president and first lady grieved the loss of their much-anticipated baby, Jackie slipped into a depression so severe that Jack suggested she go abroad for a Mediterranean cruise with her sister Lee, aboard Aristotle Onassis's yacht. Before she left, Jackie accompanied JFK to Washington's Union Station for the arrival of Ethiopia's imperial majesty Haile Selassie. Then she flew to Greece, leaving Rose to substitute for her at the White House state dinner that night.[68] "I was more important as the president's mother and wife of an ambassador than any of Jack's sisters," explained Rose.[69]

A few weeks later, President Kennedy began taping his thoughts about the American-backed coup that had toppled Vietnamese president Ngo Dinh Diem. As their father recorded his abhorrence over Diem's bloody assassination, five-year-old Caroline and two-year-old John Jr. burst into the room, giggling and bantering with their father, completely oblivious to his burdens. The president prompted his youngsters to speak into the microphone by asking them a series of questions about the four seasons. Clearly, this was a game they had played before: "When do the leaves fall?" queried the president. "Because it's winter," ventured John Jr. "No, autumn," his father gently corrected. The little boy repeated, "Autumn." "And why does the snow come on the ground?" "Because it's winter." This time the toddler, who would turn three in a few weeks, answered correctly. His dad moved to the next clue: "And why do the leaves turn green?" John ventured again, "Because it's winter." "Spring. Spring," JFK repeated for emphasis. "Spring," his son repeated. And for the fourth season, "When do we go to the Cape? Hyannis Port?" the president asked, using a familiar location as his hint. His confused son volunteered, "Oh, because it's winter." With delight in his voice, the bemused father sweetly explained, "It's summer!" Little John parroted, "It's summer."[70] Just like Rose, presiding over his childhood dinner table, JFK enjoyed instructing his own youngsters through playful quizzes. Four weeks later they were scheduled to gather around the family table again, at Hyannis Port, for the Kennedys' annual Thanksgiving celebration. But first, the president had to make a political trip to Texas, the unofficial kickoff of his 1964 reelection campaign.

Rose would always remember the crystalline autumn dawn as she left for daily Mass on Friday, November 22, 1963. Returning home, she had breakfast with Joe, and then they drove through the golden Cape Cod countryside. Rose played her usual nine holes of golf, lunched with her husband, and then lay down for a nap. Ann's blaring television interrupted her slumber, and Rose headed toward her niece's room to ask her to lower the volume. Mrs. Kennedy couldn't believe the televised bulletin: the president had been shot while riding in a motorcade through Dallas.[71] Ann saw her usually resilient aunt begin to tremble and sink into a chair. Bobby phoned. "It looks bad," the attorney general told his mother. "As far as I know, Jack can't pull through."[72] She returned to her room and paced the floor. Maybe he could survive, miraculously, like all of the other times he had stared death in the face, from his scarlet fever as a toddler to his Addisonian episodes to the ramming of PT 109 to his back surgeries. But soon Bobby phoned to confirm that Jack had succumbed to his wounds. In all of those previous instances, Joe had insulated her from worry over Jack's well-being. In her shock and grief, Rose now insisted that Joe not be told that day about their son's death. He should be allowed to have one final night of peaceful sleep, she reasoned. Then Rose went to the beach and walked along the water's edge, praying and asking herself over and over, "Why?"[73] As usual, she was alone.

Despite her anguish, Rose accepted a phone call from Lyndon and Lady Bird Johnson as they flew back to Washington from Dallas on Air Force One, bearing the body of her son. In a strong voice, she almost said, "Thanks a million," to LBJ for calling, but caught herself halfway through the last word, thinking it inappropriate, and substituted, "Thanks very much." Without missing a beat, however, she referred to the caller as "Mr. President," though he had taken the oath only thirty minutes earlier. "I wish to God there was something I could do, and I wanted you to know that we're grieving with you," Johnson told her, to which Rose replied, "I know you loved Jack, and he loved you." Those in shock often utter kind, if not truthful, words simply to get through an excruciating moment. "Here's Bird," the new president responded. Her voice breaking, Lady Bird managed to tell her former 1960 campaign partner, "Mrs. Kennedy . . . we are glad the nation had your son as long as we did." "Yes. Well, thank you, Lady Bird. Thank you very much. Good-bye." The new first lady concluded, "Love and prayers to all of you." "Yes. Thank you very much. Good-bye. Good-bye. Good-bye," Rose said firmly before hanging up the phone.[74]

Early the next morning Rose took refuge at St. Francis Xavier Church, where she attended daily Mass near the altar dedicated to Joe Jr. Two uniformed police officers escorted the tiny woman, suddenly looking very frail and elderly, past journalists and onlookers. The black net veil over her face couldn't mask dark circles under her eyes. Joe still knew nothing. Teddy and Eunice had arrived the previous evening. Joe's youngest had always been elected to tell his father about his brothers' antics, in hope that "Dad" would go easy on Teddy. Now he took on the heaviest responsibility of his life, volunteering to tell his father that another of his sons had died a violent death. Rose couldn't muster the strength to be present, "for I couldn't stand it."[75] Until the day he died, more than four decades later, Teddy's eyes would fill with tears whenever he recalled that November 23, 1963, conversation with his stroke-ridden father.[76]

On Sunday, two days after the horror in Dallas, Rose, Teddy, and Eunice flew to Washington for Jack's funeral. Joe stayed behind with Father John Cavanaugh, Notre Dame's former president. Understandably, Rose's lifelong malady, a "nervous stomach," flared in the midst of this unbearable tragedy. "I felt queasy, quite unwell" on Monday morning, she said, as the state funeral began.[77] The trauma had undoubtedly caused an attack of her irritable bowel condition. She couldn't find the strength to march six blocks from the White House to St. Matthew's Basilica with Jackie, Bobby, Teddy, and world dignitaries. "So I am not in many pictures, except at the grave," she later noted. Rose had attended Mass that morning, where she received Communion. She wanted that fact on record, so history would know why she didn't take part in the sacrament again at the funeral Mass, offered by Richard Cardinal Cushing.[78] (Church rules allow only one daily reception of Communion.)

After the service, the family clustered on the cathedral steps as military pallbearers placed Jack's flag-draped coffin on the caisson for its final trip to Arlington National Cemetery. Rose's grandson John Fitzgerald Kennedy Jr., turning three that day, honored his father with a perfect salute. Just behind Jackie, Rose appeared utterly desolate, her eyes nearly closed, her lips parted, as if she had to gasp for air. But, like most of the Kennedys that day, she never broke down in public. At Jack's final resting place, Rose watched her two surviving sons and Jackie light the eternal flame. Cardinal Cushing intoned the final blessing and committed Jack's remains to the hallowed earth. Pale and weak, Rose then returned to the White House and met with Charles de Gaulle, West German chancellor Ludwig Erhard, British prime minister Harold Macmillan, and Britain's Prince Philip, as well as Kick's in-laws, the Duke and Duchess of Devonshire. At the end of the most agonizing day of her life, a government jet flew Rose back to Cape Cod and the Kennedy compound's embrace.[79]

CHAPTER 12

Stabat Mater

"My reaction to grief is a certain kind of nervous action. I just keep moving, walking, pulling away at things, praying to myself while I move, and making up my mind that it is not going to get me. I am not going to be licked by tragedy, as life is a challenge, and we must carry on and work for the living as well as mourn for the dead," wrote Rose after Jack's death.[1]

Family nurse Rita Dallas, whose surname Rose could not utter after November 22, 1963, recalled that Rose "had trouble sleeping" after the assassination. "She would experience bad nights, during which we could hear her pacing the floor. When she finally did doze off, she was always worried she would oversleep and miss Mass. Consequently, one of the night nurse's duties was to be certain Mrs. Kennedy arose in time to go to church."[2] We know from her travel lists that Rose packed sleeping pills. Dalmane and Librium were among her prescriptions, both popular sedatives/anti-anxiety medicines in the 1960s and '70s. Not barbiturates like Seconal, they are benzodiazepines, similar to Valium, which appeared on the market in 1963. Dalmane is particularly long-acting when taken at night, producing sedation well into the next day.[3]

Rose may well have required a nurse to wake her from a deep, medicine-induced slumber. Who could blame her for turning to pharmaceuticals to reduce stress-induced insomnia in the wake of her son's horrific murder?

Trying to distract herself further, she began gathering materials for an autobiography. From Joe's New York secretary she received a shipment containing diary notes, materials she had produced about her children, correspondence with her mother, newspaper clippings, and her speeches. "It should be a wonderful book, and I am sure every woman in this country will want to read it," the secretary told her. "The potential audience is tremendous. . . ."[4] Yet nearly another decade would pass before Rose began writing her life story.

She could have rejoined Washington's social whirl. President and Mrs. Johnson invited her to attend a February 1964 dinner for new British prime minister Alec Douglas-Home. Rose declined. "It was too soon," she wrote on the invitation.[5] No doubt a White House visit would have been too painful. Only a few months earlier, she and Jack had hosted Haile Selassie there. She appreciated the Johnsons' kindness "after the tragedy," as Rose referred to Jack's death. In late February LBJ and Lady Bird visited the Kennedys at Palm Beach. "Strange to say, I was a little excited and a little sad," wrote Rose.[6] The president "seems anxious to do what he can do to assuage our grief. But whatever he does, the pro-Kennedyites say he is doing it for publicity, to get the Catholic Democratic votes." She thought that "Mrs. Johnson has always seemed to be thoughtful and eager to do the right thing and the kind thing, ever since I went campaigning with her in 1960. She is an attractive looking, well-groomed woman, but, of course, anybody who followed Jackie would be handicapped. So exceptional were Jackie's qualifications in looks and intellectual attainment."[7]

Once again a European trip would provide escape and solace. Stopping in Boston before flying to Paris, Rose visited her ninety-eight-year-old mother. Mrs. Fitzgerald was so frail that the family had kept from her the horrifying details of Jack's death. Rose expressed concern over Josie's care: "I put my head in her room in the morning, and I saw a shaft of light directly across her face where it crept in through the tiny space between the wall and the curtain." And when Rose visited at lunchtime, she discovered Josie's scrambled eggs "ice cold on an ice cold plate." Why weren't the nurses more attuned to such things? This syndrome wasn't new. Rose always kept a vigilant eye on her children's caretakers. More than once she had walked to the beach only to discover the governess "flirting with the swim instructor, while the children sat around in wet bathing suits," subjecting them to colds. Rose remembered that she "was always present during the children's meals" so that the cook varied menus.[8] As Rose's adult children passed from her life in one violent tragedy after another, she became more determined than ever to convince herself that she had done everything possible to care for them as children. Her memory of "always" being present at family meals, however, failed to account for her many trips away from home.

Rose's 1964 visit to Paris coincided with the dedication of Avenue du Président Kennedy. Only three years before, he and Jackie had been the toast of Paris; now France mourned his loss. "Every place I went the French people were most sympathetic. Mr. Zembrzuski at the Ritz Hotel said that he really dreaded to see me because his grief was so deep. These circumstances made it more difficult for me, as constant reminders often released floods of tears again. All the people at the French ceremony looked grim and solemn and sympathetic. There are many streets of the villages named after Jack."[9]

Back home, Rose began to attend tributes to her late son, especially those to raise funds for the planned John F. Kennedy Library. She now had a new charitable cause for which to attract paying fans. North Carolina's program drew so many people, at $10 per seat, that it was held in UNC's football stadium. Although Billy Graham had supported Nixon in 1960, he nonetheless gave the featured address. Rose accepted North Carolina's JFK Library contribution, and Senator Edward Kennedy spoke about Jack. Moved by the audience, Rose wrote afterward to Democratic governor Terry Sanford, "Until my arrival in North Carolina, I had not realized the great affection, admiration, and respect which the people of your state felt towards my son, and my heart was filled with gratitude and appreciation toward them."[10] Likewise, at least one audience member adored her, writing, "Dear Mrs. Kennedy, I want you to know how thrilled our family was when we realized you were sitting in front of us at St. Thomas More Church on Sunday. My husband and I so greatly admire you and your family. We strive to imitate the family spirit that you all possess among our own six children." Rose's family image resonated with this Catholic mother. "Three of my teenage children and I were honored to attend the ceremonies in Kenan Stadium yesterday. We were deeply moved by your speech. Our family has grieved with you since the death of President Kennedy. He was able to project himself in such a manner that we could identify ourselves with all of his noble ideas. We hope not to falter," the writer assured the president's mother.[11]

One month later, on June 19, 1964, yet another disaster struck the Kennedys. Traveling to a state political convention in Springfield, Massachusetts, Teddy's private plane crashed in a thick fog, killing the pilot and the senator's political aide. Kennedy's friend and colleague, Indiana senator Birch Bayh and his wife, also on the flight, dragged Teddy from the wreckage. He had suffered three fractured vertebrae, several broken ribs, and a punctured lung. Bobby could not believe the misfortune that once again befell the clan. Arriving at the hospital, he noted that if his mother had produced only her first four children, "she would have nothing now," with Joe, Jack, and Kathleen deceased and Rosemary "in a nursing home." "I guess the only reason we've survived is that there are too many of us. There are more of us than there is trouble."[12]

Teddy spent six months bedridden. Following her own life-long habit, Rose encouraged him to use his immobility for self-improvement. "When you are lying in bed, you can read a paragraph and then try to rewrite it or resay it," she suggested. "Then notice the difference between succinct, dramatic impressions of the author and your (verbose) discursive, dull recital of the same events."[13] Well, *that* must have cheered Teddy.

With Bobby in Europe and Teddy hospitalized, Rose agreed to appear at a Philadelphia ceremony honoring President Kennedy. On July 4, 1962, JFK had made a triumphant visit there: he viewed the Liberty Bell and delivered a Cold War speech at Independence Hall about the interdependence of nations. "We in Philadelphia hold especially dear the memory of President John F. Kennedy," the city's Democratic mayor told Rose. "In order that future generations may gain some measure of our love for this man, we plan to dedicate a bronze plaque to his memory at the birthplace of American independence. . . . It will be similar and adjacent to one which commemorates a visit to our nation's birthplace by President-elect Abraham Lincoln in 1861."[14] Rose could continue her comparisons of Jack to another martyred president.

Standing in front of the shrine to America's founding, Rose spoke briefly about JFK's love of history, rooted in his Boston boyhood and Honey Fitz's compelling tales of revolutionary America. "Seventy-three-year-old Mrs. Rose Kennedy appears to have triumphed over tragedy," proclaimed the *Philadelphia Bulletin*, launching an updated theme about her. Though she would have settled for a secondary position if "my son Jack, the late president," had lived, Rose now embraced center stage in his absence. "Smiling, chatting, sometimes laughing, . . . [s]he doesn't act like a woman in mourning—nor does she look or act like a woman of 73. Straight, slim, with a sprightly walk, she seems smaller than one imagines a Kennedy to be, and actually is only 5'3" tall." Ducking questions on coping with tragedy, and her late son's national contributions, Rose promoted the Joseph P. Kennedy, Jr. Foundation and stressed the importance of prenatal care to prevent mental retardation. Instead of wearing funereal black, she chose all white, from her broad-brimmed hat to her leather pumps. "Mrs. Kennedy . . . credits some of her chic to her husband," the newspaper reported. "He always steered me away from bouffant skirts—he likes simple clothes that make me look—ah, slim," explained Rose.[15] Wearing dark glasses against bright sunlight, she gazed solemnly at the plaque placed where her son had stood two years earlier. Then she left for Allentown to dedicate one of Eunice's twenty new camps for retarded children.

Rose maintained a brave public face, but that summer at Hyannis Port resurrected painful memories. Recalling the excitement President Kennedy created during visits to the compound only saddened her. "We are all at the Cape again in 1964, but it is different from other summers," she explained. Gone were helicopters signaling the president's arrival and the delight of his two children racing toward him. "Caroline and John would run and jump into his arms. He would lean over ever so affectionately and hug and embrace them. I always realized he was a little wary as to how he bent, so as not to hurt his back, and, of course, he never lifted John up into his arms," Rose explained. "Bobby is here but seems distracted by the confusion and uncertainty surrounding his own plans. . . . Ted, of course, is in the hospital, Joan with him. And if she is not there, Jean and Pat try to go up. I have not been because the day I had planned it, I had to make a speech in Philadelphia instead of Teddy. Then I had to go to Mary Moore's funeral another day." Rose tried to stay active, "as it is the only way I can keep normal and not think about the time when we were said to be the most powerful family in the world. I read and study French continually although at times I think it is foolish, as in Paris everyone in the hotel and at the couturier speaks English, and I know few French people socially." The Kennedys attempted to remain stoic, even in the confines of the Hyannis retreat, but sometimes memories overtook them. "Once or twice we gathered around the piano here at our house while Joan played and sang songs, but we hit on one of Jack's old favorites, and all dissolved into tears and left abruptly."[16]

Rather than share their grief, they hid tears until they regained their composure. Teddy remembered, "I would say to myself, 'Mother is holding up. The last thing she needs is for me to break down or give way to a flood of tears.'" "It never occurred to me to seek professional help or grief counseling of any kind. The times were different then." Before his plane crash, the young senator would take solitary beach walks and only then let the desolation over Jack's death engulf him.[17]

STILL, LIFE WENT ON. Rose slipped off to Paris to buy clothes for the fall campaigns. Bobby had decided to run for the US Senate from New York. Teddy had to contend again for the Massachusetts

seat he had won by special election two years earlier. While Rose
was abroad, her mother died. As with Honey Fitz, who had also
passed away while Rose vacationed in France, she didn't return for
the funeral. Instead, she lunched with Marc Chagall in the south of
France. Writing in French, Rose described his clear blue eyes,
twinkling like those of a laughing child. He kindly inscribed books
for family members, a request Rose made when meeting celebrated
authors. She also bestowed her own token mementos—newly
minted silver Kennedy half-dollars—as tips to elevator operators and
concierges, whose gratitude for receiving the coins touched her.[18]

Rose returned to the campaign trail, wearing her Paris fashions
at events for Teddy and Bobby. Her mid-October 1964 schedule
re-created frenetic days spent stumping for Jack in Wisconsin. At a
New York reception an atypical audience of more than a hundred
independent and Republican voters turned out to see her, most
signing on as Kennedy campaign volunteers. Ten women joined
her in a TV studio "to give the appearance of a tea" as part of a
campaign commercial. The next afternoon she attended another
reception and returned to her apartment for a rest before leaving for
an evening gathering of supporters. At the Hotel Astor Rose
appeared at a luncheon for the Johnson-Humphrey-Kennedy campaigns, and, a day later, spoke for Bobby at the Hotel Commodore's
Grand Ballroom, then joined him in a receiving line. "She's been
campaigning for something like 72 years," Bobby quipped about his
seventy-four-year-old mother. "Was it in Grover Cleveland's
administration or maybe Lincoln's that you began, Mother?"[19] A
day later Rose was off to a Staten Island luncheon, followed by a
reception the next day in Queens. Her energy was astounding. At a
lunch for Democratic women, she stood in a receiving line for
nearly an hour, shaking hands with over three thousand guests. She
took one day off (her golden wedding anniversary) before traveling
to Boston, where she and Joan substituted for still-convalescing
Teddy.[20] At "Coffee with the Kennedys," twenty-five hundred voters, mostly women, came to meet Rose and Joan. Teddy's spouse
updated the throng on his condition, noting that he hoped to walk
out of New England Baptist Hospital under his own power by

Christmas. After saying a few words, Rose traveled to two more campaign events for Bobby, in Troy and Schenectady, where thirty-five hundred Kennedy supporters turned out for a tea in her honor.[21] She assured them that Bobby would carry on President Kennedy's legacy, especially in civil rights.

Bobby faced two main problems in his New York candidacy. Some labeled him a carpetbagger from Massachusetts, and many viewed him as ruthless from his days fighting Jimmy Hoffa as a Senate Rackets Committee staffer, running Jack's campaigns, and battling the Mafia while attorney general. "Bob was a year old when we came here," Rose testified, "and has lived in New York longer than he has any place else." Without a doubt, she assured audiences, he considered himself a New Yorker. Rose humanized Bobby, telling stories about his childhood, even of those times when she "used to spank him with a rulaaa!" Bobby was approaching forty, but in some ways Rose was still in charge. After one introduction of her "seventh child, Robert Francis Kennedy," Rose took a seat behind him, and Bobby sheepishly stepped to the mike. Before he could start his speech, Rose was back at his side, stage whispering, "Tell them about your experience. . . ." "I'm going to tell them," Bobby obeyed, with a touch of faux exasperation. Smiling, he turned back to his mother, who had resumed her seat. "Why don't you give your *own* speech?" The crowd roared, and Rose giggled. "See, that's it!" Bobby exclaimed. "The reason she's never introduced us before is that we never go on the same platform with her." Gesturing back toward his mother, the seasoned pol, he declared, "We couldn't possibly compete with that!"[22] The dialogue was vintage Kennedy: warm banter, with a touch of reality about Rose's attempts to control her children. "Their presence together reminded crowds that the Kennedys were kind of an American royal family, an institution worth preserving," Evan Thomas has noted.[23]

The press embraced Rose's campaign persona. "Her Sunday audiences found her without an iota of self-pity, which is the way it has always been with the daughter of Honey Fitz," wrote Hearst reporter Bob Considine. "Mrs. Kennedy is a remarkable campaigner, tireless, cheerful, interested and with a delightful smidgeon of blarney." While campaigning for thirty-year-old Teddy in his first run for Senate, she had joshed about critics who thought he was too young. "I wanted Teddy to go into the Church. But the trouble was that he wanted to start out as bishop," Rose joked.[24] "I'd rather meet you than any queen," gushed a woman in Rochester.[25]

As the first anniversary of JFK's death approached, Joe and Rose Kennedy's two surviving sons swept to victories in their Senate campaigns. Bobby won by seven hundred thousand votes over Republican incumbent Kenneth Keating, and Teddy, still confined to a Boston hospital, trounced his opponent, earning 75 percent of the votes. A few days after the election, Rose instructed Bobby, "[You should] know that the Balfour Resolution established the Jewish home in Jerusalem, but did not make it a Jewish state." She assumed that he knew this history, "but some don't. If you don't it should be explained to you."[26]

Soon Rose departed for Europe to promote the Kennedy Library and speak about mental retardation. She appeared at a traveling exhibition of Kennedy memorabilia, including Jack's famous SOS coconut that she had urged him to preserve two decades before. He had displayed it on his desks from Capitol Hill to the Oval Office. The JFK exhibit toured fifteen cities, several behind the Iron Curtain, covering eight thousand miles. Using her French and German, Rose spoke at the Paris, Bonn, and Copenhagen venues, her message always the same: "If you have a retarded child, don't let that stop you from having more babies. If we felt that way [after Rosemary] . . . we wouldn't have two United States senators in our family today."[27]

In Copenhagen Rose laid a wreath at the graves of Resistance fighters. Marie Bruce remembered Rose's perfect instincts on this "very cold dark December day [with] heavy rain" casting a pall over the "small group of old people, shabby survivors of the Resistance." "Suddenly Mrs. Kennedy emerged from under the umbrella where the two of us stood, walked to the graves, knelt on the wet grass and began to pray quietly. The little crowd, moved, crept nearer. [The] French have an expression, 'Le mot juste.' They followed her right to the car; there were tears."[28]

BY THE MID-1960S Rose was quite comfortable using modern media to spread her message about preventing mental retardation. She did radio interviews, made public-service announcements, and began appearing on nationally syndicated talk shows to discuss her campaign and promote products made by handicapped workers. In July 1967, wearing a pink dress and her signature pearls, Rose confidently strode onto the set of Mike Douglas's syndicated TV show in Philadelphia. Describing Rosemary without mentioning her name, she observed that after two healthy sons, "we had this little girl . . . my oldest daughter, and she was mentally retarded, and I tried to get help" from family doctors, child psychiatrists, and Harvard. None offered any hope or help for Rosemary's mental deficiencies. "I was very discouraged and really heartbroken because I didn't know what to do to help the child." She then moved on to the work of the Joseph P. Kennedy, Jr. Foundation and to research indicating that viewers should vaccinate their children against measles, a major cause of retardation. The vaccinations were "not expensive," she assured them.

Douglas departed from the script Rose had prepared for him. Did parents still try to hide their retarded children? "That used to happen but not so much anymore," Rose observed. A bit dismissively, she added, "No reason now to hide them or think you have to keep them at home." Douglas wanted to know how Rose's older children reacted to their sister's affliction. "Well, there wasn't any great to-do about it. When you have a large family, some of them are brilliant and some are not so brilliant." Rosemary "was a fairly good swimmer, and we used to compliment her on her swimming or her hairdo after we'd congratulate the boys on their mental capacity." This gave her an opportunity to talk about Eunice's day camp for retarded children. Not knowing the painful truth of Rosemary's disappearance from the Kennedy family, kindly Mike

Douglas wondered aloud why she was "finally institutionalized." Rose ducked that question, generalizing, "It depends on personal circumstances." If there is a good school near the family, the child could attend it and make friends, but if she must be tutored at home, as the Kennedys had tried, then the child has no friends. "So she's better sent away to boarding school," reported Rose. When had Rosemary left the family for school? Douglas inquired. "I suppose she was probably fourteen or fifteen," Rose responded, shifting uneasily in her chair. Retarded adults can become productive citizens, she asserted. For example, "Flame of Hope Candles" had been produced by the mentally retarded. Reminiscing about past campaigns, Rose recalled how Bobby had raised her age to make Jack seem older. "I said that was the greatest sacrifice a woman can make!" she quipped.[29] Four years after Jack's death, she had rediscovered her equilibrium, wit, and life's work.

The world now began to recognize Rose not only for her large family and for overcoming President Kennedy's assassination, but also for her contributions in mental retardation. Connecticut's Saint Joseph College awarded her an honorary degree in 1965 for "womanly leadership" in encouraging the mothers of retarded children and "hastening the advent of an era of greater attack on the problems of mental retardation."[30] From Hyannis to Harvard, she presided over memorial dedications "to my beloved son, Jack, the late president." The Canadian Association for Retarded Children presented its International Award of Merit "for her personal courage which has been a source of inspiration and hope to afflicted families everywhere." She visited a Toronto school for retarded children. One child embraced her, and Rose threw her arms around him. She was particularly moved by a Canadian gift—a painting of Mount Kennedy, the Yukon peak named for JFK. She reminded her audience that Bobby had scaled its treacherous summit in tribute to his slain brother.[31]

Farther afield, Rose was invited to speak about mental retardation and support fund-raising for retarded children by the Swedish boy and girl scouts. She eagerly accepted. "Mamma Kennedy," the Swedish newspapers dubbed her. That trip's highlight was lunch at

Drottningholm Castle with King Gustaf VI Adolf, who later sent her an autographed photo of himself with her, taken on the castle's balcony. Rose appreciated the kindly king's gesture but complained to the American ambassador's wife in Stockholm, "I am sorry my coat was not buttoned properly [causing it to bulge]; but, as you recall, we were rather rushed from the inside of the castle out of doors for the picture, and I could not keep His Majesty waiting."[32] She would never relinquish her desire for flawless public images.

Rose's proudest moment in her fight against mental retardation came when she lifted a spadeful of earth at a 1966 groundbreaking for the Rose Fitzgerald Kennedy Center for Research in Mental Retardation and Human Development at Yeshiva University's Albert Einstein College of Medicine in New York. Holding the ceremonial shovel, Bobby at her side, Rose radiated pride to have, for the first time, something named for *her*. The Joseph P. Kennedy, Jr. Foundation donated $1.45 million for its construction.[33] The foundation also provided up-to-date research, statistics, and policies on mental retardation for Rose's speeches, and she added personal anecdotes about Rosemary. Through all of these efforts, she raised a curtain hiding those afflicted with developmental disabilities and gradually revealed her own internal struggles: "I remember what prayers I said, what sacrifices I offered, what tears I shed—all through my lifetime. . . . My anguished heart would again utter the eternal question, 'Dear God, why did you create my innocent child this way? What can I do to help her? What will happen to her if I die?'"[34]

Rose worried about her husband, who was racked by small strokes bringing him near death several times. In February 1967 she declined attendance at a New York fund-raising event for the foundation: "Mr. Kennedy is not very well, and all my time and efforts are centered around him here at Palm Beach."[35] Recalling Rose's devotion, John Ryan, Joe's caretaker in later years, observed, "[S]he would have breakfast with Mr. Kennedy, lunch with him or read to him and tell him what was going on. She was constantly there and constantly around him."[36]

But some events were simply too meaningful for her to miss.

Commemorations of Jack's life attracted Rose and other family members. At Choate School's Mothers' Day celebration, Rose spoke before the dedication of Robert Berks's JFK bust. (A larger rendition of the modern sculpture would eventually tower over the grand foyer of Washington's John F. Kennedy Center for the Performing Arts.) Rose reminded the audience that she and Joe selected Choate for its proximity to New York "so that we might visit the boys once in a while." In her speech, Joe Jr. earned her usual approval for studying "diligently." On the other hand, "Jack's studies were fair, his athletic participation was rather weak on account of his poor health, and he had a bit of difficulty with his masters. I say this quite frankly because, if any of you mothers have had children who have any difficulties at school, you may become discouraged. With the proper moral support, those youngsters will snap back and become exemplary students." She hailed Choate for increasing Jack's "awareness of his responsibilities" in later life—high praise indeed from Rose.[37]

During this period an old Kennedy friend, Cardinal Cushing, spoke movingly at the dedication of Boston's John F. Kennedy Federal Building: "For our generation, and the one that follows us, his memory will be a living thing—we talked to him, laughed with him, followed him, prayed with him, and finally wept over him. . . . But there will be other generations here for whom his name must be immortalized, and in this steel and stone we make his monument. . . . May the Lord, with Whom he lives today, bless all of us who loved him, and make this city, which he loved, always worthy of his memory." Boston's Catholic newspaper sent Mrs. Kennedy a photo of her and Cushing. Streaks of gray hair and facial wrinkles now revealed her age (seventy-six). She couldn't refrain from commenting, "I knew the Cardinal was younger than I, but I thought with the help of Elizabeth Arden that I could hold my own. After looking at the photo, I doubt it; so please do not show it to any of my fans."[38]

Rose needn't have worried about her appearance, vitality, or relevance as the years accumulated. Approaching seventy-eight, she still had one more national political campaign in her future. On

March 16, 1968, Robert F. Kennedy announced his candidacy for the Democratic presidential nomination. Back to work went Rose, outlining speeches to deliver for Bobby in key primary states— Indiana, Nebraska, Oregon, and California. (Democrats held only seventeen primaries in 1968, but they accounted for nearly 40 percent of the delegates. Winning early contests could attract party leaders' support.)[39] Rose emphasized Bobby's childhood, steeped in history and politics, a tack that had worked during his 1964 Senate campaign. The carpetbagger issue had disappeared, of course, but Bobby's alleged "ruthlessness" remained. "I resent" such an "epithet," Rose declared. As only a loyal mother could, she defended her son's tenacious record as attorney general, fighting "the gangsters who threatened him and his children."[40] And she did her homework. Professor Arthur Schlesinger Jr., Jack's White House historian, ran an ad in the *New York Times*, "Why I Am for Kennedy." Rose read it carefully, underlining the most convincing sections.[41]

In late April she undertook a grueling eight-day swing through Indiana, with a detour to Chicago for Kennedy Foundation events. On one-day visits to Indianapolis, Gary, La Porte, Kendallville, Fort Wayne, South Bend, and Elkhart, she wooed Hoosier voters. Rose met with the press and pressed the flesh at receptions. Teddy was at her side once; otherwise, she campaigned alone. "[I] did not campaign with Bob at all as I can get a crowd on my own," Rose asserted.[42] It was like old times. Polly Fitzgerald, the wife of Rose's nephew and organizer of the famous Kennedy teas for Jack in the 1950s, again coordinated receptions, where a new generation was eager to meet Rose. "'Bobby's Not Ruthless,' Says Rose," blared the Gary, Indiana, headlines.[43] Her message was hitting the mark.

Bobby had demonstrated true compassion in Indianapolis two weeks earlier when speaking of Martin Luther King's assassination. Only a few hours after the murder, Bobby had gently revealed the "sad news" to an audience of black supporters in words as tender and eloquent as any in American political history. Quoting from memory his favorite poet, Aeschylus, he said, "Even in our sleep, pain which cannot forget falls drop by drop upon the heart until, in our own despair, against our will, comes wisdom through the awful grace of God." Although Jackie had introduced Bobby to the Greek poets as salve for their grief after Jack's death, Bobby's simple plea for prayer reflects Rose's influence: "So I ask you tonight to return home, to say a prayer for the family of Martin Luther King . . . but more importantly to say a prayer for our own country, which all of us love—a prayer for understanding and that compassion of which I spoke."[44] Unlike other riot-torn US cities, Indianapolis remained calm that night. Rose and her mother had worried that Bobby, surrounded by five sisters, would be a "sissy." Instead, he had developed a tough political persona that only grief and despair could penetrate, revealing his vulnerability, softening his spirit. Perhaps Kick had been right when she told Marie Bruce, "[I]t is Mother who gave us our characters."[45] Bobby won Indiana with 42 percent of the votes.

After a few days at home to catch her breath, Rose was back on the trail, this time a three-day weekend in Nebraska. She spent Mother's Day appearing at two receptions (attended by three thousand voters) in Omaha. Then she was off to Girls Town (part of Father Flanagan's Boys Town) to meet with students and nuns, before visiting a nearby school for retarded children. Two days later Bobby took 51 percent of Nebraska's primary votes.

On her way to California—a crucial state, where Bobby had to defeat the other anti–Vietnam War candidate, Minnesota senator Eugene McCarthy—Rose stopped at Lake Tahoe for a few days. Her pattern of campaigning, followed by a spa visit to recharge, remained unchanged. She needed her endurance for an exhausting tour of West Coast cities. Starting in Sacramento, she held a press conference, followed by brunch and a speech for five hundred women. From the capital she flew by private plane to Fresno, spoke to a thousand senior citizens (her newest constituency), and then drove to a park to address a thousand picnickers. Day's end found her in San Francisco. The next afternoon she spoke at a reception for two thousand. Diminutive Rose kicked off her shoes and climbed onto a chair in order to be seen throughout the large ballroom.[46] The receiving line included "nuns, hippies and a topless dancer wearing nothing but 3,000 blue

Kennedy buttons." Clearly, this wasn't Buckingham Palace. "Some kissed her, some gave her gifts . . . and everyone marveled at her trim figure, firm chin line, and glossy dark hair."[47] "A charmer," one newspaper labeled her.[48] Another wrote, "Clan matriarch, Mrs. Rose Kennedy, as vigorous as any of her daughters, was deployed to Northern California to talk with the sophisticated San Francisco and Sacramento sectors. . . ."[49]

Daughter Jean and her husband, Steve Smith, Bobby's campaign manager, carried the Kennedy banner throughout the state. Pat Lawford, now divorced from Peter and living in New York, returned to Hollywood and reconnected with old friends. Teddy took time from the Senate to stump for his brother; his wife Joan was assigned to Mexican-American communities because of her Spanish-language skills. Eunice couldn't join the campaign. Her husband, Sargent Shriver, had just been named US ambassador to France. Jackie, desperately trying to maintain her family's privacy in New York, avoided the campaign trail. Bobby's wife, Ethel, with ten children and another on the way, maintained speaking engagements back east but came west when she could.[50] Rose marveled at Ethel's steadfastness: "I had never been able to be with Joe to the extent that she [Ethel] had been with Bobby. . . ." She blamed long distances, slow transportation, and a need to stay with her children in case they fell ill. "[S]o when my husband worked and went to California, I went with him only once . . . in 1927. . . ."[51] Yet Bobby and Ethel, unlike Rose and Joe, had a paradigmatic Catholic marriage, grounded on fidelity.

After a brief rest in San Francisco, Rose headed north to Oregon; its primary would be one week before California's. She held a press conference in Eugene and presided over the dedication of a school for retarded children, named for Pearl Buck, the American author, who, like Rose, was the mother of a retarded daughter. Senior citizens greeted Rose at a reception the next day, and then, in Portland, she plunged into a blur of more press conferences and receptions. This time her efforts were for naught. Bobby would become the first Kennedy to lose an election. McCarthy won 44 percent of the vote to Bobby's 38.[52]

Before the Oregon loss, Rose was back in southern California for three days of press conferences and rallies, the last one to be held in the Ambassador Hotel's ballroom. Rose flew north again for a two-day visit to Monterrey. In nearby Salinas, she presided over a reception for "Spanish and Filipinos" and was told of "great jealousy and dissension between [the] two factions . . . but we had a big crowd."[53] Leaving California for home, she waited in Hyannis for the returns from the June 4 primary.

No other American mother had faced such a prospect: that a second of her sons could be president. This would boost the concept of "republican motherhood" to its apogee. "It is wonderful to think that people have that much confidence in a member of your family. The possibility of it happening again—it's overwhelming," Rose admitted. "For one mother to have this experience twice . . . ! You almost begin to think that some other mother should have it."[54]

What Rose was about to experience, however, no one could have wished on another. Bobby had achieved his goal, defeating McCarthy, 49 to 41 percent, in the California balloting. Speaking to an ecstatic crowd of young supporters in the Ambassador Hotel ballroom, where Rose had recently appeared, Bobby thanked his sisters, mother, campaign volunteers, and "not in the order of importance," Ethel, who beamed at his side. It was the dead of night on the East Coast, and Rose didn't see or hear her son's victory speech. Calling for a win at the upcoming Democratic convention, Bobby left the podium and exited through the hotel's crowded pantry. Waiting for him was a Palestinian émigré, Sirhan Sirhan. He aimed a pistol at the senator's head and pulled the trigger. Bleeding profusely from a bullet wound behind his right ear, Kennedy lay on the floor, clutching a rosary that had been placed on his chest. An ambulance rushed him to a nearby hospital, where surgeons performed brain surgery, but Bobby remained comatose.

Back in Hyannis Port, a night nurse knocked on Rose's bedroom door. Instead of awakening her for Mass, however, she told her to turn on the television. "It's Bobby! It's Bobby!" an incredulous Rose exclaimed as the news bulletins flashed. Her niece, Ann, reported that the senator was unlikely to recover. "It seemed impossible that the same kind of disaster could befall our family twice in five years," Rose thought.[55] "If I had read it in fiction, I would have said it was incredible."[56]

Rose sought refuge at St. Francis Xavier Church, once again praying for a son felled in the prime of life while serving his country. Returning to the compound, she retreated to her room to regain her composure. This time Rose accepted the burden of informing Joe, telling him of Bobby's critical condition. Then she followed her too-familiar regimen of nervous activity, arranging and rearranging her room. By next morning, the dreaded news arrived. Bobby had died overnight, with Ethel, Teddy, Jean, Pat, Jackie, and his older children standing vigil. Rose went to her husband's room, closed the door, and told him that their third son was gone.[57] "The house was stoic after the president's death," remembered Nurse Rita Dallas, "but in chaos" when Bobby died. "My son. My son," she heard Rose repeat over and over.[58]

By the time she arrived in New York City to gather with her family before Bobby's funeral Mass, to be held at St. Patrick's Cathedral, Rose's resolve had returned. At Ethel's apartment Rose appeared "infinitely composed," Arthur Schlesinger recorded. Ethel's and Rose's certainty that "Bobby is now happier than he has ever been, that he has been reunited with Jack, that soon all will be together again," was utterly unshakable. When Jean and Eunice, who had flown in from Paris, said good-night to their mother, she responded, "I'm so glad all you children are home again."[59] At Bobby's funeral Rose meditated on Jesus's mother: "I think of the Blessed Virgin Mary. I thought of her at the crucifixion when I saw Jack [lying in state] in Washington in the Rotunda and Bobby['s coffin] again in New York. [Mary] trusted in God and bore [her pain] patiently."[60] As the medieval Catholic hymn "Stabat Mater" proclaims, "At the cross her station keeping, stood the mournful mother weeping, close to her Son to the last."[61]

With a heartbreaking quaver, Teddy delivered an eloquent

eulogy summing up Bobby as "a good and decent man, who saw wrong and tried to right it, saw suffering and tried to heal it, saw war and tried to stop it."[62] What a credit to his family, Rose thought of her last son's tribute. A twenty-one-car train bore Bobby's casket, along with his family, friends, and associates, from New York to Washington, DC, where he would be buried near Jack at Arlington National Cemetery. On the 226-mile route, through cities, towns, and countryside, thousands of mourners lined the tracks. From her seat, Rose gazed at the signs: "God Bless the Kennedys" read a young black girl's hand-lettered placard. Wanting to let people know that she saw and appreciated them, Rose occasionally waved and encouraged her children and grandchildren to do the same. She later worried that some thought her gesture "inappropriate."[63]

A few days later Teddy and Rose appeared on TV, offering their gratitude for the many condolences they had received. Wheelchairbound, Joe sat at their side, the ravages of his stroke and grief contorting his mouth. Considering her remarks "one of the best things she had ever done," Rose provided a spiritual explanation of the latest family tragedy.[64] It reflected her essence: "We cannot always understand the ways of Almighty God. The crosses which He sends us, the sacrifices which He demands of us. . . . But we accept with faith and resignation His Holy Will, with no looking back to what might have been, and we are at peace. We have courage, we are undaunted and steadfast, and we shall carry on the principles for which Bobby stood. . . ."[65]

Despite her faith, Rose grieved for Bobby. Daughter Pat, continuing a tradition started by Jack after Joe Jr. had perished, gathered family essays for a book about Bobby. Rose's tribute expressed her desolation: "How sad are our hearts when we realize that we shall never see Bobby again, with his tousled, windblown hair, his big affectionate smile, carrying one child piggyback and holding another by the hand—his dog close behind. What joy he brought us. What an aching void he has left behind, which nothing in the world can ever fill. We admired him, we loved him, and our lives are indeed bleak without him."[66] In her public tributes to Bobby, she sometimes added this sorrowful coda: "A devoted husband, beloved son, admired brother. I know I shall not look upon his like again."[67]

OUTWARDLY, ROSE WAS the soul of fortitude and steadiness. Yet her sparkle dimmed. She had recovered from Jack's passing, but the blow of a second assassination—the death of her fourth child—paired with Joe's decline had taken its toll. Correspondent Robert MacNeil inquired whether she was "glad" Jack had been president, "even though his life was cut short." "I couldn't answer that," Rose finally responded, seemingly stunned that anyone would pose such a question. "Oh, no. Oh, yes," she stumbled momentarily, processing the equation, then found her voice: "We'd much rather have him living. Oh, yes," she repeated softly. "His children and Bobby's children. Eleven children without a father. No!"[68]

Wounded she might be, but Rose's grasp on imagery remained as tight as ever. Merv Griffin persuaded her to appear on his talk show, but, as he soon discovered, she would be no ordinary guest. In fact, she immediately took charge. "I'm sending you a piece of cloth of my dress, put it in on camera and tell me how it looks," she wrote to Griffin several weeks in advance of her appearance. Arriving at the studio well ahead of taping time, she inquired, "Where do I sit?" Griffin replied, "Well, in three hours you'll be sitting right there." "OK, have your director show me the pictures he's going to take of me," Rose demanded. The director trained his camera on her, but she objected, "No, no, no, that's too close. I can't take that shot. Back up." He did, and Rose announced, "That will be fine, OK, I'm going to rest."

When the cameras rolled and Griffin asked what sustained her through incomprehensible tragedy, she replied that God "has given us, as I say, triumphs as well as ordeals." Citing Irving Stone's 1961 best-selling novel about Michelangelo, *The Agony and the Ecstasy*, she observed, "We've had great ecstatic moments, and we've had these tragedies, but the ecstasies or the triumphs are greater than the tragedies."

Rose's conversations with Griffin continued after her appearance on his talk show. She phoned periodically to tutor him about Catholicism, quizzing him about saints' feast days, as she did her children. When he fell short, Rose admonished, "You should learn about your religion!" Hearing of his mother's antics, Teddy told Griffin, "That's how she treated us. You're a Kennedy boy." Merv concluded, "Boy, she knew exactly where she was going and what she wanted for her family and what she wanted the Kennedy name to be."[69]

CHAPTER 13

❧

Times Remembered

"Few feel compassion for or understanding of Rose. She sheds no tears; her head remains up, like a small bird weathering a big storm. It is possible . . . that she is a living saint. Her God, her church, her childlike faith, take precedence over all else. No matter how heavy the repeated blows of adversity, she murmurs, 'Thy will be done' and closes the memory book," columnist Jim Bishop wrote in 1968's darkest days. "So certain was Rose's belief in an afterlife," he added, "that she sometimes shocked friends by commenting, 'I mean to speak to the president about that when I see him [in heaven].'"[1] Yet when *Look* magazine reporter Laura Bergquist interviewed Rose shortly after Bobby's death, her eyes filled with tears. "It is so very difficult to speak of him," she confessed.[2]

Bergquist followed Rose to her daily 7 a.m. Mass and watched as she stayed after the service for another twenty minutes, lost in silent prayer and meditation. An admiring parishioner pronounced her "Pope Rose" for having "the most serene faith of any human I have known . . . she's the real power and glory and strength in *that* family," he added.[3]

Adhering to Catholic teachings (as she understood them) helped her through the next family crisis: Jackie's romance with Greek millionaire divorcé Aristotle Onassis. Rose had initially met Ari in Monte Carlo, shortly before Jack's 1960 election. But fearing negative publicity if she were seen with Onassis and his mistress, opera diva Maria Callas, she had declined an invitation to dine with them. When Jackie and Onassis visited Hyannis Port in 1968, however, Rose found him charming and "rather good looking, but his figure is short and stocky, and his trousers always look voluminous." His gift of $1,500 gold bracelets to her and daughter Jean earned Rose's approval. Although she knew that her glamorous daughter-in-law preferred older men, she thought Ari, almost a quarter century Jackie's senior, much too aged.[4]

"If Jackie had asked me, I probably would have frowned upon the idea [of marrying Onassis]" because of his age (sixty-two). Rose calculated that in a decade he would be "quite an old man," nearly the same age as Joe when he suffered his debilitating stroke. "[A] man's health is apt to deteriorate and that is difficult for a woman," she reasoned. She "advised Pat, if she were ever thinking of getting married again, which I hope she is not, to consider that angle." Rose also worried about Caroline and John Jr. dividing their lives between the United States and Greece. Their grandmother favored another of Jackie's many other "guests," the widowed David Ormsby-Gore, a member of Jack and Kick's prewar London social circle.[5] Surely he would make a perfect mate for the former first lady. Interfaith marriages no longer perturbed Rose, twenty-five years removed from her vehement objection to Kathleen's marriage to an Anglican.

Rose did understand that Jackie "probably wanted companionship and a certain security, which a husband gives a woman," but she underestimated both her daughter-in-law's determination and her desire for an opulent lifestyle. In truth, the issue was divisive among the Kennedys. Believing that a Kennedy-Onassis marriage would tarnish the Camelot legend and taint his own presidential ambitions, Teddy phoned Rose to report his opposition. Jean, on the other hand, accepted Jackie's decision. Devastated by Bobby's assassination, and fearing for her children's safety, JFK's widow craved the physical and financial security that marrying Onassis would provide.[6]

It was time for Rose to consult the Church, via her old friend Cardinal Cushing. Besieged by media, who wanted to know the Kennedy family prelate's views on Jackie's decision, he himself provided little guidance, and Rose ended up advising him. Pay no attention to the reporters, she told Cushing in no uncertain terms. "[T]hey had abused my father, my husband, my sons, and now my daughter-in-law," she declared, "but I was never going to let them annihilate me."[7] Refusing to take press calls, but acknowledging the inevitable, Rose finally issued a statement wishing "the bride and groom every happiness." Jackie invited Rose, Jean, and Pat to the October 1968 wedding. Rose sent regrets: she "couldn't leave Mr. Kennedy."[8]

"Fed up" that Jackie had been labeled a "public sinner" by the Catholic Church, Rose wasn't sure if the Vatican or "some priest" had singled out her daughter-in-law. The Church, Rose believed, "had no right to pick out one person or family as an object of scandal." "Who can judge anyone?" a now more open-minded Rose asked Eunice. "My life morally has run along very smoothly, as I was fortunate enough, like you, to marry in my own milieu and religion. . . ." Yet Rose found the burdens of moral perfectionism sometimes overwhelming. "I get tired of being put in the same category as Caesar's wife [who had to be above suspicion]." She had once complained to Jack about it; he responded archly, "It's too late to change now, Mother." Letters complaining about Jackie's choice poured in, but Rose was happy to note that they were "full of praise and admiration for me and for the dignity with which I have faced all the tragedies."[9]

Roman Catholicism, her rock in troubled times, now disappointed Rose. Privately, she criticized the modern Church, calling it "a bit vague" on just what Catholics should do in such a situation. "[W]ith this new ecumenical movement, one is supposed to help one's neighbor and not adhere too much to strict, old-fashioned, bigoted, narrow-minded practices, but rather be kind to other people and try to help them in a Christian way—rather than condemn them with a strict, narrow interpretation." Like many traditional Catholics, Rose thought ecumenism, the movement launched by Pope John XXIII in 1962, uncomfortably nuanced. The clear black-and-white rules of her convent days were harsh but much more certain. Mistakenly predicting that Roman Catholicism would soon unite with Greek Orthodoxy, Rose concluded that such a partnership would recognize Onassis's divorce from his first wife and allow the Catholic Church to sanctify his marriage to Jackie.[10] Of course, they didn't unite, and even if they had, the Vatican wouldn't have recognized Onassis's divorce. Jackie and Ari's Greek Orthodox ceremony, in his private chapel on the island of Scorpios, would never be valid in the Catholic Church.

Pat, who attended the wedding, told Rose that "Jackie was very happy." "Who wouldn't be with 400 or 500 million dollars and a ruby, which is worth $1,000,000?" Rose and Pat concluded. Yet Rose observed that "[Jackie] could have worn big expensive jewelry from Van Cleef and Arpels, but she never chose to do so and was quite reserved in her choice of jewelry [while married to Jack]."[11] Praising her daughter-in-law for not being "showy" while she was Mrs. John F. Kennedy, Rose seemed miffed that Jackie would remarry for more money. Was the Kennedy fortune insufficient? Rose failed to realize that Jackie wasn't satisfied with her widow's inheritance, especially in contrast to Onassis's massive wealth and his lifestyle of private planes, yachts, and Mediterranean islands.

Despite the media frenzy surrounding Jackie's marriage to Ari, she didn't draw all of the attention from her original in-laws. Rose noted that since her television appearance eulogizing Bobby, "people have become more interested in me as a person." Tourists swarmed her after Mass in Hyannis, jockeying to snap a photo. "I thought of going out another door, but it really does not make that much difference to me, and if the people want a souvenir . . . it does not bother me too much," she concluded.[12] When she appeared on *Look*'s November cover, the magazine sold three hundred thousand more copies than its regular circulation.[13]

As the hubbub died, Rose gradually returned to her charitable work. On the fifth anniversary of Jack's assassination, she appeared on *The Today Show* to promote a new fund-raising product for the mentally retarded. Speaking with Barbara Walters, Rose touted Flame of Hope perfume; like the candles of the same name, it was produced by intellectually handicapped workers. Rose wrote on her script for the Walters interview, "I was ashamed or afraid" of Rosemary, an admission she had never previously revealed.[14]

Rose also worked to retire Bobby's campaign debt. Dunning letters had begun to arrive from vendors who had provided services to his presidential run. Hoping that she might understand the plight of small businesses, they appealed to her as family matriarch to pay the bills. Such pleas, like her own bills, went straightaway to the family's New York business office. Yet occasionally Rose returned to the banquet circuit to raise thousands of dollars to relieve Bobby's debt. In December 1968 she joined Cardinal Cushing for a Boston fund-raising dinner. What an aching void Bobby's death left in her life, she told the audience. Bob Fitzgerald, Rose's nephew, had organized the dinner, and she couldn't help offering advice after the event. Why hadn't the spotlights been fixed on celebrities as they were introduced? Shouldn't Cardinal Cushing have been seated next to her? "I get a lot of television coverage," she observed, which he missed by sitting opposite her. Why didn't someone escort the cardinal after the dinner? Instead, "he was left stranded and had to call a taxi." Trying to lessen the sting of her critiques, she wrote that "these comments are meant only to be helpful. I make a list of things in my own home, so as to correct them in the future. . . ."[15]

Indeed, Rose continued making lists of reminders for her media events:

1. Be sure dress is pulled down so it does not blouse.
2. Be sure sleeves are not wrinkled.
3. Do not gesture too much with hand while speaking on platform.
[4.] Record everything twice—voice [is] better second time.

[5.] Watch expression of mouth when speaking and answer-
ing difficult questions.[16]

Maybe 1969 would bring better days. She took comfort from a
Sybil Connolly letter. The Irish fashion designer (and creator of the
gossamer gown Jackie had worn for her official White House portrait by Aaron Shikler) reported, "I wish that you could see for
yourself, over the hearth of almost every cottage in Ireland—a picture of the Sacred Heart, the Blessed Virgin and President Kennedy."[17] What could be more fulfilling? The Sacred Heart of Jesus
(symbol of Rose's Dutch convent) and the Virgin Mary (Rose's
spiritual icon) were now grouped with her martyred son in the
Emerald Isle.

Traveling throughout the States and to Canada, Rose continued
her hectic schedule on behalf of mental retardation and the Special
Olympics. Returning to Boston, she presided over the dedication
of Jack's Brookline birthplace on what would have been his
fifty-second birthday. The Kennedys had purchased the house and
restored it with family furnishings and mementos. Now they presented its deed to the United States to create a national historic site.
In her talk Rose pointed to the room where she had given birth to
the future president: "When you hold your baby in your arms the
first time, and you think of all the things you can say and do to
influence him, it's a tremendous responsibility. What you do with
him and for him can influence not only him, but everyone he meets
and not for a day or a month or a year but for time and eternity."[18]
CBS's Harry Reasoner, who had interviewed her there two years
earlier, concluded, "When you talk to Rose Kennedy now in the
setting of his old house, which would put her in mind of the sad-
nesses of long life if anything would, what you hear is thankfulness
for the opportunities life gave her and her family—not bitterness."[19]
Rose's legend was taking hold in the public consciousness. Jack's
birthplace would provide a lasting shrine to him and the family in
just the way Rose conceived it.

Teddy, well into his six-year Senate term, now carried a huge burden. As the last surviving son, he became the family patriarch in place of his invalid father. Besides his own two, Kara and Teddy Jr., there were Jack's and Bobby's thirteen fatherless children. Not surprisingly, Teddy sometimes buckled under the strain. Always the family clown and foil, he was not accustomed to upholding the family image. He tried hard to brighten his parents' lives, "but when he wasn't with Mr. and Mrs. Kennedy, he'd get very solemn, very downcast, very alone. He would walk around the compound a lost soul," recalled Rita Dallas.[20] On his first attempt to drive to the Senate after Bobby's funeral, he suffered a panic attack. Only nighttime sailing trips from Hyannis to Maine, guided by the North Star, salved his torment.[21] An assassination nightmare haunted him. Would he meet the same violent fate as Jack and Bobby? He tried to drown his sorrows and fears in alcohol. Inebriated on a chartered flight from a fact-finding trip to Alaska, he stunned reporters with his slurred speech and adolescent behavior.[22]

A few months later, Teddy retreated to Martha's Vineyard for the annual Edgartown sailing regatta and a nostalgic party for several young women who had worked on Bobby's presidential campaign. They gathered in a cottage on Chappaquiddick, a tiny island across a narrow channel from the Vineyard. Cousin Joey Gargan had rented the cottage and planned the barbeque. Teddy joined them, contributing a bar's-worth of spirits and beer. He was genuinely grateful to the women for their loyal support in past Kennedy campaigns and knew that they would follow him into battle for the 1972 Democratic presidential nomination, should he run. Yet he often grew melancholy and "emotional" at such gatherings. They evoked too many memories of his departed brother.[23] Liquor undoubtedly aggravated his depression.

Late in the evening, Teddy left the party with one of the women, Mary Jo Kopechne. No one will ever know the exact circumstances of Teddy's late-night attempt to drive over Chappaquiddick's narrow Dike Bridge. With no guardrails to guide his Oldsmobile, it plunged over the side, into a swirling inlet. Somehow the senator escaped from the sedan, which landed on its roof in the pitch-black water. Unable to exit from the submerged, over-turned car, Kopechne drowned.[24]

As a boy, Teddy had been tapped by his older brothers as the one to tell their father about mishaps, in hopes that Joe would be lenient. When Teddy began to commit his own indiscretions, whether cheating at Harvard, or wrecking a car, Joe always helped him out of the jam. Even Rose, the model of responsibility, quoted approv-ingly her husband's advice to the errant Kennedy brothers: If you get into trouble, don't lie to me. Then I can help you. Otherwise, "I'm licked."[25] Now Joe sat silenced in Hyannis Port, across Nan-tucket Sound from where Teddy had committed the worst sin of his life. Attempting to wish away the horror as he swam across the narrow channel to Edgartown, Teddy retreated to his hotel room and failed to tell the police until the next morning.[26]

Rose encountered her son later that day, when he returned to the family compound. Distressed that he "seemed so unlike him-self," she found it "hard to believe he was my son. His usual posi-tive attitude, which he displayed so clearly at other times of difficulty, had vanished. He was disturbed, confused, and deeply distracted, and sick with grief over the death of the young woman." She attributed his behavior to the "shock" of almost drowning, as well as to the injuries, including a concussion, that he had suffered in the accident.[27] Conversely, the Edgartown police chief reported that the senator "never appeared in any kind of physical discomfort, or in shock, or confused" ten hours after the accident.[28]

Rose wrote condolences to Mary Jo's parents, telling them of the loss of her own daughter, Kathleen, also at age twenty-eight. She later asked them to meet with her at the Kennedys' New York apartment, and they discussed "the joys and sorrows that life brings to all of us."[29] Several years later, Rose explained how her husband had avoided such scandals as a businessman, particularly in meeting with starlets: Always have a trusted friend along for "protection so that if he were in an accident, like Teddy, he would not be in a dif-ficult position," Rose advised.[30]

Teddy knew that he had to tell his father about Chappaquiddick, even if Joe could no longer play the family's fixer. "Dad, I'm in some trouble," the senator explained. "There's been an accident, and you're going to hear all sorts of things about me from now on. Terrible things. But, Dad, I want you to know that they're not true. It was an accident," Teddy repeated, holding Joe's hand to his chest.[31]

Rose and the other Kennedy women, including Teddy's pregnant wife Joan, remained behind the scenes for his dramatic thirteen-minute, nationally televised speech one week after the tragedy. (Joan and Ethel had accompanied him to Mary Jo's funeral in Pennsylvania and to his court date, where he pleaded guilty to leaving the scene of an accident and received a suspended two-month sentence.) The speech's wording and themes reflected contributions from Teddy's retinue, including Robert McNamara, Ted Sorensen, Richard Goodwin, Milton Gwirtzman, Steve Smith, and John Tunney, but its stagecraft evinced Rose's touch. As *Newsweek* reported, "The Kennedys, of course, would never put on so provincial a show [as Nixon's Checkers speech of 1952, when he defended himself against a charge of financial improprieties]; their style is Roman, their taste impeccable. . . . Nor were there any tears—only a faint thickening in the senator's voice when he spoke of his family's tragic record. He was mostly the picture of discipline and probity and control, posed before the bookshelves in his father's library, his gaze level, his thick mane trimmed and combed down."[32]

Senator Kennedy asked his Massachusetts constituents to determine whether he should resign. Gwirtzman strategized that "what he meant to the Catholics as the last surviving son" would be enough to maintain Teddy's hold on the Senate seat. He was right. Ten thousand telegrams arrived at the family compound, begging him to stay in office, at a rate of 100 to 1.[33] A Senate ally predicted that Teddy would never again be a viable candidate for the presidency, but would spend the rest of his career in Congress. "I think we have finally come to the end of Camelot," reported the senator.[34] He didn't reckon on Rose's continuing image-crafting efforts.

"I am still involved with letters about Ted," she wrote to Jackie Onassis. "I am so overwhelmed with work. There seems to be always a new crisis just when we think we are at peace." Friends and family arrived at Hyannis Port to support the senator. But journalists, too, milled around the compound, cameras at the ready. "I suppose if he went to Europe, they would think he was ducking the issue, and it would be bad publicity," Rose fretted. A few weeks after the accident, she already thought Teddy seemed more relaxed. Yet she worried about the upcoming inquest on the accident, "which seems unnecessary and which people feel is a political ploy. It hangs over Ted's head and over all of us, really," Rose complained. She reminded Jackie, "You remember when you used to call him the little black sheep, but he really didn't deserve that epithet (as far as I know *then*), and he doesn't deserve it now."[35] The matriarch was standing by her wayward son.

Teddy's disaster may well have contributed to Joe's demise. Teddy certainly thought so: "The pain of that burden was almost unbearable."[36] In mid-November 1969, four months after Chappaquiddick, eighty-one-year-old Joe suffered another series of strokes that left him comatose. Holding her husband's hand, Rose knelt at his bedside, surrounded by Teddy, Joan, Eunice, Pat, Jean, Steve, Jackie, Ethel, and Ann Gargan. On November 18 Joseph P. Kennedy's heart beat its last. His body rested in a coffin at the Cape Cod mansion he had purchased in 1928. Overcome with guilt and emotion, Teddy reportedly slept under his father's casket the night before the funeral.[37]

As she did after Jack's and Bobby's deaths, Rose retreated to the beach, searching for comfort in the timeless sea and shore. This time, daughters Jean and Pat accompanied her, all of them bundled against the autumn chill. For her husband of fifty-five years, Rose requested a White Mass, symbolic of the Church's modern interpretation of death, focusing on resurrection, rather than loss.[38] Yet she dressed in funereal black, her desolate face covered with a sheer veil, as Teddy took her arm and guided her from Hyannis's St. Francis Xavier Church. Accompanied by four children, twenty-seven grandchildren, and in-laws, Rose escorted Joe's remains seventy-five miles to Brookline's Holyhood Cemetery, near JFK's birthplace, and committed his diminished body to the earth.[39] "Next to Almighty God, I had loved him . . . with all my heart, all my soul, all my mind," Rose declared.[40]

She took solace from the multitude of condolences sent by ordinary Americans. "I was amazed at the trust which they had in the mails and in the good will of the people—to enclose cash to use at our own judgment in projects of our choosing—the retarded children, Bobby Memorial, etc.—rather than designate themselves to which group the money should be given." Some mourners enclosed a dollar. One man included $5 "in memory of his own son, killed in Viet Nam just a few weeks before."[41]

Sympathy from friends and acquaintances helped. A woman who, decades before, had met Jack at Choate, wrote, "You and Mr. Kennedy had come up [to Choate] from Bronxville, with a delicious picnic for Jack and some of his friends." The young girl, eager to make a favorable impression on the elder Kennedys, had instead spilled her lunch "all over Mr. Kennedy—he was marvelous—he pretended there was nothing he loved more than having someone spill creamed chicken all over him—and you, realizing how I felt, were so kind to me." "[M]y life would not have been so full had it not been for you and your remarkable family," the note concluded.[42] Rose often received kudos for producing a famous, successful family but less frequently for displaying empathy.[43]

Robert Kennedy had complained that his father overshadowed Rose in media depictions of the family.[44] Now she would carry on without Joe. "The myth of the Kennedys is at least temporarily ended," commented *Time*.[45] But rumors of the Kennedy myth's demise were once again premature, just as they had been after Chappaquiddick. The family's mythology was now in the capable hands of its most effective creator.

Barely a month after Joe's death, Rose added to the legacy by publishing her article "Giving Children the Gifts of Faith and Courage" in the December 1969 issue of *Ladies' Home Journal*. "Mrs. Kennedy . . . is the matriarch of the century's most historic family," the magazine proclaimed. Faith, curiosity, enthusiasm, and ingenuity were the gifts Rose cited as most important for children. She believed her offspring had received them from her. "I have been ideally happy with my children. . . . Tragedies have come to a lot of other people who haven't had my compensation, and . . . I still consider myself very lucky. All I would like now is the hope of another ten active years," the seventy-nine-year-old Rose concluded.[46]

A deluge of fan letters poured in. One mother of five sons said the greatest compliment she could give them was to "tell them that they are like Jack or Bob Kennedy. . . . Your courage and your strength has [sic] been an inspiration to me and I am sure to other mothers. Thank you for teaching your children a sense of responsibility among riches."[47] Other admirers felt a need to share their tragedies. The daughter of one letter writer had been returning to college when a speeding car crashed into the auto, killing her roommate. Now the writer wanted to create a memorial plaque in honor of the roommate and inscribe it with a quote from Rose. Too many letters arrived for Rose to answer personally, but someone from the Kennedy staff always wrote to express Rose's gratitude.

Needing a break from the sadness of 1969, Rose set off to Paris to spend Christmas with the Shrivers at the American embassy, where Sarge was the ambassador. By all accounts, Eunice had the happiest and certainly the most enduring marriage of all Rose's children. Sarge adored his mother-in-law: "With much love to Grandma, who always makes everyone happy—and that is a sign of a Saint," the devout Sarge wrote to her.[48] Yet, like Teddy, because of his relaxed relationship with Rose, Sarge could tease her with impunity. He proclaimed a need for her to arrange the embassy: "I don't want that fancy china on the table with the wrong tablecloth or flowers, and somebody has got to organize the counting of the sheets and pillowcases. . . ."[49]

As the Shrivers were reliving the ambassadorial fairy tale that Joe and Rose had provided their family in prewar London, Rose couldn't resist sending unsolicited advice to Eunice. For an upcoming trip to Switzerland, Rose opined, "[Y]ou will of course have to think of getting ski clothes for the children if you take them, which is more difficult in France I suppose than here." "It would be nice if you invited Marie Bruce to spend a few days with you sometime. It would be a good change for her, and it would not be expensive," wrote Rose to her daughter. "Also, if you have any big affairs, you might like to invite the Windsors [Britain's abdicated King Edward

VIII and his wife Wallis]." Rose still fretted over Eunice's sensitive stomach, cautioning her about consommé because chefs often added sherry to it "and this might be difficult for you." In a letter about how to serve Sanka, an early brand of decaffeinated coffee, at the American embassy, Rose acknowledged her obsession with life's minutiae: "As you can see, my little mind is always busy."[50]

And it was, even regarding the Shrivers' clothing choices. To make her fashion points crystal clear, Rose clipped newspaper photos of Eunice and Sarge, circled their clothing faux pas, and indicated how to correct them. Sarge should have his shirt cuffs protrude slightly from his suit jacket (a suggestion she had also made to President Kennedy); Eunice should wear strapless shoes that didn't "break the line of the ankle." Furthermore, her dress hem was uneven. Perhaps if she held her arms "away from [her] sides as the models do," the dress would hang more evenly.[51] Ever the statesman, Sarge responded graciously: "Dear Grandma—I've sent every suit I own out for repairs! Next time you'll see me looking better!"[52]

Yet Rose didn't focus solely on appearances. She urged Sarge to investigate and correct falsities in the press about the Kennedy family. She was upset by one in *Paris Match*: "I particularly do not like the way they have talked about your father-in-law. . . . [T]hey said he was pro-Nazi, saying that he was practically willing to turn some of the countries over to the Germans. Also, I resented the way that they mentioned his being in the liquor business with Jimmy Roosevelt because I do not think that the implications were correct."[53] Now that Joe Kennedy couldn't defend himself, Rose embraced the role of protecting him and the family's reputation.

After Christmas with the Shrivers, she flew to Greece for a New Year's visit with Jackie, Ari, Caroline, and John. She would never know that Jackie had disparaged her in a 1964 interview with Arthur Schlesinger, not published until 2011. The subject was mundanity: "Mrs. Kennedy, poor little thing, was running around . . . seeing if she had enough placemats in Palm Beach, or should she send the ones from Bronxville, or had she put the London ones in storage. You know, . . . her little mind went to pieces."[54] Ironically,

Rose self-deprecatingly used the same label, "little mind," to poke fun at her obsession with trivia. Jackie also repeated JFK's view that his father was responsible for the Kennedy children's success. "Well, no one could say that it was due to my mother," Jack reportedly declared to Schlesinger in 1962.[55]

Time eventually softened Jackie's harsh view of her mother-in-law. By the early 1970s, Rose felt that "in any poll I am sure we would top any daughter–mother-in-law team." And why not? Jackie's letters to her spoke of the "pleasure" Rose brought to her and the children. "I am thrilled," exclaimed Rose, "because in this way I shall always be able to contact the children, and to know they all enjoy having me with them. . . . New Year's was possibly a little less foreign to the children because I was there," Rose assured herself. The twists of fate that had altered their lives astonished Rose, but now, perhaps, they could happily "share new experiences in an extremely different environment and atmosphere."[56] Phone calls from Jackie and her children also comforted Rose, who occasionally admitted to being lonely, though only in the third person: "It means so much to an older person to hear from the younger group in the family. [Talking to Caroline and John] lifted my spirits, and my heart sang."[57] And she loved seeing Jack's children when they visited at the Cape.

Rose apparently had charmed their stepfather: "You are one of the good Lord's most blessed children," Ari wrote, "because in the process of making an exemplary grandmother, he preceded it by making you an outstanding symbol of a man's most loyal companion and his children's mother."[58] That spring, Rose joined Jackie and Ari in Paris, where they dined at Maxim's, pursued by paparazzi, who captured Ari offering his hand to Rose as she stepped out of the limousine. Dressed in a full-length white gown topped by a dramatic black boa, Rose didn't appreciate being photographed wearing glasses, a sign that age was diminishing her eyesight. But Jackie teased that she would send to the press the picture of Rose and "Ari painting the town." Tongues would wag that "you are using your beautiful boa to seduce him away from me," Jackie joshed. She assured her mother-in-law that she was always welcome "so don't campaign all the time [for Teddy's 1970 senate reelection] because we need you too!"[59]

Accolades also accumulated back home. Her face radiating joy, she snipped the ceremonial ribbon at Yeshiva University's Rose Fitzgerald Kennedy Center for Research in Mental Retardation and Human Development, an event she labeled "one of the proudest and happiest of my entire life."[60] Her makeup sessions prior to TV appearances now took an hour, but they didn't dim her vigor once the camera's red light went on. "Your strength and energy is [*sic*] an inspiration not only to the staff of the show, but to everyone who saw you that night on television," wrote *The Dick Cavett Show* producer.[61] As one fan put it, "Watching you last night I saw the values and strength that turned out such outstanding children. It must sound like I'm suffering from an advanced case of Kennedymania, but I think your family is an incredible phenomenon. I know you are the key to it."[62]

On the fifty-third anniversary of Jack's birth, Rose found herself at another dedication, this time of his Harvard dorm room in Winthrop House. "My heart is filled with nostalgic memories of the youthful years when Jack was a happy, carefree student here," she said at the brief ceremony. "I only wish he might have lived to be with us today." It was a "very emotional but happy day" for her. "I realized how very proud and delighted the late president would have been, as a student, had he known that his rooms would serve in later years as a guest suite for use of the [Harvard] Institute of Politics."[63] How could she have known, when she had criticized Jack's irresponsibility at his 1940 Harvard graduation, that the university would honor him three decades later? Joining Rose at the dedication was Jack's roommate, Congressman Torbert Macdonald (D-MA). He recalled being in the dorm room when Rose "first chewed Jack out and then me for not having any drapes. We had curtains, I remember, but no drapes. Shortly after that we got drapes."[64]

Later in the summer of 1970, *Life*'s cover featured Rose, resplendent in a white evening gown and pearls, her hair and makeup done to perfection. At her Hyannis Port home, she stroked the baby grand's ivories, playing "Sweet Adeline" for the magazine, surrounded by framed portraits of "those giants, her menfolk." The reporter marveled at her curiosity, energy, and strength as Rose practiced iron shots on her front lawn, walked the beach with John, and even took a bicycle spin, while Caroline steadied her "whooping" grandmother. "I'm going to change my image," Grandma Kennedy joked. "I'm going to Europe again and I'm going to be seen coming out of a nightclub, or I'm going to be in a bikini on the Riviera next time!" Was she kicking off the traces in the wake of Joe's death? "I'm tired of that other image," Rose claimed—the one she had spent a lifetime crafting. "But better not make it too rollicking." Already she was rethinking her approach to life. As always, she had to consider a Kennedy male's perspective. "Teddy might not like that," she concluded. "Teddy wants me to be taken seriously."[65] No wonder. Because he had wrecked his reputation at Chappaquiddick, nearly destroying his political career, Mother would have to maintain her saintly persona.

Rose didn't barhop or wear bikinis. Instead, she embarked on an ambitious trip to Ethiopia in celebration of entering her ninth decade. Although she craved routine in her daily life, she couldn't tolerate boring predictability. Wanderlust continued to grip her. In addition to her charitable trips in the United States, and her seasonal shifts from Hyannis Port to Palm Beach, she traveled abroad three or four times a year. In July 1970 she flew to Switzerland and to Greece for another visit with the Onassises. She relaxed aboard Ari's yacht, *Christina*, observing that "my different friends have diverse ideas about their yachts." Rose was satisfied to lounge on the boat with shipmates Franklin Roosevelt Jr. and his new wife, Felicia, and then have dinner on Scorpios each evening. Soon she set off to rendezvous with Jean in Addis Ababa, but she was embarrassed to arrive after an overnight flight looking uncharacteristically disheveled. Yet everyone was "charming" to her, and "[i]f I mentioned that I am the mother of John F. Kennedy," she noted, "every facility is offered to me by the State Department, the ambassadors, and the consul generals." The trip's purpose was to visit Emperor Haile Selassie, whom she had welcomed to the White House in 1963. On that occasion, she had discovered that their birthdays were just one day apart. She would celebrate eighty, while he turned seventy-eight, in late July 1970.[66] "Whew! You become harder to catch with every birthday!" Sarge exclaimed.[67]

Staying at the emperor's guesthouse, Rose explored the bustling city with Jean and, as usual, commented on the people she encountered, noting that "their dark skin . . . is not as dark black as our blacks [in the United States]." Selassie and she marked their birthdays with gala meals at his palace. Attending Mass at a Christian Brothers church, Rose discovered that its Catholic school had been supported by a charitable American. She thought him wise to give his money to a US Catholic charity, with a stipulation to fund the Ethiopian school, in order to take the tax deduction. If he had donated directly to a foreign mission, he would lose the tax break, Rose explained.[68]

Returning to Hyannis Port after logging twenty-five thousand miles, Rose received the unsettling news that her teenaged grandsons, Robert Kennedy Jr. and Robert Shriver III, had been arrested on the Cape for marijuana possession. For the first time, Rose confronted an inconvenient family matter forthrightly: "I am not surprised because there is so much marijuana around now in all the private schools, private homes, and it is a dreadful, dreadful curse for young people. They seem to think they have to try it to be 'in.'" Media reports about the drug confused her. Some experts claimed it was "perfectly safe and doesn't do a child any more harm than some of the pills they take." Other doctors "say it is habit forming and will lead to the use of more dangerous drugs . . . what they call shooting acid or heroin." Accepting that marijuana was illegal, she "was quite disappointed as I had hoped that Bobby Shriver as one of the older boys amongst the Kennedy grandchildren would assume leadership against the drugs. In fact, I wrote to all the children and asked them to think about it—to have a big Kennedy movement against the drugs and give it enough prestige and enough excitement so that a lot would join that group, the anti-drug users, instead of being one of the users. But my hopes [of] that [have] been more or less dashed," Rose lamented.[69] In fact, the grandkids were putting the *high* in Hyannis. Coincidentally, paregoric, the opium-based drug still on Rose's 1970 travel list, was declared a Schedule III Controlled Substance by the US Drug Enforcement Administration that same year. Until then, it had been available without a prescription in Massachusetts and twenty-six other states.

After so many years of bragging about her grandchildren, Rose now puzzled over that rebellious generation as it navigated the shoals of adolescence. "I find it very difficult to argue with the young," she confided. "They seem so impatient about our ideas and assume that they know most everything." Bobby's eldest, Kathleen, now nineteen, was as headstrong as her namesake, Aunt Kick. "When I told about the high standard [of living] we have in the United States," explained Rose, "[Kathleen] immediately rejoined with the sentence, 'but that in having this high standard of living for a few people, we have trodden a lot of others under foot in this country and in other countries.'" The dismayed grandmother conceded, "[I]t is a rather difficult fight."[70]

WITH SENATOR KENNEDY'S 1970 senate reelection campaign in full swing, his staff implored Rose to campaign for him, especially among seniors. "Ted needs you at both these gatherings—[for] the older people who have lost faith in him since [Chappaquiddick] last summer."[71] The campaign sent her a litany of Teddy's legislative accomplishments for "older Americans," including Social Security increases, improved nursing home standards, and affordable housing for the elderly.[72]

Out on the hustings went Rose Kennedy again—at age eighty. In Fitchburg she spoke in French to Canadian émigrés. At a Worcester event, granddaughter Kathleen stood with her on stage, next to a photo of Teddy and Joan and their children. Better to send subliminal family images than prompt memories of "last summer." Rose mentioned that the famous Kennedy teas had begun there when Jack ran for the senate two decades before. She felt especially nostalgic when speaking for Teddy in Dorchester, where she had spent her teen years and attended high school. The Associated Press noted her vitality: "maybe no one told her that she's an octogenarian." Nevertheless, her chronic hoarseness reappeared, and cameras caught Rose dabbing her watery eyes.[73] Mild infirmities were encroaching on the aging matriarch.

Still she soldiered on. Rose asked her secretary to write to Senator Kennedy's staff, suggesting that his mother appear in New Bedford and Fall River, two more French Canadian enclaves, where she had campaigned for Jack.[74] Once there, she mentioned her visits to Canada on behalf of retarded children, and she reached out to Portuguese voters by recalling a visit she had recently made to Portugal. The campaign gently suggested that she tone down ethnic references for her forthcoming Springfield appearance. "The French felt a little slighted in New Bedford when you mentioned the Portuguese there." She was also cautioned not to single out Italians in East Boston because they only constituted 18 percent of the city's population.[75] Her East Boston visit prompted the nuns there to launch a "prayer crusade" for Teddy's victory, and they offered Masses for the repose of Jack's, Bobby's, and Joe's souls. "Who else, but his beloved Dad and brothers, could storm Heaven so efficaciously for Senator Ted?" exclaimed Sister Mary Cornelia, one of the prayer blitz's organizers.[76]

Senator Kennedy would defeat his Republican opponent, Josiah Spaulding, with 61 percent of the vote, earning a second full term in the senate.[77] Writing to Congressman Edward Boland (D-MA), who had campaigned with her for Teddy throughout the Bay State, Rose proclaimed, "Ted says I can still campaign at the age of 86, so do not be surprised to see me hit the hustings in the next campaign."[78] Boland responded, "Believe me, it was a privilege and a thrill for me to join you on the campaign trail. . . . I know that you . . . deeply sensed the love and affection for the Kennedys that flowed from the thousands of women that came to these events."[79] Rose couldn't wait to share Boland's praise with Teddy.

The next year brought another triumph—dedication of the John F. Kennedy Center for the Performing Arts, a marble temple on the Potomac River's banks. Initially Jackie told Rose she would attend and hoped that her mother-in-law would be there to put her at ease.[80] Rose emphasized her daughter-in-law's obligation to represent the Kennedys. Acknowledging the media's intrusiveness and understanding Jackie's reluctance to return to the spotlight, Rose added a pinch of guilt: "Jack would want you there."[81]

But headstrong Jackie parried Rose's pressure and decided to send regrets. Pouring out her heart in a long letter to Belle-Mère from aboard *Christina*, Jackie explained that her sister Lee and her brother-in-law were both ill in Europe. She must remain near them. Jack "never would have cared about my going to the opening of the Center anyway—It gave him so many headaches—he was never pleased with it—I worked so hard to direct it in certain ways in the first 4 years after his death. . . . That is what is important—not some opening which is all fanfare—You will be there to stand up for Jack." Jackie further explained how painful she found attending memorials to her deceased husband when all eyes were on her. That is why she asked the White House to forgo a public unveiling of her and JFK's portraits, which she attended with her children. "I really think it is the time for me to cease going to public memorials for Jack and just concentrate on bringing up his children," Jackie concluded. She knew that Rose would welcome the opportunity to speak for her and loved her mother-in-law all the more for it.[82]

Rose understood her daughter-in-law's desire to avoid hordes of attendees and press, especially after the deaths of Jack and Bobby. In fact, Rose admitted to Jackie that she still suffered pain over losing JFK: "I can never look at Jack's picture [for] a very long time."[83] Yet Rose, who craved center stage, reveled in the crowd's "enthusiasm, excitement, interest, [and] pride in the [John F. Kennedy] [C]enter." "I realized I was sitting in this presidential box in the most prestigious seat in the Center named for him. . . ." It would bring "joy and culture, pleasure and learning not only to Washington but to all the people of the country—this is what Jack would have liked this Center to represent." Reminiscing about him as an impish, undisciplined boy, Rose concluded, "How unpredictable is life!"[84]

As the Kennedy clan's leading representative, Rose remained a popular guest on television talk shows. David Frost invited her to tape a summer 1971 program, and she was more than happy to provide her script about mental retardation. She also inquired about when his show aired so that she would know whether to wear a morning, afternoon, or cocktail dress for the taping. And for color television, was she correct in choosing a "plain color" rather than a white or print dress?[85] The show went well, and Rose received a most unusual fan letter: "My labor pains started just as I watched your interview on the 'David Frost Show.' It is so very ironical how you comforted me with your words about motherhood," wrote a Yugoslavian woman. "I love all the Kennedy Family but most of all you 'Dear Rose.' You are truly [a] Child of Mary."[86] *Good Housekeeping* asked to do a cover story about Frost's guests that would picture Rose with Sophia Loren, Melba Moore, and Barbara Walters, but Rose scrawled, "Ted says no" on the invitation.[87] Men were still making some decisions for her.

Inevitably, the matriarch's prominence now spurred the first Rose Kennedy biography, by journalist Gail Cameron.[88] Its author had pleaded with Rose in 1968 (three weeks before Bobby's death) to cooperate on an authorized biography: "Neither enormous wealth nor extraordinary opportunities nor even the much written about influence of Ambassador Kennedy could ever explain your extraordinary children—in the end, much of it has to go back to you, their mother. It is for this reason that more than anything else in the world, I would love to write a book on you."[89] Unmoved, Rose had responded that because of Joe's illness she had to decline, as she had done with several other authors.[90]

Rose corrected only a few items in her copy of Cameron's book, but she was "terribly distressed" about it, especially "the way she talked about my dear Mother who was such an inspiration to me—religious, composed and conscientious—completely in control of herself and every situation—from whom I inherited my thick, lustrous hair and my petite figure. I am furious!" Rose exclaimed to Jackie.[91] Despite the book's praise for Rose, she focused on defending her mother, particularly her decision to stay at home with her six children while Honey Fitz pursued his political career and traveled abroad, sometimes with his daughters. Here was an opportunity to rationalize her own decision to leave "my youngsters in later years." She did so because transportation innovations "made distances less great, and we had the advantage of leaving our young-sters in charge of another couple, Mary and Edward Moore, who had no family responsibilities of their own."[92] Jackie tried to mol-lify her mother-in-law: "Don't be upset about *Rose*," she wrote from Greece. "It can only make your own book more interesting if you want to write one." In fact, Caroline had read Cameron's book "avidly and it sounds so nice," Jackie insisted.[93]

The Cameron biography convinced Rose to produce her own story. In the early 1940s she had thought fleetingly of writing a memoir. Later, Jack's death had prompted her to gather personal records, but again nothing came of her efforts. Editors bombarded her with pleas to choose their publishing houses. In 1967 she reported to Evan W. Thomas, then at Harper & Row, that her "autobiography ha[d] not progressed during the last few years, but I hope to work on it in the near future."[94] Later that year, Harper senior editor Cass Canfield encouraged Rose to write a "book of recollections . . . since it will be one of importance and very wide appeal. Your life is a part of the American Story." Canfield had even suggested a writer, Robert Coughlan of Time Inc., as her col-laborator on the project.[95] Moving to W. W. Norton the next year, Thomas continued to contact Rose.[96]

Rose steadfastly rejected all publisher requests until 1972, when Ted Sorensen, a successful memoirist, began to advise her. She signed a contract with Doubleday for a $1.525-million advance, the highest ever paid for a single book up to that time.[97] All proceeds would go to the Joseph P. Kennedy, Jr. Foundation. Phoning Sorensen, she chortled, "Thanks a million!" Then, pausing for comedic effect, "And a haalf!" she exclaimed in her Boston accent.[98] Sorensen delighted in that memory. Edward Kennedy, acting directly with Doubleday's executive editor, Stewart (Sandy) Rich-ardson, had concluded the deal.[99]

"For years publishers have been hoping for a first-hand account of Mrs. Kennedy's life as a doughty matriarch, daughter of a prom-inent Boston politician, wife of a multimillionaire and former dip-lomat and mother of one president and two presidential hopefuls," noted the *New York Times*. "I can't think of another person I would rather work with," Richardson crowed. "There is her magnificence in the face of adversity, her religious faith, the training and education of her children . . . she's just a tremendously admirable woman, and I know most people feel that way."[100]

After Rose rejected several volunteer writers, including Mary (Molly) Van Rensselaer Thayer, who had collaborated with Jackie on two books about the first lady, Robert Coughlan signed on as ghostwriter. A fascinating, sometimes frustrating, experience awaited him. He spent hours interviewing Rose, her family, and friends in Hyannis Port and Palm Beach. Always courteous and respectful, he found "Mrs. Kennedy" (he did not dare call her "Rose") a prickly coauthor. She treated him as she did her children and the hired help— sometimes kindly and with good humor, occasionally impatiently. Just five months after starting the project, Coughlan asked Rose's secretary to show her boss a list of her archived papers he was using "so she'll know, and will have time to object to items if she wants to." "I may or may not be good but, as you can see, I am careful," he asserted. Just in case Rose had "any damage claims" for office equipment he had rented, Coughlan concluded, "[A]ddress them to my attorney, Ted Sorensen."[101] Rose found the project tedious as she guided Coughlan step by step. Taped interviews with Rose tell the tale. Her eyes hurt, her throat is hoarse, she wants to go swimming, she tries to avoid painful topics. She's eighty-two, she's tired, life's tragedies have taken their toll, but occasionally, a lilting gaiety returns to her voice.

TIMES TO REMEMBER readers might not detect this obstacle-strewn process, except that the book is noticeably disjointed. Rose had so much territory to cover, and brought so many materials to the table, that it was difficult to organize. She could have simply given Coughlan her archives and interviews and then let the usual Kennedy handlers and her children review the drafts. Not Rose! Unlike many subjects of ghostwritten memoirs, she admirably controlled every detail of the book's production, reading each word that Coughlan painstakingly committed to paper. Here is where her lifelong attention to detail again served her well. Back to Coughlan came page after page of Rose's memos, revealing her line-by-line revisions. Anything that might hint of scandal or defilement she excised, so much so that Barbara Walters, who read the manuscript, questioned whether anyone would believe that Joe and Rose had never exchanged a cross word. Eunice, Pat, Jean, and Teddy also chimed in with their suggested revisions. Eunice and Pat didn't want so much material about Gloria Swanson, even though no mention was made of her affair with Joe. Rose asked Teddy and his staff to research prewar reactions to Nazi Germany, seeking to demonstrate that Joe's appeasement sentiments were mainstream.[102]

The memoir represented Rose's definitive attempt to burnish the family image. She did so just before Camelot's glow dimmed in the wake of revelations regarding Jack's marital infidelities and other indiscretions.[103] Rose succeeded, as had Jackie after JFK's death, in preempting negative publicity about her family.

Mass-circulation magazine *Woman's Day* serialized the memoir as "The First Book Written by a Kennedy About the Kennedys." Her face a portrait of pure joy at her son's inaugural ball, Rose appeared in a color photo, seated between Joe and Jack. "How can I have all this—and you—and still have Heaven, too!" she report-edly had written to Joe during that brief shining moment. Pub-lished in March 1974, Rose's autobiography rocketed to the top of the best-seller list. Congratulating Rose by telegram, Coughlan expressed his admiration and affection.[104] He had previously observed how much he enjoyed collaborating: "Mrs. Kennedy, you are indeed a marvel."[105] She responded blandly, "I shall always appreciate your research and editorial skill," overlooking the fact that he had written the manuscript's initial draft.[106]

To coincide with the book's release, the BBC produced *Rose Kennedy Remembers: The Best of Times . . . The Worst of Times.* The documentary highlighted her extensive interviews with correspon-dent Robert MacNeil at Hyannis Port and Palm Beach. Dressed in a white pants suit and azure blue turtleneck, Rose appeared as a gracious Palm Beach matron, showing MacNeil around her seaside estate. Describing how she and Joe had met and secretly courted, her eyes sparkled. For the Hyannis Port interviews, though, she dressed in black and spoke grimly of Jack's and Bobby's deaths.[107]

Her evident highs and lows revealed Rose's self-described "agony and ecstasy." She told *McCall's* magazine how frustrated she became in contemplating the deaths of Joe Jr., Jack, and Bobby: "I'd spent all my life, twenty-five, thirty, forty years, bringing up these children so they'd be strong, honest, capable men, self-sacrificing, devout, and willing to work, to give their talents, and then—so—it was difficult."[108] Fate had thwarted her "republican motherhood"; faith could not always sustain her.

Rose's famed composure also disappeared occasionally when she thought of Rosemary. Franklin Roosevelt Jr.'s wife, Felicia, arrived at Palm Beach in the spring of 1973 to interview Rose for the book *Doers and Dowagers*. A story of "great American women," it featured Rose, Alice Roosevelt Longworth, Clare Boothe Luce, Peggy Guggenheim, and Marjorie Merriweather Post. Dining with Rose and walking the Palm Beach golf course with her, Felicia witnessed her famous friend's mundane routine. Rose couldn't understand why people cared so much about her life: "I never had a phobia. I never had a lover. I never had a fight."[109] She repeated the well-worn story of her exalted family, but suddenly became tearful when asked about Rosemary, and why Rose never spoke about "her [daughter's] presence now." Mrs. Kennedy reiterated her memoir's reference to "psychosurgery," the family's euphemism for lobotomy. "Yes, well, she had that. Yes, and it was a heartbreak to me . . . ," Rose stammered, her voice choked with emotion.[110] Even three decades beyond the failed brain surgery, Rose still couldn't accept the disastrous results. It was bad enough to suffer the violent deaths of four children, all victims of cruel fate. But Rosemary . . . It had been Joe's perhaps well-intentioned but certainly ill-informed decision that had taken her from Rose.

Even so, Rose wanted Rosemary, long institutionalized at St. Coletta's in Wisconsin, to have her father's photograph. "Under separate cover we are mailing you an insured package," Rose's secretary wrote to Rosemary's caretaker. "[I]t contains a photograph of Rosemary's father, Ambassador Kennedy. Mrs. Kennedy brought it with her when she visited Rosemary in June [1971] but she forgot to take it out of her suitcase during her short stay with her daughter." Rose wanted to make sure it arrived safely; "it is in a rather expensive frame."[111]

Rose told St. Coletta's that she hadn't been able to supervise Rosemary's care during her husband's long illness, "as I was confined at home." Eunice had accepted that responsibility.[112] By early 1972, however, Rose asked the institution to send her quarterly reports on her daughter's progress, especially after an unspecified "accident" that Rosemary had suffered.[113]

Rosemary was much on her mother's mind. Rose sent a steady stream of letters to the nuns who cared for her. Traveling periodically to Wisconsin for one-day visits with her daughter, now in her fifties, Rose tried to make up for lost time. On one excursion, she stopped in Milwaukee to buy a $3,000 ranch-mink coat for her daughter, and before flying to Europe in fall 1972, Rose sent an artificial flower arrangement for Rosemary's living room, making sure to match her decor's color scheme. Returning from abroad, Rose went back to St. Coletta's where she had "a very pleasant visit with Rosemary. . . . I was delighted that she seemed so happy and relaxed. . . ."[114]

Rose was "deeply moved" to hear that mentally retarded students at a Long Island public school asked to rename it for Rosemary. Yet she declined to attend the dedication because so many schools were being named for her family that she simply sent regrets to such invitations.[115] Occasionally, Rosemary and her guardians visited Rose at Hyannis Port or Palm Beach. Rose, who had worked so hard with her young daughter to teach her sports, was gratified that she still enjoyed swimming and had inspired Eunice to establish the Special Olympics.

Joe had left nearly all of his estate to the Joseph P. Kennedy, Jr. Foundation.[116] While that was substantial, Rose continued to raise funds for the foundation, as well as the Robert Kennedy Memorial, and to participate in Eunice's Special Olympics projects. She appeared on Dinah Shore's daytime talk show to discuss mental retardation, accompany former big band singer Shore's rendition of "Sweet Adeline," and observe a cooking segment. Rose initially seemed bored with Dinah's preparation of crème brûlée, and cautioned that she only wanted a bit of brown sugar on the top. But then she asked to take the dessert with her. In fact, a reporter spotted frugal Rose with a doggie bag.[117] "[A]ll the members of my family and my friends said that you inspired me to give one of my best television performances," Rose reported to Shore.[118] Fans thought so, too. "Your strength, wisdom, and subtle humor just made my day," wrote a California woman, who added, "I thank you for giving the world such wonderful human beings—*your children*. My world fell apart when your Jack left us. . . ."[119] Nine years after JFK's assassination, ordinary Americans still felt his loss. Rose's steadfast public persona bolstered their spirits.

While in California to film *Dinah's Place*, Rose broadened her audience for charitable work. For decades she had spoken primarily to Catholic women's societies, but in 1972 she accepted an invitation from the Beverly Hills chapter of Hadassah, the Jewish women's philanthropic organization. Now, at age eighty-two, Rose expanded her horizons, and she made new fans beyond her previously parochial milieu. "It all seems like a beautiful dream and you a breathtaking vision in it," Hadassah's chapter president enthused. "We are the envy of the community and, indeed, the country." Hadassah endowed an Israeli medical office in Rose's honor. Obviously, Rose had moved beyond social stereotyping that marked her 1930s diary entries.

IN 1972 ANOTHER political opportunity presented itself to Rose. Sargent Shriver was running for vice president on the ticket headed by Senator George McGovern. "Now I will have to get new dresses for the campaign," Rose happily declared.[120] Speaking at a Democratic rally in New York, she finally reflected the modern women's movement, focusing on their role in American politics. Only a little more than one-third of women voters cast ballots for the doomed McGovern and Shriver ticket, which lost in a landslide to incumbent Richard Nixon.[121] Rose could take one bit of comfort—Massachusetts was the one state the Democrats carried.

As the 1976 presidential campaign approached, speculation swirled about Teddy's plans. "Would it not be too dangerous?" his mother asked Arthur Schlesinger. "It only took someone with a gun on the sixth floor. I have already lost two. . . ." Rose couldn't complete the sentence about losing Jack and Bobby.[122] She was grateful when Teddy sat out another quadrennial election, though she stumped for him in his 1976 senatorial campaign.

Now eighty-six, Rose's public life was drawing to a close. Occasionally her stout constitution failed. In 1974 a severe migraine hospitalized her. Still she found the energy to attend fund-raising dinners and balls in Palm Beach and took a part in the 1977 West Palm Beach Special Olympics. As always, she was among the first to arrive and the last to leave, congratulating the youngsters and hugging them close.[123] She also returned to her old Boston neighborhood of Dorchester in June 1977 to join Teddy, Jackie, Caroline, and John Jr. in lifting spades of dirt for the John F. Kennedy Presidential Library and Museum ground-breaking ceremony. Nothing could have pleased her more on that sunny summer day.

She went now and then to see Rosemary until the mid-1970s, but the trips were tiring. Could the St. Coletta nuns find a convent "nearer Boston where I could see Rosemary more often and where she could come to visit us frequently"?[124] Unfortunately, the sisters reported, they had no convent in Rose's vicinity. "I only wish you were nearer to us," Rose wrote dejectedly to Rosemary's caretaker.[125]

Giving up golf when her eyesight deteriorated, Rose continued to swim in the Atlantic even when she needed assistance getting in and out of the water. "Rose Kennedy is indomitable and went in swimming with a large bonnet tied under her chin," Arthur Schlesinger recorded in his journal during a 1977 Palm Beach visit.[126] Yet Rose's secretary worried about her employer's declining health. Save for staff and periodic visits from family, Rose was alone. More worrisome, she was relying increasingly on sleeping pills, one at bedtime followed by another if the first had no effect. Sometimes she was so groggy in the morning that the staff had trouble rousing her. Alarmed, her secretary wrote to Rose's children, urging them to hire a nurse for their mother. She no longer needed help with administrative tasks; they had dwindled as she had fewer public duties.[127] Schlesinger reported that despite her physical diminution, Rose was "still very bright-eyed, animated and responsive" during dinner at daughter Jean's New York home. True, Rose resorted to her standbys, posing grammar quizzes and playing "Sweet Adeline," but "[s]he went on strong till about 11 o'clock. Amazing vitality," Schlesinger marveled.[128]

In fall 1979 Rose underwent another hernia operation, a more serious one than that of 1962. This hernia was strangulated, a condition in which blood supply to part of the intestine is compromised. Still recovering from the surgery, Rose had to miss the October dedication of the JFK Library and Museum. How she would have liked to be there with Teddy, Eunice, Pat, Jean, Jackie, Sarge, Steve, the grandchildren, and President Jimmy Carter, to remember Jack by opening the towering white structure on a point of land in glistening Dorchester Bay.

Epilogue

OUT ROSE KENNEDY TODDLED, LEANING ON A CANE, SLIGHTLY stooped but impossible to miss in her jewel-tone coat and white fur hat. Her smile reflected maternal pride. What could be more historic than standing in Boston's Faneuil Hall, watching her youngest son announce his candidacy for president of the United States? She delighted in Teddy's introduction of her. Only just recovered from abdominal surgery, she relished another moment in the spotlight at the cradle of American democracy in the center of her cherished hometown.

It was November 7, 1979, and Senator Edward M. Kennedy was entering the 1980 presidential race to challenge Democratic incumbent President Jimmy Carter. Beset by a dismal economy, an energy crisis, and challenges abroad, Carter faced stiff opposition from Kennedy's left-wing insurgency. In 1971 Rose had reported that Teddy said she could campaign for him even at age ninety.[1] Now she was closing in on that milestone. A few months shy of it, she made an impassioned plea for votes in Iowa, where caucuses were scheduled for January 21.

Senator Kennedy appeared less enthusiastic. He had already

started his presidential run on the wrong foot with a halting and inarticulate response to CBS News correspondent Roger Mudd's simple query: "Why do you want to be president?" Once in Iowa, Teddy faced tough questions about Chappaquiddick, the tenuous state of his and Joan's marriage, and his chronic womanizing. Even worse, the Kennedys' traditional strategy of wooing party leaders ignored the caucuses' grassroots emphasis. Teddy experienced a decisive defeat, winning only 31 percent of precinct delegates to Carter's 59 percent. Fearing he had disappointed his mother, Teddy instead found her upbeat: "Oh, that's all right, Teddy dear. I'm sure you'll work hard and it'll get better." Then she changed the subject to a $220 sweater she had given him for Christmas. Perhaps he would like to exchange it for a cheaper one.[2] If Rose found it hard to keep her mind on the campaign, Teddy's heart wasn't in it either. Initially, he seemed to go through the motions in order to fulfill others' expectations of restoring the Kennedy presidency that had been snatched from Jack and denied Bobby.

The Iowa loss slowed contributions to a trickle, forcing brother-in-law Steve Smith to urge Teddy's withdrawal from the race. What if he lost the upcoming Massachusetts primary? The senator's legislative career might then be in jeopardy. Reluctant to be the first Kennedy brother to drop out of a presidential campaign, however, Teddy persevered all the way to the Democrats' August convention but won only a little more than one-third of the delegates to Carter's more than half. (Kennedy did, however, win his home-state primary, a positive sign for his Senate career.) By staying in the race, Teddy earned a prime-time spot on the convention's program. He made the most of it, concluding to thunderous applause, "For me, a few hours ago, this campaign came to an end. For all those whose cares have been our concern, the work goes on, the cause endures, the hope still lives, and the dream shall never die."[3]

Two weeks before the convention, Rose had turned ninety and participated in a parade through the village of Hyannis, organized by the Special Olympics. Riding in an open convertible, she clutched a bouquet of red roses and waved and smiled to the crowds.

From Gibson girl to Gracious Grandmother—how far she had traveled from the parades that Boston Mayor John Fitzgerald and she presided over seven decades ago. Yet for all her journeys, around the world and through life's vagaries, she always returned to her New England roots.

Rose's ramrod posture had deserted her, but she still managed to raise her chin, trying to defy gravity's downward force. On November 12, 1981, she returned to the White House for the first time since Jack's death. President Ronald Reagan and First Lady Nancy welcomed her and Teddy to the Oval Office. Sitting serenely on a couch, next to the president, Rose watched as Teddy presented Reagan with a plaque commending him for placing "love of country" ahead of partisanship.[4] Although he had split his own party by challenging Carter, assuring the president's 1980 loss to Reagan, Teddy could be a bipartisan master in the Senate when legislative strategy called for it. Party divisions seemed narrower in the months after March 30, 1981, when Reagan had become the only president to be seriously wounded in an assassination attempt and survive. Returning to the Oval Office, Rose had come full circle. She had first visited the White House in 1897, with Honey Fitz and her sister Agnes, to meet President William McKinley.

In July 1982 Rose turned ninety-two, and the family threw a gala party at the Hyannis Port compound, turning the occasion into a rally for Teddy's fourth Senate reelection campaign. The assembled throngs of Kennedys and their supporters serenaded Rose with an enthusiastic chorus of "When Irish Eyes Are Smiling." Wearing a white turtleneck, pearls, and a jaunty red hat, she appeared on the porch, wide-eyed at the sight of her multitiered birthday cake. Advanced age had diminished her inhibitions, and Rose blew kisses to the assembled crowd on her front lawn. When Teddy intoned somewhat too solemnly, "The poet says that the rainbow comes and goes, but the rose always remains," she staged whispered, "I never heard that before." Looking up at the senator, who now towered over his elfin mother, she smiled innocently as he ad-libbed, "It's a younger poet, Mother!"[5] Then, playfully, she held a long-stemmed rose up to his face, as if to say, "Don't take yourself so seriously. Stop and smell the roses." That Thanksgiving she urged her progeny to remember the distaff side of their family: "You are not just Kennedys. You are Fitzgeralds too."[6]

For her next birthday the Kennedys made a $1 million gift to St. Coletta's in Rose's honor, establishing a model program for senior citizens with intellectual disabilities. Rosemary was now sixty-five and still living with nuns in a small cottage at the Wisconsin institution.[7] That September of 1983 Rose made her last public appearance, enfeebled and barely ambulatory. Attending her granddaughter Sydney Lawford's wedding near Hyannis, she held tight to Pat and Teddy while slowly climbing the church steps.

Easter Sunday—Catholicism's holiest feast—was always a joyous occasion for Rose. Traditionally her family gathered around her at Palm Beach for Holy Week services and then festive meals at the Kennedy estate. But in 1984 Rose collapsed on Good Friday, and by Easter Sunday seemed near death, suffering from a severe stroke. She rallied but, like Joe after his cerebral hemorrhage, she was now confined to a wheelchair and rarely able to speak intelligibly. How she would have despised the photos taken of her when she could no longer control her facial expressions. Music and prayer continued to provide comfort, so her family brought a pianist in each week to play for her, as well as a priest to say Mass. Also like her husband, she would live nearly a decade as an invalid, cared for by nurses. Teddy's weekend visits to Hyannis Port, where she spent the last nine years of her life, brightened Rose's spirit. She had deeded him the main house at the Cape Cod compound, where he slept in his father's room, next to hers. "Let's say our prayers," he would urge Rose, and they would recite the Rosary together, even though she rarely spoke otherwise.[8]

Despite Rose's debilitation, the family celebrated her one hundredth birthday in July 1990. Her granddaughter, NBC correspondent Maria Shriver, produced a brief retrospective on the Kennedy matriarch, whose life had spanned nearly one-half of the American

Republic's history. Teddy, Eunice, Pat, and Jean provided technical assistance for "Rose Fitzgerald Kennedy: A Life to Remember," a brief video tribute to their mother, narrated by her last surviving son. By resolution, Congress designated July 22, 1990, as Rose Fitzgerald Kennedy Family Appreciation Day in honor of her maternal feats. For Rose's 104th birthday, her children published a new edition of *Times to Remember*, with her sprightly ninetieth birthday photo on the dust jacket. They felt blessed by what they called their mother's gift of politics, and they labeled her the best campaigner and politician in the celebrated Kennedy family.[9]

In 1971 Rose had written to Eunice about the Kennedy gravesite in Brookline, where one day she would join Joe Sr.: "My nephew Fred, who is in the funeral business, told me today that very often people mark their tombstones, and I said I thought it would be very appropriate to add 'Father of the President'—or put my name on and say, 'Father and Mother of the President,' leaving an open date opposite my name. I thought perhaps that you would welcome this information."[10]

After her death from pneumonia on January 22, 1995, Rose was laid to rest in a grave marked simply "Rose Fitzgerald Kennedy 1890–1995," surrounded by rose bushes. She didn't get her desired epitaph, but her twenty-first-century fans post laudatory online messages for her via social media.[11]

Her living memorial is the Rose Kennedy Greenway, linking the North End, where she was born, to downtown Boston through a series of parks, gardens, and urban green spaces created over the city's new underground traffic arteries. Dedicated in July 2004, the 1.5-mile public space epitomizes Honey Fitz's slogan "Bigger, Busier, Better Boston."

Rose was survived by Rosemary, Eunice, Pat, Jean, Teddy, all but one of her twenty-nine grandchildren, and scores of great-grandchildren. Rosemary had made her last trip to visit her mother in the summer of 1994. Eleven years later, the least visible Kennedy, but the one who inspired a worldwide movement for the disabled, died from natural causes at age eighty-six in Wisconsin, surrounded by her siblings. As Rose had hoped, Pat never remarried after her 1966 divorce from Peter Lawford. She raised four children in New York and devoted the remainder of her life to fund-raising for the arts and substance-abuse treatment. Oral cancer entailed disfiguring surgery in Pat's later years, and in 2006 she died, age eighty-two, of complications from pneumonia.[12]

Eunice and Teddy passed away only two weeks apart in August 2009: she at age eighty-eight from a series of strokes, he at seventy-nine from brain cancer. Lauded for her unparalleled work in mental retardation, Eunice left behind her Special Olympics legacy. Indeed, some observers suggested that her work on behalf of the mentally retarded was as consequential as her brothers' policy records.[13] She and Sarge were the first married couple to have received Presidential Medals of Freedom for their public service.

Teddy's colleagues, even from the opposite party, praised him as a lion of the Senate whose legislative record and longevity rivaled those of the institution's most distinguished members in its history. Expanding civil rights, lowering the voting age to eighteen, abolishing poll taxes, fighting for universal health care, ending the draft, supporting peace initiatives throughout the world, expanding education opportunities, establishing public-service projects, crafting immigration reform, and leading the charge against conservative judicial appointees were all part of his portfolio.[14]

His funeral paid homage to Rose. Traveling from Hyannis Port to Boston, the hearse bearing his remains drove through her "Dear Old North End," passing near her birthplace and St. Stephen's Church, site of Rose's baptism and funeral Mass. After being flown to Washington, Teddy was laid to rest near Jack and Bobby on a verdant Arlington hillside overlooking the nation's capital, which the three brothers had taken by storm a half century earlier. In addition to his legislative victories, Teddy's permanent monument is the Edward M. Kennedy Institute for the United States Senate, next to the John F. Kennedy Presidential Library and Museum in Rose's Dorchester neighborhood. The institute promotes civic education, particularly regarding the Senate's legislative process. It will also oversee the Kennedys' Hyannis Port mansion as a site for seminars and educational programs. Teddy had promised Rose that their home would be preserved for charitable use.[15]

When Teddy's son, Congressman Patrick Kennedy, left the House of Representatives in 2011, it marked the first time that a Kennedy was not serving in elective office since Jack took his House seat in 1947. In fact, Rose's grandson, Timothy Shriver, chairman of the Special Olympics, commented that his generation was more likely to use "soft power" in pursuing social change than formal political power.[16] By 2012, however, the Kennedys had a new star on the electoral horizon: Joseph P. Kennedy III, grandson of Robert Kennedy, won a seat in Congress from Massachusetts's Fourth District.[17] With movie-star looks, a Harvard law degree, Peace Corps service in the Dominican Republic, and the Kennedy name, Rose and Joe's great-grandson may lead his generation to political prominence.

Jean Kennedy Smith is the last of Rose's children to survive. She remains active in VSA (formerly Very Special Arts), an international organization she founded to promote arts for the disabled, based at Washington's John F. Kennedy Center for the Performing Arts. Appointed US ambassador to Ireland by President Bill Clinton in 1993, she served for five years. The only one of Rose's daughter's to hold public office, Ambassador Smith's critical role in the successful Northern Ireland peace process has been widely recognized. In 2011 President Barack Obama awarded her the Presidential Medal of Freedom for her VSA leadership and work for the disabled. Now dividing her time between homes in Manhattan and Long Island's Bridgehampton, she proudly shows visitors to her New York apartment, a veritable shrine to her brothers, complete with their photos and letters. The largest depiction is of her brother and godfather, Joe Jr.; an oil portrait of him in his Navy uniform dominates her hallway. Slim and ramrod straight, like her mother, she guides an interested scholar to a framed verse sent to her by Ireland's poet laureate Seamus Heaney. The former ambassador reads aloud its lilting stanzas and urges her visitor to join the recitation.[18] Farther removed from her immigrant roots than Rose, yet proud of the Fitzgerald/Kennedy Hibernian heritage, in 2011 Smith was inducted into the Irish America Hall of Fame.

LIFE MAGAZINE EULOGIZED Rose as "part nun, part enchantress, part ward boss and all mother."[19] Indeed, she blended her faith, femininity, political DNA, and maternal instincts into a potent formula for creating a dazzling dynasty in the modern media age. Before focus groups, consultants, and makeovers existed, Rose performed all of those roles for her family with the unswerving commitment to perfection that governed her life. When her husband and children fell short of her Victorian standards, she simply strove harder to correct, or at least mask, their flaws while touting their genuine accomplishments. Rose Kennedy's maternal ledger includes a president, three senators, a congressman, an attorney general, two World War II military heroes, an ambassador, and two Presidential Medal of Freedom winners. No wonder United Nations ambassador Adlai Stevenson introduced her at the 1962 Joseph P. Kennedy, Jr. Foundation's International Awards dinner as "the head of the most successful employment agency in America," prompting a standing ovation from President John F. Kennedy. An unwavering model of Catholic motherhood in public, Rose's private weaknesses only add dimension and depth to her persona. She emerges as even more courageous for absorbing the doubts and fears that tragedy and loss thrust upon her. Creating a template for contemporary political wives, she selected a cause—mental retardation—and made it the focus of her prodigious charitable work. Rose Fitzgerald Kennedy embraced a "family values" agenda before Reagan conservatives spawned the label. She embraced so many roles that "Mother of the President" is an inadequate epitaph. Born in the Gay Nineties, Rose gave birth to the Kennedy image that shaped twentieth-century American politics and continued to do so even as the new millennium dawned.

Commenting on the family matriarch, Jean Kennedy Smith insists, "I think it would be extremely difficult, if not impossible, in fact, to find anything negative about my mother. . . . She was and always will be a great inspiration to all of our family, and I know that we were very fortunate to have such a wonderful mother."[20] Rose would approve of her sole surviving child continuing to sustain her mother's legend and that of the political colossus she helped to create.

Acknowledgments

ROSE KENNEDY RECEIVED COUNTLESS ACCOLADES AND AWARDS for her maternal achievements. In my view, however, she could never top my own mother, Lillian Rose Perry, who helped give birth to this book in a host of ways. Mother introduced me to the Kennedy mystique when I was only four years old: on October 5, 1960, she positioned me in front of the podium where Senator John F. Kennedy spoke at a presidential campaign rally in Louisville, Kentucky. Shortly after his tragic death, she started my now extensive "Kennedy Library" by giving me my first book on JFK, a children's history of the late president and his family. For Christmas 1974 her gift to me was Rose Kennedy's memoir. Mother's love, devotion, courage, selflessness, integrity, and wisdom will always make her *mater admirabilis* in my book.

And when I wondered if I could really make it through Rose Kennedy's three hundred archival boxes covering her 104 years on this earth and complete this biography, I would hear my father's folksy assurance, "It won't be as long as it has been!" Sometimes it was, Dad. Even longer. But the perseverance that you and Mother modeled for our family must have been genetic.

Of course, Henry J. Abraham, James Hart Professor of Government, Emeritus, at the University of Virginia, is, as he loves to say, "padre de tutti." What would those of us in the Tribe of Abraham do without his guiding force? From dissertations to subsequent books, he always knows just when to declare, "Finish it!" Amid our discussions of the US Supreme Court, he had to be ever vigilant that his reference to Justice Kennedy would launch one of my endless anecdotes about *the* Kennedys! He listened with patriarchal patience.

This project began when my former student at Sweet Briar College, Rebekah Paup Martin, knowing of my lifelong Kennedy interest, e-mailed me in the fall of 2006 to say that the Kennedy Library had just released Rose's papers. Helen Davis, cheered on by Jean Newsom and Nancy Gordon, linked me to Edwin Barber, senior editor at W. W. Norton. Soon "Ed the Editor" was my new friend, gently urging me to pare down my legalistic prose to something pithier—all the while cheerfully slogging through Rose's diary with me and enduring my sermons on how Catholic doctrine had shaped Rose Kennedy's life. Halfway through, Amy Cherry, Norton vice president and senior editor, joined our team, becoming the adoptive mother of this book. Her well-placed questions, thematic suggestions, and edits provided the perfect complement to Ed's word-for-word alterations. And former Norton assistant editor Laura Romain was a delight to work with on a host of substantive and administrative details, as was her successor Anna Mageras, especially on photo acquisitions. In addition, Nancy Green worked her copyediting magic on the manuscript.

At the midway point in this project, I found a new professional family, when I accepted a position at the University of Virginia's Miller Center. As a senior fellow in its Presidential Oral History Program, I have returned to my first love in political science: the US presidency. And I have renewed my friendship with graduate-school compatriot Russell Riley, who has been the most understanding supervisor a writer could have. My new colleagues, historians Marc Selverstone, an expert on the Kennedy presidency, and Andrew Chancey, have graciously helped me find the time and funds to complete this task. The Oral History Program's administrator, Katrina Kuhn, assisted me in scheduling my Miller Center duties around my summer writing. Fellow scholar and Kennedy aficionado Emily Charnock was always ready to swap JFK stories and provide insight. Miller Center librarian Sheila Blackford acquired books for me and lent an editor's ear to my concerns over rewrites. Communications colleagues Kristy Schantz and Kim Curtis have arranged Kennedy media opportunities and offered encouraging tips on authoring biographies. Periodically I had the benefit of Professor James Sterling Young's vast knowledge from his leadership of the Edward M. Kennedy Oral History. I owe these superb resources to the Miller Center's visionary leader, Governor Gerald Baliles.

My association with the John F. Kennedy Library now spans more than a decade, starting with my book *Jacqueline Kennedy: First Lady of the New Frontier*. There is nothing I enjoy more than poring over documents and photographs and pausing to gaze out the soaring windows at Dorchester Bay and the Boston skyline. It is a close race between my neighbor, Monticello, and the John F. Kennedy Library, as to which most closely captures the spirit of its respective president. Lee Statham, of the Kennedy Library Foundation, could not have been more helpful in providing Kennedy family photos. Archivists Stephen Plotkin, Sharon Kelly, and James Hill have . expertly guided me through two projects. Maryrose Grossman's vast knowledge of Kennedy audiovisual archives and her warm friendship have combined to make my research both productive and pleasurable. She also introduced me to National Park Service rangers James Roberts and Sara Patton, who provided their specialized understanding of the John Fitzgerald Kennedy National Historic Site. They made me feel as though I had just stopped by for a visit with Rose Kennedy in 1917!

It was my good fortune to meet intern Meghan Vantine at the Kennedy Library and persuade her to serve as my research assistant. If not, I would still be copying Rose's files. Meghan couldn't have been a more skilled researcher, careful organizer, knowledgeable sounding board, or pleasant lunch partner.

Friends and family have stood by me with faith, support, and information always at the ready: Doug and Gayl Perry; David, Ellen, and Jennifer Perry; Debra DeCamillis; Suzy and Bob Brill; Simon Banner; Donna Meredith; Julia McDonough; and Diana Hess are always with me through thick and thin books. Our family's matriarch, Mary Elizabeth Perry Beckman, is my treasured Aunt Betty who convinced me that I could really complete this book before *I* turned 104.

It was my honor to interview Ambassador Jean Kennedy Smith at her Manhattan apartment in 2010. She welcomed me into her beautiful home and shared her family stories, photos, and letters. Her daughter Amanda Smith also kindly answered a question or two via e-mail. Rose Kennedy's niece, Mary Jo Gargan Clasby, kindly spoke to me by phone about her beloved "Aunt Rose" and their adventures together. The late Ted Sorensen, who helped place Mrs. Kennedy's memoir with Doubleday, discussed her and President Kennedy with me one afternoon at his stunning Central Park West apartment. I couldn't believe that I was talking to my rhetorical hero! Felicia Rogan steered me to her superb collection of Kennedy interviews at the University of Virginia Library.

Joe Graedon, of NPR's *The People's Pharmacy*, provided his vast knowledge of pharmaceuticals as I tried to comprehend Rose Kennedy's medications.

My Kentucky friends and colleagues earn special thanks. The University of Louisville's Dr. Gary Gregg and Malana Salyer brought an enthusiastic and inspirational group of teachers from the Bluegrass State to Charlottesville for a 2011 McConnell Center / Miller Center Teacher Institute on JFK. Former Kentucky secretary of state Trey Grayson, now director of Harvard's Kennedy Institute of Politics, shares my Kennedy interest and generously offered the JFK Suite (President Kennedy's Harvard dorm room in Winthrop House) for my accommodations in Cambridge. Julie Schroeder of the IOP, who oversaw the room's most recent historic face-lift, kindly made arrangements for me to stay there. What an honor to absorb the spirits of such a hallowed space, dedicated by Rose Kennedy in 1970.

And now for the two people to whom this book is dedicated with profound gratitude and love: "Rose C" and Rob Capon. They shared my excitement on productive days and bolstered me on discouraging ones. The Capons are my surrogate family, and without them, life would be so much less interesting and infinitely less joyous.

Notes

ABBREVIATIONS

Books

HTF: Amanda Smith, ed. *Hostage to Fortune: The Letters of Joseph P. Kennedy* (New York: Penguin Books, 2001).
TTR: Rose Fitzgerald Kennedy, *Times to Remember* (New York: Doubleday, 1974).
TC: Edward M. Kennedy, *True Compass: A Memoir* (New York: Twelve, 2009).

Persons

BK: Bobby Kennedy
EKS: Eunice Kennedy Shriver
EMK: Edward Moore Kennedy
ESK: Ethel Skakel Kennedy
JBKO: Jacqueline Bouvier Kennedy Onassis
JFK: John Fitzgerald Kennedy
JPK Jr.: Joseph Patrick Kennedy Jr.
JPK: Joseph Patrick Kennedy Sr.
KKH: Kathleen Kennedy Hartington
RK: Rose Kennedy
RMK: Rosemary Kennedy
RSS: Robert Sargent Shriver Jr.

Library

JFKL: John F. Kennedy Library

Papers

JPKP: Joseph P. Kennedy Papers
RFKP: Rose Fitzgerald Kennedy Papers

PROLOGUE

1. Mrs. Joseph P. Kennedy, "Giving Children the Gifts of Faith and Courage," *Ladies' Home Journal*, Dec. 1969, 120.

2. Cynthia Ann Stone, secretary to RK, to Marguerite Higgins, July 31, 1964, Box 11, RFKP.

3. Funeral Program for Rose Kennedy, Jan. 24, 1995, Box 117, RFKP. Rose's funeral mass is available on DVD from C-SPAN and on the network's Web site, www.c-span.org. Ethel Kennedy's scripture reading, as well as Eunice Kennedy Shriver's eulogy and parts of Edward Kennedy's eulogy for their mother, may be viewed on YouTube.

4. Funeral Program.

5. Eunice Shriver's eulogy.

6. Quotations from Edward Kennedy's eulogy may be found at "Excerpts from Eulogy by Sen. Kennedy," *New York Times*, Jan. 25, 1995, www.nytimes.com/1995/01/25/us/excerpts-from-eulogy-by-sen-kennedy.html, and at the recorded funeral mass cited in note 3.

CHAPTER I

1. *Rose Kennedy Remembers: The Best of Times, the Worst of Times*, BBC, 1974, JFKL. Five-minute clips may be viewed on YouTube.

2. EMK, quoted in Box 113, RFKP.

3. *TTR*, 5.

4. RK, interview by Coughlan, Jan. 19, 1972, Box 10, RFKP.

5. Ibid.

6. *TTR*, 33–34.

7. Ibid.

8. RK, interview by Coughlan, Jan. 10, 1972, Boxes 8–9, RFKP.

9. RK, interview by Coughlan, Jan. 11, 1972, Box 10, RFKP.

10. RK, interview by Coughlan, Jan. 19, 1972.

11. Gapminder, www.gapminder.org, accessed Jan. 18, 2013.

12. RK to Patricia T. Levine, Aug. 8, 1968, Box 79, RFKP.

13. *TTR*, 14.

14. "Rose Kennedy Talks about Her Life, Her Faith, and Her Children," *McCall's*, Dec. 1973, 74.

15. RK, interview by Coughlan, Jan. 21, 1972, Box 10, RFKP.

16. Susan Cheever, *American Bloomsbury: Louisa May Alcott, Ralph Waldo Emerson, Margaret Fuller, Nathaniel Hawthorne, and Henry David Thoreau: Their Lives, Their Loves, Their Work* (New York: Simon & Schuster, 2006), 191.

17. Kathryn Kish Sklar, "Victorian Women and Domestic Life: Mary Todd Lincoln, Elizabeth Cady Stanton, and Harriet Beecher Stowe," in *Women and Power in American History*, 3rd ed., ed. Kathryn Kish Sklar and Thomas Dublin (Upper Saddle River, NJ: Prentice Hall, 2009), 122, 128.

18. Linda K. Kerber, "The Republican Mother: Women and the Enlightenment—An American Perspective," *American Quarterly* 28, no. 2 (Summer, 1976): 187–205.

19. Ted Kennedy, "My Mother, Rose Kennedy," *Ladies' Home Journal*, Dec. 1975, 109.

20. RK to David Sheldon, Sept. 24, 1971, Box 59, RFKP.

21. RK, interview by Coughlan, Jan. 10, 1972.

22. Thomas H. O'Connor, *The Boston Irish: A Political History* (Old Saybrook, CT: Konecky and Konecky, 1995), 147, 158.

23. Ibid., 167.

24. RK, interview by Coughlan, Jan. 10, 1972.

25. Photograph in the Kennedy Family Photograph Collection (KFC 1223P), ca. 1910, Boston Mayor John F. Fitzgerald, daughter Rose Fitzgerald, others on reviewing stand, unidentified parade, available at http://www.jfklibray.org.

26. RK, interview by Coughlan, Jan. 7, 1972, Box 10, RFKP.

27. Ibid.

28. Nancy E. McGlen et al. *Women, Politics, and American Society,* 4th ed. (New York: Pearson Longman, 2005), 37–38.

29. "Coffee with the Kennedys," 1962, DVD, JFKL.

30. Cynthia Ann Stone, secretary to RK, to Marguerite Higgins, July 31, 1964, Box 11, RFKP.

31. RK, interview by Coughlan, Jan. 7, 1972.

32. Ibid.

33. Ibid.

34. "Boston Mayor's Daughter to Christen 'Bunker Hill'" and "Bunker Hill Steamship Christened by Miss Fitzgerald," n.d., Box 11, JFKL.

35. RK to Gladys Cook, May 17, [1907], author's collection.

36. "Miss Rose Fitzgerald's . . . ," *Boston Sunday Globe,* n.d., Box 11, JFKL.

37. *TTR,* 23–24.

38. "Who Was Rose Kennedy?" Documents and Photographs: Growing Up, A4, Photograph, Old Orchard Beach, Maine, 1907, JFKL, available online at http://www.jfklibrary.gov.

39. RK to Gladys Cook, June 27, 1907, author's collection.

40. Doris Kearns Goodwin, *The Fitzgeralds and the Kennedys: An American Saga* (New York: St. Martin's Press, 1991), 167.

41. RK, "My Ocean Trip," "1908–09 Diaries," Box 1, RFKP.

42. Robert Dallek, *An Unfinished Life: John F. Kennedy, 1917–1963* (Boston: Little, Brown, 2003), 7.

43. "My Ocean Trip."

44. Ibid.

45. RK to Patricia T. Levine.

CHAPTER 2

1. RK, interview by Coughlan, Jan. 4, 1972, Box 10, RFKP.

2. The Pew Forum on Religion & Public Life, "100th Anniversary of Secularism in France," http:// www.pewforum.org.

3. Lillian Parker Wallace, *The Papacy and European Diplomacy, 1869–1878* (Chapel Hill: University of North Carolina Press, 1948).

4. *TTR,* 31.

5. See Doris Kearns Goodwin's classic *The Fitzgeralds and the Kennedys: An American Saga* for an evocative description of life at Blumenthal (New York: St. Martin's Press, 1991), ch. 11.

6. All of the excerpts from Rose's letters may be found in her autobiography, *Times to Remember,* 35–41. Copies of the originals are in Box 12, RFKP, but they are difficult to

decipher because of Rose's sometimes illegible handwriting and the poor quality of the copies.

7. Gail Cameron, *Rose: A Biography of Rose Fitzgerald Kennedy* (New York: Putnam, 1971), 54.

8. Original emphasis.

9. Emphasis added.

10. *TTR*, 32–33.

11. Original emphasis.

12. RK, "My Ocean Trip," "1908–09 Diaries," Box 1, RFKP.

13. Ibid.

14. Original emphasis.

15. RK, "Trip on Sir Thomas Lipton's Yacht," "1908–09 Diaries," Box 1, RFKP.

16. Ibid.

17. Ibid.

18. *TTR*, 5 (photographs).

19. "Trip on Sir Thomas Lipton's Yacht."

20. Ibid.

21. RK, interview by Coughlan, Jan. 4, 1972, Box 10, RFKP.

22. "Palm Beach," "1908–09 Diaries," Box 1, RFKP.

23. Ibid.

24. RK, interview by Coughlan, Jan. 4, 1972.

25. *Rose Kennedy Remembers: The Best of Times, the Worst of Times*, BBC, 1974, JFKL. Five-minute clips may be viewed on YouTube.

26. RK, interview by Coughlan, Jan. 4, 1972; "Rose Fitzgerald to Be Bride of J. P. Kennedy," 1914 newspaper clipping, Box 12, JPKP; *Rose*, 62–65.

27. The Robert Appleton Company published volumes of the *Catholic Encyclopedia* from 1907 to 1912.

28. Thomas H. O'Connor, *The Boston Irish: A Political History* (Old Saybrook, CT: Konecky and Konecky, 1995), 178.

29. *TTR*, 48.

30. See *Rose* for illustrations, newspaper headlines, photographs, and description of the debut, 66–68.

31. *TTR*, 49.

32. RK, interview by Coughlan, Jan. 7, 1972, Box 10, RFKP.

33. Cari Beauchamp, *Joseph P. Kennedy Presents: His Hollywood Years* (New York: Knopf, 2009), ch. 1; Richard J. Whalen, *The Founding Father: The Story of Joseph P. Kennedy* (New York: New American Library, 1964), ch. 2; "The Death of a Dynasty," *Newsweek*, Dec. 1, 1969, 28–30; "Death of the Founder," *Time*, Nov. 28, 1969, 21–22.

34. *Rose Kennedy Remembers*.

35. Ibid.

36. As reported by the US Census Bureau, cited in Nancy E. McGlen et al., *Women, Politics, and American Society* (New York: Pearson Longman, 2005), 301.

37. The succeeding description of Rose's first trip to Palm Beach, Florida, in 1911, can be found in her 1951 recollections, titled "Palm Beach."

38. *Rose*, illustrations.

39. All of Rose's explanations about her father choosing her as his travel companion may be found in her interview with Coughlan, Jan. 4, 1972.

40. http://www.brainyquote.com/quotes/quotes/a/aliceroose115487.html, accessed Oct. 27, 2012.

41. *TTR*, 55.

42. Unless otherwise noted, Rose's 1911–13 trip accounts are in "My Trip Abroad," Box 1, RFKP.

43. *TTR*, 55–56.

44. *The Boston Irish*, 185.

45. *The Fitzgeralds and the Kennedys*, 234.

46. *TTR*, 44–45.

47. *Joseph P. Kennedy Presents*, 11–13.

48. *Rose Kennedy Remembers*.

49. RK, interviews by Coughlan, Jan. 4 and 7, 1972.

CHAPTER 3

1. "Ex-Mayor Fitzgerald's Daughter Rose Marries Joseph P. Kennedy," *Boston Globe*, Oct. 8, 1914, n.p., in "Who Was Rose Kennedy?" Documents and Photographs: Wife and Mother, B1, newspaper clipping, JFKL, available online at http://www.jfklibrary.gov.

2. RK's notes on *TTR* manuscript, Box 17, RFKP.

3. *HTF*, 14.

4. *TTR*, 71–72.

5. RK, interview by Coughlan, Jan. 21, 1972, Box 10, RFKP.

6. *HTF*, 14.

7. "John Fitzgerald Kennedy: National Historic Site/Massachusetts" (Washington, DC: U.S. Government Printing Office, 1973).

8. RK to Gladys Cook, Dec. 1, 1914, author's collection.

9. "Margaret Sanger," in *Encyclopedia of World Biography*, http://www.notablebiographies.com/Ro-Sc/Sanger-Margaret.html; Andrea Tone, *Devices and Desires: A History of Contraceptives in America* (New York: Hill and Wang, 2001), 4, 81.

10. *Devices and Desires*, 4, 81, and "Margaret Sanger."

11. Griswold v. Connecticut, 381 U.S. 479 (1965).

12. John Augustine Ryan, "Family," in the *Catholic Encyclopedia*, vol. 5 (New York: Robert Appleton Company, 1909), available online at http://www.newadvent.org/cathen/05782a.htm.

13. RK, interview by Coughlan, Jan. 21 and Feb. 2, 1972, Box 10, RFKP.

14. Cari Beauchamp, *Joseph P. Kennedy Presents: His Hollywood Years* (New York: Knopf, 2009), 17.

15. Andrew J. Peters to RK, Feb. 20, 1919, Box 55, RFKP.

16. RK, interview by Coughlan, Jan. 20, 1972, Box 10, RFKP.

17. *HTF*, 9.

18. RK, interview by Coughlan, Jan. 31, 1972, Box 10, RFKP.

19. Ibid.

20. RK, interview by Coughlan, Jan. 21, 1972, Box 10, RFKP.

21. "Early Married Life," dictated by Rose Kennedy, April 9, 1972, Coughlan Papers, RFKP.

22. *HTF*, 6.

23. RK, interview by Coughlan, Jan. 7, 1972, Box 10, RFKP.

24. RK, "Rosemary," "Diary Notes," Box 13, RFKP.

25. RK on *The Mike Douglas Show*, Philadelphia, taped July 6, 1967, video available in the JFKL audiovisual archives and on YouTube.

26. RK, interview by Coughlan, Jan. 14, 1972, Box 10, RFKP.

27. David L. Coulter, "Neighbors and Friends: Social Implications of Intellectual Disability," ch. 8 in *What Is Mental Retardation?: Ideas for an Evolving Disability in the 21st Century*, ed. Harvey N. Switzky and Stephen Greenspan, rev. and updated ed. (American Association on Mental Retardation, 2007), 127.

28. Buck v. Bell, 274 U.S. 200 (1927).

29. Herman H. Spitz, "How We Eradicated Familial (Hereditary) Mental Retardation—Updated," in *What Is Mental Retardation?*, 106.

30. RK, interview by Coughlan, Jan. 31, 1972, Box 10, RFKP.

31. RK, interview by Coughlan, Jan. 11, 1972, Box 10, RFKP.

32. RK, interview by Coughlan, Jan. 24, 1972, Box 10, RFKP; RK, "Diaries, 1923[–1924]," Box 1, RFKP.

33. *HTF*, 18.

34. Doris Kearns Goodwin, *The Fitzgeralds and the Kennedys: An American Saga* (New York: St. Martin's Press, 1991), 327.

35. Ibid., 369–71.

36. Ibid., 369–71.

37. *Joseph P. Kennedy Presents*, 29–30.

38. RK, interview by Coughlan, Jan. 21, 1972, Box 10, RFKP.

39. *The Fitzgeralds and the Kennedys*, 353–59.

40. RK, interview by Coughlan, Jan. 28, 1972, Box 10, RFKP.

41. "Family," *Catholic Encyclopedia*.

42. *The Fitzgeralds and the Kennedys*, 234.

43. *TTR*, 76 (original emphasis).

44. RK, interview by Coughlan, Jan. 24, 1972.

45. Ibid.

46. "Family," *Catholic Encyclopedia*.

47. RK, interview by Coughlan, Jan. 11 and 24, 1972.

48. RK, interview by Coughlan, Jan. 20 and 21, 1972.

49. RK, interview by Coughlan, Jan. 25, 1972, Box 10, RFKP.

50. "Diaries, 1923[–1924]."

51. Thomas Maier, *The Kennedys: America's Emerald Kings* (New York: Basic Books, 2003), 78.

52. RK, interview by Coughlan, Jan. 21, 1972.

53. Ibid.

54. "Diaries, 1923[–1924]."

55. RK, interview by Coughlan, Jan. 24, 1972.

56. *TTR*, 94.

57. "Diaries, 1923[–1924]."

58. *HTF*, 37.

59. *The Fitzgeralds and the Kennedys*, 374.

60. *TTR*, 79.

61. "Diaries, 1923[–1924]."

62. *HTF*, 38.

63. "Diaries, 1923[–1924]."

64. *HTF*, 39.

65. *The Fitzgeralds and the Kennedys*, 395.

66. RK, interview by Coughlan, Jan. 21, 1972.

67. RK, interview by Coughlan, Jan. 20, 1972.

68. RK, interview by Coughlan, Jan. 24, 1972.

69. Ibid.

70. RK, interview by Coughlan, Jan. 20, 1972.

71. *HTF*, 8–11.

72. Ibid., 44.

73. JPK to RK, August 1925, Box 55, RFKP.

74. RK, interview by Coughlan, Jan. 7, 1972.

75. Robert Dallek, *An Unfinished Life: John F. Kennedy, 1917–1963* (Boston: Little, Brown, 2003), 29.

76. RK, interview by Coughlan, Jan. 14, 1972.

77. RK, "David Wolper Associates Documentary on Robert F. Kennedy," Oct. 28, 1969, Box 110, RFKP.

78. *An Unfinished Life*, 29.

79. *HTF*, xx; Daniel Okrent, *Last Call: The Rise and Fall of Prohibition* (New York: Scribner, 2010), 367–71.

80. John Henry Cutler, *"Honey Fitz": Three Steps to the White House, the Colorful Life and Times of John F. ("Honey Fitz") Fitzgerald* (Indianapolis: Bobbs-Merrill, 1962), 229; Francis Russell, "Honey Fitz," *American Heritage* 19 (Aug. 1968): 28, available online at www .americanheritage.com/print/52295?page=7; *HTF*, 34.

81. Theodore C. Sorensen, author's interview, June 16, 2010.

CHAPTER 4

1. RK, interview by Coughlan, Feb. 23, 1972, Box 10, RFKP.

2. http://en.wikipedia.org/wiki/Country_Day_School_movement, accessed Oct. 27, 2012; http://www.riverdale.edu/podium/default.aspx?t=23368, accessed Oct. 27, 2012.

3. RK, interview by Coughlan, Feb. 23, 1972.

4. *HTF*, 54.

5. EKS to RK and MacSwain to RK, May 17, [1927], Box 13, RFKP.

6. Cari Beauchamp, *Joseph P. Kennedy Presents: His Hollywood Years* (New York: Knopf, 2009), 100–104.

7. RK, interview by Coughlan, Jan. 4, 1972, Box 10, RFKP.

8. RK, interview by Coughlan, Feb. 23, 1972.

9. RK, interview by Coughlan, Jan. 4, 1972.

10. *Rose Kennedy Remembers: The Best of Times, the Worst of Times*, BBC, 1974, JFKL. Five-minute clips may be viewed on YouTube.

11. RK, interview by Coughlan, Jan. 4, 1972.

12. Mary Sanford, interview by Coughlan, April 27, 1972, Coughlan Papers, JFKL.

13. RK, interview by Coughlan, Jan. 28, 1972, Box 10, RFKP.

14. RK, interview by Coughlan, Jan. 4, 1972; *Rose Kennedy Remembers*. Five-minute clips may be viewed on YouTube.

15. RK, interview by Coughlan, Jan. 7, 1972, Box 10, RFKP.

16. RK, interview by Coughlan, Jan. 10, 1972, Box 10, RFKP.

17. *TC*, 30.

18. Ibid.

19. Ibid., 44.

20. RK, interview by Coughlan, Feb. 23, 1972.

21. RK, interview by Coughlan, Jan. 21, 1972, Box 10, RFKP; *Rose Kennedy Remembers*.

22. Sanford interview.

23. RK, interview by Coughlan, Jan. 4, 1972.

24. PKL, interview by Coughlan, Sept. 3, 1972, Coughlan Papers, JFKL.

25. RK, interview by Coughlan, Jan. 18, 1972, Box 10, RFKP.

26. *TC*, 29, 44.

27. RK, interview by Coughlan, Jan. 11 and 19, 1972, Box 10, RFKP.

28. *TC*, 37, 39, 42.

29. Ibid., 40.

30. EKS, interview by Coughlan, Feb. 26, 1972, Box 10, RFKP.

31. Ibid.

32. RK, interview by Coughlan, Jan. 31, 1972, Box 10, RFKP.

33. Doris Kearns Goodwin, *The Fitzgeralds and the Kennedys: An American Saga* (New York: St. Martin's Press, 1991), 537, 542.

34. *TC*, 37; http://en.wikipedia.org/wiki/Joseph_P._Kennedy, accessed Oct. 27, 2012.

35. Gloria Swanson, quoted in Garry Wills, *The Kennedy Imprisonment: A Meditation on Power* (Boston: Little, Brown, 1981), 41.

36. RK, interview by Coughlan, Jan. 7, 1972.

37. RK to Gladys Cook, Jan. 27, 1932, author's collection.

38. Sanford interview.

39. Gloria Swanson, *Swanson on Swanson* (New York: Random House, 1980); Axel Madsen, *Gloria and Joe: The Star-Crossed Love Affair of Gloria Swanson and Joe Kennedy* (New York: Arbor House, 1988); *Joseph P. Kennedy Presents*, 146.

40. *Joseph P. Kennedy Presents*, 268; *The Fitzgeralds and the Kennedys*, 457.

41. See excerpts of Swanson from BBC 1's "Parkinson" talk show on YouTube.

42. RK, interview by Coughlan, Jan. 4, 1972.

43. KKH to JPK, Jan. 31, 1930, Box 13, RFKP

44. KK to JPK, March 23, 1930, Box 13, RFKP.

45. RK, interview by Coughlan, Jan. 4, 1972.

46. RK, interview by Coughlan, Jan. 25, 1972, Boxes 8–9, RFKP.

47. RK, interview by Coughlan, Feb. 2, 1972.

48. RK, interview by Coughlan, Jan. 4, 1972.

49. JFK to RK, undated, Box 11, RFKP.

50. "John Fitzgerald Kennedy," RK's health index cards, Box 124, RFKP.

51. JFK to JPK, undated, Box 11, RFKP.

52. JFK to RK, undated, Box 11, RFKP.

53. RK, interview by Coughlan, Jan. 4, 1972; Thomas Maier, *The Kennedys: America's Emerald Kings* (New York: Basic Books, 2003), 79–80; Robert Dallek, *An Unfinished Life: John F. Kennedy, 1917–1963* (Boston: Little, Brown, 2003), 29–33.

54. RK to Mrs. St. John, c. 1932, "Who Was Rose Kennedy?" B5-1, JFKL, www.jfk library.org/~/media/assets/Education%20and%20Public%20Programs/Education/materials /Rose%20Kennedy%20Documents%20Wife%20and%20Mother.pdf.

55. RK, interview by Coughlan, Jan. 4, 1972.

56. *HTF*, 118.

57. EKS, interview with Coughlan, Feb. 26, 1972.

58. Ibid.

59. Ibid.

60. *HTF*, 87.

61. RK, interview by Coughlan, Feb. 23, 1972.

62. *TC*, 21.

63. RK, interview by Coughlan, Jan. 7 and 17, 1972.

64. *TC*, 44.

65. *An Unfinished Life*, 25.

66. KKH to RK, March 23, 1929, Box 13, RFKP.

67. EKS to RK, March 26, 1929, Box 13, RFKP.

68. EKS to RK, Feb. 10 and March 2, 1932, Box 13, RFKP.

69. BK to RK, Oct. 9, 1934, Box 13, RFKP.

70. According to Doris Kearns Goodwin, Rose responded immediately to Joe's long telegram, saying, "I had counted my words carefully as you saw. I just wished I might have been with you today darling." *The Fitzgeralds and the Kennedys*, 495. Rose's granddaughter, Amanda Smith, however, believed that Rose sent Joe that telegram on another trip to Paris two years later, in 1936. *HTF*, 183.

71. RK to JPK, Oct. 6, 1934; JPK to RK, Oct. 6, 1934; Box 12, RFKP.

72. *HTF*, 145–46.

73. RMK to JPK, Oct. 15, 1934, Box 13, RFKP.

74. RK to RMK, undated [1933], Box 13, RFKP.

75. *HTF*, 66.

76. RK, interview by Coughlan, Jan. 7, 1972.

77. RK to EKS, April 14, 1934, Box 13, RFKP.

78. *HTF*, 129.

79. *TTR*, 175–76.

80. Hal Phyfe to RK, July 12, 1934, Box 55, RFKP; "Broadway Photographs: Art Photography and the American Stage 1900–1930," http://www.broadway.cas.sc.edu/index.php?action=showPhotographer&id=48.

81. Rose's handwritten responses to "Questions: Special to Mrs. Joseph Kennedy," from author Lucy Post Frisbee, for her book *John Fitzgerald Kennedy: Boy of the New Frontier*, Box 127, RFKP. The book's subtitle was changed to *Young Statesman* and it was published in 1964 by Bobbs Merrill.

82. JFK to JPK and RK, undated, Box 55, RFKP.

83. RK, interview by Coughlan, Feb. 23, 1972.

84. RK, "Diaries, 1934–37," Box 1, RFKP.

85. "Speeches and Appearances," Box 100, RFKP.

86. Ibid.

87. Ibid.

88. RK, interview by Coughlan, Jan. 19, 1972, Box 10, RFKP.

89. RK, interview by Coughlan, Jan. 27, 1972, Box 10, RFKP.

90. RK, "Russia," "Diaries, 1936," Box 1, RFKP.

91. Ibid.

92. RK, interview by Coughlan, Jan. 27, 1972.

93. RK, interview by Coughlan, Jan. 7, Feb. 2, and Jan. 11, 1972.

94. *TC*, 28.

95. EKS, interview by Coughlan, Feb. 26, 1972.

96. PKL, interview by Coughlan, Sept. 3, 1972, Coughlan Papers, JFKL.

97. RK, interview by Coughlan, Jan. 20, 1972, Box 10, RFKP.

98. http://en.wikipedia.org/wiki/Calendar-based_contraceptive_methods, accessed Oct. 27, 2012.

99. *The Fitzgeralds and the Kennedys*, 455.

100. EKS to Coughlan and Richardson, July 9, 1973, Box 10, RFKP.

101. *HTF*, 217.

102. RK, interview by Coughlan, Feb. 2, 1972.

103. RK, interview by Coughlan, Feb. 23, 1972.

104. RK, interview by Coughlan, Jan. 11, 1972.

105. *Rose Kennedy Remembers*.

106. RK, interview by Coughlan, Jan. 11, 1972.

107. *TTR*, 204.

108. *TC*, 42.

109. RK's notes on *TTR* Manuscript, Box 17, RFKP.

CHAPTER 5

1. "Life on the American News Front: The Kennedy Family: Nine Children and $9,000,000," *Life*, Dec. 20, 1937, 18–19.

2. Philip B. Kunhardt Jr., *Life in Camelot: The Kennedy Years* (Boston: Little, Brown, 1988), 5.

3. Ibid.

4. *HTF*, 217.

5. Max Grossman, "The Real Story of Joseph P. Kennedy's Romance," *Boston Sunday Post*, December 19, 1937, A-4; Louis M. Lyons, "Joe Kennedy Was Slow Running Bases, But He's Made Up For It Since," *Boston Post*, 1937, 6. Both are in Box 5, JPKP.

6. Will Swift, *The Kennedys Amidst the Gathering Storm: A Thousand Days in London, 1938–1940* (New York: Smithsonian Books, 2008), 13.

7. Marjorie Means, "Children's Voices Will Soon Enliven American Ambassador's Residence in London," *New York Sun*, March 8, 1938, 22.

8. RK, "Diary 1938," Box 2, RFKP.

9. "Kennedy Family Leaves for England," with AP photo, "News clippings/articles collected by Rose Kennedy," Box 12, JPKP.

10. Luella R. Hennessey, as told to Margot Murphy, "Bringing Up the Kennedys," *Good Housekeeping*, Aug. 1961, 114.

11. RK, "1938 Diary," Box 1, RFKP.

12. RK, interview by Coughlan, Jan. 4, 1972, Box 10, RFKP.

13. Deborah Mitford, "The Dowager Duchess of Devonshire with Charlotte Mosley," lecture at the Frick Collection, New York, NY, Nov. 10, 2010, http://www.youtube.com/watch?v=25IO32AxGq4. See Mitford, *Wait for Me! Memoirs* (New York: Farrar, Straus and Giroux, 2010), 204.

14. *The Kennedys Amidst the Gathering Storm*, 35.

15. RK, "Diary of Rose F. Kennedy, Year-1939, London," Box 2, RFKP.

16. "1938 Diary," Box 1.

17. "Speeches and Appearances, 1935–1977, " Box 100, RFKP.

18. Lemuel F. Parton, "Mrs. J. P. Kennedy Has One of Her Few Bits of Publicity," *New York Sun*, May 5, 1938, in "Diary 1938," Box 2, RFKP.

19. "1938 Diary," Box 1.

20. Ibid.

21. Ibid.

22. *TTR*, 221.

23. *HTF*, 252.

24. Ibid.

25. RK to Mrs. Vincent Grene, April 10, 1938, author's collection.

26. Cynthia Ann Stone, RK's secretary, to Marguerite Higgins, July 31, 1964, Box 11, RFKP.

27. "1938 Diary," Box 1.

28. RK, interview by Coughlan, Jan. 25, 1972, Box 8, RFKP.

29. Ibid.

30. Ibid.

31. "Diary 1938," Box 2.

32. "Romantic Dresses at the First Court," *Evening Standard*, May 12, 1938, in "Diary 1938," Box 2.

33. "Seven Americans Presented to King," *New York Times*, May 12, 1938.

34. Charles Higham, *Rose: The Life and Times of Rose Fitzgerald Kennedy* (New York: Pocket Books, 1996), 183; Laurence Leamer, *The Kennedy Women: The Saga of an American Family* (New York: Villard Books, 1994), 256.

35. *TTR*, 230.

36. Theodora Benson, "Woman to Woman: The Children's Zoo," *Country Life*, undated clipping in "Diary 1938," Box 2.

37. Unsourced newspaper clipping in "1938 Diary," Box 2, RFKP.

38. *Evening Standard* clipping, ibid.

39. Ambassador Kennedy had hoped to receive an honorary degree from Harvard. When he learned that he wouldn't, he found an excuse to boycott his eldest son's commencement ceremony, though he attended Class Day, an event Joe Jr. chaired. The ambassador wrote in his unpublished memoir that he skipped commencement because he wanted to spend time with Jack, who was ill, at Hyannis Port. *HTF*, 265. The apple of his parents' eye, Joe Jr. had neither mother nor father in the audience on his graduation day.

40. "Diary 1938," Box 2.

41. RK, interview by Coughlan,, Jan. 17, 1972, Box 10, RFKP.

42. RK, interview by Coughlan, Jan. 25, 1972.

43. Ibid.

44. "Mr. Eden Americans' Guest," *Manchester Daily Dispatch*, July 5, 1938, in "Diary 1938," Box 2.

45. Lesley Blanch, "Family Fugue: Theme and Variations on the Kennedys," *Vogue*, July 1938, in "Diary 1938," Box 2.

46. A. Fraser to Sir [Ambassador Joseph Kennedy], in "Diary 1938," Box 2.

47. Grace Cowardin Dammann to RK, August 25, 1938, in "Diary 1938," Box 2.

48. Marianne Mayfayre, "The Kennedys at Cannes," unsourced and undated clipping in "Diary 1938," Box 2.

49. "At the Races," unsourced and undated clipping in "Diary 1938," Box 2.

50. "The Dowager Duchess of Devonshire with Charlotte Mosley"; *Wait for Me!*, 204.

51. "Diary 1938," Box 2.

52. "Diary 1938," Box 2.

53. Cari Beauchamp, *Joseph P. Kennedy Presents: His Hollywood Years* (New York: Knopf, 2009), 360; "It Happened at the Hôtel du Cap," *Vanity Fair*, March 2009, www.vanity fair.com/style/features/2009/03/dietrich-kennedy200903.

54. "Diary 1938," Box 2.

55. Unsourced newspaper clipping in "1938 Diary," Box 2.

56. "Tension Over Czechoslovakia Eases; British Cabinet Maps Compromise Plan to Organize State on Switzerland Lines," *New York Herald Tribune*, August 31, 1938.

57. "Diary 1938," Box 2.

58. Ibid.

59. Ibid.

60. Unsourced newspaper clipping in "1938 Diary," ibid.; *HTF*, 273.

61. *TTR*, 236.

62. "Diary 1938," Box 2.

63. Ibid.

64. Ibid.

65. RK, interview by Coughlan, Jan. 21, 1972, Box 10, RFKP.

66. "Diary 1938," Box 2.

67. *The Kennedys Amidst the Gathering Storm*, 108.

68. "Diary 1938," Box 2.

69. Ibid.

70. Unsourced newspaper clipping in "1938 Diary," ibid.

71. "Diary 1938," Box 2.

72. Ibid.

73. Unsourced newspaper clipping in "1938 Diary," ibid.

74. "Diary 1938," Box 2.

75. Ibid.

76. Ibid.

77. Ibid.

78. Ibid.

79. "World's Workers Pay for Arms Race," (London) *Daily Herald*, October 18, 1938, n.p.; "How an Ambassador's Wife Makes His Speech," (London) *Times*, October 18, 1938, both in "Diary 1938," Box 2.

80. *HTF*, 294.

81. Ibid.; *TTR*, 242.

82. *TTR*, 243.

83. "Diary 1938," Box 2.

84. Ibid.

85. RK to PKL, undated, on American Embassy stationery, Box 13, RFKP.

86. Jean Kennedy Smith, author's interview, Sept. 20, 2010.

87. http://en.wikipedia.org/wiki/Mater_Admirabilis, accessed Oct. 27, 2012.

88. Wilhela Cushman, "With the Kennedy Family in London Town," *Ladies' Home Journal*, Oct. 1938, 30, 82.

89. Richard Tregaskis, "Kennedy's Son Takes Look at Europe," *Boston Sunday Advertiser Green*, Oct. 2, 1938, 2.

90. "Diary 1938," Box 2.

91. Ibid.

CHAPTER 6

1. RK to S. Richardson, Sept. 11, 1973, Box 10, RFKP.
2. Martin Gilbert, *Kristallnacht: Prelude to Destruction* (New York: Harper Perennial, 2007), 13–14.
3. RK, "Diary 1938," Box 2, RFKP.
4. See James A. Bill and Carl Leiden, *Politics in the Middle East*, 2nd ed. (Boston: Little, Brown, 1984); Clyde Sanger, *Malcolm MacDonald: Bringing an End to Empire* (Liverpool, UK: Liverpool University Press, 1995).
5. "Diary 1938."
6. Ibid.
7. Ibid.
8. Ibid.
9. Mary Jo Gargan Clasby, author's interview, Sept. 7, 2011.
10. "Diary 1938."
11. RK to Josie Fitzgerald, undated, Addington Golf Club stationery, Box 12, RFKP.
12. RK, "Diary of Rose F. Kennedy, Year 1939, London," Box 2, RFKP.
13. "Diary 1938."
14. RK to Josie Fitzgerald.
15. "Diary 1938."
16. Ibid.
17. Ibid.
18. RK, "Diary 1939," Box 2.
19. RK to Josie Fitzgerald, undated, Suvretta House stationery, Box 12, RFKP.
20. "1938 Diary."
21. *HTF*, 306.
22. "Diary 1939."
23. *HTF*, 306.
24. "Diary 1939."
25. RK to JPK Sr., undated, Hotel Ritz stationery, Box 5, JPKP.
26. Will Swift, *The Kennedys Amidst the Gathering Storm: A Thousand Days in London, 1938–1940* (New York: Smithsonian Books, 2008), 134–35.
27. RK to Josie Fitzgerald, undated, American Embassy stationery, Box 12, RFKP.
28. Marie Bruce, "Reflections on Rose," July 1972, Box 15, RFKP.
29. "Diary 1939."
30. Ibid.
31. Ibid.
32. Ibid.
33. RK, "Notes and Memoirs, Mrs. Kennedy," "Diary 1939," Box 3, RFKP.
34. *HTF*, 318.
35. *TC*, 56.
36. *HTF*, 321.
37. RK, "Diary 1939," Box 3.
38. Ibid.
39. *The Kennedys Amidst the Gathering Storm*, 135.
40. RK, "Second Visit to Windsor Castle," "1939," Box 3, RFKP.
41. Ibid.
42. "Education: The Monkeys," *Time*, March 2, 1953.

43. Mother Isabel to JPK, April 3, 1939, Box 13, RFKP.

44. JPK to RMK, undated, Box 13, RFKP.

45. "Diary 1939," Box 2.

46. *TTR*, 245.

47. Jerome Beatty, "The Nine Little Kennedys and How They Grew," *Reader's Digest* 34, no. 204 (April 1939): 16.

48. "Diary 1939," Box 2.

49. *HTF*, 332.

50. Ibid.

51. Ibid.

52. "Diary 1939," Box 2.

53. Ibid.

54. Ibid.

55. *TTR*, 249.

56. "Speeches and Appearances, 1935–1977," Box 100, RFKP.

57. *HTF*, 341.

58. RK to JPK, undated, S.S. *Normandie* stationery, Box 5, JPKP, JFKL.

59. Cari Beauchamp, *Joseph P. Kennedy Presents: His Hollywood Years* (New York: Knopf, 2009), 363. Biographer Sylvia Jukes Morris writes that Clare Boothe Luce initially attracted Kennedy's "libidinous interest" in May 1938. *Rage for Fame: The Ascent of Clare Boothe Luce* (New York: Random House, 1997), 318.

60. "Diary 1939," Box 2.

61. "Speeches and Appearances," Box 100; "Diary 1939," Box 2.

62. RK to JPK, undated, Westchester Country Club stationery, "Hyannis Port," JPKP.

63. "Diary 1939," Box 2.

64. Ibid.

65. Ibid.

66. Ibid.

67. Ibid.

68. *Joseph P. Kennedy Presents*, 363.

69. *TC*, 56–57.

70. *HTF*, 360.

71. *TTR*, 251.

CHAPTER 7

1. *HTF*, 366.

2. The photograph (PC 89) of Joe Jr., Kathleen, and Jack is available on the John F. Kennedy Library and Museum Web site, www.jfkl.org; Rose's photo is in Will Swift, *The Kennedys Amidst the Gathering Storm: A Thousand Days in London, 1938–1940* (New York: HarperCollins, 2008), three pages before text on 263.

3. *TTR*, 252.

4. RK, interview by Coughlan, Jan. 26, 1972, Box 10, RFKP.

5. RK to S. Richardson, Sept. 11, 1973, 10, RFKP.

6. RK, interview by Coughlan, Jan. 26, 1972.

7. RMK to JPK, Aug. 31, [1939], Box 13, RFKP.

8. RMK to JPK, Sept. 12, 1939, Box 13, RFKP.

9. *HTF*, 515. Belmont House was located in Hereford, and Rosemary vacationed there. Her Hertfordshire school was Boxmoor.

10. JPK to RK, Sept. 18, 1939, in *HTF*, 380.

11. RK to JPK, undated [1940?], on Bronxville stationery, RFKP.

12. JPK to RK, Oct. 11, 1939, in *HTF*, 394.

13. RK to JPK, on Bronxville stationery, with [1940?] added, JPKP.

14. *TTR*, 257.

15. JPK to RK, Sept. 18, 1939, in *HTF*, 379–80; E. F. Waldron to JPK, conveying RK's message, Oct. 5, 1939, Box 13, RFKP.

16. Dorothy Gibbs to JPK, Sept. 13, 1939, Box 13, RFKP.

17. JPK to RK, March 20, 1940, in *HTF*, 411.

18. JPK to RK, Oct., 11, 1939, in *HTF*, 394; RMK to JPK, [April 4(?), 1940], ibid., 412.

19. RMK to JPK, [April 4(?), 1940], in *HTF*, 412.

20. JPK to RK, Oct. 11, 1939, in *HTF*, 394.

21. Edward Shorter, *The Kennedy Family and the Story of Mental Retardation* (Philadelphia: Temple University Press, 2000), 1.

22. JPK to RK, Oct. 2, 1939, in *HTF*, 391; JPK to RK, Oct. 11, 1939, in *HTF*, 393.

23. RK, interview by Coughlan, Jan. 26, 1972.

24. Sylvia Jukes Morris, *Rage for Fame: The Ascent of Clare Boothe Luce* (New York: Random House, 1997).

25. JPK to RK, March 14, 1940, in *HTF*, 409.

26. Letters from JPK to RK, April 5, 1940, in *HTF*, 413, 415.

27. JPK to RK, April 26, 1940, in *HTF*, 419.

28. RMK to JPK, April 13/14, 1940, Box 13, RFKP.

29. *TC*, 41–42.

30. *HTF*, 432, n. 504.

31. RK to Robert Coughlan and S. Richardson, July 21, 1973, Box 10, RFKP.

32. JPK to RK, May 20, 1940, in *HTF*, 432–33.

33. RK to JPK, June 1, 1940, in *HTF*, 436; RK to JPK, June 24, 1940, ibid., 447.

34. RK to JPK, June 24, 1940, in *HTF*, 446–47.

35. Copied for RK, "Hold for Possible Use in Autobiography," Box 10, RFKP.

36. Christie's Oct. 9, 2002, auction of inscribed copy of *Why England Slept*, http://www.christies.com/Lotfinder/LotDetailsPrintable.aspx?intObjectID=3980457.

37. E.g., Chris Matthews, *Jack Kennedy: Elusive Hero* (New York: Simon & Schuster, 2011), 16; Nigel Hamilton, *JFK: Reckless Youth* (New York: Random House, 1991), 49–50.

38. Edward E. Moore to RK, June 7, 1940, Box 13, RFKP.

39. RMK to JPK, July 4, 1940, Box 13, RFKP.

40. JPK to RMK, Aug. 2, 1940, Box 13, RFKP.

41. JPK to RMK, Sept. 10 and 12, 1940, Box 13, RFKP.

42. JPK to RK, Aug. 2, 1940, in *HTF*, 455.

43. JPK to RK, Sept. 10, 1940, in *HTF*, 466–67.

44. RK to JPK, "1940" added, JPKP, JFKL. Amanda Smith believes Rose wrote it on Oct. 7, 1940. *HTF*, 474. John Burns was a Harvard Law professor, Massachusetts state court judge, and the first legal counsel for the Securities and Exchange Commission and the Maritime Commission, working for Joe Kennedy when he chaired those commissions; he was in private practice by 1940 when RK met with him. "Judge John Burns," Franklin and Eleanor Roosevelt Institute, http://newdeal.feri.org/kiosk/profile.cfm?QID=2870.

45. FDR to JPK, Oct. 17, 1940, in *HTF*, 475.

46. RK's untitled remembrance of visit with President Roosevelt, and "Visit to Washington, Oct. 29, 1940," "Diaries 1939–1941, 1951," Box 3, RFKP.

47. JPK Diary, in *HTF*, 481.

48. *TTR*, 275.

49. JPK, Radio Address, Oct. 29, 1940, in *HTF*, 482–89.

50. "For Mrs. Kennedy, Speech," "Speeches and Appearances," 1935–77, Box 100, RFKP.

51. *TTR*, 275.

52. "For Mrs. Kennedy, Speech."

53. Louis Lyons, *Boston Globe*, Nov. 9, 1940, 1.

54. "Diaries, 1939–41, 1951."

55. RK, interview by Coughlan, Jan. 11, 1972, Box 10, RFKP.

56. RK to "My darlings," Dec. 5, 1941, Box 55, RFKP.

57. *TC*, 60–65.

58. RK, interview by Coughlan, Jan. 11, 1972.

59. RK to children, Jan. 5, 1941, Box 55, RFKP.

60. EKS, interview by Coughlan, Feb. 26, 1972, Box 10, RFKP.

61. Ibid.

62. EKS, "Hope for Retarded Children," *Saturday Evening Post*, Sept. 22, 1962, http://www.eunicekennedyshriver.org/articles/print_article/148.

63. Doris Kearns Goodwin, *The Fitzgeralds and the Kennedys: An American Saga* (New York: St. Martin's Press, 1991), 741.

64. RK to JPK, [May 13, 1940], in *HTF*, 530.

65. "Diaries, 1935–1941, 1951."

66. Ibid.

67. Ibid.

68. Ibid.

69. Hank Searls, *The Lost Prince: Young Joe, the Forgotten Kennedy* (New York: World, 1969).

70. Robert Dallek, *An Unfinished Life: John F. Kennedy, 1917–1963* (Boston: Little, Brown, 2003), 82–83.

71. Jack El-Hai, *The Lobotomist: A Maverick Medical Genius and His Tragic Quest to Rid the World of Mental Illness* (Hoboken, NJ: Wiley, 2005), 139.

72. *The Kennedy Family and the Story of Mental Retardation*, 33.

73. Michael O'Brien, *John F. Kennedy: A Biography* (New York: St. Martin's, 2005), 173.

74. "Hope for Retarded Children." In late 1960, just after the presidential election, the National Association for Retarded Children revealed that JFK had a retarded sister institutionalized in Wisconsin.

75. Laurence Leamer, *The Kennedy Women: The Saga of an American Family* (New York: Villard Books, 1994), 319.

76. Goodwin quoted in *John F. Kennedy: A Biography*, 173–74.

77. RK, interview by Coughlan, Jan. 21 and Jan. 7, 1972, Box 10, RFKP.

78. EKS, interview by Coughlan, Feb. 7, 1972, Box 10, RFKP. I am grateful to the Kennedy Library for granting my request to remove redactions from Mrs. Shriver's interview.

79. RK, interview by Coughlan, Jan. 7, 1972.

80. *The Kennedys Amidst the Gathering Storm*, 299–300.

81. RK to children, March 27, 1942, Box 55, RFKP.

82. RK to children, May 9, 1942, Box 55, RFKP.
83. http://www.thefreedictionary.com/pluperfect, accessed Oct. 27, 2012.
84. JFK to RK, Washington, DC, in *HTF*, 538.
85. RK to BK, Jan. 12, 1942, in *HTF*, 535.
86. RK to JPK Jr., Feb. 19, 1942, in *HTF*, 541.
87. JPK Jr., undated, on US Naval Air Station, Banana River, Florida, stationery, Box 56, RFKP.
88. RK to children, Feb. 2, 1943, Box 55, RFKP.
89. *TC*, 68.
90. Ibid., 65–66.
91. RK to KKH, undated, on Beverly-Wilshire stationery, Box 57, RFKP.
92. JFK to RK, undated, United States Navy Yard, SC, Box 56, RFKP.
93. RK to JPK Jr., Feb. 9, 1943, Box 56, RFKP.
94. Robert J. Donovan, *PT 109: John F. Kennedy in World War II* (New York: McGraw-Hill, 2001).
95. JFK to RK and JPK, [May 15, 1943], in *HTF*, 554; JFK to family, June 24, 1943, Box 56, RFKP.
96. RK, interview by Coughlan, Jan. 20, 1972, Box 10, RFKP.
97. JFK to family, received Aug. 29, 1943, Box 56, RFKP.
98. RK to KKH and JFK, Sept. 2, 1943, Box 56, RFKP.
99. JPK to JPK Jr., Aug. 31, 1943, Box 56, RFKP.
100. RK to JPK Jr., Sept. 16, 1943, Box 56, RFKP.
101. JPK Jr. to JPK and RK, Nov. 9, 1943, Box 56, RFKP.

CHAPTER 8

1. RK, "Diary Note," in *HTF*, 573.
2. RK to children, Jan. 31, 1944, Box 55, RFKP.
3. Coconut Shell Paperweight, John F. Kennedy Library and Museum, http://www.jfklibrary.org/Asset-Viewer/Ey5l6Vagyk2dwA6BTctDZg.aspx.
4. KKH to JPK and RK, March 22, 1944, in *HTF*, 580.
5. JPK to KKH, April 3, 1944, in *HTF*, 581.
6. RK, "Notes on My Reaction to Kick's Marriage," "Diaries," Box 3, RFKP.
7. Telegram draft, RK to KKH, in *HTF*, 584.
8. "Notes on My Reaction to Kick's Marriage."
9. Thomas Maier, *The Kennedys: America's Emerald Kings* (New York: Basic Books, 2003), 157.
10. KKH to RK, April 30, 1943, in *HTF*, 584–85.
11. KKH to JPK, May 5, 1944, in *HTF*, 586.
12. Deborah Mitford, "The Dowager Duchess of Devonshire with Charlotte Mosley," Lecture at the Frick Collection, New York, NY, Nov. 10, 2010, http://www.youtube.com/watch?v=25IO32AxGq4.
13. Marie Bruce and Lady Astor to RK, May 7, 1944, in *HTF*, 587.
14. JPK Jr. to JPK, May 7, 1944, in *HTF*, 587.
15. KKH to JPK, May 8, 1944, in *HTF*, 587.
16. JPK Jr. to JPK and RK, May 8, 1944, in *HTF*, 587–89.
17. *The Kennedys*, 136.
18. KKH to RK, May 9, 1944, in *HTF*, 589–91.

19. RK to KKH, June 30, 1944, in *HTF*, 595.

20. Robert Dallek, *John F. Kennedy: An Unfinished Life, 1917–1963* (Boston: Little, Brown, 2003), 102.

21. RK to KKH, June 30, 1944.

22. KKH to RK, July 6, 1944, in *HTF*, 597.

23. Marie Bruce's Notes on RK, July 1972, Box 15, RFKP.

24. JPK Jr. to JPK and RK, July 26, 1944, in *HTF*, 598. See also *HTF*, n. 144, about Joe Jr.'s romance with Pat Wilson.

25. JPK Jr. to JPK and RK, August 4, 1944, in *HTF*, 598. JPK Jr. to JFK, August 10, 1944, Box 56, RFKP.

26. RK, "Joe Jr.'s Death," in *HTF*, 599.

27. *TC*, 85–86.

28. Edward J. Renehan Jr., *The Kennedys at War, 1937–1945* (New York: Doubleday, 2002), 304; Hank Searls, *The Lost Prince: Young Joe, the Forgotten Kennedy* (New York: World Publishing Co., 1969), 283; John Kelly, "For Joe Kennedy, Memorial Wall Had to Substitute for Burial Site," *Washington Post*, September 6, 2009, C3; John Kelly, "Readers Fill in the Story Surrounding Death of Lt. Joseph Kennedy," *Washington Post*, October 4, 2009, C3; "Lt. Joe Kennedy," Norfolk and Suffolk Aviation Museum," http://www .aviationmuseum.net/Joe_Kennedy.htm, accessed Oct. 27, 2012.

29. Clara St. John to RK, Aug. 25, 1944, Box 10, RFKP. I am grateful to Mrs. St. John's grandchildren, Margaret and Gordon St. John, for their gracious permission to publish the letter in full.

30. Mary Jo Gargan Clasby, author's interview, Sept. 7, 2011.

31. Major Lord Hartington to KKH, Sept. 4, 1944, Box 57, RFKP.

32. KKH to JPK and RK, [Sept. 20, 1944], in *HTF*, 601.

33. RK to KKH, Sept. 25, 1944, in *HTF*, 602.

34. KKH to Kennedy family, Sept. 23, 1944, in *HTF*, 603.

35. RK, interview by Coughlan, Jan. 20, 1972, Box 10, RFKP.

36. Joey Gargan, interview by Coughlan, Aug. [27?], 1972, Robert Coughlan Papers, Northwestern University, MS 82-5: 11, JFKL.

37. Mary Jo Gargan Clasby and Richard Clasby, interview by Coughlan, Feb. 18, 1972, Box 10, RFKP.

38. Mary Jo Gargan Clasby, author's interview, Sept. 7, 2011.

39. JPK to KKH, May 1, 1945, in *HTF*, 618.

40. JPK to Cissy Patterson, Nov. 26, 1945, in *HTF*, 622.

41. Edward Shorter, *The Kennedy Family and the Story of Mental Retardation* (Philadelphia: Temple University Press, 2000), 35–36.

42. JPK to Sir James Calder, July 31, 1946, in *HTF*, 629.

43. JPK to Cissy Patterson, Nov. 26, 1945, in *HTF*, 622.

44. RK, interview by Coughlan, Jan. 4, 1972, Box 10, RFKP.

45. "John F. Kennedy on Politics and Public Service," White House Tapes, Miller Center Presidential Recordings Program, University of Virginia, http://whitehousetapes .net/exhibit/john-f-kennedy-politics-and-public-service.

46. RK, interview by Coughlan, Jan. 7, 1972, Box 10, RFKP.

47. RK to her children, April 11, 1946, in *HTF*, 626.

48. RK to KKH, June 6, 1946, Box 58, RFKP.

49. RK to KKH, June 6, 1946, Box 58, RFKP.

50. Ibid.

51. "Diaries," [circa 1946], Box 3, RFKP.

52. RK to KKH, June 6, 1946, Box 58, RFKP.

53. *TTR*, 314–15.

54. RK, interview by Coughlan, Jan. 7, 1972, Box 10, RFKP.

55. "John F. Kennedy on Politics and Public Service."

56. *An Unfinished Life*, 128.

57. Kenneth P. O'Donnell and David F. Powers with Joe McCarthy, *"Johnny, We Hardly Knew Ye": Memories of John Fitzgerald Kennedy* (Boston: Little, Brown, 1970), 54.

58. RK, interview by Coughlan, Jan. 10, 1972, Box 9, RFKP.

59. *An Unfinished Life*, 131.

60. Barbara Leaming, *Jack Kennedy: The Education of a Statesman* (New York: Norton, 2006), opposite 252.

61. "John F. Kennedy on Politics and Public Service."

62. RK, "Diaries 1947," Box 3, RFKP.

63. RK to JPK, Sept. 1947, "Diaries," Box 3, RFKP.

64. RK to JPK, undated, from Lismore Castle, Box 5, JPK Papers, JFKL.

65. "Diaries 1947."

66. *Finian's Rainbow*, http://en.wikipedia.org/wiki/Finian's_Rainbow.

67. RK to JPK, from Lismore Castle.

68. *HTF*, 636, n. 227.

69. *An Unfinished Life*, 153.

70. Ibid., 152–53; *Jack Kennedy*, 191–92.

71. RK, interview by Coughlan, Feb. 23 and Jan. 11, 1972, Box 10, RFKP.

72. Doris Kearns Goodwin in *The Kennedys*, American Experience, PBS Home Video, DVD, 2003; *An Unfinished Life*, 322.

73. RK, interview by Coughlan, Jan. 19, 1972, Box 10, RFKP.

74. *An Unfinished Life*, 105.

75. Maier, *The Kennedys*, 227.

76. Doris Kearns Goodwin, *The Kennedys and the Fitzgeralds: An American Saga* (New York: St. Martin's Press, 1991), 853–54.

77. *The Kennedys*, American Experience.

78. "Kennedy Tragedy Family's Second," *Boston Traveler*, May 14, 1948.

79. *Jack Kennedy*, 193.

80. Ibid.

81. *Times to Remember* background material, "Newspaper Clippings and Correspondence on KKH's Death, 1948," Box 13, RFKP.

82. JPK to Duchess of Devonshire, Sept. 1, 1948, in *HTF*, 637.

83. RK, interview by Coughlan, Jan. 11, 1972, Box 10, RFKP. The blank lines' meaning is unclear. They could be inaudible material on the recordings or redactions.

84. May 14, 1948. In addition to Kathleen's death, the *Globe* counted Joe Jr.'s and Billy's wartime casualties. Of course, the paper didn't know about Rosemary's tragic lobotomy.

CHAPTER 9

1. RK to Hélène Arpels, July 10, 1950, in *HTF*, 640.

2. RK to BK and ESK, July 13, 1950, in *HTF*, 644.

3. RK, interview by Coughlan, Jan. 20, 1972, Box 10, RFKP.

4. John Henry Cutler, *"Honey Fitz": Three Steps to the White House* (New York: Bobbs-Merrill, 1962), 322.

5. Doris Kearns Goodwin, *The Fitzgeralds and the Kennedys: An American Saga* (New York: St. Martin's Press, 1991), 864.

6. *TC*, 78–79.

7. Gail Cameron, *Rose: A Biography of Rose Fitzgerald Kennedy* (New York: G. P. Putnam's Sons, 1971), 137.

8. RK to Marie Bruce, July 23, 1951, in *HTF*, 655.

9. Robert Dallek, *An Unfinished Life: John F. Kennedy, 1917–1963* (Boston: Little, Brown, 2003), 157; William Manchester, *One Brief Shining Moment: Remembering Kennedy* (Boston: Little, Brown, 1983), 60.

10. "John F. Kennedy on Politics and Public Service," White House Tapes, Miller Center Presidential Recordings Program, University of Virginia, http://whitehousetapes .net/exhibit/john-f-kennedy-politics-and-public-service.

11. "Coffee Hour Notes, First Time," in "Speeches and Appearances, 1935–78," Box 100, RFKP.

12. Gloria Negri, "Pauline Fitzgerald: The Force Behind JFK Tea Parties," *Boston Globe*, February 18, 2008.

13. Philip B. Kunhardt Jr., ed., *Life in Camelot: The Kennedy Years* (Boston: Little, Brown, 1988), 34–37.

14. EMK, interview by Coughlan, Nov. 13, 1972, Robert Coughlan Papers, Northwestern University, MS 82-5: 11, JFKL.

15. RK, interview by Coughlan, Jan. 17, 1972, Box 10, RFKP.

16. Ibid.

17. RK, interview by Coughlan, Jan. 4, 1972, Box 10, RFKP.

18. Ibid.

19. Burton Hersh, *The Education of Edward Kennedy: A Family Biography* (New York: William Morrow, 1972).

20. *TC*, 102–103 (original emphasis).

21. "French Notes," "Old French Speech," and "Translation of French Speech," in "Speeches and Appearances, 1935–78," Box 100, RFKP.

22. "Italian Speech," Box 100, RFKP; *HTF*, 653, n. 269.

23. RK, interview by Coughlan, Jan. 21, 1972, Box 10, RFKP.

24. *An Unfinished Life*, 171–72, 174–75.

25. RK, interview by Coughlan, Jan. 21, 1972, Box 10, RFKP.

26. JPK to Sir James Calder, Dec. 31, 1952, in *HTF*, 661.

27. "Pauline Fitzgerald: The Force Behind Famed JFK Tea Parties."

28. RK, interview by Coughlan, Jan. 18, 1972, Box 10, RFKP.

29. Barbara A. Perry, *Jacqueline Kennedy: First Lady of the New Frontier* (Lawrence: University Press of Kansas, 2004), 36.

30. David Pitts, *Jack and Lem: John F. Kennedy and Lem Billings: The Untold Story of an Extraordinary Friendship* (New York: Carroll and Graf, 2007). After gaining access to eight hundred previously closed letters between Jack and Lem, Pitts concludes that Lem was gay but that his friendship with JFK was nonsexual.

31. *Jacqueline Kennedy*, 32–33.

32. RK, interview by Coughlan, Jan. 20, 1972.

33. *Jacqueline Kennedy*, 35–36.

34. JBKO to RK, [June 29, 1953], in *HTF*, 662.

35. RK, interview by Coughlan, Jan. 19, 1972, Box 10, RFKP.

36. *Jacqueline Kennedy*, 37.

37. JFK to RK and JPK, Sept. 15, 1953, in *HTF*, 663.

38. RSS to RK and JPK, Feb. 8, 1953, Box 55, RFKP.

39. Mark K. Shriver, *A Good Man: Rediscovering My Father, Sargent Shriver* (New York: Henry Holt, 2012), 76–78.

40. RK to JPK, undated [1951?], on Ritz Hotel stationery, Box 5, JPKP. Rose's references in the letter to "Your little darlings," and Jack's leaving for "the Orient" probably indicate that she wrote it in the fall of 1951 when Jack, Bobby, and Pat went on a trip to Israel, Iran, Pakistan, India, Singapore, Thailand, French Indochina, Korea, and Japan. *An Unfinished Life*, 165.

41. RK to JPK, undated [erroneously dated 1953 in JFKL files], on United States Lines stationery, Box 5, JPKP.

42. "Travel List–Mrs. Kennedy, 1957," "Speeches and Appearances," Box 100, RFKP. Redactions removed on Sept. 14, 2011, per my request. I am grateful to the Kennedy Library for releasing the unredacted version.

43. Joe Graedon, cohost of public radio's *The People's Pharmacy*, author's interview, Aug. 13, 2011; "Paregoric," National Center for Biotechnology Information and U.S. National Library of Medicine, http://www.ncbi.nlm.nih.gov/pubmedhealth/PMH0000083/#a6 01090-brandNames, accessed Oct. 27, 2012.

44. P. W. Brown, "The Irritable Bowel Syndrome," *Rocky Mountain Medical Journal* 40 (May 1950): 343–46; Ronald Kessler, in *The Sins of the Father: Joseph P. Kennedy and the Dynasty He Founded* (New York: Warner Books, 1996), 372–73, lists Rose's drug prescriptions and cites a 1976 reference to her IBS, dating to 1933. For Lomotil, see http://en.wikipedia.org/wiki/Lomotil.

45. Graedon interview; William Schack, *Art and Argyrol: The Life and Career of Albert C. Barnes* (New York: Thomas Yoseloff, 1960).

46. Graedon, e-mail to author, July 10, 2012.

47. www.pharmaoffshore.com/index.php?cPath=334.

48. RK to JPK, undated [erroneously dated 1953 in JFKL files], on United States Lines stationery, Box 5, JPKP.

49. RK to JPK, undated [erroneously dated 1953 in JFKL files], on Christian Dior stationery, Box 5, JPKP. Based on the days of the week and dates that Rose mentions, this letter cannot be from 1953. Moreover, she would not likely have still been in Paris a few days before Jack's wedding on Sept. 12, 1953. The trip was more likely in 1957, when September 9, to which she refers, was indeed on a Monday.

50. RK to JPK, undated [1951?], on Ritz Hotel stationery, Box 5, JPKP; *An Unfinished Life*, 165.

51. RK, interview by Coughlan, Jan. 14 and 17, 1972, Box 10, RFKP.

52. Invitation from the Christ Child Society to attend Mrs. Joseph P. Kennedy's speech, Oct. 25, [1953], "Speeches and Appearances," Box 100, RFKP. The "suggested minimum donation" was two dollars per person.

53. Jan DesRosiers, Secretary to RK, to the British Consulate General, Oct. 19, 1953, "Speeches and Appearances," Box 100, RFKP.

54. Allon Barker to Jan DesRosiers, Oct. 22, 1953, Box 100, RFKL.

55. RK, Speech to Christ Child Society, Oct. 25, 1953, Box 100, RFKP.

56. Catherine Dennehy to RK, undated, "Speeches and Appearances," Box 100, RFKP.

57. "Future Speaking Dates," [1954], "Speeches and Appearances," ibid.

58. Ralph H. Reed to RK, Feb. 9, 1954, "Speeches and Appearances," ibid.

59. JF [James Fayne] to Thomas J. Walsh, Nov. 23, 1964, "Speeches and Appearances," Box 100, RFKP.

60. Cholly Knickerbocker, "Powers Picks Eight American Beauties Over 40," *Miami Herald*, Feb. 21, 1954.

61. Nancy Randolph, "Mrs. Kennedy to Get Youth Award," New York *Daily News*, April 29, 1954.

62. "CYO Award Goes to Mrs. Kennedy," and Associated Press Photo "Mrs. Kennedy Honored by CYO," uncited and undated newspaper clippings in "Articles Collected by Rose Kennedy," Box 12, JPKP.

63. Edward Shorter's *The Kennedy Family and the Story of Mental Retardation* (Philadelphia: Temple University Press, 2000) is the definitive history of the Kennedys' philanthropy. Shorter observes that Rose's participation has virtually no paper trail (except, I would note, for her many fund-raising appearances and speeches), 50–51.

64. Speech to CYO, May 10, 1954, "Speeches and Appearances," Box 100, RFKP.

65. Ibid.

66. Mary Jo Gargan Clasby, author's interview, Sept. 7, 2011.

67. Christopher Kennedy Lawford, *Symptoms of Withdrawal: A Memoir of Snapshots and Redemption* (New York: HarperCollins, 2005), 4.

68. Mary Jo Gargan Clasby interview.

69. Ibid.

70. Minna Littmann, "Mrs. Kennedy Home from World Tour," *Standard-Times*, undated, "Articles Collected by Rose Kennedy," Box 12, JPKP.

71. RK to JPK, [July 1955], in *HTF*, 666.

72. RK to JPK, undated, on Ritz Hotel stationery, Box 5, JPKP. Probably from 1951, when Rose was in Paris with Jack, Bobby, and Pat.

73. *An Unfinished Life*, 195–96.

74. *Jacqueline Kennedy*, 44–45.

75. Ibid.

76. RK, interview by Coughlan, Jan. 20, 1972.

77. As quoted in *The Fitzgeralds and the Kennedys*, 904.

78. RK, interview by Coughlan, Jan. 21, 1972.

79. *Jacqueline Kennedy*, 47–48.

80. RK, interview by Coughlan, Jan. 19, 1972, Box 10, RFKP.

81. RK, interview by Coughlan, Feb. 23, 1972, ibid.

82. RK, interview by Coughlan, Jan. 14, 1972, ibid.

83. JPK to EMK, July 19, 1957, Box 55, RFKP.

84. JPK to EMK, Sept. 3, 1955, in *HTF*, 670.

85. JPK to JBKO, Aug. 23, 1957, "Family Correspondence," Box 55, RFKP.

86. JPK to Joseph Kinneen, Aug. 6, 1955, in *HTF*, 667.

87. RK, *Reader's Digest* manuscript, "Articles Written by RK, 1956," Box 116, RFKP.

88. Ibid.

89. Robert F. Kennedy Jr., author's conversation, April 27, 2006.

90. *TC*, 117–18, 126.

91. Monsignor Newman Flanagan to JFK, Dec. 17, 1956, "Speeches and Appearances," Box 100, RFKP.

92. RK to Flanagan, Feb. 4, 1957, ibid.

93. Flanagan to RK, Feb. 7, 1957, ibid.

94. RK to Flanagan, Feb. 15, 1957, ibid; RK to Flanagan, Feb. 22, 1957, ibid.

95. RK to Marge Kayser, Nov. 5, 1957, ibid.

96. Marge Kayser, "C.R. Audience Charmed by Mrs. Kennedy," *Cedar Rapids Gazette*, Oct. 24, 1957.

97. *The Kennedy Family and the Story of Mental Retardation*, 50–51. See also Allison C. Carey, *On the Margins of Citizenship: Intellectual Disability and Civil Rights in Twentieth-Century America* (Philadelphia: Temple University Press, 2010), ch. 6, on the rise of the parents' movement and the influence of the Kennedy family in intellectual-disability rights.

98. "List of People to Receive Autographed Copies of Profiles in Courage from Mrs. Kennedy for Christmas 1957," "Speeches and Appearances," Box 100, RFKP.

CHAPTER 10

1. Barbara A. Perry, *Jacqueline Kennedy: First Lady of the New Frontier* (Lawrence: University Press of Kansas, 2004), 56.

2. CJS to Frank K. Eldridge, March 3, 1958, "Speeches and Appearances," Box 101, RFKP.

3. RK to John J. Ford, Feb. 25, 1958, ibid.

4. Frank [no surname] to C. J. Shaw, on Star Theatre stationery, March 27, 1958, ibid.

5. Doris Kearns Goodwin, *The Fitzgeralds and the Kennedys: An American Saga* (New York: St. Martin's Press, 1991), 916.

6. RK to Cardinal McIntyre, Feb. 13, 1958, Box 101, RFKP.

7. RK to Reverend Mother Mulqueen, April 2, 1958, ibid.

8. RK, interview with Paul Coates, [Los Angeles, 1958], ibid.

9. *The Fitzgeralds and the Kennedys*, 916.

10. "At Home with the Kennedys," Oct. 28, 1958, IFP 156, JFKL.

11. Ibid.

12. Robert Dallek, *An Unfinished Life: John F. Kennedy, 1917–1963* (Boston: Little, Brown, 2003), 225.

13. "The Trinity Award," Oct. 24, 1959, Box 101, RFKP.

14. RK, interview with Coates.

15. "Trinity College," Oct. 24, 1959, New York, NY, Box 101, RFKP.

16. RK to JBKO, June 15, 1959, in *HTF*, 685.

17. "New York Diary, May 9, 1959," "Diaries 1959–1970," Box 4, RFKP.

18. Yolada Maurer, "Spellbound Audience Captivated by 'Court,'" *Fort Lauderdale News*, Feb. 5, 1960.

19. JPK to Enrico Galeazzi, March 9, 1960, in *HTF*, 686.

20. "Kennedy for President Advisory Campaign Committee," Manchester, NH, Box 101, RFKP.

21. RK, Wisconsin diary entry, "Diaries 1959–1970," Box 4, RFKP.

22. Ibid.

23. Ibid.

24. "Excerpts from Cardinal Cushing Article," Box 101, RFKP.

25. "The 1960 Presidential Campaign," *Jubilee* 7 (March 1960): 8–15.

26. Wisconsin itineraries, Box 101, RFKP.

27. Wisconsin diary entry.

28. *Jacqueline Kennedy*, 55.

29. "Recommendations," Box 101, RFKP.

30. RK, "Easter 1960," "Diaries 1959–1970," Box 4, RFKP.

31. Carolyn Sayler, *Doris Fleeson: Incomparably the First Political Journalist of Her Time* (Santa Fe, NM: Sunstone Press, 2010), 11.

32. "Easter 1960," "Diaries 1959–1970."

33. Baltimore speech, Box 101, RFKP.

34. "Itinerary for Mrs. Rose Kennedy [Maryland]," Box 101, RFKP.

35. Ruth Montgomery, "Mama Stumps for Kennedy," *New York Journal-American*, June 4, 1960.

36. RK, "Presidency," June 23, 1960, "Diaries 1959–1970."

37. RK to JBKO, July 10, [1960], marked "never sent," "Diaries 1959–1970."

38. "Supporting Kennedy: Kennedy's Mother to Campaign," *New York Times*, July 13, 1960.

39. Gwen Gibson, "A Mother's Greatest Sacrifice: For Son, Country, Ma Kennedy Tells Age," *Daily News*, July 13, 1960, 6.

40. Mary McGarey, "Kennedy's Mother Is Tan, Trim, Fashionable at 70," *Columbus Dispatch*, July 13, 1960.

41. "A Mother's Greatest Sacrifice."

42. RK, diary entry, July 12, [1960], "Diaries 1959–1970," Box 4, RFKP.

43. Diary entry, July 13, [1960], ibid.

44. Diary entry, July 14, [1960], ibid.

45. "Mother's Day," AP Wirephoto, "Newspaper Clippings," Box 14, RFKP.

46. RK to children, Aug. 23, 1960, in *HTF*, 691.

47. Mrs. J. Paul Richardson to RK, Sept. 28, 1960, Box 101, RFKP.

48. RK, interview by Coughlan, Jan. 10, 1972, Box 8, RFKP.

49. "1960 Campaign: Louisville and Lexington, Kentucky Campaign Trip," "Diaries 1959–1970."

50. Ibid.

51. RK, "1960 Campaign," "Diaries 1959–1970."

52. RK, "1960 Campaign: October 7–9." "Diaries 1959–1970."

53. "1960 Campaign: Louisville and Lexington."

54. "1960 Campaign," "Diaries 1959–1970."

55. "1960 Campaign: October 7–9."

56. *Jacqueline Kennedy*, 63.

57. "Mrs. Joseph P. Kennedy: Cities Visited During Campaign," Box 101, RFKP.

58. Philip B. Kunhardt Jr., ed., *Life in Camelot: The Kennedy Years* (Boston: Little, Brown, 1988), 156–57.

59. *Life*, Nov. 21, 1960.

60. "Post Election," "Diaries 1959–1970."

61. *Jacqueline Kennedy*, 63–64.

62. RK, "Between Christmas and the Inauguration, 1960," "Diaries 1959–1970," Box 4, RFKP.

63. Ibid.

64. Ibid.

65. Ibid.

66. Ibid.

67. Richard Avedon, *The Kennedys: Portrait of a Family* (New York: Collins Design, 2007), 28–32.

68. Ibid.

69. Jeff Greenfield, *Then Everything Changed: Stunning Alternate Histories of American Politics: JFK, RFK, Carter, Ford, Reagan* (New York: G.P. Putnam's Sons, 2011), xiii.

70. RK, "Jackie, Avedon, Hairdressers," "Diaries 1959–1970."

71. Ibid.

72. RK, "January 19, before the Inauguration," "Diaries 1959–1970."

73. Ibid.

74. *Life in Camelot,* 172, 176.

75. RK, interview by Coughlan, Jan. 10, 1972, Box 8, RFKP.

76. "Rose Fitzgerald Kennedy: A Life to Remember," produced by Freida Lee Mock and Terry Sanders, American Film Foundation, 1990; *TTR,* 391.

77. *TTR,* 391.

CHAPTER 11

1. David McCullough, *Truman* (New York: Simon & Schuster, 1992), 970.

2. *TTR,* 394.

3. James A. Abbott and Elaine M. Rice, *Designing Camelot: The Kennedy White House Restoration* (New York: Van Nostrand Reinhold, 1998), 175–80.

4. *TTR,* 395–96.

5. "Travel List–Mrs. Kennedy," undated, "Speeches and Appearances," Box 100, RFKP.

6. Rose Kennedy's handwritten description of April 19, 1961, visit to White House, Box 14, RFKP. In late 1962 Castro released nearly all the captives in return for food and medicine from the United States.

7. RK, "Jack's Trip Abroad," "Diaries 1959–1970," Box 4, RFKP.

8. Ibid.

9. Michael Gerson, "Trig's Breakthrough," *Washington Post,* Sept. 8, 2008.

10. "Jack's Trip Abroad."

11. Ibid.

12. RK to JPK, June 1961, Ritz stationery, Box 14, RFKP.

13. RK, "Hall of Mirrors at Versailles," "Diaries 1959–1970," Box 4, RFKP.

14. Ibid.

15. Marguerite Higgins, "Rose Fitzgerald Kennedy," *McCall's,* May 1961, 103.

16. Barbara A. Perry, *Jacqueline Kennedy: First Lady of the New Frontier* (Lawrence: University Press of Kansas, 2003), 2.

17. RK to BK, October 4, 1961, Box 13, RFKP.

18. *TTR,* 407.

19. Mary Jo Gargan Clasby, author's interview, Sept. 7, 2011.

20. JFK to RK, Nov. 3, 1962, "Family Correspondence," Box 57, RFKP.

21. RK to JFK, Nov. 10, 1962, ibid. Emphasis added.

22. Ibid.

23. Hamish Bowles, Arthur M. Schlesinger Jr., and Rachel Lambert Mellon, *Jacqueline Kennedy: The White House Years, Selections from the John F. Kennedy Library and Museum* (Boston: Bulfinch Press, 2001), 88.

24. Marta Casals Istomin, author's interview, Jan. 22, 2011; RK, "Casals Concert, November 13, 1961," "Diaries 1959–1970"; JBKO to RK, undated, White House stationery, ibid. Jackie referred to her mother-in-law by the French term belle mère (literally, "beautiful mother").

25. RK, "Thanksgiving '61," "Diaries 1959–1970."

26. Ibid.

27. "Winchester Chapter Guild of the Infant Saviour Presents Mrs. Joseph P. Kennedy," November 19, 1961, "Speeches and Appearances," Box 101, RFKP.

28. "My Reactions to My First Visit at the White House," ibid.

29. "Thanksgiving '61."

30. *TTR*, 416.

31. Laurence Leamer, *The Kennedy Men: 1901–1963* (New York: William Morrow, 2001), 336–39.

32. *TTR*, 418. The family chauffeur claimed that Rose insisted on playing her daily golf game, even as Joe was rushed to the hospital (quoted in *The Kennedy Men*, 590–91). Teddy stated emphatically, "My mother went to the hospital immediately" (*TC*, 178).

33. Luella Hennessey-Donovan, Oral History Interview, Sept. 25, 1991, JFKL; Rita Dallas, with Maxine Cheshire, "My 8 Years as the Kennedys' Private Nurse," *Ladies' Home Journal*, March 1971, 106.

34. Diane Winter, secretary to RK, to Roger Vaurs, press secretary, French consulate, Jan. 9, 1962, "Speeches and Appearances," Box 101, RFKP.

35. RK to Mrs. Lane, Jan. 18, 1962, ibid.

36. RK to Franz Pein, Jan. 9, 1962, ibid.; Franz Pein to RK, Jan. 12, 1962, ibid.

37. Charles J. Lewin to RK, Feb. 5, 1962, ibid.

38. Francis X. Morrissey to RK, Feb. 26, 1962.

39. RK, interview by Coughlan, Jan. 25, 1972, Box 8, RFKP.

40. Henry Betts, interview by Coughlan, July 6, 1972, Robert Coughlan Papers of Northwestern University, MS 82-5:8, JFKL; "My 8 Years as the Kennedys' Private Nurse," 106.

41. *TTR*, 423.

42. Betts, interview by Coughlan, July 6, 1972, Coughlan Papers.

43. Ibid.

44. Ibid.

45. Arthur M. Schlesinger Jr., *Robert Kennedy and His Times* (New York: Ballantine Books, 1979), 634.

46. Ibid.

47. Ibid.

48. Ibid.

49. Peter S. Canellos, ed. *Last Lion: The Fall and Rise of Ted Kennedy* (New York: Simon & Schuster, 2009), 94.

50. RK to BK, July 10, 1962, "Family Correspondence," Box 58, RFKP.

51. Diane Winter to ESK, June 7, 1962, ibid.

52. RK to JBKO and EK, Nov. 1, 1962, Box 14, RFKP.

53. RK to JFK, November 10, 1962, "Family Correspondence," Box 57, RFKP.

54. RK, "Retreat at Noroton, June 24, 1962," "Diaries 1959–1970."

55. Edward Shorter, *The Kennedy Family and the Story of Mental Retardation* (Philadelphia: Temple University Press, 2000), 83–88.

56. EKS, "Hope for Retarded Children," *Saturday Evening Post*, Sept. 22, 1962.

57. Undated and unsourced interview with RK, "Speeches and Appearances." Based on information in the interview, Rose likely gave it in 1963.

58. *The Kennedy Family and the Story of Mental Retardation*, ch. 5.

59. "Coffee with the Kennedys," 1962, video, IFP 156, JFKL.

60. RK to Mrs. Carl Ludwig, Jan. 7, 1963; RK to Mr. and Mrs. Robert P. Fitzgerald, Jan. 15, 1963, "Speeches and Appearances."

61. Eleanor O'Byrne to RK, March 12, 1963, Box 58, RFKP.

62. BK to RK, April 15, 1963, "Family Correspondence," ibid.

63. RK, "Saturday–April 6, 1963," "Diaries 1959–1970."

64. RK to BK, April 29, 1963, "Family Correspondence," Box 58, RFKP.

65. RK to ESK, Sept. 24, 1963, ibid.

66. ESK to RK, Oct. 9, 1962, ibid.

67. "Luncheon Given at White House for President and Señora," July 23, 1962, Box 14, RFKP.

68. *Jacqueline Kennedy,* 169–73.

69. "Haile Selassie," "Speeches and Appearances."

70. "President Kennedy on the South Vietnamese Coup," Nov. 4, 1963, Miller Center Presidential Recordings Program, University of Virginia, http://millercenter.org/presidentialclassroom/exhibits/jfks-memoir-dictation-on-the-assassination-of-diem.

71. *TTR,* 441–42.

72. William Manchester, *The Death of a President: November 1963* (New York: Harper and Row, 1967), 238–39.

73. *TTR,* 444.

74. Max Holland, ed., *The Presidential Recordings: Lyndon B. Johnson: The Kennedy Assassination and the Transfer of Power, November 1963–January 1964,* 3 vols. (New York: W. W. Norton, 2005), 1: 63–66.

75. *TTR,* 446.

76. *TC,* 210.

77. *TTR,* 446.

78. RK, "Reaction to Grief, 1964," "Diaries 1959–1970," Box 4, RFKP.

79. Ibid.

CHAPTER 12

1. RK, "Reaction to Grief, 1964," "Diaries 1959–1970," Box 4, RFKP.

2. Rita Dallas with Maxine Cheshire, "My 8 Years as the Kennedys' Private Nurse," *Ladies' Home Journal,* March 1971, 164.

3. "Travel List–Mrs. Kennedy 1957," "Speeches and Appearances," Box 100, RFKP. Rose's prescription medicines are listed in Ronald Kessler's *The Sins of the Father: Joseph P. Kennedy and the Dynasty He Founded* (New York: Warner Books, 1996), 372–73. Joe Graedon of NPR's *The People's Pharmacy,* provided the history of popular sedatives / antianxiety medicines; e-mail to author, July 10, 2012.

4. Gertrude Bell to RK, Jan. 22, 1964, Box 14, RFKP.

5. Invitation to dinner for Sir Alec Douglas-Home, Feb. 13, 1964, "Speeches and Appearances," Box 101, RFKP.

6. RK, "March 1964," "Diaries 1959–1970," Box 4, RFKP.

7. "Reaction to Grief, 1964."

8. Ibid.

9. Ibid.

10. RK to Terry Sanford, May 21, 1964, "Speeches and Appearances," Box 103, RFKP.

11. Evelyn Blackburn to RK, May 18, 1964, ibid.

12. Peter S. Canellos, ed., *Last Lion: The Fall and Rise of Ted Kennedy* (New York: Simon & Schuster, 2009), 103.

13. Ibid., 104; *TC*, 218–25.

14. James H. J. Tate to JPK and RK, May 29, 1964, "Speeches and Appearances," Box 103, RFKP.

15. Eileen Foley, "The Indomitable Mrs. Rose Kennedy," *Philadelphia Bulletin*, June 30, 1964.

16. RK, "Summer, 1964–Recall Jack's Arrival at Hyannis," "Diaries 1959–1970."

17. *TC*, 213.

18. RK, "August 1964," "Diaries 1959–1970."

19. Marquis Childs, "Kennedy's Mother Real Star of Campaign," clipping in "Speeches and Appearances," Box 103, RFKP.

20. Polly Fitzgerald to RK, "Robert F. Kennedy for U.S. Senator," Oct. 21, 1964, ibid.

21. "2500 Sip Coffee with Kennedys," [Oct. 1964], unsourced newspaper clipping, ibid; Virginia Spain Spring, "Rose Kennedy Calls on Long Experience for Her Campaigning," *Schenectady Union-Star*, Oct. 26, 1964.

22. *The Kennedys*, American Experience, PBS Home Video, 2003.

23. Evan Thomas, *Robert Kennedy: His Life* (New York: Touchstone, 2000), 301.

24. Bob Considine, "My Son, the Candidate," Hearst Headline Service, Oct. 8, 1964.

25. Judy Bennett, "RFK Gets Boost from Mother," Rochester *Democrat and Chronicle*, Oct. 30, 1964, 5B.

26. RK's secretary to BK, Nov. 10, 1964, Box 57, RFKP.

27. Helen Keyes, "Europe Remembers JFK," *This Week*, n.d.

28. Marie Bruce, "Reflections on Rose, 1972," Box 15, RFKP.

29. *The Mike Douglas Show*, July 1967, JFKL. May be viewed on YouTube.

30. President of Saint Joseph College to RK, March 22, 1965, "Speeches and Appearances," Box 104, RFKP.

31. Bruce West, "Award Dinner Launches $15,00,000 Crusade," Toronto *Globe and Mail*, [undated], 2–4; RK to Donald Anderson, Sept. 23, 1965, Box 104, RFKP.

32. RK to Peggy Parsons, Aug. 2, 1966, ibid.

33. Peter Hikss, "Ground Broken for Kennedy Center for Retarded: Mother of Late President Is Praised by the Head of Yeshiva at Ceremony," *New York Times*, May 1, 1966; untitled and undated clippings about the center, ibid. The center is now the Rose F. Kennedy University Center for Excellence in Developmental Disabilities.

34. Speech at Yeshiva University, May 1, 1966, Box 104, RFKP.

35. RK to Andrew A. Lynn, Feb. 2, 1967, "Speeches and Appearances, Regretted," Box 107, RFKP.

36. John Ryan, interview by Coughlan, Sept. 3, 1972, Coughlan Papers, JFKL.

37. Speech at Choate Dedication of Robert Berks's Bust of John F. Kennedy, May 20, 1967, "Speeches and Appearances," Box 107, RFKP; RK to Harold L. Tinker, May 23, 1967, ibid.

38. Cushing, "Prayer at the Opening Ceremony of the John Fitzgerald Kennedy Federal Building," Sept. 9, 1966; RK to Francis J. Lally, Sept. 20, 1966, "Speeches and Appearances," Box 104, RFKP.

39. Stephen J. Wayne, *The Road to the White House 2004: The Politics of Presidential Elections* (Belmont, CA: Thomson/Wadsworth, 2004), 12; Thurston Clarke, *The Last Campaign: Robert F. Kennedy and 82 Days that Inspired America* (New York: Henry Holt, 2008), 25–26.

40. RK, "Outline of my Speech for Bob 1968," "'68 Campaign," Box 108, RFKP.

41. Arthur Schlesinger Jr., "Why I Am for Kennedy," *New York Times*, May 8, 1968, C33, "'68 Campaign," ibid.

42. RK, "Bob's Campaign," "Diaries, 1959–1970," Box 4, RFKP.

43. Associated Press clipping, dateline Gary, Indiana, in "Robert F. Kennedy Presidential Campaign, Indiana and Illinois," Box 108, RFKP.

44. "Robert F. Kennedy, Remarks on the Assassination of Martin Luther King, Jr., Delivered April 4, 1968, Indianapolis, IN," "American Rhetoric: Top 100 Speeches," www.americanrhetoric.com/speeches/rfkonmlkdeath.html.

45. "Reflections on Rose, 1972."

46. "Rose Kennedy a Charmer," *San Francisco Examiner*, May 20, 1968, 10.

47. Frances Moffat, "The Indefatigable Kennedy Girls," *Los Angeles Chronicle*, May 20, 1968, 16.

48. "Rose Kennedy a Charmer."

49. Myrna Oliver, "How the Kennedys Invaded California," *Los Angeles Herald Examiner*, n.d.

50. Ibid.

51. RK, "Diaries, 1968," Box 4, RFKP.

52. *Robert Kennedy*, 382.

53. "Robert F. Kennedy Presidential Campaign, California," Box 108, RFKP.

54. Kitty Hanson, "Her Son the Candidate: At 77, Rose Kennedy Hits the Campaign Trail for Bobby," clipping in "Presidential Campaign, Oregon," ibid.

55. *TTR*, 475.

56. "Diaries, 1968."

57. "My 8 Years as the Kennedys' Private Nurse," 165.

58. *The Kennedys*, American Experience.

59. Arthur M. Schlesinger Jr., *Journals: 1952–2000* (New York: Penguin Press, 2007), 293.

60. *The Best of Times, the Worst of Times: Rose Kennedy Remembers*, BBC, 1974, JFKL. Five-minute clips may be viewed on YouTube: http://www.youtube.com/watch?v =J1QqbYM24XE&feature=related.

61. "Stabat Mater," *Catholic Encyclopedia*, http://www.newadvent.org/cathen/14239b .htm.

62. "Edward M. Kennedy: Public Address at Memorial Service for Robert F. Kennedy," June 8, 1968, http://www.americanrhetoric.com/speeches/ekennedytributetorfk .html.

63. Bill Eppridge and Hay Gorley, *Robert Kennedy: The Last Campaign* (New York: Harcourt Brace, 1993), 124–31; *TTR*, 476–77.

64. Sue Salad, secretary to RK, to Coughlan, Nov. 17, 1972, Box 13, RFKP.

65. *TTR*, 478.

66. Warren Rogers, *When I Think of Bobby: A Personal Memoir of the Kennedy Years* (New York: HarperCollins, 1993), 185–86.

67. *The Journey of Robert F. Kennedy*, David L. Wolper, producer, ABC, 1970. Rose had delivered the poignant tribute to Bobby at a December 1968 fund-raising dinner in Boston, organized to retire his campaign debt.

68. *The Best of Times, the Worst of Times.*

69. Quotes from *CNN Larry King Live*, interview with Merv Griffin, May 11, 2006, with excerpts of Rose Kennedy on *The Merv Griffin Show*, http://transcripts.cnn.com /TRANSCRIPTS/0605/11/lkl.01.html.

CHAPTER 13

1. Jim Bishop, "The Subject Was Rose," unsourced newspaper clipping in Box 108, RFKP. Based on the article's text and its placement in Rose's files, it was likely published in October 1968. Bishop, a syndicated columnist, appeared in more than two hundred newspapers.

2. Laura Bergquist, "A Visit with the Indomitable Rose Kennedy," *Look*, Nov. 26, 1968, 25.

3. Ibid. (original emphasis).

4. RK, "Diaries 1959–1970," Box 4, RFKP. All of the references to Rose's thoughts about the wedding derive from this source.

5. Ibid.

6. Ibid.

7. RK to EKS, Oct. 29, 1968, "Family Correspondence, Eunice Kennedy Shriver, 1978–1975," Box 58, RFKP.

8. RK, "Jackie's Wedding to Onassis," Box 4, RFKP.

9. RK to EKS, Oct. 29, 1968.

10. "Jackie's Wedding to Onassis."

11. Ibid.

12. RK, "Oct. 17, 1968," "Diaries 1959–1970."

13. Diane Winter to Stephen Smith, Feb. 11, 1969, "Edward M. Kennedy Senate Campaign, September–November," Box 112, RFKP.

14. "Sample Questions and Answers for Mrs. Joseph P. Kennedy, *The Today Show*, Nov. 22, 1968," Box 108, RFKP.

15. RK to Mrs. Robert Fitzgerald, Jan. 7, 1969, Box 108, RFKP.

16. RK, "Notes and Arrangements for Speaking," Box 108, RFKP.

17. RK, "The Irish and John F. Kennedy," "Diaries 1959–1970."

18. National Park Service, "New Strategic Plan to Be Developed for John Fitzgerald Kennedy National Historic Site," Newsletter 1, Spring, US Department of Interior, 2009.

19. *JFK—The Childhood Years*, CBS News Special, Oct. 31, 1967, Box 12, RFKP.

20. Peter S. Canellos, ed., *Last Lion: The Fall and Rise of Ted Kennedy* (New York: Simon & Schuster, 2009), 137.

21. *TC*, 273–74.

22. *Last Lion*, 138, 146.

23. Ibid., 148–50; *TC*, 290.

24. *Last Lion*, 152–53.

25. RK, interview by Coughlan, Feb. 23, 1972, Box 10, RFKP.

26. *Last Lion*, 154–55.

27. *TTR*, 491.

28. Joe McGinniss, *The Last Brother: The Rise and Fall of Teddy Kennedy* (New York: Simon & Schuster, 1993), 544.

29. *TTR*, 492.

30. RK, interview by Coughlan, Jan. 25, 1972, Box 8, RFKP.

31. *Last Lion*, 177.

32. "'Grief, Fear, Doubt, Panic'—and Guilt," *Newsweek*, Aug. 3, 1969, http://www.thedailybeast.com/newsweek/1969/08/03/grief-fear-doubt-panic-and-guilt.html.

33. *Last Lion*, 172.

34. *Newsweek*, Aug. 3, 1969.

35. RK to JBKO, Aug. 18, 1969, Box 57, RFKP (original emphasis).

36. *TC*, 293.

37. *TTR*, 479. *Last Lion*, 177.

38. "Joseph P. Kennedy Dead; Forged Political Dynasty," *New York Times*, Nov. 19, 1969.

39. "The Death of a Dynasty," *Newsweek*, Dec. 1, 1969, 28.

40. *TTR*, 479.

41. RK, "Following Joseph P. Kennedy's Death," "Diaries 1959–1970."

42. Olive Watson to RK, undated, Box 124, RFKP.

43. Chris Matthews, *Jack Kennedy: Elusive Hero* (New York: Simon & Schuster, 2011), 16, 400. Matthews believes that Rose withheld affection from young Jack, a claim Jacqueline Kennedy also made in her famous "Camelot" discussion with journalist Theodore White one week after her husband's assassination. According to Matthews, Rose never visited Jack at Choate, even when he was seriously ill in the infirmary. The latter may be true, in part because Rose had seven children at home to care for, including an infant. In addition, as we have seen, she began to suffer her own health problems about this time, diagnosed many years later as irritable bowel syndrome. But she came at least once to see Jack at boarding school (for the picnic) and kept close tabs on his health through correspondence with the headmaster's wife.

44. "The Death of a Dynasty."

45. "Death of the Founder," *Time*, Nov. 28, 1969, 21.

46. Mrs. Joseph P. Kennedy, "Giving Children the Gifts of Faith and Courage," *Ladies' Home Journal*, Dec. 1969.

47. Peggie O'Neill to RK, Jan. 7, 1970, "Letters from the Public," Box 111, RFKP.

48. RSS to RK, undated, Box 57, RFKP.

49. RSS, jokingly signed "Yul Brenner," to RK, March 12, 1968, Box 58, RFKP. Yul Brynner starred in stage and screen versions of *The King and I*. Why Shriver chose the actor's name to sign this note is unclear.

50. RK to EKS, Oct. 1, 1968; RK to EKS, June 3, 1968; RK to EKS, Oct. 27, 1969; RK to EKS, Sept. 29, 1969, Box 58, RFKP.

51. RK to EKS, June 10, 1970, ibid.

52. RSS to RK, July 8, 1964, ibid.

53. RK to RSS, Aug. 2, 1968, ibid.

54. *Jacqueline Kennedy: Historic Conversations on Life with John F. Kennedy* (New York: Hyperion, 2011), 51.

55. Arthur M. Schlesinger Jr., *Journals 1952–2000* (New York: Penguin Press, 2007), 150.

56. RK, "Jackie's Relationship with Rose Kennedy," "Diaries 1959–1970," Box 4, RFKP.

57. RK to JBKO, July 8, 1971, Box 57, RFKP.

58. JBKO and Ari Onassis to RK, postmarked Feb. 13, 1970, ibid.

59. JBKO to RK, April 1970, ibid.

60. RK to Samuel Belkin, June 4, 1970, "Speeches and Appearances, 1970," Box 112, RFKP.

61. Bridgett Potter to RK, May 21, 1970, ibid.

62. Jim Neel to RK, May 20, 1970, ibid.

63. RK to Don Price, June 3, 1970, ibid.

64. Quoted in Andrew Blake, "JFK's Rooms at Harvard Dedicated as Memorial Site," *Boston Globe*, June 1970, in "Speeches and Appearances, 1970," Box 112, RFKP.

65. "Rose Kennedy at 80," *Life*, July 17, 1970, 21–25.

66. RK, "Trip to Ethiopia," "Diaries 1959–1970."

67. RSS to RK, Aug. 11, 1970, Box 58, RFKP.

68. "Trip to Ethiopia."

69. RK, "Summer in Hyannis," "Diaries 1959–1970."

70. Ibid.

71. Sally Fitzgerald to RK, undated, "Dorchester," "Edward M. Kennedy Senate Campaign, September–November," Box 112, RFKP.

72. "Edward M. Kennedy Senate Campaign."

73. Associated Press, "Rose Kennedy Campaigns Again for One of Her Sons," Sept. 22, 1970.

74. Diane Winter, secretary to RK, to Mary Frackelten, June 1, 1970, "Edward M. Kennedy Senate Campaign."

75. "Edward M. Kennedy Senate Campaign."

76. Sister Mary Cornelia to RK, Oct. 29, 1970, "Edward M. Kennedy Senate Campaign."

77. *TC*, 294.

78. RK to Edward Boland, Nov. 16, 1970, "Edward M. Kennedy Senate Campaign."

79. Boland to RK, Nov. 23, 1970, "Edward M. Kennedy Senate Campaign."

80. JBKO to RK, undated, Box 57, RFKP. This missive begins, "How we all enjoyed your letter!"

81. RK to JBKO, July 8, 1971, Box 57, RFKP.

82. JBKO to RK, undated, ibid.

83. RK to JBKO, Dec. 27, 1971, ibid.

84. "Opening of JFK Center for the Performing Arts," "Diaries 1971," Box 5, RFKP.

85. Madeline Sulad, secretary to RK, to Jeanne Vanderbilt (Frost's producer), Feb. 10, 1971, "Speeches and Appearances," Box 113, RFKP.

86. Joyce Yablan to RK, Aug. 25, 1972, ibid.

87. Peter Baker (Frost's producer) to RK, July 1, 1971, ibid.

88. Gail Cameron, *Rose: A Biography of Rose Fitzgerald Kennedy* (New York: G. P. Putnam's Sons, 1971).

89. Gail Cameron to RK, May 18, 1968, "Correspondence," Box 97, RFKP.

90. RK to Mrs. Robert Wise Wescott (Gail Cameron), May 31, 1968, ibid.

91. RK to JBKO, July 8, 1971, Box 57, RFKP.

92. RK, "Reactions After Book 'Rose,'" "Diaries 1971," Box 4, RFKP.

93. JBKO to RK, undated, Box 57, RFKP.

94. RK to Evan Thomas, July 30, 1967, Box 11, RFKP.

95. Cass Canfield to RK, Nov. 20, 1967, ibid.

96. Evan Thomas to RK, April 22, 1968, ibid; Cass Canfield to RK, April 24, 1968, ibid.

97. Stewart Richardson to RK, Jan. 18, 1973, ibid.

98. Ted Sorensen, *Counselor: A Life at the Edge of History* (New York: Harper, 2008), 256.

99. Ted Sorensen, author's conversation, April 15, 2010; Henry Raymont, "Doubleday Gets Rose Kennedy's Book," *New York Times*, Dec. 1, 1971.

100. "Doubleday Gets Rose Kennedy's Book."

101. Coughlan to Sue Sulad, secretary to RK, April 13, 1972, Box 11, RFKP.

102. "Comments and Corrections on the *Times to Remember* Manuscript," Box 19, RFKP.

103. In the mid-1970s, congressional committees investigating President Kennedy's assassination uncovered his liaisons with Mafia moll Judith Campbell Exner.

104. Coughlan to RK, May 19, 1974, Box 11, JFKP.

105. Coughlan to RK, Dec. 1963, ibid.

106. RK to Coughlan, June 3, 1974, ibid.

107. *Rose Kennedy Remembers: The Best of Times . . . the Worst of Times,* BBC, 1974, JFKL. Five-minute clips may be viewed on YouTube.

108. "Rose Kennedy Talks About Her Life, Her Faith, and Her Children," *McCall's,* Dec. 1973, 121.

109. RK, interview by Felicia Warburg Roosevelt, April 6, 1973, "Mrs. Joseph P. Kennedy," Box 1, Felicia Rogan Papers, University of Virginia.

110. Ibid.

111. Madeline Sulad, secretary to RK, to Sister Mary Charitas, July 30, 1971, Box 57, RFKP.

112. RK to redacted recipient, March 28, 1972, ibid.

113. Madeline Sulad to Felice Lenz, Jan. 5, 1972, ibid. References to Rosemary's health issues are redacted at the Kennedy Library.

114. RK to Sister Paulus, Oct. 25, 1972, ibid.

115. Madeline Sulad to William Callahan, Feb. 23, 1972, ibid.; William Callahan letter, Feb. 8, 1972, ibid.

116. Joseph Kennedy left up to $1 million to Rose, along with real estate investments; $50,000 to his two sisters; and the remainder of his $2- to $4-million estate to the Kennedy Foundation. "A Kennedy Will Aids Foundation," *New York Times,* Aug. 26, 1970.

117. Eleanor Roberts, "Rose Kennedy Visits Dinah—and Shows She's Super-Organized," *Boston Herald Traveler,* April 3, 1972, B31.

118. RK to Dinah Shore, April 14, 1972, "Speeches and Appearances," Box 113, RFKP.

119. Betty Long to RK, April 12, 1972, ibid. (original emphasis).

120. *Journals 1952–2000,* 358.

121. Nancy E. McGlen et al., *Women, Politics, and American Society,* 4th ed. (New York: Pearson Longman, 2005), 82.

122. *Journals 1952–2000,* 410.

123. Linda Corley, photographs by Bob Davidoff, *The Kennedy Family Album: Personal Photos of America's First Family* (Philadelphia: Running Press, 2008).

124. RK to Sister Sheila, June 11, 1975, Box 57, RFKP.

125. RK to Sister Julaine, Aug. 5, 1975, ibid.

126. *Journals 1952–2000,* 430.

127. Barbara Gibson and Ted Schwarz, *Rose Kennedy and Her Family: The Best and Worst of Their Lives and Times* (New York: Birch Lane, 1995), ch. 14.

128. *Journals 1952–2000,* 449.

Epilogue

1. *David Frost Show,* "Speeches and Appearances," Box 113, RFKP.

2. Adam Clymer, *Edward M. Kennedy: A Biography* (New York: William Morrow, 1999), 286–300; *TC,* 371–75. See also Timothy Stanley, *Kennedy v. Carter: The 1980 Battle for the Democratic Party's Soul* (Lawrence: University Press of Kansas, 2010).

3. *Edward M. Kennedy,* 300–19; *TC,* 373–80.

4. *Edward M. Kennedy,* photograph, between pp. 272 and 273.

5. Maria Shriver's tribute to her grandmother on her one hundredth birthday included clips from the 1982 party. They may be viewed on YouTube.

6. Charles Higham, *Rose: The Life and Times of Rose Fitzgerald Kennedy* (New York: Pocket Books, 1995), 427.

7. www.stcolettawiorg/about/history.php, accessed Oct. 27, 2012.

8. Peter S. Canellos, ed. *Last Lion: The Fall and Rise of Ted Kennedy* (New York: Simon & Schuster, 2009), 308.

9. *TTR*, 2004 ed., xii.

10. RK to EKS, March 2, 1971, "Family Correspondence, Eunice Kennedy Shriver, 1968–75," Box 58, RFKP.

11. www.findagrave.com, accessed Oct. 27, 2012.

12. Martin Weil, "Rosemary Kennedy, 86; President's Disabled Sister," *Washington Post*, Jan. 8, 2005; Andrew Jacobs, "Patricia Kennedy Lawford Dies at 82," *New York Times*, Sept. 18, 2006.

13. *U.S. News and World Report*, Nov. 15, 1993, cited by Carla Baranauckas, "Eunice Kennedy Shriver, Influential Founder of Special Olympics, Dies at 88," *New York Times*, Aug. 11, 2009.

14. Barbara A. Perry, "The First Family," in *Companion to the John F. Kennedy Presidency*, ed. Marc Selverstone (Malden, MA: Wiley-Blackwell, forthcoming).

15. "Kennedys' Oceanfront Compound House Donated to Edward M. Kennedy Institute," *Huffington Post*, Jan. 30, 2012.

16. Vincent Bzdek, *The Kennedy Legacy: Jack, Bobby and Ted and a Family Dream Fulfilled* (New York: Palgrave Macmillan, 2009), 248.

17. Glen Johnson, Travis Andersen, and Martine Powers, "Joseph Kennedy III Announces Congressional Campaign," *Boston Globe*, Feb. 16, 2012.

18. Jean Kennedy Smith, author's interview, Sept. 20, 2010.

19. Brad Darrach, "The Sorrow and the Strength: Rose Fitzgerald Kennedy 1890–1995," *Life*, February 1995, 52.

20. Jean Kennedy Smith, e-mail to author, Feb. 23, 2012.

Photograph Credits

Frontispiece: Photo by Abbie Rowe, White House, JFK Library, Boston.

Mary Josephine Hannon Fitzgerald. Courtesy of JFK Presidential Library and Museum, Boston.

John Francis Fitzgerald. Courtesy of JFK Presidential Library and Museum, Boston.

Rose Fitzgerald with her siblings. Courtesy of JFK Presidential Library and Museum, Boston.

Rose and her classmates. Courtesy of JFK Presidential Library and Museum, Boston.

Rose christening the *Bunker Hill*. Courtesy of JFK Presidential Library and Museum, Boston.

Mayor John F. Fitzgerald and Rose at Boston parade. Courtesy of JFK Presidential Library and Museum, Boston.

Rose and Joseph P. Kennedy on their wedding day. ©CORBIS.

Rose's first three children. Copyright © John F. Kennedy Library Foundation.

Rose's card file. Courtesy of JFK Presidential Library and Museum, Boston.

Rose, three months pregnant, with family. Copyright © John F. Kennedy Library Foundation.

Rose's visit to California. Copyright © John F. Kennedy Library Foundation.

K. LeMoyne Billings, Kiko, and Jack. Copyright © John F. Kennedy Library Foundation.

Kick, Rose, Rosemary, US Embassy Residence, London. Courtesy of JFK Presidential Library and Museum, Boston.

Family portrait on the Cannes beach. Copyright © John F. Kennedy Library Foundation.

Rose, Jack, and Eunice on Mount Corcovado. Copyright © John F. Kennedy Library Foundation.

Rosemary, Bobby, Pat, Jean, Teddy, and Rose at the launching of the USS *President Polk*. Courtesy of United States Navy and JFK Presidential Library and Museum, Boston.

Joe Jr. escorts Kick to her wedding. Courtesy of JFK Presidential Library and Museum, Boston.

Rose accepts the Navy Cross for Joe Jr. Courtesy of United States Navy and JFK Presidential Library and Museum, Boston.

Rose during 1946 Democratic primary. Courtesy of JFK Presidential Library and Museum, Boston.

Jack with Grandfather Fitzgerald. Copyright © John F. Kennedy Library Foundation.

Bobby, his first child (Kathleen), Josie Fitzgerald, and Rose. Copyright © John F. Kennedy Library Foundation.

Jack and Jean, Pat and Rose, and Eunice. Courtesy of JFK Presidential Library and Museum, Boston.

Pope Pius XII and Rose. Courtesy of JFK Presidential Library and Museum, Boston, and www.fotografiafelici.com.

Rose campaigning for Jack. Courtesy of JFK Presidential Library and Museum, Boston.

Rose with Jack and Lyndon Johnson. Copyright © Bettman/CORBIS.

Joe and Rose at the airport. Copyright © Bettman/CORBIS.

Rose at Inaugural Ball. Copyright © John F. Kennedy Library Foundation.

Pablo Casals kisses Jackie Kennedy's hand. Photo by Robert Knudsen, White House, JFK Library, Boston.

Rose at a state dinner. Photo by Cecil Stoughton, White House, JFK Library, Boston.

Rose with twenty-one of her grandchildren. Photo by Cecil Stoughton, White House, JFK Library, Boston.

Rose receives an honorary degree. Copyright © John F. Kennedy Library Foundation.

President Kennedy's Arlington grave site. Photo by Cecil Stoughton, White House, JFK Library, Boston.

Rose and Marc Chagall. Copyright © John F. Kennedy Library Foundation.

Rose Fitzgerald Kennedy Center groundbreaking. NY Daily News Archive, Getty Images.

Rose on the *Mike Douglas Show*. Copyright © Michael Leshnov.

Rose and Teddy at the Hyannis Port rink. Copyright © John F. Kennedy Library Foundation.

Rose campaigning in Indiana. Copyright © John F. Kennedy Library Foundation.

Eulogy for Bobby. AP/J. Walter Green.

Index